OLIVER GOLDSMITH'S

History
OF THE
Natural World

OLIVER GOLDSMITH'S

History OF THE *Natural World*

THE ANIMAL KINGDOM DESCRIBED AND ILLUSTRATED WITH 200 COLOUR ENGRAVINGS

FOREWORD BY GERALD DURRELL

STUDIO EDITIONS
LONDON

Originally published 1774 as
A History of the Earth and Animated Nature
by Oliver Goldsmith

Illustrations originally published 1849
in *Dictionnaire Universel d'Histoire Naturelle*
by M. Charles D'Orbigny

This edition published 1990 by Studio Editions Ltd.
Princess House, 50 Eastcastle Street
London W1N 7AP, England

Printed and bound in Malaysia

ISBN 1 85170 352 7

CONTENTS

PUBLISHER'S NOTE

Oliver Goldsmith's *History of the Earth and Animated Nature* was first published in 1774, the year of his death. It was an instantaneous success and many editions were produced throughout the late-eighteenth and nineteenth centuries.

The original is very large, with many hundreds of thousands of words and to produce this edition economically we have greatly abridged the original text. In particular we have omitted the first section of the book on the earth and the races of mankind entirely and we have concentrated on the animals, birds, fish, insects and other creatures that Goldsmith describes so beautifully.

Goldsmith was not a natural historian by training. He drew heavily on previously published works, in particular Buffon's massive and impressive scientific works of the eighteenth century, but as Gerald Durrell writes in his introduction to this edition, "Although he plundered other men's works and stole shamelessly, he knew, as a good alchemist should, the art of turning base metal into gold, of turning dull prose into fine, elegant writing."

Goldsmith had little regard for the scientific classifications of other naturalists, adopting a haphazard system which contained a multitude of errors. In the light of recent scientific developments this system seems even more simplistic. However, since it is for his fine prose, not his scientific prowess that Goldsmith would wish to be remembered, we have not attempted to correct his inaccuracies and his original system of scientific classification has been maintained.

The majority of the colour plates are taken from Charles d'Orbigny's *Dictionnaire Universel d'Histoire Naturelle* whose great twenty volume work was published in 1849. D'Orbigny's illustrators contain some of the best known names of the nineteenth century, a period when French natural history illustration was at its height. Their quality is superb.

Other illustrations include the colour plates by J. Stewart, taken from the Blackie & Son edition of Goldsmith published circa 1873, and the A. Fullarton & Co. edition published in 1848. The black and white illustrations are taken from Bell's *A History of British Quadrupeds* published in 1874, *The Watercolours and Drawings of Thomas Bewick*, the 1810 edition of *The Encyclopedia Britannica*, *An History of the Earth and Animated Nature* by Oliver Goldsmith (1774), the Blackie & Son edition of Goldsmith published circa 1873, Kirby's *Elementary Text-Book of Entomology*, Marchington's *A Portrait of Shooting*, Yarrell's *A History of British Fishes* and Cassell's *Popular Natural History*.

The captions to the illustrations have been taken from the original plates. The Latin nomenclature has been left as it appeared in d'Orbigny's *Histoire Universel d'Histoire Naturelle*. Many of these have variations, or have been altered later, and also differ from present-day scientific descriptions. For some of the rarer species it has not been possible to identify common names, and in these cases only Latin names are given. The colour illustrations, taken from the Blackie and Fullarton editions of Goldsmith, were not originally published with Latin names, and therefore only appear with common names.

ACKNOWLEDGEMENTS

The Publishers would like to thank the following for their help in preparing this edition:

Gerald Durrell for his foreword, and all those who have given editorial help – Geoffrey N. Swinney, S. Peter Dance, The Zoological Society of London, The Department of Invertebrates, London Zoo, and the Royal Society for the Protection of Birds.

FOREWORD BY
GERALD DURRELL

All over the world there lie vast archives, acres and acres of paper, a billion rustling documents that are an immense forest of discovery. All this represents our knowledge of the world around us, a world whose secrets we are rapidly destroying even as we unravel them.

In the early stages of our career as mankind, one supposes that Neanderthal Man, for example, only had an interest in the natural world around him in order to eat and not to be eaten. But to preserve himself from the dismal fate of becoming another mammal's *foie gras*, he had to learn the ways of the Mammoth and the Sabre-toothed Tiger, learn how to hunt and not be hunted, learn, as it were, the habits of his lunch if he was to have a lunch at all and not become lunch. These were the beginnings of amassing knowledge, although it was stored in the skull and not in a filing cabinet. Then when man become more sedentary, learnt to plant crops, domesticate animals and to read and write and not pass on his knowledge in a series of (to us) incomprehensible grunts, we were on the way towards what today we call, ironically, civilisation. Knowledge could be accumulated and passed on by tablets, papyrus, parchment, so that a different form of communication from speech could be used about the then known world.

If you examine the way we have acquired knowledge, it has a very uneven pattern, and you will find a blindingly brilliant idea embedded like a diamond in a bed of superstition and mythology. It is quite possible that the man who invented the wheel believed in dragons.

However, our investigation of the world around us did hiccough its way along. When you read some of the earlier investigators like Aristotle and Pliny you may be amused by their naivety, but you must always remember that a lot of the so-called facts they were told were transmitted by word of mouth, and we all know how a story or description, flipped from tongue to tongue, grows like a bud and expands into a multi-coloured flower. Even the written word can sometimes create a strange version of the truth.

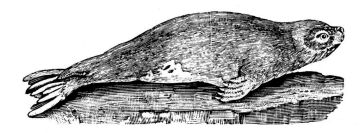

During our efforts to unravel the natural world we did, of course, waste a lot of energy on side issues. In the Middle Ages men spent a long time in pondering the problem whether or not Adam and Eve had navels. A lot of argument and thought was given to the thorny problem of whether or not swallows hibernated in the mud at the bottom of ponds when they disappeared in autumn – migration had not been discovered. But the fact that the swallows' absence was noticed and that people were sufficiently interested to question their whereabouts was a step forward in the garnering of knowledge.

Long after Aristotle and Pliny, of course, came a wealth of books about the world we live in. This was the time of the medieval bestiaries, and enchanting books they were, filled with misinformation and misnomers. But in spite of this they were an attempt to understand nature around us, even if the attempt fell very short of the truth in many cases. In the fantastically funny and delightful bestiary translated by T. H. White, for example, we are told many strange things about animal habits. This is how the whale was believed to behave:

'This animal lifts its back out of the open sea above the watery waves, and then it anchors itself in the one place; and on its back, what with the shingle of the ocean drawn there by the gales, a level lawn gets made and bushes begin to grow there. Sailing ships that happen to be going that way take it to be an island, and land on it. Then they make themselves a fireplace. But the whale, feeling the hotness of the fire, suddenly plunges down into the depths of the deep, and pulls down the anchored ship with it into the profound.'

As our knowledge expanded, more serious works than the bestiaries came into being, although it must be realised that the early works were considered serious scientific tomes in their day. However, by the eighteenth century scientific works like the massive and impressive volumes of Buffon were being produced. Nevertheless, these works were usually written in a ponderous and dull style that would not appeal to that poor, much maligned being, the Man in the Street. What was needed was an illuminator, and this is where Oliver Goldsmith excelled.

Goldsmith has, unkindly and unfairly, been described as a hack, but if he was a hack then I wish I had his hack's talent. He was an alchemist, for although he plundered other men's works and stole shamelessly, he knew, as a good alchemist should, the art of turning base metal into gold, of turning dull prose into fine, elegant writing, and he did this not with a lode-stone but with his pen.

We are in urgent need of people like Goldsmith today, for as our knowledge and horizons have widened, science has split up into numerous groups and each of these groups has developed its own language to describe its findings. Thus the language of the zoologist might be so different as to be almost incomprehensible to an astrophysicist, whereas some of the astrophysicist's jargon would puzzle a geologist and baffle a botanist. To our poor Man in the Street, all of them might just as well be talking Patagonian. Just recently there was an interesting series of experiments done on how those charming crustaceans, the Hermit crabs, choose

their shells. The paper when published was entitled 'How animals make assessments: information gathering by the hermit crab *Pagurus bernhardus*', and on reading it, one section in particular leapt from the page, metaphorically speaking, and seized me by the throat. It was this:

> 'Each prediction of the model was upheld in these experiments and the model is also congruent with previous observations, particularly that crabs housed in poor shells will persist for longer with shells with blocked apertures than will those in good shells. Being housed in a poor shell would result in higher initial levels of causal factors at the start of investigation, as the causal factors for shell acquisition are a combination of factors from the occupied shell and from the shell under investigation. In our presentation of changes in motivational state we have plotted straight lines over time but this is undoubtedly incorrect. First, there is likely to be an element of decreasing return in terms of additional information. Second, there is likely to be an increasing ease of distraction during any phase of continuing investigation . . .'

Now if scientists are going around writing things that only another scientist can understand, how on earth are we to get Mr Smith the butcher or Mr Jones the candlestick maker to take a deep and abiding interest in the problems that face the Hermit crab in its daily life? What we need are more Oliver Goldsmiths around to re-write such observations in clear, beautiful prose that we can all enjoy and comprehend. For Goldsmith could take words and use them to construct a wonderful picture in our minds, as a painter can take a palette covered with a multitude of colours like a Persian carpet and, by dipping his brush into it, produce, miraculously, a scene or a portrait of delicacy and beauty.

We talk a lot about education now, as if it were a panacea for all ills, but we don't, I think, pay enough attention to the way that it is taught, which is by the manipulation of words. In a delightful book called *Mr Fortune's Maggot*, the missionary hero spends a long time trying to describe an umbrella to a Polynesian boy. The description is enchanting but incomprehensible to the person who has never known the need for an umbrella. I found myself in a similar predicament in West Africa once, when I was sitting round a camp-fire with my helpers in a temperature that felt – even if it was not – about 200F in the shade. Somehow or other the subject of snow and ice came up. I tried my best to explain this phenomenon to people who had never seen it and I felt I was talking like a bestiary. White things that fell out of the sky and if enough of them fell they might make you so cold you could die? Rivers and ponds *hard* so that you could walk on them? As I listened to myself I thought I must sound like Baron Münchausen.

The man who first described the Duck-billed Platypus (unfortunately not Goldsmith) might have had similar difficulties.

'Well, gentlemen,' I can hear him saying, 'here we have an undoubted mammal, with a duck's beak, webbed feet, fur and tail somewhat like a beaver and poison spurs on its hind legs like the fangs of a snake. It lays eggs and yet suckles its young with milk.' Even the compiler of a bestiary might have flinched a bit. But I am quite sure that the Hermit crabs, umbrella, the snow and ice and the Duck-billed Platypus could have been handled most adroitly by Oliver Goldsmith and described in lovely prose that even the greatest sceptic would have accepted.

Goldsmith's work is important. Although it is peppered with inaccuracies and is slightly confusing because of his own – somewhat haphazard – method of classification, it lets us appreciate the many rungs of the ladder of knowledge we have climbed. In this present volume, to have thought to combine Goldsmith's prose with the extraordinary illustrations from the *Dictionnaire Universel d'Histoire*

Naturelle by Charles d'Orbigny (of which I am most proud to have an edition in my library) was a masterstroke. This magnificent work published in 1849 was a major contribution to our knowledge of the natural world. Not only was it packed with information but it was illustrated by a team of superb artists including Prêtre, Blanchard, Baron, Oudart and Travies. Their plates are of the most exquisite accuracy and colouring. They were done in the heyday of French science, beautifully conceived and executed in the days when France took its science seriously. So now we have a wonderful amalgam, the prose of Goldsmith and the work of the best natural history painters of the nineteenth century.

Goldsmith, we are told, was not a handsome man but rather an ugly one. His manner in society was lumbering and uncouth, not smooth and witty as one would have expected from one who wrote such polished prose. Yet no less a person than Dr. Johnson said 'He did not touch anything that he did not adorn.' After he was buried his coffin was disinterred so that the two most beautiful women in London society could cut locks from his hair. Not really bad for a hack.

This new presentation of Goldsmith's work is a book to be cherished.

GERALD DURRELL
JERSEY,
26th JANUARY 1990

PREFACE

Oliver Goldsmith

Natural History, considered in its utmost extent, comprehends two objects. First, that of discovering, ascertaining, and naming all the various productions of nature. Secondly, that of describing the properties, manners and relations, which they bear to us, and to each other. The first, which is the most difficult part of this science, is systematical, dry, mechanical, and incomplete. The second is more amusing, exhibits new pictures to the imagination, and improves our relish for existence, by widening the prospect of nature around us.

Both, however, are necessary to those who would understand this pleasing science, in its utmost extent. The first care of every enquirer, no doubt should be, to see to visit and examine every object, before he pretends to inspect its habitudes or its history. From seeing and observing the thing itself, he is most naturally led to speculate upon its uses, its delights, or its inconveniences.

Numberless obstructions, however, are found in this part of his pursuit, that frustrate his diligence and retard his curiosity. The objects in nature are so many, and even those of the same kind are exhibited in such a variety of forms, that the enquirer finds himself lost, in the exuberance before him, and, like a man who attempts to count the stars unassisted by art, his powers are all distracted in the barren superfluity.

To remedy this embarrassment, artificial systems have been devised which, grouping into masses those parts of nature more nearly resembling each other, refer the enquirer for the name of the single object he desires to know to some one of those general distributions, where it is to be found by further examination.

If, for instance, a man should, in his walks, meet with an animal, the name, and consequently the history of which, he desires to know, he is taught by systematic writers of natural history, to examine its most obvious qualities, whether a quadruped, a bird, a fish, or an insect. Having determined it, for explanation sake, to be an insect, he examines whether it has wings; if he finds it possessed of these, he is taught to examine whether it has two or four; if possessed of four, he is taught to observe whether the two upper wings are of a shelly hardness and serve as cases to those under them; if he finds the wings composed in this manner, he is then taught to pronounce, that this insect is one of the beetle kind: of the beetle kind, there are three different classes, distinguished from each other by their feelers; he examines the insect before him, and finds that the feelers are clavated or knobbed at the ends; of beetles, with feelers thus formed, there are ten kinds; and among those, he is taught to look for the precise name of that which is before him. If, for instance, the knob be divided at the ends and the belly be streaked with white, it is no other than the Dor or the Maybug; an animal, the noxious qualities of which give it a very distinguished rank in the history of the insect creation. In this manner a system of natural history may, in some measure, be compared to a dictionary of words. Both are solely intended to explain the names of things; but with this difference, that in the dictionary of words we are led from the name of the thing to its definition; whereas in the system of natural history, we are led from the definition to find out the name.

Such are the efforts of writers, who have composed their works with great labour and ingenuity, to direct the learner in his progress through nature, and to inform him of the name of every animal, plant, or fossil substance, that he happens to meet with; but it would be only deceiving the reader, to conceal the truth, which is, that books alone can never teach him this art in perfection; and the solitary student can never succeed. Without a master, and a previous knowledge of many of the objects in nature, his book will only serve to confound and disgust him. Few of the individual plants or animals, that he may happen to meet with, are in that precise state of health, or that exact period of vegetation, from whence their descriptions were taken. Perhaps he meets the plant only with leaves, but the systematic writer has described it in flower. Perhaps he meets the bird before it has moulted its first feathers, while the systematic description was made in its state of full perfection. He thus ranges without an instructor, confused and with sickening curiosity from subject to subject, till at last he gives up the pursuit, in the multiplicity of his disappointments.

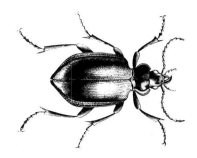

Some practice therefore, much instruction and diligent reading are requisite to make a ready and expert naturalist, who shall be able, even by the help of a system, to find out the name of every object he meets with. But when this tedious, though requisite, part of study is attained, nothing but delight and variety attends the rest of his journey. Wherever he travels, like a man in a country where he has many friends, he meets with nothing but acquaintances and allurements in all the stages of his way. The mere uninformed spectator passes on in gloomy solitude; but the naturalist, in every plant, in every insect, and every pebble, finds something to entertain his curiosity, and excite his speculation.

From hence it appears, that a system may be considered as a dictionary in the study of nature. The ancients, however, who have all written most delightfully on this subject, seem entirely to have rejected those humble and mechanical helps to science. They contented themselves with seizing upon the great outlines of history and passing over what was common, as not worth the detail; they only dwelt upon what was new, great and surprising, and sometimes even warmed the imagination at the expense of truth. Such of the moderns as revived this science in Europe undertook the task more methodically, though not in a manner so pleasing. Aldrovandus, Gesner and Johnson, seemed desirous of uniting the entertaining and rich descriptions of the ancients with the dry and systematic arrangement, of which they were the first projectors. This attempt, however, was extremely imperfect, as the great variety of nature was, as yet, but very inadequately known. Nevertheless, by attempting to carry on both objects at once; first, of directing us to the name of the thing; and then, giving the detail of its history, they drew out their works into a tedious and unreasonable length; and thus mixing incompatible aims they have left their labours, rather to be occasionally consulted than read with delight by posterity.

The later moderns, with that good sense which they have carried into every other part of science, have taken a different method in cultivating natural history. They have been content to give, not only the brevity, but also the dry and disgusting air of a dictionary to their systems. Ray, Klin, Brisson and Linnæus, have had only one aim, that of pointing out the object in nature, of discovering its name, and where it was to be found in those authors that treated of it in a more prolix and satisfactory manner. Thus natural history at present is carried on, in two distinct and separate channels, the one serving to lead us to the thing, the other conveying the history of the thing, supporting it as already known.

The following Natural History is written, with only such an attention to system as serves to remove the reader's embarrassments, and allure him to proceed. It can make no pretensions in directing him to the name of every object he meets with; that belongs to works of a very different kind, and written with very different aims. It will fully answer my design, if the reader, being already possessed of the name of any animal, shall find here a short, though satisfactory history of its habitudes, its subsistence, its manners, its friendships and hostilities. My aim has been to carry on just as much method, as was sufficient to shorten my descriptions by generalizing them, and never to follow order where the art of writing, which is but another name for good sense, informed me that it would only contribute to the reader's embarrassment.

Still, however, the reader will perceive, that I have formed a kind of system in the history of every part of animated nature, directing myself by the great obvious distinctions that she herself seems to have made, which, though too few to point exactly to the name, are yet sufficient to illuminate the subject, and remove the reader's perplexity. Mr. Buffon, indeed, who has brought greater talents to this part of learning than any other man, has almost entirely rejected method in classing quadrupeds. This, with great deference to such a character, appears to me running into the opposite extreme; and, as some moderns have of late spent much time, great pains, and some learning, all to very little purpose, in systematic arrangement, he seems so much disgusted by their trifling, but ostentatious efforts, that he describes his animals, almost in the order they happen to come before him. This want of method seems to be a fault; but he can lose little by a criticism which every dull man can make, or by an error in arrangements, from which the dullest are the most usually free.

In other respects, as far as this able philosopher has gone, I have taken him for my guide. The warmth of his style, and the brilliancy of his imagination, are inimitable. Leaving him therefore without a rival in these, and only availing myself of his information, I have been content to describe things in my own way; and though many of the materials are taken from him, yet I have added, retrenched, and altered, as I thought proper. It was my intention at one time, whenever I differed from him, to have mentioned it at the bottom of the page; but this occurred so often, that I soon found it would look like envy, and might perhaps, convict me of those very errors which I was wanting to lay upon him. I have therefore, as being every way his debtor, concealed my dissent, where my opinion was different; but wherever I borrow from him, I take care at the bottom of the page to express my obligations. But though my obligations to this writer are many, they extend but to the smallest part of the work, as he has hitherto compleated only the history of quadrupeds. I was therefore left to my own reading alone, to make out the history of birds, fishes and insects, of which the arrangement was so difficult, and the necessary information so widely diffused and so obscurely related when found, that it proved by much the most laborious part of the undertaking. Thus having made use of Mr. Buffon's lights in the first part of the work, I may, with some share of confidence, recommend it to the public. But what shall I say to that part, where I have been entirely left without his assistance? As I would affect neither modesty nor confidence, it will be sufficient to say, that my reading upon this part of the subject has been very extensive; and that I have taxed my scanty circumstances in procuring books which are on this subject, of all others, the most expensive. In consequence of this industry, I here offer a work to the public, of a kind, which has never been attempted in ours, or any other modern language, that I know of. The ancients, indeed, and Pliny in particular, have anticipated me, in the present manner of treating natural history. Like those historians who describe the events of a campaign, they have not condescended to give the private particulars of every individual that formed the army; they were content with characterizing the generals, and describing their operations, while they left it to meaner hands to carry the muster-roll. I have followed their manner, rejecting the numerous fables which they adopted, and adding the improvements of the moderns, which are so numerous, that they actually make up the bulk of natural history.

The delight which I found in reading Pliny, first inspired me with the idea of a work of this nature. Having a taste rather classical than scientific, and having but little employed myself in turning over the dry labours of modern system-makers, my earliest intention was to translate this agreeable writer, and by the help of a commentary to make my work as amusing as I could. Let us dignify natural history never so much with the grave appellation of a useful science, yet still we must confess that it is the occupation of the idle and the speculative, more than the busy and the ambitious part of mankind. My intention therefore was to treat what I then conceived to be an idle subject, in an idle manner; and not to hedge round plain and simple narratives with hard words, accumulated distinctions, ostentatious learning, and disquisitions that produced no conviction. Upon the appearance however of Mr. Buffon's work, I dropped my former plan, and adopted the present, being convinced by his manner, that the best imitation of the ancients was to write from our own feelings, and to imitate nature.

It will be my chief pride therefore, if this work may be found an innocent amusement for those who have nothing else to employ them, or who require a relaxation from labour. Professed naturalists will, no doubt, find it superficial; and yet I should hope that even these will discover hints, and remarks, gleaned from various reading, not wholly trite or elementary. I would wish for their approbation. But my chief ambition is to drag up the obscure and gloomy learning of the cell to open inspection; to strip it from its garb of austerity, and to show the beauties of that form, which only the industrious and the inquisitive have been hitherto permitted to approach.

Anredouche. sc.

BOOK I

MAMMALS

OF RUMINATING ANIMALS

Of all animals, those that chew the cud are the most harmless, and the most easily tamed. As they live entirely upon vegetables, it is neither their interest nor their pleasure to make war upon the rest of the brute creation; content with the pastures where they are placed, and fearing nothing from each other, they generally graze in herds for their mutual security. All the fiercest of the carnivorous kinds seek their food in gloomy solitude; these, on the contrary, range together; the very meanest of them are found to unite in each other's defence; and the hare itself is a gregarious animal, in those countries where it has no other enemies but the beasts of the forest to guard against.

As the food of ruminant animals is entirely of the vegetable kind, and as this is very easily procured, so these animals seem naturally more indolent and less artful than those of the carnivorous kind; and as their appetites are more simple, their instincts seem to be less capable of variation. The fox or the wolf are for ever prowling; their long habits of want give them a degree of sharpness and cunning; their life is a continued scene of stratagem and escape: but the patient ox, or the deer, enjoy the repast that Nature has abundantly provided; certain of subsistence, and content with security.

As Nature has furnished these animals with an appetite for such coarse and simple nutriment, so she has enlarged the capacity of the intestines, to take a greater supply. In the carnivorous kinds, as their food is nourishing and juicy, their stomachs are small, and their intestines short; but in these, whose pasture is coarse, and where much must be accumulated before any quantity of nourishment can be obtained, their stomachs are large and their intestines long and

GIRAFFE *Camelopardalis girafa*

muscular. The bowels of a ruminating animal may be considered as a laboratory, with vessels in it, fitted for various transmutations. It requires a long and tedious process before grass can be transmitted into flesh; and for this purpose, Nature, in general, has equipped herbivores with four stomachs, through which the food successively passes, and undergoes the proper separations.

The first is called the paunch, which receives the food after it has been slightly chewed; the second is called the honeycomb, and is a continuation of the former; these two, which are very capacious, the animal fills as fast as it can, and then lies down to ruminate, which may be properly considered as a kind of vomiting without effort or pain. Like quadrupeds of the cow, sheep or deer kind, the rhinoceros, the camel, the horse, the rabbit, the marmot, and the squirrel, all chew the cud by intervals, although they are not furnished with stomachs like the former. Numberless other animals appear to ruminate; not only birds, but fishes, and insects. Among birds are the pelican, the stork, the heron, the pigeon, and the turtle dove; these are able to disgorge their food to feed their young. Among fishes are lobsters, crabs, and that fish called the dorado. The salmon also is said to be of this number: and, if we may believe Ovid, the scarus likewise; of which he says:

Of all the fish that graze beneath the flood,
He only ruminates his former food.

Of insects, the ruminating tribe is still larger: the cricket, the wasp, the drone, the bee, the grasshopper, and the beetle. All these animals either actually chew the cud, or seem at least to ruminate. They have the stomach composed of muscular fibres, by which means the food is ground up and down, in the same manner as in those which are particularly distinguished by the appellation of ruminants.

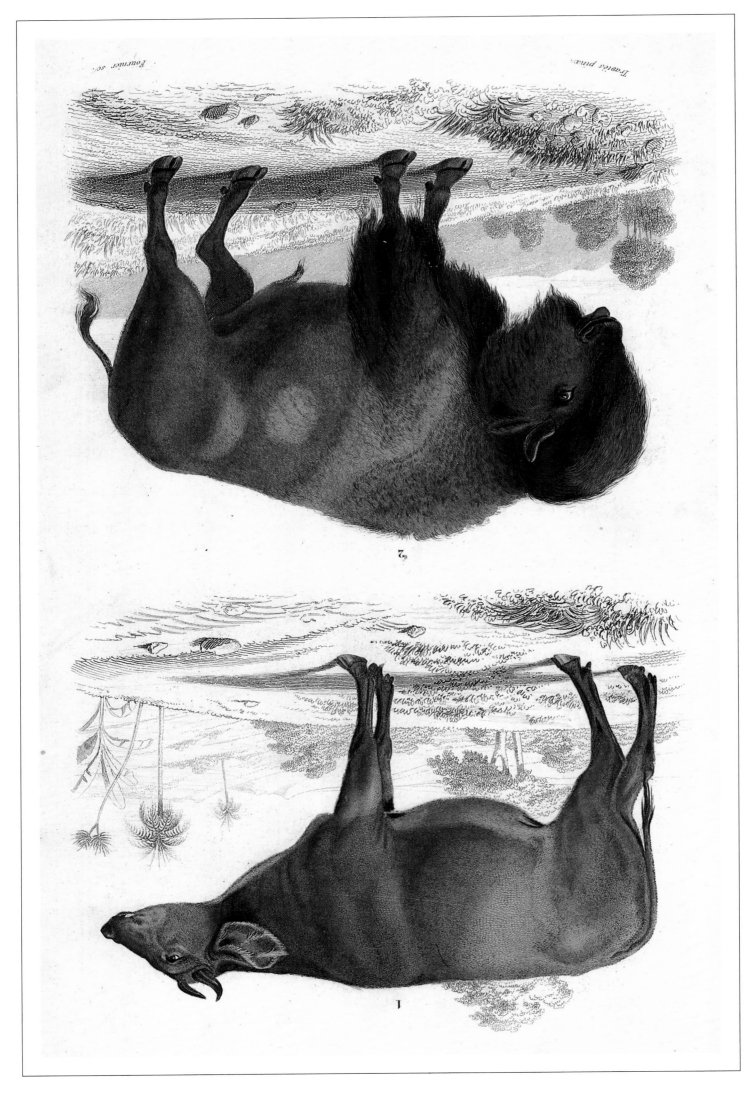

ANIMALS OF THE COW KIND

THE COW

Of all ruminant animals, those of the Cow kind deserve the first rank, both for their size, their beauty, and their services; providing beef and veal for the table while its very milk is wrought into butter and cheese.

The climate and pasture of Great Britain, is excellently adapted to this animal's moderate nature; and the verdure and the fertility of our plains are perfectly suited to the manner of its feeding; for wanting the upper fore teeth, it loves to graze in a high rich pasture.

They in return enrich the pasture; for, of all animals, the cow seems to give back more than it

takes from the soil. The horse and the sheep are known, in a course of years, to impoverish the ground. The land where they have fed becomes weedy, and the vegetables coarse and unpalatable: on the contrary, the pasture where the cow has been bred, acquires a finer softer surface, and becomes every year more beautiful and even.

The age of the cow is known by the teeth and horns. This animal is furnished with eight cutting teeth in the lower jaw; at the age of ten months, the two middlemost of these fall out, and are replaced by others, that are not so white, but broader; at the age of sixteen months, the two next milk-white teeth fall out likewise, and others come up in their room: thus, at the end of every six months, the creature loses and gains, till, at the age of three years, all the cutting teeth are renewed, and then they are long, pretty white and equal.

The horns are another, and a surer method of determining this animal's age. At three years old, it sheds its horns, and new ones arise in their place, which continue as long as it lives; at four years of age, the cow has small pointed neat smooth horns, thickest near the head; at five the horns become larger, and are marked round with the former year's growth. Thus, while the animal continues to live, the

1 OX *Bos brachyceros* 2 BISON *Bos americanus*

horns continue to lengthen; and every year a new ring is added at the root; so that allowing three years before their appearance, and then reckoning the number of rings, we have in both together the animal's age exactly.

The breed of cows has been entirely improved by a foreign mixture, properly adapted to supply the imperfections of our own. Such as are purely British, are far inferior in size to those on many parts of the continent; but those which we have thus improved, by far excel all others. Our Lincolnshire kind derive their size from the Holstein breed: and the large hornless cattle that are bred in some parts of England, came originally from Poland.

The breed of the Isle of Man, and most parts of Scotland, is much less in general than in England or Ireland: they are differently shaped also, the dewlap being much smaller, and, as the expression is, the beast has more of the ewe neck. This, till some years ago, was considered in cattle as a deformity; and the cow was chosen, according to Virgil's direction, with a large dewlap: however, at present it is the universal opinion, that the cow wants in udder what it has in neck, and the larger the dewlap, the smaller is the quantity of its milk. Our graziers now, therefore, endeavour to mix the two breeds; the large Holstein with the small northern; and from both results that fine milch breed, which excels the cattle of any other part of the world.

Africa is remarkable for the largest and the smallest cattle; as is also India, Poland, Switzerland, and several other parts of Europe. Among the Eluth Tartars, where the pastures are remarkably rich and nourishing, the cow becomes so large, that he must be a tall man who can reach the tip of its shoulder. On the contrary, in France, where the animal is stinted in

its food, and driven from the most flourishing pastures, it greatly degenerates.

But the differences in the size of this animal are not so remarkable as those which are found in its form, its hair, and its horns. The difference is so very extraordinary in many of them, that they have been even considered as a different kind of creature, and names have been given them as a distinct species, when in reality they are all the same. In this manner the urus and bison have been considered, from the variety in their make, to be distinct in their production; but they are all in fact the descendants of one common stock, as they have that certain mark of unity, they breed and propagate among each other.

Naturalists have therefore laboured under an obvious error, when, because of the extreme bulk of the urus, or because of the hump upon the back of the bison, they assigned them different places in the creation, and separated a class of animals which was really united. It is true, the horse and the ass do not differ so much in form, as the cow and the bison; nevertheless, the former are distinct animals, as their breed is marked with sterility; the latter are animals of the same kind, as their breed is fruitful, and a race of animals is produced, in which the hump belonging to the bison is soon worn away. The differences, therefore, between the cow, the urus, and the bison, are merely accidental.

The urus, or wild bull, is chiefly to be met with in the province of Lithuania; and grows to a size, that scarce any other animal, except the elephant, is found to equal. It is quite black, except a stripe mixed with white, that runs from the neck to the tail, along the top of the back; the horns are short, thick and strong; the eyes are fierce and fiery; the forehead is adorned with a kind of garland of black curled hair, and some of them are found to have beards of the same; the neck is short and strong, and the skin has an odour of musk. The female, though not so big as the male, exceeds the largest of our bulls in size; nevertheless, her udder and teats are so small, that they can scarcely be perceived.

THE BISON

The Bison, which is another variety of the cow kind, differs from the rest in having a lump between its shoulders. If we should compare the shape of our common cow with that of the bison, the difference will appear very great. The shaggy mane, the beard, the curled forehead, the inverted horns, the broad breast and the narrow hind parts give the bison the appearance rather of a lion than a cow; and fit it more for a state of war than a state of servitude. Yet both animals are found to be so similar as to breed among each other, propagating a race that continues the kind.

These animals are of various kinds; some very large, other as diminutively little. In general, to regard this animal's fore parts, he has somewhat the look of a lion, with a long shaggy mane, and a beard under his chin; his head is little, his eyes red and fiery, with a furious look; the forehead is large, and the horns so big, and so far asunder, that three men might often fit between them. On the middle of the back there grows a bunch almost as high as that of a camel, covered with hair, and which is considered a great delicacy by those that hunt him.

The breed of the bison, is found in all the southern parts of the world; throughout India; throughout Africa, from Mount Atlas to the Cape of Good Hope. In all these countries, the bison seems chiefly to prevail; where they are found to have a smooth soft hair, are very nimble of foot, and in some measure supply the want of horses.

In America, especially towards the north, the bison is well known. The American bison, however, is found to be rather less than that of the ancient continent; its hair is longer and thicker, its beard more remarkable, and its hide more lustrous and soft.

The wild cow and tame, the animal belonging to Europe, and that of Asia, Africa, and America, the bonafus and the urus, the bison and the zebu, are all one and the same, propagate among each other, and, in the course of a few generations, the hump wears away, and scarce any vestiges of savage fierceness are found to remain. Of all animals, therefore, except man alone, the cow seems most extensively propagated. Its nature seems equally capable of the rigours of heat and cold. It is an inhabitant as well of the frozen fields of Iceland, as the burning deserts of Libya. It seems an ancient inmate in every climate, domestic and tame in those countries which have been civilized, savage and wild in the countries which are less peopled, but capable of being made useful in all: able to defend itself in a state of nature against the most powerful enemy of the forest; and only subordinate to man.

Above 1 2 COMMON ZEBU 3 SMALL ZEBU
Below 1 ADDAX ANTELOPE 2 SABLE ANTELOPE (A Fullarton & Co.)

ANIMALS OF THE SHEEP AND GOAT KIND

The goat and the sheep are apparently different in the form of their bodies, in their covering, and in their horns. They may, from hence, be considered as two different kinds with regard to all common and domestic purposes. But if we come to examine them closer, and observe their internal conformation, no two animals can be more alike; their feet, their four stomachs, their suet, their appetites, all are entirely the same, and show the similitude between them; but what makes a much stronger connection is, that they propagate with each other. The sheep and the goat, therefore, may be considered as belonging to one family; and were the whole races reduced to one of each, they would quickly replenish the earth with their kind.

THE SHEEP

The Sheep, in its servile state, seems to be divested of all inclinations of its own, and of all animals it appears the most stupid. Every quadruped has a peculiar turn of countenance, a physiognomy, if we may so call it, that generally marks its nature. The sheep seems to have none of those traits that betoken either courage or cunning; its large eyes, separated from each other, its ears sticking out on each side, and its narrow nostrils, all testify the extreme simplicity of this creature; and the position of its horns also, shows that Nature designed the sheep rather for flight than combat. It appears a large mass of flesh, supported upon four small straight legs, ill fitted for carrying such a burden; its motions are awkward, it is easily fatigued, and often sinks under the weight of its own corpulency. In proportion as the marks of human transformation are numerous, the animal becomes more helpless and stupid. Those which live upon a fertile pasture, and grow fat, become entirely feeble; those that want horns are found more dull and heavy than the rest; those whose fleeces are longest and finest are most subject to a variety of disorders; and, in short, whatever changes may have been wrought in this animal by the industry of man are entirely calculated for human advantage, and not for that of the creature itself. It might require a succession of ages before the sheep could be restored to its primitive state of activity, so as to become a match for its pursuers in the forest.

But this animal, in its domestic state, is too well known to require a detail of its peculiar habits, or the arts which have been used to improve the breed.

If we are to look for this animal in its noblest state, we must seek for it in the African desert, or the extensive plains of Siberia. The variety is so great, that scarcely any two countries have their sheep of the same kind; there is found a manifest difference in all, either in the size, the covering, the shape, or the horns.

The woolly sheep, as it is seen among us, is found only in Europe, and some of the temperate provinces of Asia. When transported into warmer countries, either into Florida or Guinea, it loses its wool, and assumes a covering fitted to the climate, becoming hairy and rough; it there also loses its fertility, and its flesh no longer has the same flavour. In the same manner, in the very cold countries, it seems equally helpless and a stranger, it still requires the unceasing attention of mankind for its preservation; and although it is found to subsist as well in Greenland as in Guinea, it seems a natural inhabitant of neither.

Of the domestic kinds to be found in the different parts of the world, besides our own, which is common in Europe, the first variety is to be seen in Iceland, Muscovy, and the coldest climates of the north. This, which may be called the Iceland sheep, resembles our breed in the form of the body and the tail; but differs in a very extraordinary manner in the number of the horns, being generally found to have four, and sometimes even eight, growing from different parts of the forehead. These are large and formidable, and the animal seems thus fitted by nature for a state of war, however, it is of the nature of the rest of its kind, being mild, gentle and timid. Its wool is very different also from that of the common sheep, being long, smooth, and hairy.

The second variety to be found in this animal, is that of the Broad-tailed sheep, so common in Tartary, Arabia, Persia, Barbary, Syria, and Eygpt. This sheep is only remarkable for its large and heavy tail, which is often found to weigh from twenty to thirty pounds. It sometimes grows a foot broad, and is obliged to be supported by a kind of board, that goes upon wheels.

The third observable variety is that of the sheep called *Strepsicheros*. This animal is a native of the islands of the archipelago, and only differs from our sheep, in having straight horns, surrounded with a spiral furrow.

The last variety is that of the Guinea sheep, which

is generally found in all the tropical climates, both of Africa and the East Indies. They are of a large size, with a rough hairy skin, short horns, and ears hanging down, with a kind of dewlap under the chin. They differ greatly in form from the rest, and might be considered as animals of another kind, were they not known to breed with other sheep. These of all the domestic kinds, seem to approach the nearest to the state of nature. They are larger, stronger, and swifter than the common race, and, consequently, better fitted for a precarious forest life.

At the same time, while man thus cultivates the domestic kinds, he drives away and destroys the savage race, which are less beneficial, and more headstrong. These, therefore, are to be found in but a very small number, in the most uncultivated countries, where they have been able to subsist by their native swiftness and strength. It is in the more uncultivated parts of Greece, Sardinia, Corsica, and particularly in the deserts of Tartary, that the Moufflon is to be found, that bears all the marks of being the primitive race, and that has been actually known to breed with the domestic animal.

The moufflon, or musmon, though covered with hair, bears a stronger similitude to the ram, than to any other animal: like the ram, it has the eyes placed near the horns, and its ears are shorter than those of

GOATS *Capra aegagrus*

the goat; it also resembles the ram in its horns, in all the particular contours of its form. The horns also are alike, they are of a yellow colour, they have three sides, as in the ram, and bend backwards in the same manner, behind the ears; the muzzle and the inside of the ears are of a whitish colour, tinctured with yellow; the other parts of the face are of a brownish grey. The general colour of the hair over the body is of a brown, approaching to that of the red deer. The inside of the thighs and the belly are of a white, tinctured with yellow. The form, upon the whole, seems more made for agility and strength than that of the common sheep; and the moufflon is actually found to live in a savage state, and maintain itself, either by force or swiftness, against all the animals that live by rapine.

Such is the sheep in its savage state; a bold, noble, and even beautiful animal: but it is not the most beautiful creatures that are always found most useful to man. Human industry has therefore destroyed its grace, to improve its utility.

THE GOAT

The Goat seems, in every respect, more fitted for a life of savage liberty than the sheep. It is naturally more lively, and more possessed with animal instinct. It easily attaches itself to man, and seems sensible of his caresses. It is also stronger and swifter, more courageous and more playful, lively, capricious, and vagrant: it is not easily confined to its flock, but chooses its own pastures, and loves to stray remote from the rest. It chiefly delights in climbing precipices, in going to the very edge of danger; it is often seen suspended upon an eminence hanging over the

sea, upon a very little base, and even sleeps there in security. Nature has in some measure fitted it for traversing these declivities with ease; the hoof is hollow underneath, with sharp edges, so that it walks as securely on the ridge of a house, as on the level ground. It is a hardy animal, and very easily sustained; for which reason it is chiefly the property of the poor, who have no pastures with which to supply it. Happily, however, it seems better pleased with the neglected wild, than the cultivated fields of art; it chooses the healthy mountain, or the shrubby rock; its favourite food is the tops of boughs, or the tender bark of young trees; it seems less afraid of immoderate heat, and bears the warm climates better than the sheep; it sleeps exposed to the sun, and seems to enjoy its warmest fervours, neither is it terrified at the storm, or incommoded by the rain; immoderate cold alone seems to affect it, and it is said to produce a vertigo, with which this animal is sometimes incommoded. The inconstancy of its nature is perceivable in the irregularity of its gait; it goes forward, stops, runs, approaches, flies, merely from caprice, and with no other seeming reason than the extreme vivacity of its disposition.

THE CHAMOIS AND IBEX

The Chamois and the Ibex both bear very near approaches to the goat in figure; have horns that never shed; and, at the same time, are more different from each other than from the animal in question. From which of these two sources our domestic goat is derived is not easy to settle. Mr. Buffon is of opinion that the ibex is the principal source, that our

domestic goat is the immediate descendant, and that the chamois is but a variety from that stock, a sort of collateral branch of the same family. His principal reason for giving the preference to the ibex is its having a more masculine figure, large horns, and a large beard; whereas the chamois wants these marks of primitive strength and wildness. He supposes, therefore, in their original savage state, that our goat has taken after the male of the parent stock, and the chamois after the female.

They are both natives of the Alps, the Pyrenees and the mountains of Greece; both well fitted for their precarious lives among the ledges of precipices.

The ibex resembles the goat in the shape of its body but differs in the horns, which are much larger, some two yards long, and bent backwards, full of knots. The ibex has a large black beard, is of brown colour, with a thick warm coat of hair. A streak of black runs along the top of the back; and the belly and backing of the thighs are of a fawn colour.

The chamois is the size of a domestic goat and is most agreeably lively, and active beyond expression. The chamois hair is short, like that of a doe; in spring an ash colour, and in autumn a dun colour, inclining to black, and in winter blackish brown. It has two small circular horns, about half a foot long, of a beautiful black and rising from the forehead, almost between the eyes. The ears are placed in an elegant manner, near the horns with two stripes of black on each side of the face. They run along the rocks with great ease and seeming indifference and leap from one to another to escape pursuit, mounting or descending in an oblique direction; and throw themselves down a rock of thirty feet, to light with great security upon some fragment on the side of the precipice. To see them jump in this manner, they seem rather to have wings than legs.

They are peaceful, gentle creatures, and live in society with each other. They are found in flocks of from four to fourscore, and even a hundred, dispersed upon the crags of the mountains. The large males are seen feeding detached from the rest, except in rutting time, when they approach the females, and drive away the young. The time of their coupling is from the beginning of October to the end of November; and they bring forth in April and March. The young keeps with the dam for above five months, and it is asserted that they live between twenty and thirty years. Their flesh is good to eat; and they are found to have ten or twelve pounds of suet, which far surpasses that of the goat in hardness and goodness. The chamois has a kind of feeble bleat, by which the parent calls its young. But in cases of danger, and when it is to warn the rest of the flock, it uses a hissing noise, which is heard at a great distance. For it is to be observed that this creature is extremely vigilant, and has an eye the quickest and most piercing in nature. Its smell also is not less distinguishing. Upon any alarm, therefore, or any apprehensions of danger, the chamois begins his hissing note with such force, that the rocks and the forests re-echo to the sound. The hissing of the male is much louder and sharper than that of the female; it is performed through the nose; and is properly no more than a very strong breath, driven violently through a small aperture. The chamois feeds upon the best herbage, and chooses the most delicate parts of the plants, the flower and the tender buds. It is not less delicate with regard to several aromatic herbs, which grow upon the sides of the mountains. It drinks but very little while it feeds upon the succulent herbage, and chews the cud in the intervals of feeding. This animal is greatly admired for the beauty of its eyes, which are round and sparkling, and which mark the warmth of its constitution.

THE GAZELLES

The Gazelles, of which there are several kinds, resemble the roe-buck in size and delicacy of form; they have deep pits under the eyes like that animal; they resemble the roe-buck in the colour and nature of their hair; they resemble him in the bunches upon their legs, which only differ in being upon the fore-legs in these, and on the hind legs in the other.

The distinguishing marks of this tribe of animals, by which they differ both from the goat and deer, are these: their horns are made differently, being annulated or ringed round, at the same time that there are longitudinated depressions running from the bottom to the point. They have bunches of hair upon their fore-legs; they have a streak of black, red or brown, running along the lower part of their sides, and three streaks of whitish hair in the internal side of the ear. These are characters that none of them are without; besides these, there are others which, in general, they are found to have, and which are more obvious to the beholder. Of all animals in the world, the gazelle has the most beautiful eye, extremely brilliant, and yet so meek that all the eastern poets compare the eyes of their mistresses to those of this animal. A gazelle-eyed beauty is considered as the highest compliment

BUSHBOK *Antilope scripta*

that a lover can pay; and, indeed, the Greeks themselves thought it no inelegant piece of flattery to resemble the eyes of a beautiful woman to those of a cow. The gazelle, for the most part, is more delicately and finely limbed than even the roe-buck; its hair is as short, but finer and more glossy. Its hind legs are longer than those before, as in the hare, which gives it greater security in ascending or descending steep places. Their swiftness is equal, if not superior to that of the roe; but as the latter bounds forward, so these run along in an even uninterrupted course. Most of them are brown upon the back, white under the belly, with a black stripe, separating these colours between. Their tail is of various lengths, but in all covered with pretty long hair; and their ears are beautiful, well placed, and terminating in a point. They all have a cloven hoof, like the sheep; they all have permanent horns; and the female has them smaller than the male.

Of these animals, Mr. Buffon makes twelve varieties, which, however, is much fewer than what other naturalists have made them. The first is the Gazella, properly so called, which is of the size of the roe-buck, and very much resembling it in all the proportions of its body, but entirely differing, as was said, in the nature and fashion of the horns, which are black and hollow, like those of the ram, or the goat, and never fall. The second he calls the Kevel, which is rather less than the former; its eyes also seem larger; and its horns, instead of being round, are flattened on the sides, as well in the male as the female. The third he calls the Corin, which very much resembles the two former, but that it is still less than either. Its horns also are smaller in proportion, smoother than those of the other two, and the annular prominences

belonging to the kind are scarce discernable, and may rather be called wrinkles than prominences. Some of these animals are often seen streaked like a tiger. These three are supposed to be of the same species. The fourth he calls the Zeiran, the horns only of which he has seen; which, from their size, and the description of travellers, he supposes to belong to a larger kind of the gazelle, found in India and Persia, under that denomination.

The fifth he calls the Koba, and the sixth the Kob; these two differ from each other only in size, the former being much larger than the latter. The muzzle of these animals is much longer than those of the ordinary gazelle; the head is differently shaped, and they have no depressions under the eyes. The seventh he calls after its Egyptian name, the Algazel; which is shaped pretty much like the ordinary gazelle, except that the horns are much longer, being generally three feet from the point to the insertion; whereas, in the common gazelle, they are not above a foot; they are smaller also, and straiter, till near the extremities, when they turn short, with a very sharp flexure: they are black and smooth, and the annular prominences are scarcely observable. The eighth is called the Pazan; or, by some, the Bezoar goat, which greatly resembles the former, except a small variety in their horns; and also with this difference, that as the algazel feeds upon the plains, this is only found in the mountains. They are both inhabitants of the same countries and climate; being found in Egypt, Arabia, and Persia. This last is the animal famous for that

concretion in the intestines or stomach, called the Oriental Bezoar, which was once in such repute all over the world for its medicinal virtues. The word bezoar is supposed to take its name either from the pazan or pazar, which is the animal that produces it; or from a word in the Arabic language, which signifies antidote, or counter-poison. It is a stone of a glazed blackish colour, found in the stomach, or the intestines of some animal, and brought over to us from the East-Indies.

The ninth is called the Ranguer, and is a native of Senegal. This differs somewhat in shape and colour from the rest; but particularly in the shape of its horns, which are straight to near the points, where they crook forward, pretty much in the same manner as in the chamois they crook backward. The tenth variety of the gazelle is the Antelope, so well known to the English, who have given it the name. This animal is of the size of a roe-buck, and resembles the gazelle in many particulars, but differs in others: it has deeper eye pits than the former; the horns are formed differently also, being about sixteen inches long, almost touching each other at the bottom, and spreading as they rise, so as at their tips to be sixteen inches asunder. They have the annular prominences of their kind, but not so distinguishable as in the gazelle: however, they have a double flexure, which is very remarkable, and serves to distinguish them from all others of their kind. At the root they have a tuft of hair, which is longer than that of any part of the body. Like others of the same kind, the antelope is brown on the back, and white under the belly; but these colours are not separated by the black streak which is to be found in all the rest of the gazelle kinds. There are different sorts of this animal, some with larger horns than others, and others with less. The one which makes the eleventh variety in the gazelle kind, Mr. Buffon calls the Lidme, which has very large horns; and the other, which is the twelfth and last, he calls the Indian Antelope, the horns of which are very small.

ANIMALS OF THE DEER KIND

The stag is one of those innocent and peaceable animals that seems made to embellish the forest, and animate the solitudes of nature. The easy elegance of his form, the lightness of his motions, those large branches that seem made rather for the ornament of his head than its defence, the size, the strength and the swiftness of this beautiful creature, all sufficiently rank him among the first of quadrupeds, among the most noted objects of human curiosity.

THE STAG

The Stag, or Hart, whose female is called a *hind*, and the young a *calf*, differs in size and in horns from a fallow-deer. He is much larger, and his horns are round; whereas in the fallow kind they are broad and palmated. By these the animal's age is known. The first year, the stag has no horns, but a horny excrescence, which is short, rough, and covered with a thin hairy skin. The next year the horns are single and straight; the third year they have two antlers, three the fourth, four the fifth, and five the sixth.

These horns, large as they seem, are, notwithstanding, shed every year, and new ones come in their place. The old horns are of a firm solid texture, and usually employed in making handles for knives and other domestic utensils. But, while young, nothing can be more soft or tender; and the animal, as if conscious of his own imbecility, at those times, instantly upon shedding his former horns, retires from the rest of his fellows, and hides himself in solitudes and thickets, never venturing out to pasture, except by night. During this time, which most usually happens in the spring, the new horns are very

painful, and have a quick sensibility of any external impression. The flies also are extremely troublesome to him. When the old horn is fallen off, the new does not begin immediately to appear; but the bones of the skull are seen covered only with a transparent periosteum, or skin, which, as anatomists teach us, covers the bone of all animals. After a short time, however, this skin begins to swell, and to form a soft tumour, which contains a great deal of blood, and which begins to be covered with a downy substance that has the feel of velvet, and appears nearly of the same colour with the rest of the animal's hair. This tumour every day buds forward from the point like the graft of a tree; and, rising by degrees from the head, shoots out the antlers on either side, so that in a few days, in proportion as the animal is in condition, the whole head is completed. However, when the whole head has received its full growth, the extremities then begin to acquire the solidity; the velvet covering, or bark, with its blood-vessels, dry up, and then begin to fall; and this the animal hastens, by rubbing its antlers against every tree it meets. In this manner, the whole external surface being stripped off by degrees, at length the whole head acquires its complete hardness, expansion, and beauty.

A short time after they have furnished their horns, they begin to feel the impressions of the rut, or the desire of copulation. The old ones are the most forward; and about the end of August, or the beginning of September, they quit their thickets, and return to the mountain in order to seek the hind to whom they call with a loud tremulous note. At this time their neck is swollen; they appear bold and furious; fly from country to country; strike with their

horns against the trees and obstacles, and continue restless and fierce until they have found the female; who at first flies from them, but is at last compelled and overtaken. When two stags contend for the same female, however timorous they may appear at other times, they then seem agitated with an uncommon degree of ardour. They paw up the earth, menace each other with their horns, bellow with all their force, and striking in a desperate manner against each other, seem determined upon death or victory. This combat continues till one of them is defeated or flies; and it often happens that the victor is obliged to fight several of those battles before it remains undisputed master of the field. The old ones are generally the

1 & 2 RED DEER 3 ROE BUCK 4 TIBETAN MUSK-DEER
5 & 6 REIN-DEER 7 GUAZUPUCO DEER 8 STAG OF PALESTINE 9 AXIS
10 GUAZUTI DEER 11 GREAT RUSA 12 N. EUROPEAN STAG 13 WAPITI
14 FALLOW DEER (J. Stewart)

conquerors upon these occasions, as they have more strength and greater courage; and these also are preferred by the hind itself to the young ones, as the latter are more feeble, and less ardent. However, they are all equally inconstant, keeping to the female but a few days, and then seeking out for another not to be enjoyed, perhaps, without a repetition of their former danger.

In this manner the stag continues to range from one to the other for about three weeks, the time the rut continues; during which he scarce eats, sleeps, or rests, but continues to pursue, to combat, and to enjoy. At the end of this period of madness, for such in this animal it seems to be, the creature that was before fat, sleek, and glossy, becomes lean, feeble, and timid. He then retires from the herd to seek plenty and repose; he frequents the side of the forest, and chooses the most nourishing pastures, remaining there till his strength is renewed. Thus is his whole life passed in the alternations of plenty and want, of corpulence and inanition, of health and sickness, without having his constitution much affected by the violence of the change. As he is above five years coming to perfection, he lives about forty years; and it is a general rule, that every animal lives about seven or eight times the number of years which it continues to grow.

The usual colour of the stag in England is red; nevertheless, the greater number in other countries are brown. Of all the animals that are natives of this climate, there are none that have such a beautiful eye as the stag: it is sparkling, soft, and sensible. His senses of smelling and hearing are in no less perfection. When he is in the least alarmed, he lifts the head and erects the ears, standing for a few minutes as if in a listening posture. Whenever he ventures upon some unknown ground, or quits his native covering, he first stops at the skirt of the plain to examine all around; he next turns against the wind to examine by the smell if there be any enemy approaching. If a person should happen to whistle or call out, at a distance, the stag is seen to stop short in his slow measured pace, and gazes upon the stranger with a kind of awkward admiration: if the cunning animal perceives neither dogs nor fire-arms preparing against him, he goes forward, quite unconcerned, and slowly proceeds without offering to fly. The cry of the hind, or female, is not so loud as that of the male, and is never excited but by apprehension for herself or her young. When once they have conceived, they separate from the males, and then they both herd together apart. The time of gestation continues between eight and nine months, and they generally produce but one at a time. Their usual season for bringing forth is about the month of May, or the beginning of June, during which they take great care to hide their young in the most obscure thickets. Almost every creature is a formidable enemy, but, the stag himself is a professed enemy, and she is obliged to use all her art to conceal her young from him as from the most dangerous of her pursuers. At this season, therefore, the courage of the male seems transferred to the female; she defends her young against her less formidable opponents by force; and when pursued by the hunter, she ever offers herself to mislead him from the principal object of her concern. She flies before the hounds for half the day, and then returns to her young, whose life she has thus preserved at the hazard of her own.

The calf never quits the dam during the whole summer; and in winter the hind, and all the males under a year old, keep together, and assemble in herds, which are more numerous in proportion as the season is more severe. In the spring they separate; the hinds to bring forth, while none but the year olds remain together; however, these animals are in general fond of herding and grazing in company; it is danger or necessity alone that separates them.

The dangers they have to fear from other animals, are nothing when compared to those from man. The men of every age and nation have made the chases of the stag one of their most favourite pursuits; and those who first hunted from necessity, have continued it for amusement. In our own country, in particular, hunting was ever esteemed as one of the principal diversions of the great. At first, indeed, the beasts of the chase had the whole island for their range, and knew no other limits than those of the ocean.

Those who hunt this animal have their peculiar terms for the different objects of their pursuit. The professors in every art take a pleasure in thus employing a language known only to themselves, and thus accumulate words which to the ignorant have the appearance of knowledge. In this manner, the stag is called the first year, a *calf*, or *hind calf*; the second year, a *knobber*, the third, a *brock*; the fourth, a *staggard*; the fifth, a *stag*; the sixth, a *hart*. The female is called a *hind*; the first year she is a *calf*; the second, a *hearse*; the third, a *hind*. This animal is said to *harbour* in the place where he resides. When he cries he is said to *bell*; the print of his hoof is called the *slot*; his tail is called the *single*; his excrement the *fewmet*; his horns are called his *head*; when simple, the first year, they are called *broches*; the third year, *spears*; the fourth year, that part which bears the antlers is called the *beam*, and the little impressions upon its surface *glitters*; that which rise from the crust of the *beam* are called *pearls*. The antlers also have distinct names: the first that branches off is called the *antler*; the second the *sur antler*; all the rest which grow afterwards, till you come to the top, which is called the *crown*, are called *royal antlers*. The little buds about the tops are

called *croches*. The impression on the place where the stag has lain, is called the layer. If it be in covert or thicket, it is called his *harbour*. Where a deer has passed into a thicket, leaving marks whereby his bulk may be guessed, it is called an *entry*. When they cast their heads, they are said to *mew*. When they rub their heads against trees, to bring off the peel of their horns, they are said to *fray*. His last refuge, when every other method of safety has failed him, is to take the water, and to attempt an escape by crossing whatever lake or river he happens to approach. While

swimming, he takes all possible care to keep in the middle of the stream, lest, by touching the bough of a tree, or the herbage on the banks, he may give scent to the hounds. He is also ever found to swim against the stream; whence the huntsmen have made it into a kind of proverb, *That he that would his chace find, must up with the river and down with the wind.* When a stag hard hunted takes to swimming in the water, he is said to *go sail.* When he turns his head against the hounds, he is said to *bay*; and when the hounds pursue upon the scent, until they have unharboured the stag, they are said to *draw on the slot.*

Now to seek out a stag in his haunt, it is to be observed, that he changes his manner of feeding every month. From the conclusion of rutting-time, which is November, he feeds in heaths and broomy places. In December they herd together, and withdraw into the strength of the forests, to shelter themselves from the severer weather, feeding on holm, elder trees, and brambles. The three following months they leave herding, but keep four or five in a company, and venture out to the corners of the forest, where they feed on winter pasture, sometimes making their incursions into the neighbouring cornfields, to feed upon the tender shoots, just as they peep above ground. In April and May they rest in thickets and shady places, and seldom venture forth, unless roused by approaching danger. In September and October their annual ardour returns; and then they leave the thickets, boldly facing every danger, without any certain place for food or harbour.

The stags of China are of a particular kind, for they are no taller than a common housedog; and hunting them is one of the principal diversions of the great.

The stag of Corsica is a very small animal, being not above half the size of those common among us. His body is short and thick, his legs short, and his hair of a dark brown.

There is in the forests of Germany, a kind of stag,

named by the ancients the Tragelaphus, and which the natives call the Bran Deer, or the Brown Deer. This is of a darker colour than the common stag, of a lighter shade upon the belly, long hair upon the neck and throat, by which it appears bearded, like the goat.

There is also a very beautiful stag, which by some is said to be a native of Sardinia; but others (among whom is Mr. Buffon) are of opinion that it comes from Africa or the East Indies. He calls it the Axis, after Pliny; and considers it as making the shade between the stag and the fallow deer. The horns of the axis are round, like those of the stag; but the form of its body entirely resembles that of the buck, and

the size also is exactly the same. The hair is of four colours; namely, fallow, white, black, and grey. The white is predominant under the belly, on the inside of the thighs, and the legs. Along the back there are two rows of spots in a right line; but those on other parts of the body are very irregular. A white line runs along each side of this animal, while the head and neck are grey. The tail is black above, and white beneath; and the hair upon it is six inches long.

Although there are but few individuals of the deer kind, yet the race seems diffused over all parts of the earth. The new continent of America, in which neither the sheep, the goat, nor the gazelle, have been originally bred, nevertheless produces stags, and other animals of the deer kind, in sufficient plenty. The Mexicans have a breed of white stags in their parks, which they call Stags Royal. The stags of Canada differ from ours in nothing except the size of the horns, which in them is greater; and the direction of the antlers, which rather turn back, than project forward, as in those of Europe. The same difference of size that obtains among our stags, is also to be seen in that country; and, as we are informed by Ruysch, the Americans have brought them into the same state of domestic tameness that we have our sheep, goats, or black cattle. They send them forth in the day-time to feed in the forests; and at night they return home with the herdsman who guards them. The inhabitants have no other milk but what the hind produces; and use no other cheese but what is made from thence.

THE FALLOW DEER

The Fallow Deer are much smaller, so they seem of a nature less robust, and less savage than those of the stag kind. They are found but rarely wild in the forests; they are, in general, bred up in parks, and kept for the purposes of hunting, or of luxury, their flesh being preferred to that of any other animal. The horns of the buck make its principal distinction, being broad and palmated. They seek the female at their second year, and, like the stag, are fond of variety. The doe goes with young above eight months, like the hind; and commonly brings forth one at a time: but they differ in this, that the buck comes to perfection at three, and lives till sixteen; whereas the stag does not come to perfection till seven, and lives till forty.

As this animal is a beast of chase, like the stag, so the hunters have invented a number of names relative to him. The buck is the first year called a *fawn*; the second, a *pricket*; the third, a *sorel*; the fourth, a *sore*; the fifth, a *buck of the first head*; and the sixth, a *great buck*. The female is called a *doe*; the first year a *fawn*; and the second a *tegg*. The manner of hunting the buck is pretty much the same as that of stag hunting, except that less skill is required in the latter. The buck is more easily roused; it is sufficient to judge by the view, and mark what grove or covert it enters, as it is not known to wander far from thence; nor, like the stag, to change his *layer*, or place of repose.

There are two varieties of the fallow deer in England, which are of foreign origin. The beautiful spotted kind, originally brought from Bengal; and the very deep brown sort, that are now so common in several areas. These were introduced by King James the First, from Norway: for having observed their hardiness, and that they could endure the winter, even in that severe climate, without fodder, he brought over some of them into Scotland, and disposed of them among his chases. Since that time, they have multiplied in many parts of the World, and England is famous for its venison. The Spanish fallow-deer are as large as stags, but of a darker colour, and a more slender neck: their tails are longer than those of ours, they are black above, and white below. The deer are larger and stronger than ours, with great necks, and their colour inclined to grey.

THE ELK

The Elk is an animal of great stature, rather of the buck than the stag kind, as its horns are slatted towards the top, with a span of between three – ten feet from one antler tip to the other. It is known in Northern Europe and Asia under the name of Elk, and in North America, where it is extremely common, by that of the Moose-deer.

There is very little difference between the European elk, and the American moose-deer, as they are but varieties of the same animal. It may be rather larger in America achieving a height of between nine – fourteen feet. There are two kinds of American moose, the common light grey, not very large; and the black moose, which grows to an enormous height with antlers proportionate to size. Both kinds have flat palmed horns, not unlike the fallow deer, only the palm is much larger, having a short trunk on the head and then immediately spreading about a foot broad with a kind of small antler-like foot, on one edge. The grey moose is about the size of a horse, and although it has large buttocks, its tail is not above an inch long. As in all kinds, the upper lip is much longer than the under and their nostrils the span of a man's hand. In all places, however, it is timorous and gentle; content with its pasture, and never willing to disturb any other animal, when supplied itself.

The European elk grows to above seven or eight feet high.

THE REIN-DEER

Of all animals of the deer kind, the Rein-Deer is the most extraordinary and the most useful. It is a native of the icy regions of the north and nature seems to have fitted it entirely to answer the necessities of that hardy race of mankind that live near the pole. As these would find it impossible to subsist among their barren snowy mountains without its aid, so this animal can live only there, where its assistance is most absolutely necessary. From it alone the inhabitants of Lapland and Greenland supply most of their wants; it answers the purposes of a horse, to convey them from one mountain to another; it answers the puposes of a cow, in giving milk; and it answers the purposes of the sheep, in providing them with a warm, though a homely kind of clothing. From this quadruped alone, therefore, they receive as many

advantages as we derive from three of our most useful creatures.

The rein-deer, also a native of North America under the name of Caribou, resembles the American elk in the fashion of its horns. Both have browantlers, very large, and hanging over their eyes; palmated towards the top, and bending forward, like a bow. But here the similarity between these two animals ends; for, as the elk is much larger than the stag, so the rein-deer is much smaller. It is lower and stronger built than the stag; its legs are shorter and thicker, and its hoofs much broader than in that animal; its hair is much thicker and warmer, its horns much larger in proportion, and branching forward over its eyes; its ears are much larger; its pace is rather a trot than a bounding, and thus it can continue for a whole day; its hoofs are cloven and moveable, so that it spreads them abroad as it goes, to prevent its sinking in the snow. When it proceeds on a journey, it lays its great horns on its back, while there are two branches which always hang over its forehead, and almost cover its face. One thing seems peculiar to this animal and the elk; which is, that as they move along, their hoofs are heard to crack with a pretty loud noise. This arises from their manner of treading; for as they rest upon their cloven hoof, it spreads on the ground, and the two divisions separate from each other; but when they lift it, the divisions close again,

1 MOUSE-DEER *Moschus pygnueus*

2 MOOSE *Cervus alces*

and strike against each other with a crack. The female also of the rein-deer has horns as well as the male, by which the species is distinguished from all other animals of the deer kind whatsoever.

When the rein-deer first shed their coat of hair, they are brown; but, in proportion as summer approaches, their hair begins to grow whitish; until, at last, they are nearly grey. They are, however, always black about the eyes. The neck has long hair, hanging down, and coarser than upon any other part of the body. The feet, just at the insertion of the hoof, are surrounded with a ring of white. The hair in general stands so thick over the whole body, that if one should attempt to separate it, the skin will nowhere appear uncovered: whenever it falls also, it is not seen to drop from the root, as in other quadrupeds but seems broken short near the bottom; so that the lower part of the hair is seen growing, while the upper falls away.

The horns of the female are made like those of the male, except that they are smaller and less branching. As in the rest of the deer kind, they sprout from the points; and also in the beginning, are furnished with a hairy crust, which supports the blood-vessels, of most exquisite sensibility. The rein-deer shed their horns, after rutting-time, at the latter end of November; and they are not completely furnished again till towards autumn. The female always retains hers till she brings forth, and then sheds them, about the beginning of November. If she is barren, however, which is not unfrequently the case, she does not shed them till winter.

ANIMALS OF THE HORSE KIND

THE HORSE

Of all the quadruped animals, the Horse seems the most beautiful; the noble largeness of his form, the glossy smoothness of his skin, the graceful ease of his motions, and the exact symmetry of his shape, have taught us to regard him as the most perfectly formed; and yet, what is extraordinary enough, if we examine him internally, his structure will be found the most different from that of man of all other quadrupeds whatsoever. As the ape approaches us the nearest in internal conformation, so the horse is the most remote.

With six cutting teeth before, and single hoofed, the horse is a native of Europe and the East; a generous, proud, and strong animal, fit either for the draught, the course, or the road; he is delighted with woods, he takes care of his hind parts; defends himself from the flies with his tail; scratches his fellow; defends its young; calls by neighing; sleeps after nightfall; fights by kicking, and by biting also; rolls on the ground when he sweats; eats the grass closer than the ox; distributes the feed by dunging; lacks a gall bladder; never vomits. The mare goes with foal two hundred and ninety days. The placenta is not fixed, and the foal is produced with the feet stretched out. He acquires the canine teeth not till the age of five years. In those boundless tracts, whether of Africa, or South America, where he runs at liberty, he seems no way incommoded with the inconveniences to which he is subject in Europe. The continual verdure of the fields supplies his wants; and the climate that never knows a winter suits his constitution, which naturally seems adapted to heat.

In these countries, therefore, the horses are often seen feeding in droves of five or six hundred. As they do not carry on war against any other race of animals, they are satisfied to remain entirely upon the defensive, and they have always one among their number that stands as sentinel, to give notice of any approaching danger; and this office they take by turns. If a man approaches them while they are feeding by day, their sentinel walks up boldly near him, as if to examine his strength, or to intimidate him from proceedings; but, as the man approaches within pistol shot, the sentinel then thinks it high time to alarm his fellows; this he does by a loud kind of snorting, upon which they all take the signal, and fly off with the speed of the wind; their faithful sentinel bringing up the rear.

We have the testimony of the ancients that there were wild horses once in Europe; at present, however, they are totally brought under subjection; and even those which are found in America are of a Spanish breed, which being sent thither upon its first discovery, have since become wild, and have spread over all the south of the vast continent, almost to the Straits of Magellan. These, in general, are a small breed, of about fourteen hands high. They have thick jaws and clumsy joints; their ears and neck also are long; they are easily tamed; for the horse by nature is a gentle complying creature, and resists rather from fear than obstinancy.

It is not in the new, but the old world that we are to

look for this animal, in a true state of nature; in the extensive deserts of Africa, in Arabia, and those widespread countries that separate Tartary from the more Southern nations. Vast droves of these animals are seen wild among the Tartars: they are of a small breed, extremely swift, and very readily evade their pursuers. As they go together, they will not admit of any strange animals among them, though even of their own kind. Whenever they find a tame horse attempting to associate with them, they instantly gather round him, and soon oblige him to seek safety by flight. There are vast numbers also of wild horses to the north of China, but they are of a weak timid breed; small of stature and useless in war.

At the Cape of Good Hope also there are numbers of horses, in a state of nature, but small, vicious, and untameable.

But of all countries in the world, where the horse runs wild, Arabia produces the most beautiful breed, the most generous, swift, and persevering. They are found, though not in great numbers, in the deserts of that country. Although they are active and beautiful, they are not so large as those that are bred up tame and rather inclined to leanness than fat; they are of a brown colour; their mane and tail very short, and the

ARAB HORSE *Equus caballus*

hair black and tufted. Their swiftness is incredible.

The Arabians, as we are told by historians, first began the management of horses in the time of Sheik Ismael. Before that they wandered wild along the face of the country until the natives first began to tame their fierceness, and to improve their beauty; so that at present they possess a race of the most beautiful horses in the whole world, with which they drive a trade, and furnish the stables of princes at immense prices.

Mares support fatigue, thirst, and hunger, better than the horses are found to do. They are also less vicious, of a gentler nature, and are not so apt to neigh. They are more harmless also among themselves, not so apt to kick or hurt each other, but remain whole days together without the least mischief. The Arabians preserve the pedigree of their horses with great care, and for several ages back. They know their alliances and all their genealogy; they distinguish the races by different names, and divide them into three classes. The first is that of the nobles, the ancient breed, and unadulterated on either side: the second is that of the horses of the ancient race, but adulterated; and the third is that of the common and inferior kind: the last they sell at a low price; but those of the first class, and even of the second, amongst which are found horses of equal

value to the former, are sold extremely dear. They know, by long experience, the race of a horse by his appearance; they can tell the name, the surname, the colour, and the marks properly belonging to each. When they are not possessed of stallions of the noble race themselves, for their mares, they borrow from their neighbours, paying a proper price as with us, and receive a written attestation of the whole. In this attestation is contained the name of the horse and the mare, and their respective genealogies. When the mare has produced her foal, new witnesses are called, and a new attestation signed, in which are described the marks of the foal, and the day noted when it was brought forth. These attestations increase the value of the horse; and they are given to the person who buys him. The most ordinary mare of this race sells for five hundred crowns; there are many that sell for a thousand; and some of the very finest kinds for fourteen or fifteen hundred pounds.

They at present seem sensible of the great advantage their horses are to the country; there is a law, therefore, that prohibits the exportation of the mares, and such stallions as are brought into England are generally purchased on the eastern shores of Africa, and come round by the Cape of Good Hope. They are in general less in stature than our own, being not above fourteen, or fourteen hands and a half high; their motions are much more graceful and swifter than of our own horses; but, nevertheless, their speed is far from being equal; they run higher from the ground; their stroke is not so long and close; and they are far inferior in bottom. Still, however, they must be considered as the first and finest breed in the world; and that from which all others have derived their principal qualifications. It is even probable that Arabia is the original country of horses; since there, instead of crossing the breed, they take every precaution to keep it entire.

The Arabian breed has been diffused into Egypt as well as Barbary, and into Persia also; where, it is said, there are studs of ten thousand white mares all together, very fleet, and with the hoof so hard that shoeing is unnecessary. The horses of these countries a good deal resemble each other. They are usually of a slender make; their legs fine, bony, and far apart; a thin mane; a fine crest; a beautiful head; the ear small and well pointed; the shoulder thin; the side rounded, without any unsightly prominence; the croup is a little of the longest, and the tail is generally set high.

Next to the barb, travellers generally rank the Spanish Genette. These horses, like the former, are little, but extremely swift and beautiful. The head is something of the largest; the mane thick; the ears long, but well pointed; the eyes filled with fire; the shoulder thickish, and the breast full and large; the croup round and large; the legs beautiful, and without hair; the pastern a little of the longest, as in the barb, and the hoof rather too high. Nevertheless, they move with great ease, and carry themselves extremely well. Their most usual colour is black, or a dark bay. They seldom or never have white legs, or white snip. The Spaniards, who have a groundless aversion to these marks, never breed from such as have them. They are all branded on the buttock with the owner's name; and those of the province of Andalusia pass for the best. These are said to possess courage, obedience, grace, and spirit, in a greater degree than even the barb; and, for this reason, they have been preferred as war horses to those of any other country.

The Italian horses were once more beautiful than they are at present, for they have greatly neglected the breed. Nevertheless, there are still found some beautiful horses among them, particularly among the Neapolitans, who chiefly use them for the draught. In general, they have large heads and thick necks. They are also restive, and consequently unmanageable. These faults, however, are recompensed by the largeness of their size, by their spirit, and the beauty of their motion. They are excellent for show, and have a particular aptitude to prance. The Italians have a peculiar sport, in which horses of this breed run against each other. They have no riders, but saddles so formed as to slap against the horses' sides as they move, and thus to spur them forward. They are set to run in a kind of railed walk, about a mile long out of which they never attempt to escape; but, when they once set forward, they never stop, although the walk from one end to the other is covered with a crowd of spectators, which opens and gives way as the horses approach.

The Danish horses are of such an excellent size and so strong a make, that they are preferred to all others for the draught. There are some of them perfectly well shaped; but this is but seldom seen, for in general they are found to have a thick neck, heavy shoulders, long and hollow back, and a narrow croup: however, they all move well, and are found excellent both for parade and war. They are of all colours, and often of

Above ONAGER, Below COUAGGA (A Fullarton & Co.)

whimsical ones, some being streaked like the tiger, or mottled like the leopard.

The German horses are originally from Arabian and Barbary stocks; nevertheless, they appear to be small and ill shaped: it is said also, that they are weak and washy, with tender hooves. The Hungarian horses, on the other hand, are excellent for the draught, as well as the saddle. The Hussars, who use them in war, usually slit their nostrils; which is done, as it is said, to prevent their neighing, but, perhaps, without any real foundation.

The Dutch breed is good for the draught, and is generally used for that purpose over Europe: the best come from the province of Friesland. The Flanders horses are much inferior to the former; they have most commonly large heads, flat feet, and swollen legs; which are an essential blemish in horses of this kind.

The French horses are of various kinds; but they have few that are good. The best horses of that country come from Limosin; they have a strong resemblance to the barb, and, like them, are excellent for the chase; but they are slow in coming to perfection: they are to be carefully treated while young, and must not be backed till they are eight years old. Normandy furnishes the next best; which, though not so good for the chase, are yet better for war. In general, the French horses have the fault of being

heavy shouldered, which is opposite to the fault of the barb, which is too thin in the shoulder, and is, consequently, apt to shoulder-slipt.

The Persian horses are, in general, the most beautiful and most valuable of all the east. They are in general of a middle size; and they have all a thin head, a fine crest, a narrow breast, small ears well placed, the legs fine, the hoof hard, and a beautiful croup; they are docile, spirited, nimble, hardy, courageous, and capable of supporting a very great fatigue; they run very swiftly, without being easily fatigued; they are strong, and easily nourished, being only supplied with barley and chopped straw; they are put to grass only for six weeks in the spring; they have always the tail at full length, and there are no geldings among the number; they are protected from the air, as in England, by body clothes; they are attended with the most punctual exactness; and they are ridden generally in a snaffle, without spurs. Great numbers of

these are every year transported into Turkey, but chiefly into the East Indies: however, travellers agree that they are not to be compared to the Arabian horses, either for courage, force, or beauty; and that the latter are greatly sought, even in Persia.

The horses of India are of a very indifferent kind, being weak and washy. Those which are used by the grandees of the country, come from Persia and Arabia; they are fed with a small quantity of hay during the day; and at night they have boiled peas, mixed with sugar and butter, instead of oats or barley: this nourishment supports them, and gives them strength; otherwise, they would soon sink and degenerate. Those naturally belonging to the country, are very small and vicious. Some are so very little, it is said, that the young Mogul prince, at the age of seven or eight, rode one of those little horses, not much larger than a greyhound: and it is not long since one of these was brought over into this country, as a present to our Queen, that measures no more than nine hands high; and is not much larger than a common mastiff. It would seem, that climates excessively hot, are unfavourable to this animal. It is a common exercise with the grandees of that country, who are excellent horsemen, to dart out their lances before them upon full gallop, and to catch them again before they come to the ground. They have a sport also on horseback, that requires great dexterity in the rider, and a great share of activity in the horse; they strike off a ball, with a battledore, while they are upon a full gallop, and pursuing it, strike it again before it comes to the ground; and this they continue for a mile together, striking sometimes to the right, and sometimes to the left, with amazing speed and agility.

If we consult the ancients on the nature and qualities of the horses of different countries, we learn, that the Grecian horses, and particularly those of Thessaly, had the reputation of being excellent for war; that those of Achaia were the largest that were known; that the most beautiful came from Egypt, which bred great numbers; that the horses of Ethiopia were not in esteem from the heat of the country; that Arabia and Africa furnished very beautiful horses, and very fit for the course; that those of Italy, and particularly of Apulia, were very good; that in Sicily, Capadocia, Syria, Armenia, Media, and Persia, there were excellent horses, equally esteemed for their speed and vigour; that those of Sardinia and Corsica, though small, were spirited and courageous; that those of Spain resembled the Parthian horses, in being very well adapted for war; that in Walachia and Transylvania, there were horses with bushy tails, and manes hanging down to the ground, which, nevertheless, were extremely swift and active; that the Danish horses were good leapers; those of Scandinavia, though little, were well shaped, and possessed of great agility; that the Flanders breed was strong; that the Gaulish horses were good for carrying burdens; that the German breeds were so bad, so diminuitive, and ill shaped, that no use could be made of them;

that the Swiss and Hungarian horses were good; and, lastly, that those of India were very diminutive and feeble.

I have hitherto omitted making mention of one particular breed, more excellent than any that either the ancients or moderns have produced; and that is our own. It is not without great assiduity, and unceasing application, that the English horses are now become superior to those of any part of the world, both for size, strength, swiftness, and beauty. It was not without great attention, and repeated trials of all the best horses in different parts of the world, that we have been thus successful in improving the breed of this animal, so that the English horses are now capable of performing what no others ever could attain to. By a judicious mixture of the several kinds, by the happy difference of our soils, and by our superior skill in management, we have brought this animal to its highest perfection. An English horse, therefore, is now known to excel the Arabian, in size and swiftness; to be more durable than the barb, and more hardy than the Persian. An ordinary racer is known to go at the rate of a mile in two minutes: and we had one instance, in the admirable Childers, of still greater rapidity. He has been frequently known to move about eighty-two feet and a half in a second, or almost a mile in a minute: he had run also round the course of Newmarket, which is very little less than four miles, in six minutes and forty seconds.

English hunters are considered as the noblest and the most useful horses in the world. Our geldings are, therefore, sent over to the continent in great numbers, and sell at very great prices; as for our mares and stallions, there is a law prohibiting their exportation; and one similar to this, obtained even as early as the times of Athelstan, who prohibited their exportation, except where designed as presents.

Roger de Belegme, created Earl of Shrewsbury by William the Conqueror, is the first who is recorded to have made attempts towards improving our native breed. He introduced Spanish stallions into his estate at Powys in Wales, from which that part of the country was for many ages after famous for a swift and generous race of horses: however, at that time, strength and swiftness were more regarded than beauty; the horses' shapes, in time of action, being entirely hid by a coat of armour, which the knights then usually put upon them, either by way of ornament or defence.

To conclude, I will content myself with just mentioning the description of Camerarius, in which he professes to unite all the perfections which a horse ought to be possessed of. 'It must,' says he, 'have three parts like those of a woman; the beast must be broad, the hips round, and the mane long: it must, in three things resemble a lion; its countenance must be fierce, its courage must be great, and its fury irresistible: it must have three things belonging to the sheep; the nose, gentleness, and patience: it must have three of a deer; head, leg, and skin: it must have three of a wolf; throat, neck, and hearing: it must have three of a fox; ear, tail, and trot: three of a serpent; memory, fight, and flexibility: and, lastly, three of a hare; running, walking, and perseverance.'

THE ZEBRA

The Zebra is the most beautiful, but at the same time the wildest animal in nature. Nothing can exceed the delicate regularity of this creature's colour, or the lustrous smoothness of its skin; but, on the other hand, nothing can be more timid or more untameable.

It is chiefly a native of the southern parts of Africa; and there are whole herds of them often seen feeding in those extensive plains that lie towards the Cape of Good Hope. However, their watchfulness is such, that they will suffer nothing to come near them; and their swiftness is so great, that they readily leave every pursuer far behind. The zebra, in shape, rather resembles the mule, its head is large, its ears long, its back straight, its legs finely placed, and its tail tufted at the end; like the horse, its skin is smooth and close, and its hind quarters round and fleshy. But its greatest beauty lies in the amazing regularity and elegance of its colours. In the male, they are white and brown; in the female, white and black. These colours are disposed in alternative stripes over the whole body, and with such exactness and symmetry, that one would think Nature had employed the rule and compass to paint them. These stripes, which, like so many ribbands, are laid all over its body, are narrow, parallel, and exactly separated from each other. It is not here as in other parti-coloured animals, where the tints are blended into each other;

every stripe here is perfectly distinct, and preserves its colour round the body, or the limb, without any diminution. In this manner are the head, the body, the thighs, the legs, and even the tail and the ears beautifully streaked, so that at a little distance one would be apt to suppose that the animal was dressed out by art, and not thus admirably adorned by Nature.

In the male zebra, the head is striped with fine bands of black and white, which in a manner centre in the forehead. The ears are variegated with a white and dusky brown. The neck has broad stripes of the same dark brown running round it, leaving narrow white stripes between. The body is striped also across the back with broad bands, leaving narrower spaces of white between them, and ending in points at the sides of the belly, which is white, except a black line pectinated on each side, reaching from between the forelegs, along the middle of the belly, two thirds of its length. There is a line of separation between the trunk of the body and the hind quarters, on each side; behind which, on the rump, are bands of narrow stripes, joined together, by a stripe down the middle, to the end of the tail. The colours are different in the female; and in none the stripes seem entirely to agree in form, but in all they are equally distinct; the hair equally smooth and fine; the white shining and unmixed; and the black, or brown, thick and lustrous.

Such is the beauty of this creature, that it seems by nature fitted to satisfy the pride and the pleasure of man; and formed to be taken into his service. Hitherto, however, it appears to have disdained servitude, and neither force nor kindness have been able to wean it from its native independence and ferocity. Its extraordinary beauty is not the only motive we have

for wishing this animal among the number of our dependents: its swiftness is said to surpass that of all others; so that the speed of a zebra has become a proverb among the Spaniards and Portuguese. It stands better upon its legs also than a horse; and is consequently stronger in proportion. Thus, if by proper care we improved the breed, as we have in other instances, we should probably in time to come have a race as large as the horse, as fleet, as strong, and much more beautiful.

The zebra, as was said, is chiefly a native of the Cape of Good Hope. It is also found in the kingdom of Angola; and, as we are assured by Lopez, in several provinces also of Barbary. In those boundless forests it has nothing to restrain its liberty; it is too shy to be caught in traps, and therefore seldom taken alive. It would seem, therefore, that none of them has ever been brought into Europe, that were caught sufficiently young, so as to be untinctured by their original state of wildness. The Portuguese, indeed, pretend that they have been able to tame them, and that they have sent four from Africa to Lisbon, which were so far brought under as to draw the King's coach. Of those which were sent to Brazil, not one could be tamed; they would permit one man only to approach them; they were tied up very short; and one of them, which had by some means got loose, actually killed his groom, having bitten him to death.

This animal, which is neither to be found in Europe, Asia, or America, is nevertheless very easily fed. That which came over into England some years ago, would eat almost anything, such as bread, meat, and tobacco; that which is now among us, subsists entirely upon hay. The noise they make is neither like that of a horse or an ass, but more resembling the confused barking of a mastiff dog. In the two which I saw, there was a circumstance that seems to have escaped naturalists; which is, that the skin hangs loose below the jaw upon the neck, in a kind of dewlap, which takes away much from the general beauty.

These animals are often sent as presents to the princes of the east. We are told, that one of the governors of Batavia gave a zebra, which had been sent to him from Africa, to the Emperor of Japan, for which he received as an equivalent for the company, a present, to the value of sixty thousand crowns. Teller

ZEBRA *Equus montanus*

1 WILD BOAR 2 COLLARED PECCARY 3 CHINESE SOW 4 CAPIBARA
5 BABYROUSSA (J. Stewart)

also relates, that the Great Mogul gave two thousand ducats for one of them. And it is frequent with the African ambassadors to the court of Constantinople, to bring some of these animals with them, as presents for the Grand Seignoir.

ANIMALS OF THE HOG KIND

Animals of the hog kind seem to unite in themselves all those distinctions by which others are separated. They resemble those of the horse kind in the number of their teeth, which in all amount to forty-four, in the length of their head, and in having but a single stomach. They resemble the cow kind in their cloven hoofs, and the position of their intestines; and they resemble those of the claw-footed kind in their appetite for flesh, in their not chewing the cud, and in their numerous progeny. Like the rapacious kinds, they have short intestines. Thus this species serves to fill up that chasm which is found between the carnivorous kinds and those that live upon grass; being possessed of the ravening appetite of the one, and the inoffensive nature of the other.

THE WILD BOAR

The Wild Boar, which is the original of all the varieties of this creature is neither a solitary nor a gregarious animal. The three first years the whole litter follows the sow, and the family lives in a herd together. The sow brings forth, till the age of fifteen, ten to twenty young a litter, once a year. The hog, in a natural state, is found to feed chiefly upon roots and vegetables; it seldom attacks any other animals, being content with such provisions as it procures without danger. He is much smaller than the tame hog-pig, and does not vary in his coarse haired coat colour as those of the domestic kind do, being an iron grey,

inclining to black, including the cloven feet, and tail. He roots the ground in a different manner from the common hog, ploughing it up like a furrow. The tusks, issuing from both the upper and lower jaw, grow to almost a foot long and are exceedingly sharp at the points. These tusks never fall and the teeth are never shed as in other animals.

THE PECCARY OR TAJACU

That animal which of all others most resembles a hog, and yet is of a formation very distinct from it, is called the Peccary, or Tajacu. It is a native of South America, and is seen in herds, grazing among the woods, and inoffensive, except when offended.

The peccary resembles a small hog; the form of its body, the shape of its head, the length of its snout, and the form of its legs, are entirely alike: but the body is not so bulky; its legs not so long; its bristles much thicker and stronger than those of the hog, resembling rather the quills of a porcupine, than hair; instead of a tail, it has only got a little fleshy protuberance, which does not even cover its posteriors; but that which is still more extraordinary, and in which it differs from all other quadrupeds whatsoever, is, that it has got upon its back a lump resembling the navel in other animals which is found to separate a liquor of a very strong smell. The peccary is the only creature that has those kind of glands

which discharge the milky substance, on that part of its body. This lump, or navel is situated over the hind legs, obscured by long bristles. The whitish liquor distilled from the small glands under the skin resembles that obtained from the civet, but Mr. Buffon affirms that the smell is strong and offensive.

The colour of the body is grizzly, with bristles, thicker and stronger than those of a common hog; though not as thick as those of a porcupine, and they are variegated with black and white rings. The belly is almost bare; and the short bristles on the sides, gradually increase in length, as they approach the ridge of the back, to five inches long. On the head also, between the ears, there is a large tuft of bristles, that are chiefly black. The ears are about two inches and a half long, and stand upright; and the eyes resemble those of a common hog, only they are smaller. From the lower corner of the eye to the snout, is usually six inches; and the snout itself is like that of a hog's, though it is smaller. One side of the lower lip is generally smooth, by the rubbing of the tusk of the upper jaw. The feet and hoofs are perfectly like those of a common hog; but it has no tail. The peccary may be tamed like the hog, and has pretty nearly the same habits and natural inclinations.

It is numerous in parts of Southern America. They go in large herds together; and unite, like hogs, in each other's defence. They are particularly fierce when their young are attempted to be taken from them, when they threaten with their tusks, and their rough bristles standing erect, as in the hog kind, they assume a very terrible appearance.

The peccary is rather fond of the mountainous parts of the country; it seems to delight neither in the marshes nor the mud, but keeps among the woods, where it subsists upon wild fruits, roots, and vegetables.

The peccary, like the hog, is very prolific; the young ones follow the dam, and do not separate till they have come to perfection.

THE CAPIBARA OR CABIAI

The Capibara resembles a hog of about two years old, in the shape of its body, and the coarseness and colour of its hair. Like the hog, it has a thick short neck, and a rounded bristly back; like the hog, it is fond of the water and marshy places, brings forth many at a time, and, like it, feeds upon animal and vegetable food. But, when examined more nearly, the differences are many and obvious. The head is

1 WILD BOAR *Sus scropha*

2 COLLARED PECCARY *Dicotyles torquatus*

longer, the eyes are larger, and the snout, instead of being rounded, as in the hog, is split, like that of a rabbit or hare, then furnished with thick strong whiskers; the mouth is not so wide, the number and the form of the teeth are different, for it is without tusks: like the peccary, it wants a tail; and, unlike to all others of this kind, instead of a cloven hoof, it is in a manner web-footed, and thus entirely fitted for swimming and living in the water. The hoofs before are divided into four parts; and those behind, into three; between the divisions, there is a prolongation of the skin, so that the foot, when spread in swimming, can beat a greater surface of water.

As its feet are thus made for the water, so it is seen to delight entirely in that element; and some naturalists have called it the Water-hog for that reason. It is a native of South America, and is chiefly seen frequenting the borders of lakes and rivers, like the otter. It seizes the fish upon which it preys, with its hoofs and teeth, and carries them to the edge of the lake, to devour them at its ease. It lives also upon fruits, corn, and sugar-canes. As its legs are long and broad, it is often seen sitting up, like a dog that is taught to beg. Its cry more nearly resembles the braying of an ass, than the grunting of a hog. It seldom goes out, except at night, and that always in company. It never ventures far from the sides of the river or the lake in which it preys; for as it runs ill, because of the length of its feet, and the shortness of its legs, so its only place of safety is the water, into which it immediately plunges when pursued, and keeps so long at the bottom, that the hunter can have no hopes of taking it there. The capibara, even in a state of wildness, is of a gentle nature, and, when taken young, is easily tamed. It comes and goes at command, and even shows an attachment to its keeper. Its flesh is said to be fat and tender, but, from the nature of its food, it has a fishy taste, like that of all those which are bred in the water. Its head, however, is said to be excellent; and, in this, it resembles the beaver, whose fore parts taste like flesh, and the hind like the fish it feeds on.

ANIMALS OF THE CAT KIND

All the class of the cat kind are chiefly distinguished by their sharp and formidable claws, which they can hide and extend from their sheaths when seizing their prey. Their teeth also, thirty in number, are very formidable; but are rather calculated for tearing their prey than for chewing it; for this reason they feed slowly, and while they eat, generally continue growling, to deter others from taking a share. They lead a solitary ravenous life, neither uniting for their mutual defence, like vegetable feeders, nor for their mutual support, like those of the dog kind. The whole of this cruel and ferocious tribe seek their food alone; and, except at certain seasons, are even enemies to each other. The

dog, the wolf, and the bear, are sometimes known to live upon vegetable or farinaceous food; but all of the cat kind, such as the lion, the tiger, the leopard, and the ounce, devour nothing but flesh, and starve upon any other provision.

They are, in general, fierce, rapacious, subtle and cruel, unfit for society among each other, and incapable of adding to human happiness. They are not less remarkable for the shortness of their snout, the roundness of their head, and the large whiskers which grow on the upperlip.

THE CAT

The Cat, which is the smallest animal of this kind, is the only one that has been taken under human protection, and may be considered as a faithless friend, brought to oppose a still more insidious enemy. It is, in fact, the only animal of this tribe whose services can more than recompense the trouble of their education, and whose strength is not sufficient to make its anger formidable.

THE LION

Most terrestrial animals are found larger, fiercer, and stronger, in the warm than in the cold or temperate climates. They are also more courageous and enterprizing; all their dispositions seeming to partake of the ardour of their native soil. The Lion, produced under the burning sun of Africa, is, of all others, the most terrible, the most undaunted. It is particularly in these frightful deserts, that those enormous and terrible beasts are found, that seem to be the scourge and the terror of the neighbouring kingdoms. Happily, indeed, the species is not very numerous; and it seems to be diminishing daily; for those who have travelled through these countries, assure us, that there are by no means so many there at

present, as were known formerly; and Mr. Shaw observes, that the Romans carried fifty times as many lions from Libya, in one year, to combat in their amphitheatres, as are to be found in the whole country at this time. However, numberless accounts assure us that his anger is noble, his courage magnanimous, and his disposition grateful. He has been often seen to despise contemptible enemies, and pardon their insults when it was in his power to punish them. He has been seen to spare the lives of such as were thrown to be devoured by him, to live peaceably with them, to afford them a part of his subsistence, and sometimes to want food himself rather than deprive them of that life which his generosity had spared.

It may also be said that the lion is not cruel, since he is so only from necessity, and never kills more than he consumes. When satiated, he is perfectly gentle; while the tiger, the wolf, the fox, the pole-cat, and the ferret, kill without remorse, are fierce without cause, and, by their indiscriminate slaughter, seem rather to satisfy their malignity than their hunger.

The outward form of the lion seems to speak his internal generosity. His figure is striking, his look confident and bold, his gait proud, and his voice terrible. His stature is not overgrown, like that of the elephant, or rhinoceros; nor is his shape clumsy, like that of the hippopotamus, or the ox. It is compact, well proportioned, and sizeable; a perfect model of strength joined with agility. It is muscular and bold, neither charged with fat nor unnecessary flesh. To see

LION *Felis leo*

him is to be assured of his superior force. His large head surrounded with a dreadful mane; all those muscles that appear under the skin swelling with the slightest exertions; and the great breadth of his paws, with the thickness of his limbs, plainly evince that no other animal is capable of opposing him. He has a very broad face that, as some have imagined, resembles the human. It is surrounded with very long hair, which gives it a very majestic air. The top of the head, the temples, the cheeks, the under jaw, the neck, the breast, the shoulder, the hind legs, and the belly, are covered with it, while all the rest of the body is covered with very short hair, of a tawny colour.

The lion's mane, grows longer every year as the animal grows older: the lioness is without this ornament at every age. She goes with young no more than five months; the young ones, which are never more than two in number when brought forth, are about the size of a large pug dog, harmless, pretty, and playful; they continue the teat for twelve months, and the animal is more than five years in coming to perfection.

LIONESS *Felis leo*

THE TIGER

The ancients had a saying, *That as the peacock is the most beautiful among birds, so is the tiger among quadrupeds*. In fact, no quadruped can be more beautiful than this animal; the glossy smoothness of his hair, which lies much smoother, and shines with greater brightness than even that of the leopard; the extreme blackness of the streaks with which he is marked, and the bright yellow colour of the ground which they diversify, at once strike the beholder. To this beauty of colouring is added an extremely elegant form, much larger indeed than that of the leopard, but more slender, more delicate, and bespeaking the most extreme swiftness and agility. Unhappily, however, this animal's disposition is as mischievous as its form is admirable, as if Providence was willing to show the small value of beauty, by bestowing it on the most noxious of quadrupeds.

The chief and most observable distinction in the tiger, and in which it differs from all others of the mottled kind, is in the shape of its colours, which run in streaks or bands in the same direction as his ribs from the back down to the belly. The Tiger is much larger, and often found bigger even than the lion himself: it is much slenderer also in proportion to its size; its legs shorter, and its neck and body longer. In short, of all other animals, it most resembles the cat in shape.

In classing carnivorous animals, we may place the lion foremost; and immediately after him follows the tiger, which seems to manifest all the noxious qualities of the lion without sharing any of his good ones. To pride, courage, and strength, the lion joins greatness, clemency, and generosity; but the tiger is fierce without provocation, and cruel without necessity. The lion seldom ravages except when excited by hunger; the tiger, on the contrary, though glutted with slaughter, is not satisfied, still continues the carnage, and seems to have its courage only enflamed by not finding resistance. In falling in among a flock or a herd, it gives no quarter, but levels all with indiscriminate cruelty, and scarce finds time to appease its appetite while intent upon satisfying the malignity of its nature.

THE PANTHER AND THE LEOPARD

Of all this tribe, whose skins are so beautifully spotted, and whose natures are so mischievous, the Panther may be considered as the foremost. This animal has been by many naturalists mistaken for the tiger; and, in fact, it approaches next to it in size, fierceness and beauty. It is distinguished, however,

JAGUAR *Felis onca*

by one obvious and leading character; that of being spotted, not streaked; for, in this particular, the tiger differs from the panther, the leopard, and almost all other ranks of this mischievous family.

This animal, which Mr. Buffon calls simply the Panther, Linnaeus the Pard, Gesner the Pardalis, and the modern Latins the Leopardus, is a native of Africa and South Asia, yellow with dark spots in colour and sometimes black.

Next to the great panther is the animal which Mr. Buffon calls the Leopard, or Panther of Senegal, where it is chiefly found. The differences between this animal and the former are these: the large panther is often found to be six feet long, from the tip of the nose to the insertion of the tail; the panther of Senegal is not above four. The large panther is marked with spots in the manner of a rose, that is, five or six make a kind of circle, and there is generally a large one in the middle. The leopard of Senegal has a much more beautiful coat, the yellow is more brilliant, and the spots are smaller, and not disposed in rings, but in clusters. As to the rest, they are whitish under the belly; the tail in both is pretty long, but rather longer in proportion in the latter, than the former. To these two animals, whose differences seem to be so very minute, we may add a third; namely, the Jaguar or Panther of America. This, in every respect, resembles the two former, except in the disposition of its spots, and that its neck and head are rather streaked than spotted. The jaguar is also said to be lower upon its legs, and less than the leopard of Senegal. These three quadrupeds have but very slight differences, and the

principal distinction used by Mr. Buffon, is taken from the size; the first, as he says, is usually six feet long; the second, four feet; and the last, about three.

From what has been said of this rapacious tribe, we perceive a similitude in the manners and dispositions of them all, from the lion to the cat. The similitude of their internal conformation, is still more exact; the shortness of their intestines, the number of their teeth, and the structure of their paws. The first of this class is the Lion, distinguishable from all the rest by his strength, his magnitude, and his mane. The second is the Tiger, rather longer than the lion, but not so tall, and known by the streaks and the vivid beauty of its robe; including also the American tiger or cougar; distinguishable by its size, next that of the tiger, its tawny colour, and its spots. The third is the Panther and the Leopard. The fourth is the Ounce, not so large as any of the former, spotted like them, but distinguishable by the cream coloured ground of its hair, and the great length of its tail, being above the length of its body. The fifth is the Catamountain or Tiger cat, less than the ounce, but differing particularly in having a shorter tail, and being streaked down the back like a tiger. The sixth is the short tailed kind; namely, the Lynx, of the size of the former, but with a short tail, streaked, and the tips of its ears tufted with black. The seventh is the Syagush, differing from the lynx in not being mottled like it, in not being so large, and in having the ears longer, though tipped with black, as before. The eighth is the

1 ASIATIC LION 2 LIONESS 3 BENGAL TIGER 4 LEOPARD
5 JAGUAR (J. Stewart)

Serval, resembling the lynx in its form, and the shortness of its tail; streaked also like it, but not having the tips of its ears tufted. Lastly, the Cat, wild and tame, with all its varieties; all less than any of the former, but, like them, equally insidious, rapacious, and cruel.

ANIMALS OF THE DOG KIND

The second class of carnivorous quadrupeds may be denominated those of the dog kind. This class is neither so numerous nor so powerful as the former, and yet neither so treacherous, rapacious, or cowardly. This class may be principally distinguished by their claws, which have no sheath, like those of the cat kind, but still continue at the point of each toe, without a capability of being stretched forward, or drawn back. The nose also, as well as the jaw, of all the dog kind, is longer than in the cat; the body is, in proportion, more strongly made, and covered with hair instead of fur. There are many internal distinctions also; as in the intestines, which are much longer in the dog kind, than in those of the cat; the eye is not formed for night vision; and the olfactory nerves are diffused, in the dog kinds, upon a very extensive membrane within the skull, resulting in a very strong sense of smelling: by which they pursue their prey.

If we compare the natural habitudes of this class with the former, we shall find that the dog kinds are not so solitary as those of the cat, but love to hunt in company, and encourage each other with their mutual cries. In this manner the dog and the jackal pursue their prey; and the wolf and fox, which are of this kind, though more solitary and silent among us, yet, in countries where less persecuted, and where they can fearlessly display their natural inclinations, they are found to keep together in packs, and pursue their game with alternate howlings.

THE DOG

Of all this tribe, the Dog has every reason to claim the preference, being the most intelligent of all known quadrupeds, and the acknowledged friend of mankind. The dog, independant of the beauty of his form, his vivacity, force and swiftness, is possessed of all those internal qualifications that can conciliate the affections of man, and make the tyrant a protector. A natural share of courage, an angry and ferocious disposition, renders the dog, in its savage state, a formidable enemy to all other animals: but these readily give way to very different qualities in the domestic dog, whose only ambition seems the desire to please; he is seen to come crouching along, to lay his force, his courage, and all his useful talents, at the feet of his master; he waits his orders, to which he pays implicit obedience; he consults his looks, and a single glance is sufficient to put him in motion; he is more faithful even than the most boasted among men; he is constant in his affections, friendly without interest, and grateful for the slightest favours; much more mindful of benefits received, than injuries offered; he is not driven off by unkindness; he still continues humble, submissive, and imploring; his only hope to be serviceable, his only terror to displease; he licks the hand that has been just lifted to strike him, and at last disarms resentment, by submissive perseverance.

More docile than man, more obedient than any other animal, he is not only instructed in a short time, but he also conforms to the dispositions and the manners of those who command him. He takes his tone from the house he inhabits. When at night the guard of the house is committed to his care, he seems proud of the charge, he continues a watchful sentinel, he goes his rounds, scents strangers at a distance, and gives them warning of his being upon duty. If they attempt to break in upon his territories, he becomes more fierce, flies at them, threatens, fights, and either conquers alone, or alarms those who have most interest in coming to his assistance; however, when he has conquered, he quietly reposes upon the spoil, and abstains from what he has deterred others from abusing; giving thus at once a lesson of courage, temperance, and fidelity.

The dog, thus trusted, exerts a degree of superiority over all animals that require human protection. The flock and the herd obey his voice more readily even than that of the shepherd or the herdsman; he conducts them, guards them, keeps them from capriciously seeking danger, and their enemies he considers as his own. Nor is he less useful in the pursuit; when the sound of the horn, or the voice of the huntsman calls him to the field, he testifies his pleasure by every little art, and pursues with perseverance, those animals, which, when taken, he must not expect to divide.

Few quadrupeds are less delicate in their food; and yet there are many kinds of birds which the dog will not venture to touch. It should seem that water is more necessary to the dog than food; he drinks often, though not abundantly; and it is commonly believed, that when abridged in water, he runs mad. This dreadful malady, the consequences of which are so well known, is the greatest inconvenience that results from the keeping this faithful domestic.

THE WOLF

The Wolf, from the tip of the nose, to the tail, is about three feet seven inches long, and about two feet five inches high; which shows him to be larger than our great breed of mastiffs, which are seldom found to be above three feet by two. His colour is a mixture of black, brown, and grey, extremely rough and hard, but mixed towards the roots with a kind of ash coloured fur. In comparing him to any of our well known breed of dogs, the great Dane, or mongrel greyhound, for instance, he will appear to have the legs shorter, the head larger, the muzzle thicker, the eyes smaller and more separated from each other, and the ears shorter and straighter. He appears, in every respect, stronger than the dog; and the length of his hair contributes still more to his robust appearance. The feature which principally distinguishes the visage of the wolf from that of the dog, is the eye, which opens slantingly upwards, in the same direction with the nose; whereas, in the dog, it opens more at right angles with the nose, as in man. The tail also, in this animal, is long and bushy; and he carries it rather more between his hind legs than the dog is seen to do. The colour of the eye-balls in the wolf are of a fiery green, and give his visage a fierce and formidable air, which his natural disposition does by no means contradict.

The wolf is one of those animals whose appetite for animal food is the most vehement; and whose means of satisfying this appetite are the most various. Nature has furnished him with strength, cunning, agility, and all those requisites which fit an animal for pursuing, overtaking, and conquering its prey; and yet, with all these, the wolf most frequently dies of hunger, for he is the declared enemy of man. Scarce any thing belonging to him is good, except his skin. Of this the furrier's make a covering that is warm and durable, tough coarse and unsightly. His flesh is very indifferent, and seems to be disliked by all other animals, no other creature being known to eat the wolf's flesh except the wolf himself. He breathes a most foetid vapour from his jaws, as his food is indiscriminate, often putrid, and seldom cleanly. In short, every way offensive, a savage aspect, a frightful howl, an insupportable odour, a perverse disposition, fierce habits, he is hateful while living, and useless when dead.

The male and female seek each other only once a year, always in winter, and the coupling does not continue above twelve or fifteen days; usually commencing among the oldest, those which are young being later in their desires. The males have no fixed time for engendering; they pass from one female to the other, beginning at the end of December, and ending at the latter end of February. The time of pregnancy is about three months and an half; and the young wolves are found from the latter end of April to the beginning of July. When the she-wolves are near their time of bringing forth, they seek some very tufted spot, in the thickest part of the forest; in the middle of this they make a small opening, cutting away the thorns and briars with their teeth, and afterwards carry thither a great quantity of moss, which they form into a bed for their young ones. They generally bring forth five or six, and sometimes even to nine at a litter. The cubs are brought forth, like those of the bitch, with the eyes closed; the dam suckles them for some weeks, and teaches them betimes to eat flesh, which she prepares for them, by chewing it first herself. They do not leave the den where they have been littered, till they are six weeks, or two months old. They then follow the old one, who leads them to drink to the trunk of some old tree where the water has settled, or at some pool in the neighbourhood. If she apprehends any danger, she instantly conceals them in the first convenient place, or brings them back to their former retreat. In this manner they follow her for some months; when they are attacked, she defends them with all her strength, and more than usual ferocity. Although, at other times, more timorous than the male, at that season she becomes bold and fearless; willing perhaps to teach the young ones future courage by her own example. It is not till they are about ten or twelve months old, and until they have shed their first teeth, and completed the new, that she thinks them in a capacity to shift for themselves.

THE FOX

The Fox is of smaller and of a slenderer make than the wolf, being above two feet three inches. The tail of the fox also is longer in proportion and more bushy; its nose is smaller and approaching more nearly to that of the grey-hound, and its hair softer. It differs from the dog in having its eyes obliquely situated, like those of the wolf; its ears are directed also in the same manner as those of the wolf, and its head is equally large in proportion to its size. It differs still more from the dog in its strong offensive smell, which is peculiar to the species, and often the cause of its death.

The fox has since the beginning been famous for his cunning and his arts, and he partly merits his reputation. Patient and prudent, he waits the oppor-

1 ORIENTAL JACKAL *Canis aureus*

2 HYAENA *Hyaena vulgaris*

tunity for depredation, and varies his conduct with every occasion. His whole study is his preservation; although nearly as indefatigable, and actually more swift than the wolf, he does not entirely trust to either, but makes himself an asylum, to which he retires in case of necessity; where he shelters himself from danger, and brings up his young.

As among men, those who lead a domestic life are more civilized and more endued with wisdom than those who wander from place to place, so, in the ranks of animated nature, the taking possession of a home supposes a degree of instinct which others are without. The choice of the situation for this domicile, the art of making it convenient, of hiding its entrance, and securing it against more powerful animals, are all marks of superior skill and industry. The fox possesses both, and turns them to his advantage. He generally keeps his kennel at the edge of the wood, and yet within an easy journey of human habitation. From thence he listens to the crowing of the cock, and the cackling of the domestic fowls. He scents them at a distance; he seizes his opportunity, conceals his approaches, creeps slyly along, makes the attack, and seldom returns without his booty. If able to get into the yard, he begins by levelling all the poultry without remorse, and carrying off a part of

47

the spoil, hides it at some convenient distance, and again returns to the charge. Taking off another fowl in the same manner, he hides that also, but not in the same place; and this he practices for several times together, until the approach of day, or human voices give him warning to retire. He is equally alert in seizing the young hares and rabbits, and in the same manner he finds out birds nests, seizes the partridge and the quail while sitting, and destroys a large quantity of game. The wolf is most hurtful to the peasant, but the fox to the gentleman. In short, nothing that can be eaten seems to come amiss; rats, mice, serpents, toads, and lizards. He will, when urged by hunger, eat carrots and insects; and those that live near the sea-coasts will, for want of other food, eat crabs, shrimps, and shell-fish. The hedge-hog in vain rolls itself up into a ball to oppose him, this determined glutton seizes it until it is obliged to appear uncovered, and then he devours it. The wasp and the wild bee are attacked with equal success. Although at first they fly out upon their invader, and actually oblige him to retire, this is but for a few minutes, until he has rolled himself upon the ground, and thus crushed such as stick to his skin; he then returns to the charge, and at last, by perserverance, obliges them to abandon their combs; which he greedily devours, both wax and honey.

This animal also brings forth once a year. Its litter is generally from four to six, and seldom less than three. The female goes with young about six weeks, and seldom stirs out while pregnant, but makes a bed for her young, and takes every precaution to prepare for their production. When she finds the place of their retreat discovered, and that her young have been disturbed during her absence, she removes them one after the other in her mouth, and endeavours to find them out a place of better security.

The cubs of the fox are born blind, like those of the dog; they are eighteen months or two years in coming to perfection, and live about twelve or fourteen years.

In general, foxes found in Europe, Asia and America are red; but in the colder countries round the pole, the foxes are of all colours; black, blue, grey, iron grey, silver grey, white, white with red legs, white with black heads, white with the tip of the tail black, red with the throat and belly entirely white, and lastly with a stripe of black running along the back.

THE JACKAL

The species of the Jackal is found all over Asia and parts of Africa. The size of a middling dog, resembling the fox in the hind parts, particularly the tail; and the wolf in the fore parts, especially the nose; its legs are shorter than those of the fox, and its colour is of a bright yellow, or sorrell, as we express it in horses. Those of the warmest climates are the largest, and their colour is rather of a reddish brown than of that beautiful yellow by which the smaller jackal are chiefly distinguished.

To the savage fierceness of the wolf the jackal adds the impudent familiarity of the dog. Its cry is a howl, mixed with barking, and a lamentation resembling that of human distress. It is more noisy in its pursuits even than the dog, and more voracious than the wolf. The jackal never goes alone, but always in a pack of forty or fifty together. Nothing then can escape them; they are content to take up with the smallest animals; and yet, when thus united, have they courage to face the largest. They seem very little afraid of mankind; but pursue their game to their very doors, without testifying either attachment or apprehension. They enter insolently into the sheep-folds, the yards, and the stables, and, when they can find nothing else, devour the leather harness, boots, and shoes, and run off with what they have not time to swallow. They watch the burying grounds, follow armies, and keep in the rear of caravans. They may be considered as the vulture of quadruped kind; every thing that once had animal life, seems equally agreeable to them.

They hide themselves in holes by day and seldom appear abroad till night-fall, when the jackal that has first hit upon the scent of a gazelle or some larger beast gives notice to the rest by a howl, which it repeats as it runs; while all the rest, that are within hearing, pack in to its assistance.

But man is not the only intruder upon the jackal's industry and pursuits. The lion, the tiger, and the panther, whose appetites are superior to their swiftness, attend to its call, and follow in silence at some distance behind. The jackal pursues the whole night with unceasing assiduity, keeping up the cry, and with great perseverance at last tires down its prey; but just at the moment it supposes itself going to share the fruits of its labour, the lion or the leopard comes in, satiates himself upon the spoil, and his poor provider must be content with the bare carcass he leaves behind. It is no wonder, therefore, the jackal is voracious, since it so seldom has sufficiency; nor that it feeds on putrid substances, since it is not permitted to feast on what it has newly killed.

THE HYAENA

The Hyaena is similar to the wolf both in the shape of its head and body. The ears of the hyaena are longer, with less hair, the head broader, the nose flatter, and not so pointed. The eyes are not placed obliquely, but more like those of a dog. Longer in the leg than the dog or the wolf, it is different from all other quadrupeds whatsoever, in having four toes, on both the fore and hind feet. Its hair is of a dirty grey, marked with black, disposed in waves down its body. Its tail is short, with pretty long hair; and immediately under it, above the anus, there is an opening into a kind of glandular pouch, which separates a substance of the consistence, but not of the odour, of civet. This opening might have given rise to the error of the ancients, who asserted, that this animal was every year, alternately, male and female. When pursuing the scent, the head is held low, with the nose near the ground and the back appears elevated, like that of the hog, with a long bristly band of hair that runs all along, gives an impression of that animal; and, it is probable that, from this similarity it first took its name, the word *huoine* being Greek, and derived from *hus*, which signifies a sow.

But no words can give an adequate idea of this animal's figure, deformity, and ferocity, more savage and untameable than any other quadruped, it seems to be for ever in a state of rage or rapacity, for ever growling, except when receiving its food. Its eyes then glisten, the bristles of its back all stand upright, its head hangs low, and yet its teeth appear; all which give it a most frightful aspect, which a dreadful howl tends to heighten. This, which I have often heard, is very peculiar: its beginning resembles the voice of a man moaning, and its latter part as if he were making a violent effort to vomit. As it is loud and frequent, it

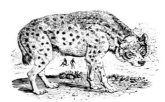

might, perhaps, have been sometimes mistaken for that of a human voice in distress, and have given rise to the accounts of the ancients, who tell us, that the hyaena makes its moan, to attract unwary travellers, and then to destroy them: however this be, it seems the most untractable, and, for its size, the most terrible of all other quadrupeds; nor does its courage fall short of its ferocity; it defends itself against the lion, is a match for the panther, and attacks the ounce, that it seldom fails to conquer.

It is an obscene and solitary animal, to be found chiefly in the most desolate and uncultivated parts of the torrid zone, of which it is a native. It resides in the caverns of mountains, in the clefts of rocks, or in dens that it has formed for itself under the earth. It lives by

1 EUROPEAN WOLF 2 N. AMERICAN BLACK WOLF 3 ST BERNARD'S MASTIFF 4 HIGHLAND GREY HOUND 5 GREAT DOG OF NEPAL
(J. Stewart)

depredation, like the wolf, but is much stronger, and more courageous. It sometimes attacks man, carries off cattle, follows the flock, breaks open the sheep cots, and ravages with insatiable voracity. It eyes shine by night; and it is asserted, not without great appearance of truth, that it sees better by night than by day. When desitute of other provision, it devours the dead.

ANIMALS OF THE WEASEL KIND

Having described the bolder ranks of carnivorous animals, we now come to a smaller and more feeble class, less formidable indeed than any of the former, but far more numerous, and, in proportion to their size, more active and enterprising. The weasel kind may be particularly distinguished from other carnivorous animals, by the length and slenderness of their bodies, which are so fitted as to wind, like worms, into very small openings, after their prey; and hence also they have received the name of vermin, from their similitude to the worm in this particular. These animals differ from all of the cat kind, in the formation and disposition of their claws, which, as in the dog kind, they can neither draw in nor extend at will as cats are known to do. They differ from the dog kind, in being clothed rather with fur than hair; and although some varieties of the fox may resemble them in this particular, yet the coat of the latter is longer, stronger, and always more resembling hair. Beside these distinctions, all animals of the weasel kind have glands placed near the anus, that either open into it, or beneath it issuing a substance that, in some, has the most offensive smell in nature, in others, the most pleasing perfume. All of this kind are still more marked by their habits and dispositions, than their external form; cruel, voracious, and cowardly, they subsist only by theft, and find their chief protection in their minuteness. They are all, from the shortness of their legs, slow in pursuit; and, therefore, owe their support to their patience, assiduity, and cunning. As their prey is precarious, they live a long time without food; and if they happen to fall in where it is in plenty, they instantly destroy all about them before they begin to satisfy their appetite, and suck the blood of every animal before they begin to touch its flesh.

THE WEASEL

The Weasel is the smallest of this numerous tribe; its length not exceeding seven inches, from the tip of the nose to the tail. This length, however, seems to be very great, if we compare it with the height of the animal, which is not above an inch and a half. In measuring the wolf, we find him to be not above once and a half as long as he is high, in observing the weasel, we find it near five times as long as it is high, which shows an amazing disproportion. The tail also, which is bushy, is two inches and a half long, and adds to the apparent length of this little animal's body. The colour of the weasel is of a bright red on the back and sides, but white under the throat and the belly. It has whiskers like a cat; and thirty-two teeth, which is two more than any of the cat kind; and these also seem better adapted for tearing and chewing, than those of the cat kind are. The eyes are little and black. The ears short, broad, and roundish; and have a fold at the lower part, which makes them look as if they were double. Beneath the corners of the mouth, on each jaw, is a spot of brown.

This animal, though very diminutive to appearance, is, nevertheless, a very formidable enemy to quadrupeds a hundred times its own size. It is very common and well known in most parts of the British Isles. Hunting after dark, it does not eat its prey immediately, but, after killing it by a single bite near the head, and with a wound so small as to be invisible it carries it off to its young, or its retreat. It also breaks and sucks the eggs, and sometimes kills the hen that attempts to defend them. It is remarkably active; and, in a confined place, scarce any animal can escape it. It will run up the sides of walls with such facility, that no place is secure from it; and its body is so small, that there is scarce any hole it cannot wind through. During the summer, its excursions are more extensive; but in winter, it chiefly confines itself in barns and farm-yards, where it remains till spring, and where it brings forth its young. All this season it makes war upon the rats and mice, with still greater success than the cat; for being more active and slender, it pursues them into their holes, and, after a short resistance, destroys them. It creeps also into pigeon-holes, destroys the young, catches sparrows, and all kind of small birds; and, if it has brought forth its young, hunts with still greater boldness and avidity. In summer, it ventures farther from the house; and particularly goes into those places where the rat, its chiefest prey, goes before it. Accordingly, it is found in the lower grounds, by the side of waters, near mills, and often is seen to hide its young in the hollow of a tree.

The female takes every precaution to make a comfortable bed for her little ones; she lines the bottom of her hole with grass, hay, leaves, and moss, and generally brings forth from three to five at a time. All animals of this, as well as those of the dog kind, bring forth their young with closed eyes; but they very soon acquire strength sufficient to follow the dam in her excursions, and assist in her projects of petty rapine. The weasel, like all others of its kind does not run on equably, but moves by bounding; and when it climbs a tree, by a single spring it gets a good way from the ground. It jumps in the same manner upon its prey; and, having an extremely limber body, evades the attempts of much stronger animals to seize it.

This animal, like all of its kind, has a very strong smell; and that of the weasel is peculiarly foetid. The weasel smells more strongly in summer than in winter; and more abominably when irritated or pursued, than when at its ease. It always preys in silence, and never has a cry except when struck, and then it has a rough kind of squeaking, which at once expresses resentment and pain.

THE ERMINE OR STOAT

The Stoat, or Ermine, differs from the weasel in size, being usually nine inches long; whereas the former is not much above six. The tail of the ermine is always tipped with black, and is longer in proportion to the body. The edges of the ears and the ends of the toes in this animal are of a yellowish white; and although it is of the same colour with the weasel, being of a lightish brown, and though both this animal, as well as the weasel, in the most northern parts of Europe, changes its colour in winter, and becomes white; yet even then the weasel may be easily distinguished from the ermine by the tip of the tail, which in the latter is always black.

It is well known that the fur of the ermine is the most valuable of any hitherto known; and it is in winter only that this little animal has it of the proper colour and consistence. In summer, the ermine, as was said before, is brown, and it may at that time more properly be called the stoat.

In the north of Europe and Siberia, their skins make a valuable article of commerce. This animal is sometimes found white in Great Britain, and is then called a white weasel. Its furs, however, among us are of no value, having neither the thickness, the closeness, nor the whiteness of those which come from Siberia. The fur of the ermine, in every country, changes by time; for, as much of its beautiful whiteness is given it by certain arts known to the furriers, so its natural colour returns, and its former whiteness can never be restored again.

THE FERRET

The animal next in size to the ermine, is the Ferret; which is domestic to Europe, though said to be originally brought from Africa into Spain, which being a country abounding in rabbits, required an animal of this kind, more than any other: however it is not to be found at present in the British Isles except in its domestic state; and it is chiefly kept tame, for the purposes of the warren.

The ferret is about one foot long, being nearly four inches longer than the weasel. It resembles that animal in the slenderness of its body, and shortness of its legs; but its nose is sharper, and its body more slender, in proportion to its length. The ferret is commonly of a cream colour; but they are also found of all the colours of the weasel kind; white, blackish, brown, and parti-coloured. Those that are of the whitish kind, have their eyes red, as is almost general with all animals entirely of that colour. But its principal distinction from the weasel, is the length of the hair on its tail, which is much longer in the ferret than the weasel.

As this animal is a native of Africa, it cannot bear the rigours of our climate, without care and shelter; and it generally repays the trouble of its keeping, by its great agility in the warren. It is naturally such an enemy of the rabbit kind, that if a dead rabbit be presented to a young ferret, although it has never seen one before, it instantly attacks and bites it with an appearance of rapacity. If the rabbit be living, the ferret is still more eager, seizes it by the neck, winds itself round it, and continues to suck its blood, till it be satiated.

Their chief use in warrens, is to enter the holes, and drive the rabbits into the nets that are prepared for them at the mouth. For this purpose, the ferret is muzzled; otherwise, instead of driving out the rabbit, it would content itself with killing and sucking its blood at the bottom of the hole; but, by this contrivance, being rendered unable to seize its prey, the rabbit escapes from its claws, and instantly makes to the mouth of the hole with such precipitation, that it is inextricably entangled in the net placed there for its reception.

The female of this species, is smaller than the male, whom she seeks with great ardour, and they breed twice a year. Some of them devour their young as soon as brought forth; and then they become fit for the male again. Their number is usually from five to six at a litter. They are very easily irritated; and, although at all times their smell is very offensive, it then is much more so; and the bite is very difficult of cure.

THE POLECAT

The Polecat is larger than the weasel, the ermine, or the ferret, being one foot five inches long; whereas, the weasel is but six inches, the ermine nine, and the ferret eleven inches. It so much resembles the ferret in form, that some have been of opinion they were one and the same animal; nevertheless, there are a sufficient number of distinctions between them: it is, in the first place, larger than the ferret; it is not quite so slender, and has a blunter nose; it differs also internally, having fourteen ribs, whereas the ferret has fifteen; and missing one of the breast bones, which is found in the ferret.

The polecat, for the most part, is of a deep chocolate colour; it is white about the mouth; the ears are short, rounded, and tipped with white; a little beyond the corners of the mouth a stripe begins, which runs backward, partly white and partly yellow: its hair, like that of all this class, is of two sorts; the long and the furry: but, in this animal, the two kinds are of different colours; the longest is black, and the shorter yellowish: the throat, feet and tail, are blacker than any other parts of the body: the claws are white underneath, and brown above; and its tail is about two inches and an half.

It is very destructive to young game of all kinds: but the rabbit seems to be its favourite prey; a single polecat is often sufficient to destroy a whole warren; for, with that insatiable thirst for blood which is natural to all the weasel kind, it kills much more than it can devour.

The female brings forth her young in summer, to the number of five or six at a time; these she soon trains to her own rapacious habits, supplying the want of milk, which no carnivorous quadruped has in plenty, with the blood of such animals as she happens to seize. The fur of this animal is considered as soft and warm; yet it is less in demand than some of a much inferior kind, from its offensive smell, which can never be wholly removed, or suppressed. The polecat seems to be an inhabitant of the temperate climates, scarce any being found towards the north, and but very few in the warmer latitudes. The species is found in North America and parts of Europe.

THE SABLE

Most of the classes of the weasel kind would have continued utterly unknown and disregarded were it not for their furs, which are finer, more glossy and soft, than those of any other quadruped. Their dispositions are fierce and untameable; their scent generally offensive; and their figure disproportioned and unpleasing. The knowledge of one or two

MARTEN *Mustela martes*

of them would, therefore, have sufficed curiosity; and the rest would probably have been confounded together, under one common name, as things useless and uninteresting, had not their skins been coveted by the vain, and considered as capable of adding to human magnificence or beauty.

Of all these, however, the skin of the Sable is the most coveted, and held in the highest esteem. It is of a brownish black, and the darker it is it becomes the more valuable. A single skin, though not above four inches broad, is often valued at ten or fifteen pounds; the fur differing from others in this, that it has no grain; so that, rub it which way you will, it is equally smooth and unresisting. Nevertheless, though this little animal's robe was so much coveted by the great, its history till of late was but very little known; and we are obliged to Mr. Jonelin for the first accurate description of its form and nature. From him we learn that the sable resembles the martin in form and size, and the weasel in the number of its teeth; for it is to be observed, that whereas the martin has thirty-eight teeth, the weasel has but thirty-four; in this respect, therefore, the sable seems to make the shade between these two animals; being shaped like the one, and furnished with teeth like the other. It is also furnished with very large whiskers about the mouth; its feet are broad and, as in the rest of its kind, furnished with five claws on each foot. These are its constant marks; but its fur, for which it is so much valued, is not always the same. Some of the species are of a dark brown over all the body, except the ears and the throat, where the hair is rather yellow; others are more of a yellowish tincture, their ears and throat being also much paler. These in both are the colours they have in winter, and which they are seen to change in the beginning of the spring; the former becoming of a yellow brown, the latter of a pale yellow. In other respects they resemble their kind, in vivacity, agility, and inquietude; in sleeping by day and seeking their prey by night; in living upon smaller animals, and in the disagreeable odour that chiefly characterizes their race.

They generally inhabit along the banks of rivers, in shady places, and in the thickest woods. They leap with great ease from tree to tree, and are said to be afraid of the sun, which tarnishes the lustre of their robes. They are chiefly hunted in winter for their skins, during which part of the year they are only in season. They are mostly found in Siberia, and but very few in any other country of the world; and this scarcity it is which enhances their value. The hunting of the sable chiefly falls to the lot of the condemned criminals, who are sent from Russia into these wild and extensive forests that, for a great part of the year, are covered with snow; and in this instance, as in many others, the luxuries and ornaments of the vain, are wrought out of the dangers and the miseries of the wretched. These are obliged to furnish a certain number of skins every year, and are punished if the proper quantity be not provided.

The sable is also killed by the Russian soldiers, who are sent into those parts to that end. They are taxed a certain number of skins yearly, like the former, and are obliged to shoot with only a single ball, to avoid spoiling the skin, or else with cross-bows and blunt arrows. As an encouragement to the hunters, they are allowed to share among themselves the surplus of those skins which they thus procure; and this, in the process of six or seven years, amounts to a very considerable sum. A colonel, during his seven years' stay, gains about four thousand crowns for his share, and the common men six or seven hundred each for theirs.

THE ICHNEUMON

The Ichneumon, which some have injudiciously denominated the Cat of Pharoah, is one of the boldest and most useful animals of all the weasel kind. In the kingdom of Egypt, where it is chiefly bred, it is used for the same purposes that cats are in Europe, and is even more serviceable, as being more expert in catching mice than they. This animal is usually of the size of the martin, and greatly resembles it in appearance, except that the hair, which is of a grizzly black, is much rougher and less downy. The tail also is not so bushy at the end; and each hair in particular has three or four colours, which are seen in different dispositions of its body. Under its rougher hairs, there is a softer fur of a brownish colour, the rough hair being about two inches long, but that of the muzzle extremely short, as likewise that on the legs and paws. However, being long since brought into a domestic state, there are many varieties in this animal, some being much larger than the martin, others much less; some being of a lighter mixture of colours, and some being streaked in the manner of a cat.

The ichneumon, with all the strength of a cat, has more instinct and agility; a more universal appetite for carnage, and a greater variety of powers to procure it. Rats, mice, birds, serpents, lizards and insects, are all equally pursued; it attacks every living thing which it is able to overcome, and indiscriminately preys on flesh of all kinds. Its courage is equal to the vehemence of its appetite. It fears neither the force of the dog nor the insidious malice of the cat; neither the claws of the vulture nor the poison of the viper. It makes war upon all kinds of serpents with great avidity, seizes and kills them how venomous forever they be; and we are told that when it begins to perceive the effects of their rage, it has recourse to a certain root, which the Indians call after its name, and assert to be an antidote for the bite of the asp or the viper.

But what this animal is particularly serviceable to the Egyptians for is, that it discovers and destroys the eggs of the crocodile. It also kills the young ones that have not as yet been able to reach the water, and, as fable usually goes hand in hand with truth, it is said that the ichneumon sometimes enters the mouth of the crocodile, when it is found sleeping on the shore, boldly attacks the enemy in the inside, and at length, when it has effectually destroyed it, it eats its way out again.

The ichneumon when wild generally resides along the banks of rivers; and in times of inundation makes to the higher ground, often approaching inhabited places in quest of prey. It goes forward silently and cautiously, changing its manner of moving according to its necessities. Sometimes it carries the head high, shortens its body, and raises itself upon its legs; sometimes it lengthens itself and seems to creep along the ground; it is often observed to sit upon its hind legs, like a dog when taught to beg; but more commonly it is seen to dart like an arrow upon its prey, and seize it with inevitable certainty. Its eyes are sprightly and full of fire, its physiognomy sensible, its body nimble, its tail long, and its hair rough and various. Like all of its kind, it has glands that open behind and furnish an odorous substance. Its nose is too sharp and its mouth too small to permit its seizing things that are large; however, it makes up by its courage and activity its wants of arms; it easily strangles a cat though stronger and larger than itself; and often fights with dogs, which, though never so bold, learn to dread the ichneumon as a formidable enemy. It also takes the water like an otter, and, as we are told, will continue under it much longer.

This animal grows fast and dies soon. It is found in great numbers in all the southern parts of Asia, from Egypt to Java; and it is also found in Africa, particularly at the Cape of Good Hope.

This animal was one of those formerly worshipped by the Egyptians, who considered every thing that was serviceable to them as an emanation of the Deity, and worshipped such as the best representatives of God below. Indeed, if we consider the number of eggs which the crocodile lays in the sand at a time, which often amount to three or four hundred, we have reason to admire this little animal's usefulness as well as industry in destroying them, since otherwise the crocodile might be produced in sufficient numbers to over-run the whole earth.

THE STINKARDS

This is a name which our sailors give to one or two animals of the weasel kind, which are chiefly found in America. All the weasel kind, as was already observed, have a very strong smell; some of them indeed approaching to a perfume, but the greatest number most insupportably foetid. But the smell of our weasels, and ermines, and polecats, is fragrance itself when compared to that of the skunk.

The Skunk resembles a polecat in shape and size, but particularly differs in the length of its hair and colour. The hair is above three inches and an half long, and that at the end of the tail above four inches. The colour is partly black and partly white, variously disposed over the body, very glossy, long, and beautiful. There seem to be two varieties of this animal, which Mr. Buffon calls the Conepate and the Zorille. The conepate differs from the zorille in the disposition of its colours, which are more exact, having five white stripes upon a black ground, running longitudinally from the head to the tail. The zorille is rather smaller and more beautifully coloured, its streaks of black and white being more distinct, and the colours of its tail being black at its insertion and white at the extremity.

But whatever differences there may be in the figure or colour of these little animals, they all agree in one common affection, that of being intolerably foetid and loathsome. I have already observed that all the weasel kind have glands furnishing an odorous matter, near the anus, the conduits of which generally have their aperture just at its opening. That substance which is stored up in these receptacles is in some of this kind, such as in the martin, and also in the genet and the civet, a most grateful perfume; but in the weasel, the ermine, the ferret, and the polecat, it is extremely foetid and offensive. These glands in the animals now under consideration are much larger, and furnish a matter sublimed to a degree of putrescence that is truly amazing. As to the perfumes of musk and civet, we know that a single grain will diffuse itself over a whole house, and continue for months to spread an agreeable odour, without diminution. However, the perfume of the musk or the civet is nothing, either for strength or duration, to the insupportable odour of these.

It has been said that they take this method of ejecting their excrement to defend themselves against their pursuers; but it is much more probable that this ejection is the convulsive effect of terror, and that it serves as their defence without their own concurrence. Certain it is that they never smell thus horridly except when enraged or affrighted, for they are often kept tame about the houses of the planters of America

TREE SHREW *Tupaia ferruginea*

without being very offensive.

The habits of all these animals are the same, living like all the rest of the weasel kind, as they prey upon smaller animals and birds eggs.

"In the year 1749," says Kalm, "one of these animals came near the farm where I lived. It was in winter time, and during the night; and the dogs that were upon the watch, pursued it for some time, until it discharged against them. Although I was in my bed a good way off, I thought I should have been suffocated; and the cows and oxen themselves, by their lowings, showed how much they are affected by the stench. About the end of the same year, another of these animals crept into our cellar, but did not exhale the smallest scent, because it was not disturbed. A foolish woman, however, who perceived it at night, by the shining of its eyes, killed it, and at that moment its stench began to spread. The whole cellar was filled with it to such a degree, that the woman kept her bed for several days after; and all the bread, meat, and other provisions, that were kept there, were so infected, that they were obliged to be thrown out of doors."

THE GENETT

From the skunk, which is the most offensive animal in nature, we come to the Genett, which is one of the most beautiful and pleasing. Instead of the horrid stench with which the former affects us, this has a most grateful odour; more faint than civet, but to some, for that reason, more agreeable. This animal is rather less than the martin; though there are genetts of different sizes; and I have seen one rather larger. It also differs somewhat in the form of its body. It is not easy, in words, to give an idea of the distinction. It resembles all those of the weasel kind, in its length, compared to its height; it resembles them in having a soft beautiful fur, and in its appetite for petty carnage. But then it differs from them in having the nose much smaller and longer, rather resembling that of a fox than a weasel. The tail also, instead of being bushy, tapers to a point, and is much longer; its ears are larger, and its paws smaller. As to its colours, and figure in general, the genett is spotted with black, upon a ground mixed with red and grey. It has two sorts of hair, the one shorter and softer, the other longer and stronger, but not above half an inch long on any part of its body, except the tail. Its spots are distinct and separate upon the sides, but unite towards the back, and form black stripes, which run longitudinally from the neck backwards. It has also along the back a kind of mane or longish hair, which forms a black streak from the head to the tail, which last is marked with rings, alternately black and white, its whole length.

The genett, like all the rest of the weasel kinds, has glands, that separate a kind of perfume, resembling civet, but which soon flies off. These glands open differently from those of other animals of this kind; for, as the latter have their apertures just at the opening of the anus, these have their aperture immediately under it; so that the male seems, for this reason, to the superficial observer, to be of two sexes.

It resembles the martin very much in its habits and disposition; except, that it seems tamed much more easily. Bellonius assures us, that he has seen them in the houses at Constantinople as tame as cats; and that they were permitted to run every where about; without doing the least mischief. For this reason they have been called the Cats of Constantinople; although they have little else in common with that animal, except their skill in spying out and destroying vermin. Naturalists pretend that they inhabit only the moister grounds, and chiefly reside along the banks of rivers, having never been found in mountains, nor dry places. The species is not much diffused; it is not to be found in any part of Europe, except Spain and Turkey; it requires a warm climate to subsist and multiply in; and yet it is not to be found in the warmer regions either of India or Africa. From such as have seen its uses at Constantinople, I learn, that it is one of the most beautiful, cleanly, and industrious animals in the world; that it keeps whatever house it is in, perfectly free from mice and rats, which cannot endure its smell. Add to this, its nature is mild and gentle, its colours various and glossy, its fur valuable; and, upon the whole, it seems to be one of those animals that, with proper care, might be propagated amongst us, and might become one of the most serviceable of our domestics.

THE CIVET

The Civet resembles animals of the weasel kind in the long slenderness of its body, the shortness of its legs, the odorous matter that exudes from the glands behind, the softness of its fur, the number of its claws, and their incapacity of being sheathed. It differs from them in being much larger than any hitherto described; in having the nose lengthened, so as to resemble that of the fox; the tail long, and tapering to a point; and its ears straight, like those of a cat. The colour of the civet varies: it is commonly ash, spotted with black; though it is whiter in the female, tending to yellow; and the spots are much larger, like those of a panther. The colour on the belly, and under the throat, is black; whereas the

other parts of the body are black or streaked with grey. This animal varies in its colour, being sometimes streaked, as in our kind of cats called Tabbies. It has whiskers, like the rest of its kind; and its eye is black and beautiful.

The opening of the pouch or bag, which is the receptacle of the civet, differs from that of the rest of the weasel kind, not opening into but under the anus. Beside this opening, which is large, there is still another lower down. The pouch itself is about two inches and an half broad, and two long; its opening makes a chink, from the top downwards, that is about two inches and an half long; and it is covered on the edges, and within, with short hair: when the two sides are drawn asunder, the inward cavity may be seen, large enough to hold a small pullet's egg; all round this are small glands, opening and furnishing that strong perfume which is so well known, and is found, in this pouch, of the colour and consistence of pomatum. Those who make it their business to breed these animals for their perfume, usually take it from them twice a week, and sometimes oftener. The animal is kept in a long sort of a box, in which it cannot turn round. The person, therefore, opens this box behind, drags the animal backwards by the tail, keeps it in this position by a bar before, and, with a wooden spoon, takes the civet from the pouch, as carefully as he can; then lets the tail go, and shuts the box again. The perfume, thus procured, is put into a vessel, which he takes care to keep shut; and when a sufficient quantity is procured, it is sold to very great advantage.

It is not only bred among the Turks, the Indians, and Africans, but great numbers of these animals are also bred in Holland, where in general, it is sold for about fifty shillings an ounce; though, like all other commodities, its value alters in proportion to the demand. The perfume of Amsterdam is reckoned the purest of any; the people of other countries adulterating it with gums.

The perfume of the civet is so strong that it communicates itself to all parts of the animal's body; the fur is impregnated thereby, and the skin penetrated to such a degree that it continues to preserve the odour for a long time after it is stripped off. If a person be shut up with one of them in a close room, he cannot support the perfume, which is so copiously diffused. When the animal is irritated, as in all the weasel kind, its scent is much more violent than ordinary; and if it be tormented so as to make it sweat, this also is a strong perfume, and serves to adulterate or increase what is otherwise obtained from it.

Native only of the old Continent, the civet is said to be a wild fierce animal; and, although sometimes tamed, is never thoroughly familiar. Its teeth are strong and cutting, although its claws be feeble and inflexible. It is light and active, and lives by prey, as the rest of its kind, pursuing birds, and other small animals that it is able to overcome. They are sometimes seen stealing into the yards and outhouses, to seize upon the poultry: their eyes shine in the night, and it is very probable that they see better in the dark than by day. When they fail of animal food, they are found to subsist upon roots and fruits, and very seldom drink; for which reason they are never found near great waters. They breed very fast in their native climates, where the heat seems to conduce to their propagation; but in our temperate latitudes, although they furnish their perfume in great quantities, yet they are not found to multiply – a proof that their perfume has no analogy with their appetite for generation.

ANIMALS OF THE HARE KIND

The hare is the swiftest animal in the world for the time it continues; and few quadrupeds can overtake even the rabbit when it has but a short way to run.

If we were methodically to distinguish animals of the hare kind from all others, we might say that they have but two cutting teeth above and two below, that they are covered with a soft downy fur, and that they have a bushy tail.

Animals of the hare kind, like all others that feed entirely upon vegetables, are inoffensive and timorous. The hare, the rabbit, and the squirrel, are placed (by Pyerius, in his Treatise of Ruminating Animals) among the number of those that chew the cud; certainly their lips continually move whether sleeping or waking, they chew their food very much before they swallow it. All these animals use their forepaws like hands; they are remarkably salacious, and are furnished by Nature with more ample powers than most others for the business of propagation. They are so very prolific, that were they not thinned by the constant depredations made upon them by most other animals, they would quickly over-run the earth.

THE HARE

Of all these the Hare is the largest, the most persecuted, and the most timorous; all its muscles are formed for swiftness; and all its senses seem only given to direct its flight. It has very large prominent eyes, placed backwards in its head, so that it can almost see behind it as it runs. These are never wholly closed; but as the animal is continually upon the watch, it sleeps with them open. The ears are still more remarkable for their size; they are moveable and capable of being directed to every quarter; so that the smallest sounds are readily received, and the animal's motions directed accordingly. The muscles of the body are very strong, and without fat, so that it may be said to carry no superfluous burden of flesh about it; the hind feet are longer than the fore, which still adds to the rapidity of its motions.

An animal so well formed for a life of escape might be supposed to enjoy a state of tolerable security; but as every rapacious creature is its enemy, it but very seldom lives out its natural term. Pursued and persecuted on every side, the race would long since have been totally extirpated, had it not found a resource in its amazing fertility.

The hare multiplies exceedingly; it is in a state of engendering at a few months old; the females go with young but thirty days, and generally bring forth three or four at a time. As soon as they have produced their young they are again ready for conception, and thus do not lose any time in continuing the breed.

The young of these animals are brought forth with their eyes open, and the dam suckles them for twenty days, after which they leave her, and seek out for themselves. From this we observe, that the education these animals receive is but trifling, and the family connection but of short duration. They seldom, however, separate far from each other, or from the place where they were produced; but make each a form at some distance, having a predilection rather for the place than each other's society. They feed during the night rather than by day, choosing the most tender blades of grass, and quenching their thirst with the dew. They live also upon roots, leaves, fruits and corn, and prefer such plants as are furnished with a milky juice. They also strip the bark of trees during the winter, there being scarce any that they will not feed on, except the lime or the alder. They are particularly fond of birch, pinks, and parsley.

They do not pair, however, but in the rutting season, which begins in February; the male pursues and discovers the female by the sagacity of its nose. They are then seen, by moonlight, playing, skipping, and pursuing each other; but the least motion, the slightest breeze, the falling of a leaf is sufficient to disturb their revels.

As their limbs are made for running, they easily outstrip all other animals in the beginning; and could they preserve their speed it would be impossible to overtake them; but as they exhaust their strength at their first efforts, and double back to the place they started from, they are more easily taken than the fox, which is a much slower animal than they. As their hind legs are longer than the fore, they always choose to run up hill, by which the speed of their pursuers is diminished. Their motions are also without any noise, as they have the sole of the foot furnished with hair; and they seem the only animals that have hair on the inside of their mouths.

They seldom live above seven or eight years at the utmost; they come to their full perfection in a year, and it is said, that the females live longer than the males. They are not so wild as their dispositions and their habits seem to indicate; but are of a complying nature, and easily tamed, though they regain their native freedom at the first opportunity.

Their natural instincts for their preservation are extraordinary; they make themselves a form particularly in those places where the colour of the grass most resembles that of their skin; they are naturally fonder of the open country, and are constrained only by fear to take shelter in places that afford them neither a warm sun nor an agreeable pasture.

THE RABBIT

The hare and the Rabbit, though so very nearly resembling each other in form and disposition, are yet distinct kinds, as they refuse to mix with each other. Yet, it has been actually known that the rabbit couples with animals of a much more distant nature; and there is at present in the Museum at Brussels, a creature covered with feathers and hair, and said to be bred between a rabbit and a hen.

The fecundity of the rabbit is still greater than that of the hare: they breed seven times a year, and bring eight young ones each time. On a supposition, therefore, that this happens regularly, at the end of four years, a couple of rabbits shall see a progeny of almost a million and a half. From hence we might justly apprehend being overstocked by the increase; but, happily for mankind, their enemies are numerous, and their nature inoffensive; so that their destruction bears a near proportion to their fertility.

But although their numbers are diminished by every beast and bird of prey, and still more by man himself, yet there is no danger of their extirpation. Whereas the hare is a poor defenceless animal, that

has nothing but its swiftness to depend on for safety; its numbers are, therefore, every day decreasing; it is otherwise with the rabbit, its fecundity being greater, and its means of safety more certain. The hare seems to have more various arts and instincts to escape its pursuers, by doubling, squatting, and winding; the rabbit has but one art of defence alone, but in that one finds safety; by making itself a hole, where it continues a great part of the day, and breeds up its young; there it continues secure from the fox, the hound, the kite, and every other enemy.

Nevertheless, though this retreat is safe and convenient, the rabbit does not seem to be naturally fond of keeping there. It loves the sunny field and the open pasture; it seems to be a chilly animal, and dislikes the coldness of its under-ground habitation. It is, therefore, continally out, when it does not fear disturbance; and the female often brings forth her young, at a distance from the warren, in a hole, not above a foot deep at the most. There she suckles them for about a month; covering them over with moss and grass whenever she goes to pasture, and scratching them up at her return. This external retreat seems a kind of country house, at a distance from the general habitation. To this both male and female often retire from the warren; led their young by night and, if not disturbed, continue there till they are fully grown. There they find a greater variety of pasture than near the warren, which is generally eaten bare; and enjoy a warmer sun, in this shallower hole.

They usually bring forth their young in the warren, in a space, separate from the male. On these

occasions, the female digs herself a hole, at the bottom of which she makes a more ample apartment. This done, she pulls off from her belly a good quantity of her hair, with which she makes a kind of bed for her young. During the two first days she never leaves them; and stirs out only to procure nourishment, in this manner suckling her young, for near six weeks. During all this time, the male seldom visits their separate apartment; but when they are grown up, so as to come to the mouth of the hole, he then seems to acknowledge them as his offspring, takes them between his paws, smooths their skin, and licks their eyes; all of them, have an equal share in his caresses.

The rabbit, though less than the hare, generally

FLYING SQUIRREL *Sciuropterus americanus*

lives longer. As these animals pass the greater part of their lives in their burrow, where they continue at ease and unmolested, they have nothing to prevent the regularity of their health, or the due course of their nourishment. They are, therefore, generally found fatter than the hare; but their flesh is, notwithstanding, much less delicate.

THE SQUIRREL

The Squirrel is a beautiful little animal, which is but half savage. We might give some idea of its form by comparing it to a rabbit, with shorter ears, and a longer tail. The tail, suffices to distinguish it from all others, as it is extremely long, beautiful and bushy, spreading like a fan, and which, when thrown up behind, covers the whole body. This serves the little animal for a double purpose; when erected, it serves, like an umbrella, as a secure protection from the injuries of the heat and cold; and when extended, promotes these vast leaps that the squirrel takes from tree to tree.

It is neither carnivorous nor hurtful; its usual food is fruits, nuts and acorns; it is cleanly, nimble, active, and industrious. It generally, like the hare and rabbit, sits up on its hind legs, and uses the fore paws as hands; these have five claws or toes, as they are called, and one of them is separated from the rest like a thumb. It seldom descends to the ground, except in case of storms, but jumps from one branch to another; feeds, in spring, on buds and young shoots; in summer, on ripening fruits particularly young pinecones; in autumn acorns, filberts, chestnuts and wildings. This season of plenty, however, is not spent in idle enjoyment; the provident little animal gathers at that time its provisions for winter.

Its nest is generally formed among the large branches of a great tree, where they begin to fork off into small ones. After choosing the place where the timber begins to decay, and a hollow may the more easily be formed, the squirrel begins by making a kind of level between the forks; and then bringing moss, twigs, and dry leaves, it binds them together with great art, so as to resist the most violent storm. This is covered up on all sides; and has but a single opening at top, just large enough to admit the little animal; and this opening is itself defended from the weather by a kind of canopy, made in the fashion of a cone, so that it throws off the rain. The nest thus formed, with a very little opening above, is, nevertheless, very commodious and roomy below; soft, well knit together, and every way convenient and warm. In this retreat the little animal brings forth its young and shelters itself from the sun and the storm. Its provision of nuts and acorns is seldom in its nest, but in the hollows of the tree, laid up carefully together, and never touched but in case of necessity. Thus one single tree serves for a retreat and a store-house; and without leaving it during the winter, the squirrel possesses all those enjoyments that its nature is capable of receiving.

Of all other animals, the squirrel leads the most frolicsome playful life; being surrounded with abundance, and having few enemies to fear. They are in heat early in the spring; when, it is very diverting to see the female feigning an escape from the pursuit of two or three males, and to observe the various proofs of their agility, which is then exerted in full force. They seldom bring forth above four or five young at a time; and that but once a year. The time of their gestation seems to be about six weeks; they are pregnant in the beginning of April, and bring forth about the middle of May.

The squirrel is never found in the open fields; it always keeps in the midst of the tallest trees, and, as much as possible, shuns the habitations of men. It is extremely watchful, if the tree in which it resides be but touched at the bottom, the squirrel instantly quits its nest, flies off to another tree and travels, with great ease, along the tops of the forest, until it is perfectly out of danger. Its usual way of moving is by bounds from one tree to another, at forty feet distance it is obliged to descend, it runs up the side of the next tree with amazing facility.

In Lapland, and the extensive forests to the north, the squirrels are observed to change their habitation, and to remove in vast numbers from one country to another. In these migrations they are generally seen by thousands, travelling directly forward, when nothing can stop their progress. What I am going to relate, appears so extraordinary, that were it not attested by Klein and Linnaeus, it might be rejected. When squirrels, in their progress, meet with broad rivers, or extensive lakes, they take an extraordinary method of crossing them. Upon approaching the banks, and perceiving the breadth of the water, they return as if by common consent, into the neighbouring forest, each in quest of a piece of bark. When the whole company are fitted in this manner, they boldly commit their little fleet to the waves; every squirrel fitting on its own piece of bark, and fanning the air with its tail, to drive the vessel to its desired port. It too often happens that the poor mariners are not aware of the dangers of their navigation; for although at the edge of the water it is generally calm, in the middle it is always more turbulent. There the slightest additional gust of wind oversets the little

sailor and his vessel together. The whole navy, that but a few minutes before rode proudly and securely along, is now overturned, and a shipwreck of two or three thousand sailors ensues. This, which is so unfortunate for the little animal, is generally the most lucky accident in the world for the Laplander on the shore; who gathers up the dead bodies as they are thrown in by the waves, eats the flesh, and sells the skins for about a shilling the dozen.

THE GUINEA-PIG

The Guinea-Pig is a native of the warmer climates, but has been so long rendered domestic, and so widely diffused, that it is now become common in every part of the world. There are few unacquainted with the figure of this little animal; in some places it is considered as the principal favourite, and is often found even to displace the lap-dog. It is smaller than a rabbit, and its legs are shorter; they are scarcely seen, except when it moves; and the neck, also, is so short, that the head seems stuck upon the shoulders. The ears are short, thin and transparent; the hair is like that of a sucking-pig, from whence it has taken the name; and it wants even the vestiges of a tail. In other respects, it has some similitude to the rabbit. When it moves, its body lengthens like that animal; and when it is at rest, it gathers up in the same manner. Its nose is formed with the rabbit lip, except that its nostrils are much farther asunder. Like all other animals in a domestic state, its colours are different; some are white, some are red, and others both red and white. It differs from the rabbit in the number of its toes, having four toes on the feet before, and but three on those behind. It strikes its head with the fore feet like the rabbit; and, like it, sits upon the hind feet; for which purpose there is a naked callous skin on the back part of the legs and feet.

These animals are of all others the most helpless and inoffensive. They are scarce possessed of courage sufficient to defend themselves against the meanest of all quadrupeds, a mouse. Their only animosity is exerted against each other; for they will often fight very obstinately; and the stronger is often known to destroy the weaker. But against all other aggressors, their only remedy is patience and non-resistance. How, therefore, these animals, in a savage state, could contrive to protect thenselves, I have not been able to learn; as they want strength, swiftness, and even the natural instinct so common to almost every other creature.

As to their manner of living among us, they owe their lives entirely to our unceasing protection. They must be constantly attended, shielded from the exces-

1 BLACK SQUIRREL 2 ARIEL PETAURUS 3 SQUIRREL-LIKE PETAURUS
4 LESSER FLYING SQUIRREL 5, 6 GREY SQUIRREL 7 BRITISH SQUIRREL
8 GROUND SQUIRREL 9 AGIUMP SQUIRREL (J. Stewart)

sive colds of the winter, and secured against all other domestic animals, which are apt to attack them, from every motive, either of appetitie, jealousy, or experience of their pusillanimous nature. Such indeed is their stupidity, that they suffer themselves to be devoured by the cats, without resistance; and, different from all other creatures, the female sees her young destroyed without once attempting to protect them. Their usual food is bran, parsley, or cabbage leaves; but there is scarce a vegetable cultivated in our gardens that they will not gladly devour. The carrot-top is a peculiar dainty; as also salad; and those who would preserve their healths, would do right to vary their food; for if they be continued on a kind too succulent or too dry, the effects are quickly perceived upon their constitutions. When fed upon recent vegetables, they seldom drink. But it often happens that, conducted by nature, they seek drier food, when the former disagrees with them. They then gnaw cloths, paper, or whatever of this kind they meet with; and, on these occasions, they are seen to drink like most other animals, which they do by lapping. They are chiefly fond of new milk; but, in case of necessity, are contented with water.

They move pretty much in the manner of rabbits, though not near so swiftly; and when confined in a room, seldom cross the floor, but generally keep along the wall. The male usually drives the female on before him, for they never move abreast together; but constantly the one seems to tread in the footsteps of the preceding. They chiefly seek for the darkest recesses, and the most intricate retreats; where, if hay be spread as a bed for them, they continue to sleep together, and seldom venture out but when they suppose all interruption removed. On those occasions they act as rabbits; they swiftly move forward from their bed, stop at the entrance, listen, look round, and, if they perceive the slightest approach of danger, they run back with precipitation. In very cold weather, however, they are more active, and run about in order to keep themselves warm.

They are a very cleanly animal, and very different from that whole name they go by. If the young ones happen to fall into the dirt, or be any other way discomposed, the female takes such an aversion to them that she never permits them to visit her more. Indeed, her whole employment, as well as that of the male, seems to consist in smoothing their skins, in disposing their hair, and improving its gloss. The male and female take this office by turns; and when they have thus brushed up each other, they then bestow all their concern upon their young, taking particular care to make their hair lie smooth, and biting them if they appear refractory. As they are so solicitous for elegance themselves, the place where they are kept must be regularly cleaned, and a new bed of hay provided for them at least every week.

When they go to sleep, they lie flat on their bellies, pretty much in their usual posture; except that they love to have their fore feet higher than their hind. For this purpose, they turn themselves several times around before they lie down, to find the most convenient situation. They sleep, like the hare, with their eyes half open; and continue extremely watchful, if they suspect danger.

These animals are exceedingly salacious, and generally are capable of coupling at six weeks old. The female never goes with young above five weeks; and usually brings forth from three to five at a time; and this not without pain. But what is very extraordinary, the female admits the male the very day she has brought forth, and becomes again pregnant; so that their multiplication is astonishing. She suckles her young but about twelve or fifteen days; and during that time does not seem to know her own; for if the young of any other be brought, though much older, she never drives them away, but suffers them even to drain her, to the disadvantage of her own immediate offspring. They are produced with the eyes open, and in about twelve hours, equal even to the dam in agility. Although the dam has but two teats, yet she abundantly supplies them with milk: and they are also capable of feeding upon vegetables, almost from the very beginning. Their manner of eating is something like that of the rabbit; and, like it, they appear also to chew the cud. Although they seldom drink, they make water every minute. They grunt somewhat like a young pig; and have a more piercing note to express pain.

ANIMALS OF THE RAT KIND

Were it necessary to distinguish animals of the rat kind from all others, we might describe them as having two large cutting teeth, like the hare kind, in each jaw; as covered with hair; and as not ruminating. These distinctions might serve to guide us, had we not too near an acquaintance with this noxious

race to be mistaken in their kind. Their numbers, their minuteness, their vicinity, their vast multiplication, all remind us of their existence. The elephant, the rhinoceros, or the lion, we have driven into their native solitudes. But it is otherwise with the little teasing race I am now describing: no force can be exerted against their unresisting timidity; no arts can

diminish their amazing propagation: millions may be at once destroyed, and yet the breach be repaired in the space of a very few weeks; and, in proportion as Nature has denied them force, it has supplied the defect by their fecundity.

THE GREAT RAT

Of these, the animal best known at present, and in every respect the most mischievous, is the Great Rat; which, though but a newcomer into this country, has taken too secure a possession to be ever removed. This hateful and rapacious creature, though sometimes called the Rat of Norway, is utterly unknown in all the northern countries, and, by the best accounts I can learn, comes originally from the Levant. Its first arrival, as I am assured, was upon the coasts of Ireland, in those ships that traded in provisions to Gibraltar; and perhaps we owe to a single pair of these animals, the numerous progeny that now infests the whole extent of the British Empire.

This animal is in length about nine inches; its eyes are large and black; the colour of the head, and the whole upper part of the body, is of a light brown, mixed with tawny and ash colour. The end of the nose, the throat and belly, are of a dirty white, inclining to a grey; the feet and legs are almost bare, and of a dirty pale flesh colour; the tail is as long as the body, covered with minute dusky scales, mixed with a few hairs, and adds to the general deformity of its detestable figure. It is chiefly in the colour that this animal differs from the Black Rat. This new invader, in a very few years after its arrival, found means to destroy almost the whole species, and to possess itself of their retreats.

The Norway rat has the same disposition to injure us, with much greater power of mischief. It burrows in the banks of rivers, ponds, and ditches; and is every year known to do incredible damage to those mounds that are raised to conduct streams, or to prevent rivers from overflowing. In these holes, which it forms pretty near the edge of the water, it chiefly resides during the summer, where it lives upon small animals, fish, and corn. At the approach of winter, it comes nearer the farm houses; burrows in their corn, eats much, and damages still more than it consumes. But nothing that can be eaten, seems to escape its voracity. It destroys rabbits, poultry, and all kinds of game; and, like the polecat, kills much more than it can carry away. It swims with great ease, dives with great celerity, and easily thins the fish

1 MALABAR GIANT SQUIRREL *Sciurus maximus*

2 HAMSTER *Cricetus vulgaris*

Ed Traviès pinx.

Manceau sc.

pond. In short, scarce any of the feebler animals escape its rapacity, except the mouse, which shelters itself in its little hole, where the Norway rat is too big to follow.

These animals frequently produce from fifteen to thirty at a time; and usually bring forth three times a year. This great increase would quickly be found to overrun the whole country, were it not, happily for us, that they eat and destroy each other. The same insatiable appetite that impels them to indiscriminate carnage, also incites the strongest to devour the weakest, even of their own kind. The large male rat generally keeps in a hole by itself, and is as dreaded by its own species, as the most formidable enemies. In this manner the number of these vermin is kept within due bounds. Mankind has contrived several other methods of destroying these noxious intruders; ferrets, traps, and particularly poison: but of all other poisons, I am told that the nux vomica, ground and mixed with meal, is the most certain, as it is the least dangerous.

The black rat, greatly resembling the great rat in figure, is very distinct in nature, as appears from their mutual antipathy. This animal was formerly as mischievous as it was common; but at present it is almost utterly extirpated by the great rat, one malady often expelling another. It is become so scarce, that I do not remember ever having seen one. It is said to be possessed of all the voracious and unnatural appetites of the former; though, as it is less, they may probably be less noxious! Its length is about seven inches; and the tail is near eight inches long. The colour of the body is a deep iron grey, bordering upon black, except the belly, which is a dirty cinereous hue. They have propagated in America in great numbers, being originally introduced from Europe; and as they seem to keep their ground wherever they get footing, they are now become the most noxious animals in that part of the world.

The Black Water Rat is about the same size as the latter, with a larger head, a blunter nose, smaller eyes, and shorter ears, and the tip of its tail a little white. It never frequents houses; but is usually found on the banks of rivers, ditches and ponds, where it burrows and breeds. It feeds on fish, frogs, and insects; and in some countries it is eaten on fasting days.

THE MOUSE

Fearful by nature, but familiar from necessity, the Mouse attends upon mankind, and comes an unbidden quest to his most delicate entertainments. Fear and necessity seem to regulate all its motions; it never leaves its hole but to seek provision, and seldom ventures above a few paces from home. Different from the rat, it does not go from one house to another, unless forced; and, as it is more easily satisfied, it does much less mischief.

Almost all animals are tamed with more difficulty in proportion to the cowardice of their natures. The mouse being the most feeble, and consequently the most timid of all quadrupeds, except the guinea-pig, is never rendered thoroughly familiar; and, even though fed in a cage, retains its natural apprehensions. No animal has more enemies, and few are so incapable of resistance. The owl, the cat, the snake, the hawk, the weasel, and the rat itself, destroy this species by millions, and it only subsists by its amazing fecundity.

The mouse brings forth at all seasons, and several times in the year. Its usual number is from six to ten. These in less than a fortnight are strong enough to run about for themselves. They are chiefly found in farm yards and among the corn, but are seldom in those ricks that are much infested with rats. The early growth of this animal implies also the short duration of its life, which seldom lasts above two or three years. This species is very much diffused, being found in almost all parts of the world. They are animals that, while they fear human society, closely attend it; and, although enemies to man, are never found but near those places where he has fixed his habitation.

THE LONG TAILED FIELD MOUSE

The Long Tailed Field Mouse is larger than the common mouse, of a colour very nearly resembling the Norway rat, and chiefly found in fields and gardens. They are extremely voracious, and hurtful

in gardens and young nurseries, where they are killed in great numbers. However their fecundity quickly repairs the destruction.

THE SHORT TAILED FIELD MOUSE

Nearly resembling the former, but larger, (for it is six inches long) is the Short Tailed Field Mouse; which, as its name implies, has the tail much shorter than the former, it being not above an inch and a half long, and ending in a small tuft. Its colour is more inclining to that of the domestic mouse, the upper part being blackish and the under of an ash colour. This, as well as the former, are remarkable for laying up provision against winter (and Mr. Buffon assures us) they sometimes have a store of above a bushel at a time.

THE SHREW MOUSE

We may add also the Shrew Mouse to this species of minute animals, being about the size of the domestic mouse, but differing greatly from it in the form of its nose, which is very long and slender. The teeth also are of a very singular form, and twenty-eight in number; whereas the common number in the rat kind is usually not above sixteen. The two upper fore-teeth are very sharp, and on each side of them there is a kind of wing or beard, like that of an arrow, scarce visible but on a close inspection. The other teeth are placed close together, being very small, and seeming scarce separated; so that with respect to this part of its formation, the animal has some resemblance to the viper. However, it is a very harmless little creature, doing scarce any injury. On the contrary, as it lives chiefly in the fields, and feeds more upon insects than corn, it may be considered rather as a friend than an enemy. It has a strong disagreeable smell, so that the cat, when it is killed, will refuse to eat it. It is said to bring four or five young at a time.

THE DORMOUSE

These animals may be distinguished into three kinds; the Greater Dormouse, which Mr. Buffon calls the Loir; the middle, which he calls the Lerot; the less, which he denominates the Muscardin. They differ from each other in size, the largest being equal to a rat, the least being no bigger than a mouse. They all differ from the rat in having the tail tufted with hair, in the manner of a squirrel, except that the squirrel's tail is flat, resembling a fan; and theirs round, resembling a brush. The lerot differs from the loir by having two black spots near the eyes; the muscardin differs from both in the whitish colour of its hair on the back. They all three agree in having black sparkling eyes, and the whiskers partly white

1 EUROPEAN SHREW *Sorex araneus*
2 MOLE *Talpa asiatica*

and partly black. They agree in their being stupefied during the winter, and in their hoarding up provisions to serve them in case of a temporary revival.

They inhabit woods or very thick hedges, forming their nests in the hollow of some tree, or near the bottom of a close shrub, humbly content with continuing at the bottom, and never aspiring to sport among the branches. Towards the approach of the cold season they form a little magazine of nuts, beans, or acorns; and, having laid in their hoard, shut themselves up with it for the winter. As soon as they feel the first advances of the cold they prepare to lessen its effect, by rolling themselves up in a ball, and thus exposing the smallest surface to the weather. But it often happens that the warmth of a sunny day, or an accidental change from cold to heat, thaws their nearly stagnant fluids, and they revive. On such occasions they have their provisions laid in, and they have not far to seek for their support. In this manner they continue usually asleep, but sometimes waking, for above five months in the year, seldom venturing from their retreats, and consequently but rarely seen.

Their nests are lined with moss, grass and dead leaves; they usually bring forth three or four young at a time, and that but once a year, in the spring.

THE LEMMING

Having considered various kinds of these noxious little animals that elude the indignation of mankind, and subsist by their number, not their strength, we come to a species more bold, more dangerous, and more numerous than any of the former. The Lemming, which is a native of Scandinavia, is often seen to pour down in myriads from the northern mountains, and, like a pestilence, destroy all the productions of the earth. It is described as being larger than a dormouse, with a bushy tail, though shorter. It is covered with thin hair of various colours. The extremity of the upper part of the head is black, as are likewise the neck and shoulders, but the rest of the body is reddish, intermixed with small, black sport of various figures, as far as the tail, which is not above half an inch long. The eyes are little and black, the ears round and inclining towards the back, the legs before are short, and those behind longer, which gives it a great degree of swiftness. But what it is much more remarkable for than its figure are, its amazing fecundity and extraordinary migrations.

In wet seasons, all of the rat kind are known to propagate more than in the dry; but this species in particular is so assisted in multiplying by the moisture of the weather, that the inhabitants of Lapland sincerely believe that they drop from the clouds, and that the same magazines that furnish hail and snow pour the lemming also upon them. In fact, after long rain, these animals set forward from their native mountains, and several millions in a troop deluge the whole plain with their numbers. They move, for the most part, in a square, marching forward by night and lying still by day. Thus, like an animated torrent, they are often seen more than a mile broad covering the ground, and that so thick that the hindmost touches its leader. It is in vain that the poor inhabitant resists or attempts to stop their progress, they still keep moving forward; and, though thousands are destroyed, myriads are seen to succeed and make their destruction impracticable. They generally move in lines, which are about three feet from each other and exactly parallel. Their march is always directed from the north-west to the south-west, and regularly conducted from the beginning. Wherever their motions are turned nothing can stop them; they go directly forward, impelled by some strange power; and, from the time they first set out, they never once think of retreating. If a lake or a river happens to interrupt their progress, they all together take the water and swim over it; a fire, a deep well, or a torrent, does not turn them out of their straight lined direction; they boldly plunge into the flames, or leap down the well, and are sometimes seen climbing up on the other side. If they are interrupted by a boat across a river while they are swimming, they never attempt to swim round it, but mount directly up its sides; and the boat-men, who know how vain resistance in such a case would be, calmly suffer the living torrent to pass over, which it does without further damage. If they meet with a stack of hay or corn that interrupts their passage, instead of going over it they gnaw their way through; if they are stopped by a house in their course, if they cannot get through it, they continue there till they die. It is happy, however, for mankind that they eat nothing that is prepared for human subsistence; they never enter a house to destroy the provisions, but are contented with eating every root and vegetable that they meet. If they happen to pass through a meadow, they destroy it in a very short time, and give it an appearance of being burnt up and strewed with ashes. If they are interrupted in their course, and a man should imprudently venture to attack one of them, the little animal is no way intimidated by the disparity of strength, but furiously flies up at its opponent, and, barking somewhat like a puppy, wherever it fastens does not easily quit the hold. If at last the leader be forced out of its lane, which it defends as long as it can, and be separated from the rest of its kind, it sets up a plaintive cry different from that of anger, and, as some pretend to say, gives itself a voluntary death, by hanging itself on the fork of a tree. The two divisions continue their engagements and animosity until one party overcomes the other. From that time they utterly disappear, nor is it well known what becomes of either the conquerors or the conquered. Some suppose that they rush headlong into the sea, others that they kill themselves, as some are found hanging on the forked branches of a tree.

THE MOLE

The Mole is formed to live wholly under the earth. It is bigger than a mouse some six inches long with a coat of short, glossy hair. Its nose is long and pointed, resembling that of a hog, but much longer. Its eyes are so small that it is scarce possible to discern them. Instead of ears it has only holes in the place. Its neck is so short that the head seems stuck upon the shoulders. The body is thick and round, terminating in a very small short tail, and its legs also are so very short that the animal seems to lie flat on its belly.

From under its belly, as it rests in this position, the four feet appear just as if they immediately grew out of the body. Thus the animal appears to us at first view as a mass of flesh covered with a fine shining black skin, with a little head, and scarce any legs, eyes, or tail. On a closer inspection, however, two little black points may be discerned, that are its eyes. The fore-legs appear very short and strong, and furnished with five claws each. These are turned outwards and backwards, as the hands of a man when swimming. The hind legs are longer and weaker than the fore, being only used to assist its motions; whereas the others are continually employed in digging. The teeth are like those of a shrew-mouse, and there are five on both sides of the upper jaw, which stand out; but those behind are divided into points.

Such is the extraordinary figure and formation of this animal; which, if we compare with its manner of living, we shall find a manifest attention in Nature to adapt the one to the other. As it is allotted a subterraneous abode, the seeming defects of its formation vanish, or rather are turned to its advantage. The breadth, strength, and shortness of the fore feet, which are inclined outwards, answer the purposes of digging, serving to throw back the earth with great ease, and to pursue the worms and insects which are its prey. The form of the body is not less admirably contrived for its way of life. The fore part is thick and very muscular, giving great strength to the action of the fore feet, enabling it to dig its way with amazing force and rapidity, either to pursue its prey, or elude the search of the most active enemy. I have seen it, when let loose in the midst of a field, like the ghost on a theatre stage, instantly sink into the earth; and the most active labourer, with a spade, in vain attempted to pursue.

The smallness of its eyes, which induced the ancients to think it was blind, is, to this animal, a peculiar advantage. A more extensive fight would only have served to show the horrors of its prison, while Nature had denied it the means of escape. Had this organ been larger, it would have been perpetually liable to injuries, by the falling of the earth into it; but Nature, to prevent that inconvenience, has not only made them very small, but very closely covered them with hair. Anatomists mention, beside these advantages, another, that contributes to their security; namely, a certain muscle, by which the animal can draw back the eye whenever it is in danger.

As the eye is thus perfectly fitted to the animal's situation, so also are the sense of hearing and smelling. The first gives it notice of the most distant appearance of danger; the other directs it, in the midst of darkness, to its food.

Thus admirably is this animal fitted for a life of darkness and solitude; with no appetites but what it can easily indulge, with no enemies but what it can easily evade or conquer. As soon as it has once buried itself in the earth, it seldom stirs out, unless forced by violent rains in summer, or when in pursuit of its prey, it happens to come too near the surface. In general, it chooses the looser softer grounds, beneath which it can travel with greater ease; in such also it generally finds the greatest number of worms and insects, upon which it chiefly preys. It is observed to be most active, and to cast up most earth, immediately before rain; and, in winter, before a thaw: at those times the worms and insects begin to approach the surface, whither this industrious animal pursues them. On the contrary, in very dry weather, the mole seldom or never forms any hillocks; for then it is obliged to penetrate deeper after its prey, which at such seasons retire far into the ground.

As the moles very seldom come above ground, they have but few enemies; and very readily evade the pursuit of animals stronger and swifter than themselves. Their greatest calamity is an inundation, when they are seen, swimming, and using every effort to reach the higher grounds. The greatest part, however, perish, as well as their young, which remain in the holes behind. Were it not for such accidents, from their great fecundity, they would become extremely troublesome; and as it is, they are considered by the farmer as his greatest pest. They couple towards the approach of spring; and their young are found about the beginning of May. They generally have four or five at a time; and it is easy to distinguish among other mole-hills, that in which the female has brought fourth her young. These are made with much greater art than the rest; and are usually larger. The female, in order to form this retreat, begins by erecting the earth into a tolerably spacious apartment, which is supported within by partitions, at proper distances, that prevent the roof from falling. She beats the earth very firm, so as to make it capable of keeping out the rain. As the hillock in which this apartment is thus formed, is raised above ground, the apartment itself is above the level of the plain, and less subject to inundations. The place being thus fitted, she then procures grass and dry leaves, as a bed for her young. There they lie secure from wet, and she continues to make their retreat equally so from danger: for all round this hill of her own raising, are holes running into the earth, that part from the middle apartments, like rays from a centre, and extend about fifteen feet in every direction; as the mole is very quick of hearing, the instant she perceives her burrow attacked, she takes to her tunnels and unless the earth be dug away by several men at once, she and her young always make good their retreat.

ANIMALS OF THE HEDGEHOG KIND

THE HEDGEHOG

The Hedgehog, with an appearance the most formidable, is one of the most harmless animals in the world: unable or unwilling to offend, all its precautions are for its own security; and it is armed with a thousand points, to keep off the enemy, not to invade him. While other creatures trust to their force, their cunning, or their swiftness, this animal, has but one expedient for protection. As soon as it perceives itself attacked, it withdraws all its vulnerable parts, rolls itself into a ball, and presents nothing but its defensive thorns to the enemy; thus, while it attempts to injure no other quadruped, they are equally incapable of injuring it: like those knights, who were armed in such a manner, that they could neither conquer others, nor be themselves overcome.

This animal is of two kinds; one with a nose like the snout of a hog; the other, more short and blunt, like that of a dog. That with the muzzle of a dog is the most common, being about six inches in length, from the tip of the nose to the insertion of the tail. The tail is little more than an inch long; and so concealed by the spines, as to be scarce visible; the head, back, and sides, are covered with prickles; the nose, breast, and belly, are covered with fine soft hair; the legs are short, of a dusky colour, and almost bare; the toes on each foot are five in number, long and separated; the prickles are about an inch in length, and very sharp pointed; their lower part is white, the middle black, and the points white; the eyes are small, and placed high in the head; the ears are round, pretty large, and naked; the mouth is small, but well furnished with teeth; which it only

uses in chewing its food. Its only reliance in cases of danger, is on its spines; the instant it perceives an enemy, it puts itself into a posture of defence, and patiently waits till its enemy passes by, or is fatigued with fruitless attempts to annoy it. The cat, the weasel, the ferret, and the stoat quickly decline the combat; and the dog himself generally spends his time in empty menaces, rather than in effectual efforts. Every increase of danger only increases the animal's precautions to keep on its guard; its assailant vainly attempts to bite, since he thus more frequently feels than inflicts a wound; he stands enraged and barking, and rolls it along with his paws; still, however, the hedgehog patiently submits to every indignity, but continues secure; and still more to disgust its enemy with the contest, sheds its urine, the smell of which is alone sufficient to send him away.

The hedgehog, like most other wild animals, sleeps by day, and ventures out by night. It generally resides in small thickets, in hedges, or in ditches covered with bushes; there it makes a hole of about six or eight inches deep, and lies well wrapped up, in moss, grass, or leaves. Its food is roots, fruits, worms, and insects. It is also said to suck cattle, and hurt their udders; but the smallness of its mouth will serve to clear it from this reproach. It is said also to be hurtful in gardens and orchards, where it will roll itself in a heap of fruit, and so carry a large quantity away upon its prickles; but this imputation is also ill grounded, since the spines are so disposed, that no fruit will stick upon them. It rather appears to be a very serviceable animal, in ridding our fields of insects and worms, which are so prejudicial to vegetation.

They couple in spring, and bring forth about the beginning of summer. They sleep during the winter; and what is said of their laying up provisions for that season, is consequently false. They at no time eat much, and can survive a long time without any food whatsoever. Their blood is cold, like all hibernating animals.

THE PORCUPINE

Those arms which the hedgehog possesses in miniature, the Porcupine has in a more enlarged degree. The short prickles of the hedgehog are in this animal converted into shafts. In the one the spines are about an inch long; in the other, a foot. The porcupine is about two feet long, and fifteen inches high. Like the hedgehog, it appears a mass of misshapen flesh, covered with quills, from ten to fourteen inches long, tapering and sharp at both ends. These, whether considered separately or together, afford sufficient subject to detain curiosity. Each quill is

EUROPEAN HEDGEHOG *Erinaceus europaeus*

thickest in the middle; and inserted into the animal's skin, in the same manner as feathers are found to grow upon birds. It is spongy inside like the top of a goose-quill; and of different colours, being white and black alternately, from one end to the other. The biggest are often found fifteen inches long, and a quarter of an inch in diameter; extremely sharp, and capable of inflicting a mortal wound. They seem harder than common quills, being difficult to cut, and solid at that end which is not fixed in the skin. If we examine them in common, as they grow upon the animal, they appear of two kinds; the one such as I have already described; the other, long, flexible and slender, growing here and there among the former. There is still another fort of quills, that grow near the tail, white and transparent, and that seem to be cut short at the end. All these quills, incline backwards, like the bristles of a hog; but when the animal is irritated, they stand upright, as bristles are seen to do.

As to the rest of its figure, the muzzle bears some resemblance to that of a hare, but black; the legs are very short, and the feet have five toes, both before and behind; and these, as well as the belly, the head, and all other parts of the body, are covered with a sort of short hair, like prickles, there being no part, except that the ears and the sole of the foot, that is free from them: the ears are thinly covered with very fine hair; and are in shape like those of mankind: the eyes are small, like those of a hog, being only one third of an inch from one corner to the other.

This animal seems to partake very much of the nature of the hedgehog; having this formidable apparatus of arms rather to defend itself, than annoy the enemy. Many naturalists supposed that it was capable of discharging them at its foes, and killing at a great distance but, it is now universally believed that its quills remain firmly fixed in the skin, and are then only shed when the animals moults them, as birds do their feathers. It is true, we are told by Ellis, that a wolf at Hudson's Bay was found dead, with the quills of a porcupine fixed within its mouth; which might have very well happened, from the voraciousness of the former, and not the resentment of the latter.

The porcupine is seldom the aggressor; and when attacked by the bolder animals, it only directs its quills so as to keep always pointing towards the enemy. These are an ample protection; even the lion himself will not venture to make an attack. From such, therefore, the porcupine can defend itself; and chiefly hunts for serpents, and all other reptiles, for subsistence. Travellers universally assure us that, between the serpent and the porcupine there exists an irreconcileable enmity, and that they never meet without a mortal engagement. The porcupine, on these occasions, is said to roll itself upon the serpent, and thus destroy and devour it.

The Americans (who hunt this animal) assure us that the porcupine lives from twelve to fifteen years. During the time of coupling, which is in the month of September, the males become very fierce and dangerous, and often are seen to destroy each other with their teeth. The female goes with young seven months, and brings forth one at a time; this she suckles but about a month, and accustoms it betimes to live, like herself, upon vegetables and the bark of trees; she is very fierce in its defences, but, at other seasons, she is fearful, timid, and harmless. The porcupine never attempts to bite, nor any way to injure its pursuers: if hunted by a dog or a wolf, it instantly climbs up a tree, and continues there until it has wearied out the patience of its adversary.

The Couando is to be found chiefly in the southern parts of America, its quills are four times shorter, its snout more unlike that of a hare; its tail is long enough to catch by the branches of trees, and hold by them.

The Urson, which Mr. Buffon calls after our countryman Hudson, is a native of Hudson's Bay. The shape of this animal is not so round as that of the two former, but somewhat resembling the shape of a pig. It is covered with long bristly hair, with a shorter hair underneath; and under this the quills lie concealed very thick; they are white, with a brown point, and bearded, and the longest do not exceed four inches. They make their nest under the roots of great trees, sleep very much, and chiefly feed upon the bark of the juniper. In winter the snow serves them for drink; and in summer they lap water, like a dog.

AMPHIBIOUS QUADRUPEDS

The gradations of Nature from one class of beings to another are made by imperceptible deviations.

As we saw in the foregoing chapters quadrupeds almost degraded into the insect tribe, or mounted among the inhabitants of the air. We are to observe their approach to fishes, to trace the degrees by which they become more unlike terrestrial animals, till the similitude of the fish prevails over that of the quadruped.

Between terrestrial and aquatic animals there are tribes that can scarce be referred to any rank, but lead an amphibious life between them. Sometimes in water, sometimes on land, they seem fitted for each element, and yet completely adapted to neither. Lacking the agility of quadrupeds upon land, and the perseverance of fishes in the deep, the variety of their powers only seems to diminish their force; and, though possessed of two different methods of living, they are more inconveniently provided than such as have but one.

All quadrupeds of this kind, though covered with hair in the usual manner, are furnished with membranes between the toes, which assist their motion in the water. Their paws are broad and their legs short, by which they are more completely fitted for swimming. Some of these animals are more adapted to live in the water than others; but, as their power increases to live in the deep, their unfitness for living upon land increases in the same proportion. Some, like the otter, resemble quadrupeds in every thing except in being in some measure web-footed; others depart still further, in being, like the beaver, not only web-footed, but having the tail covered with scales, like a fish. Others depart yet farther, as the seal by having the hind feet stuck to the body like fins. Such are the gradations of the amphibious tribe. They all, however, live in water, either by habit or conformation; they all continue a long time under water; they all consider that element as their proper abode; whenever prest by danger, they fly to the water for security; and, when upon land, appear watchful, timorous, and unwieldy.

THE OTTER

In the first step of the progression from land to amphibious animals, we find the Otter, resembling those of the terrestrial kind in shape, hair, and internal conformation; resembling the aquatic tribes in its manner of living, and in having membranes between the toes to assist it in swimming. From this peculiar make of its feet, which are very short, it swims faster than it runs, and can overtake fishes in

Top EUROPEAN OTTER *Mustela lutra*
Bottom EUROPEAN BEAVER *Castor fiber*

1.

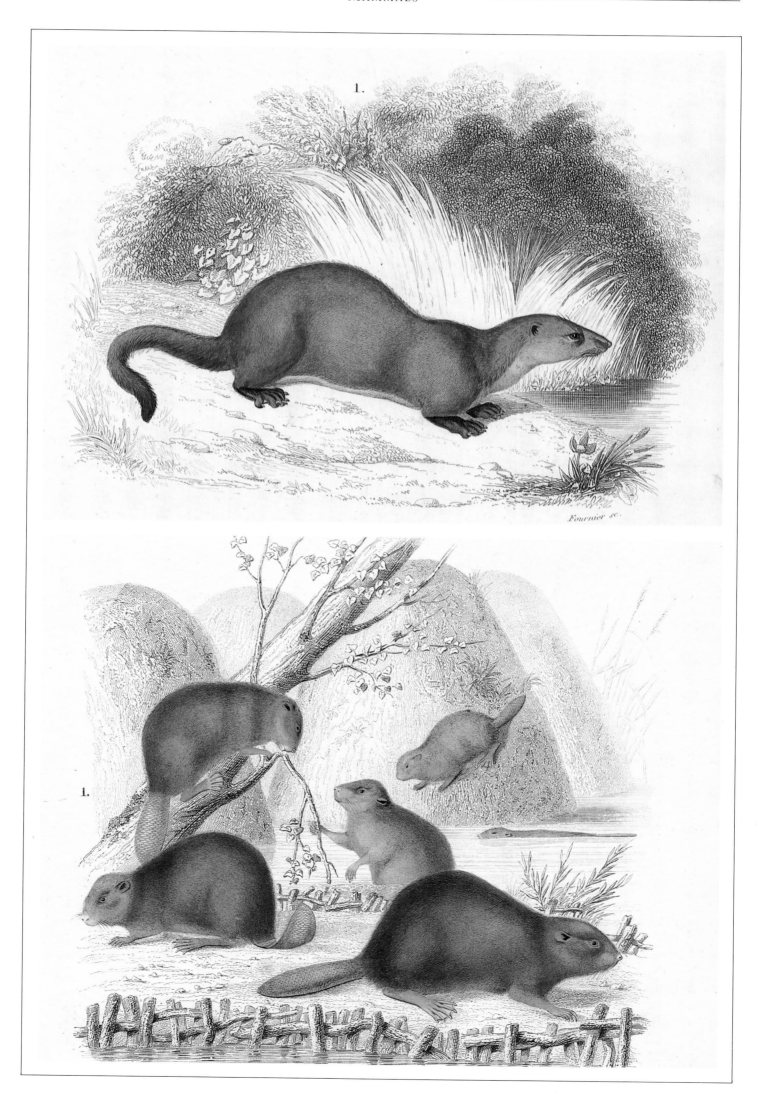

Fournier sc.

1.

their own element. The colour of this animal is brown; and it is somewhat of the shape of an overgrown weasel, being long, slender, and soft skinned. Its usual length is about two feet long, from the tip of the nose to the insertion of the tail; the head and nose are broad and flat; the mouth bears some similitude to that of a fish; the neck is short, and equal in thickness to the head; the body long; the tail broad at the insertion, but tapering off to a point at the end; the eyes are very small, and placed nearer the nose than usual in quadrupeds. The legs are very short, but remarkably strong, broad, and muscular. The joints are articulated so loosely, that the animal is capable of turning them quite back, and bringing them on a line with the body, so as to perform the office of fins. Each foot is furnished with five toes, connected by strong broad webs like those of water fowl.

This voracious animal is found at the sides of lakes and rivers, but particularly the former, for it is seldom fond of fishing in a running stream, for the current of the water having more power upon it than upon the fishes it pursues. However, when in rivers, it is always observed to swim against the stream, and to meet the fishes it preys upon rather than to pursue them. In lakes it destroys more than it devours, and is often seen to spoil a pond in the space of a few nights. But the damage they do by destroying fish is not so great as their tearing in pieces the nets of the fishers, which they infallibly do whenever they become entangled. The instant they find themselves caught, they go to work with their teeth, and in a few minutes destroy nets of very considerable value.

The otter has two different methods of fishing; the one by catching its prey from the bottom upward, the other by pursuing it into some little creek and seizing it there. In the former case, as this animal has larger lungs than most other quadrupeds, it can remain for some minutes at the bottom; and whatever fish passes over at that time is certainly taken; since the eyes of fish are placed so as not to see under them, the otter attacks them from below; and, seizing them at once by the belly, drags them on shore, where it often leaves them untouched, to continue the pursuit for hours together. The other method is chiefly practised in lakes and ponds, where there is no current; the fish thus taken are rather small, for the

great ones will never be driven out of deep water.

In the rivers and the lakes frequented by the otter, the bottom is generally stony and uneven, with many trunks of trees, and roots underneath the water. The shore also is hollow, scooped inward by the waves. These are the places the otter chiefly chooses for its retreat; and there is scarce a stone which does not bear the mark of its residence, as upon them its excrements are always made.

The otter couples about the middle of summer and brings forth at the end of nine weeks, three to four young, generally under the hollow banks, upon such weeds as the place affords. The young ones are always found at the end of the water; and the dam, teaches them instantly to plunge into the deep, and escape among the rushes or weeds that fringe the stream. They swim with great rapidity, and in such a manner that no part of them is seen above water, except the tip of the nose. It is only when the dam is absent that they can be taken; and converted to fishing for men and in some places there are dogs purposely trained for discovering their retreats. The manner of training them up to hunt for fish requires not only assiduity but patience; however, their use, when taught, greatly repays the trouble of teaching; and, perhaps, no other animal is more beneficial to its master.

Otters are to be met with in most parts of the world, and rather differ in size and colour from each other, than in habitudes or conformation. In North America and Carolina they are usually found white, inclining to yellow. The Brazilian otter is much larger than ours, with a roundish head, almost like a cat. The tail is shorter, being but five inches long; and the hair is soft, short, and black, except on the head, where it is of a dark brown, with a yellowish spot under the throat.

THE BEAVER

The Beaver seems to be the only remaining monument of brutal society. From the result of its labours, which are still to be seen in the remote parts of America, we learn how far instinct can be aided by imitation. We thence perceive to what a degree animals, without language or reason, can concur and attain by numbers those advantages which each, in a state of solitude, seems unfitted to possess. The beaver is the only creature among quadrupeds that has a flat broad tail, covered with scales, which serves as a rudder to direct its motions in the water. It is the sole quadruped that has membranes between the toes on the hind feet only, and none on the fore feet, which supply the place of hands, as in the squirrel. In short, it is the only animal that in its fore parts entirely resembles a quadruped, and in its hind parts seems to approach the nature of fishes, by having a scaly tail. In other respects, it is about two feet long and near one foot high; it is somewhat shaped like a rat, except the tail, which, as has been observed, is flat and scaly. Its colour is of a light brown; the hair of two sorts; the one longer and coarser; the other, soft, fine, short, and silky. The teeth are like those of a rat or a squirrel, but longer stronger, and admirably adapted to cutting timber or stripping bark, to which purposes they are constantly applied. One singularity more may be mentioned in its conformation; which is, that, like birds, it has but one and the same vent for the emission of its excrements and its urine.

The beavers begin to assemble about the months of June and July, to form a society that is to continue for the greatest part of the year. They arrive in numbers from every side, and generally form a company of above two hundred. The place of meeting is commonly the place where they fix their abode, and this is always by the side of some lake or river. If it is a lake in which the waters are always upon a level, they dispense with building a dam; but if it be a running stream, which is subject to floods and falls, they then set about building a dam, that crosses the river, so that it forms a dead water in that part which lies above and below. This dam, or pier, is often fourscore or a hundred feet long, and ten or twelve feet thick at the base. If we compare the greatness of the

work with the powers of the architect, it will appear enormous; but the solidity with which it is built is still more astonishing than its size. The part of the river over which this dam is usually built, is where it is most shallow, and where some great tree is found growing by the side of the stream. This they use for making the principal part in their building; and, although it is often thicker than a man's body, they instantly set about cutting it down. For this operation they have no other instrument but their teeth, which soon lay it level, so that it falls across the stream.

This dike, is sometimes ten, and sometimes twelve feet thick at the foundation. It descends in a slope, on that side next the water, which gravitates upon the work in proportion to the height, and presses it with a prodigious force towards the earth. The opposite side is erected perpendicular, like our walls; and that declivity, which, at the bottom, is about twelve feet broad, diminishes towards the top, where it is no more than two feet broad, or thereabouts. The materials whereof this mole consists, are wood and clay. The beavers cut, with suprising ease, large pieces of wood, some as thick as one's thigh, and four to six feet in length. They drive one end of these stakes into the ground, at a small distance one from the other, intermingling a few with them that are smaller and more pliant. As the water, however, would find a passage through the intervals or spaces between them, and leave the reservoir dry, they have recourse to a clay, which they know where to find, and with which they stop up all the cavities both within and without, so that the water is duly con-

DUCK-BILLED PLATYPUS *Ornithorhynchus paradoxus*

fined. They continue to raise the dike in proportion to the elevation of the water. They are conscious like-wise that the conveyance of their materials by land would not be so easily accomplished as by water; and therefore they take the advantage of its increase, and swim with their mortar on their tails, and their stakes between their teeth, to the places where there is most occasion for them. If their works are in the least damaged, the breach is instantly reviewed, and, with the utmost diligence and application, perfectly repaired.

The dike, or mole, being thus completed, their next care is to erect their several apartments, which are either round or oval, and divided into three stories: the first below the level of the causeway, which is for the most part full of water; the other two above it. This little fabric is built in a substantial manner, on the edge of their reservoir, and always in such divisions as above-mentioned, that in case of the water's increase, they may move up a story higher, and be no ways incommoded. If they find any little island contiguous to their reservoir, they fix their mansion there, which is then more solid, and not so frequently exposed to the overflowing of the water. If they cannot find so commodious a situation, they drive piles into the earth, to fence and fortify their habitation against the wind as well as the water. They make two apertures, at the bottom, to the stream; one is a passage to their bagnio, which they always keep neat and clean; the other leads to that part of the building where every thing is conveyed, that will either soil or damage their upper apartments. They have a third opening, much higher, for the prevention of their being shut up and confined, when snow has closed the apertures of the lower floors. Sometimes they build their houses altogether upon dry land; but then they sink trenches five or six feet deep, in order to descend into the water when convenient. They make use of the same materials; and are equally industrious in the erection of their lodges, as their dikes. Their walls are perpendicular, and about two feet thick. As their teeth are more serviceable than saws, they cut off all the wood that projects beyond the wall. After this, when they have mixed clay and dry grass together, they work it into a kind of

mortar, with which, by the help of their tails, they plaster all their works, both within and without.

The inside is vaulted, and is large enough for the reception of eight or ten beavers.

All these works, especially in northern parts, are finished by August, or September; at which time they begin to lay in their stores. During the summer, they are perfect epicures; and regale themselves every day on the choicest fruits and plants the country affords. Their provisions, in the winter season, principally consist of the wood of the birch, and other trees, which they steep in water, from time to time. They cut down branches from three to ten feet in length. The largest branches are conveyed to their magazines by a whole body of beavers; but the smallest by one only; each of them, however, takes a different way in order that no one labourer should interrupt another in the prosecution of his work. Their wood-yards are larger or smaller, in proportion to the number in family. These logs are not thrown up in one continual pile, but laid one across the other, with small spaces between them, in order to take out just such a quantity as they shall want for their immediate consumption. This timber is cut again into small particles, and conveyed to one of their largest lodges, where the whole family meet, to consume their respective dividends, in equal portions. Sometimes they travese the woods, and regale their young with a more novel and elegant entertainment.

THE SEAL

The Seal resembles a quadruped in some respects, and a fish in others. The head is round, like that of a man; the nose broad, like that of the otter; the teeth like those of a dog; the eyes large and sparkling; no external ears, but holes that serve for that purpose; the neck is well proportioned, and of a moderate length; but the body thickest where the neck is joined to it. From thence the animal tapers down to the tail, growing all the way smaller, like a fish. The whole body is covered with a thick bristly shining hair, which looks as if it were rubbed over with oil; and thus far the quadruped prevails over the aquatic. But it is in the feet that this animal greatly differs from all the rest of the quadruped kind; for, though furnished with the same number of bones as other quadrupeds, they are so stuck on the body, and so covered with a membrane, that they more resemble fins than feet; and might be taken for such, did they not have claws. In the fore feet all the arm and cubit, are hid under the skin, and nothing appears but the hand from the wrist downwards. These hands are covered in a thick skin, which serves, like a fin, for swimming; and are

1, 2 HARP SEAL 3 PENNANTS PIED SEAL 4 MARBLED SEAL
5 SEAL OF SCOTCH COASTS 6 WALRUS 7, 8 FUR SEAL
(J. Stewart)

distinguished by five claws, which are long, black, and piercing. As to the hind feet, they are stretched out on each side of the short tail, covered with a hairy skin like the former, and both together almost joining at the tail; the whole looks like the broad flat tail of a fish. The dimensions of this animal are various, being found from four feet long to nine. They differ also in their colours; some being black, others spotted, some white, and many more yellow.

The water is the seal's usual habitation, and whatever fish it can catch its food. Though not equal in instinct and cunning to some terrestrial animals, it is greatly superior to the mute tenants of that element in which it chiefly resides. Although it can continue for several minutes under water, it is not able, like fishes, to remain there for any length of time; and a seal may be drowned like any other terrestrial animal. Thus it seems superior in some respects to the inhabitants of both elements, and inferior in many more. Although furnished with legs, it is deprived of all the advantages of them. The hind feet, indeed, being turned backwards, are entirely useless upon land; so that when the animal is obliged to move, it drags itself forward like a reptile, and with an effort more painful. For this purpose it is obliged to use its fore feet, which, though very short, serve to give it such a degree of swiftness that a man cannot readily overtake it; and it runs towards the sea. As it is thus awkwardly formed for going upon land, it is seldom found at any distance from the sea-shore.

The females in our climate bring forth in winter, and rear their young upon some sand-bank, rock, or desolate island, at some distance from the continent. When they suckle their young they lie on their sides while these, which are at first white with woolly hair, cling to the teats, of which there are four in number, near the navel. In this manner the young continue in the place where they are brought forth, for twelve or fifteen days; after which the dam brings them down to the water, and accustoms them to swim and get their food on their own. As each litter never exceeds above three or four, so the animal's cares are not much divided, and the education of her little ones is soon completed. In fact, the young are particularly docile; they recognise the mother's voice among the rest of the old ones; they assist each other in danger, and are perfectly obedient to her call. Thus early accustomed to subjection, they continue to live in society, hunt and herd together, and have a variety of tones by which they encourage to pursue or warn each other of danger. All along the shore, each has its own peculiar rock, of which it takes possession, and where it sleeps. The only season when their social spirit seems to forsake them, is that when they feel the influences of natural desire. They then fight most desperately; and the male that is victorious, keeps all the females to himself. Their combats on these occasions are managed with great obstinacy, and yet great justice: two are never seen to fall upon one together.

As their chief food is fish, so they are very expert at

SEAL *Phoca vitulina*

pursuing and catching it. In those places where herrings are in shoals, the seals frequent and destroy them by thousands. When the herring retires, the seal is then obliged to hunt after fish that are more capable of evading the pursuit. However, they are very swift in deep waters, dive with great rapidity, and, while the spectator eyes the spot at which they disappear, they are seen to emerge at above a hundred yards distance.

The seal is taken for the sake of its skin, and for the oil its fat yields. The former is very useful in covering trunks, making waistcoats, shot-pouches, and several other conveniences. The flesh of this animal formerly found place at the tables of the great. At a feast provided by Archbishop Nevell, for Edward the Fourth, there were twelve seals and porpoises provided, among other extraordinary rarities.

The seal is a social animal, and gathers in large numbers. They are found in every climate, but in the

north and icy seas they are particularly numerous. It is on those shores, which are less inhabited than ours, and where the fish resort in greater abundance, that they are seen by thousands, barking on the rocks, and suckling their young. There they keep watch like other gregarious animals; and, if an enemy appears, instantly plunge altogether into the water. In fine weather they more usually employ their time in

fishing; and generally come onshore in tempests and storms.

As seals are gregarious, so are they also animals of passage, and migrate from one part of the world to another. Most quadrupeds are contented with their native plains and forests, and seldom stray except

when necessity or fear impels them. But seals change their habitation; and are seen in vast multitudes directing their course from one continent to another. On the northern coasts of Greenland they are seen to retire in July, and to return again in September. This time it is supposed they go in pursuit of food. But they make a second departure in March to cast their young, and return in the beginning of June, young and all, in a great body together, observing in their route a certain fixed time and track, like birds of passage. When they go upon this expedition, they are seen in great droves for many days together, making towards the north, taking that part of the sea most free from ice, and going still forward into those seas where man cannot follow. When they leave the coasts to go upon this expedition they are all extremely fat, but on their return they come home excessively lean.

ANIMALS OF THE MONKEY KIND

Quadrupeds may be considered as a numerous group, terminated on every side by some that but in part deserve the name. On one quarter we see a tribe covered with quills, or furnished with wings, that lift them among the inhabitants of air; on another, we behold a diversity clothed with scales and shells, to rank with insects; on a third, we see them descending into the waters, to live among the mute tenants of that element. There is also a numerous tribe, that, leaving the brute creation, seem to make approaches even to humanity; that bear an awkward resemblance to the human form, and discover some faint efforts at intellectual sagacity.

Animals of the monkey class are furnished with hands instead of paws; their ears, eyes, eyelids, lips, and breasts, are like those of mankind; their internal conformation also bears some distant likeness; and the whole offers a picture that may well mortify the pride of such as make their persons alone the principal object of their admiration.

These approaches, however, are gradual; and some bear the marks of this our boasted form, more strongly than others.

In the Ape kind we see the whole external machine strongly impressed with the human likeness, and capable of the same exertions: these walk upright, have no tail, have fleshy posteriors, have calves to their legs, and feet nearly like ours.

In the Baboon kind we perceive a more distant approach to the human form; the quadruped mixing in every part of the animal's figure: these generally go upon all fours; but some, when upright, are as tall as a man; they have short tails, long snouts, and are possessed of brutal fierceness.

The Monkey kind are removed a step further: these are much smaller than the former, with tails as long, or longer than their bodies, and flattish faces.

ORANG-UTAN

The foremost of the ape kind is the Orang-utan, or Wild Man of the Woods, found in Borneo and Sumatra. The orang-utan of all other animals, most nearly approaches to the human race. Sometimes achieving a height of 7 feet, in general, its stature is less than that of a man; but its strength and agility much greater. Travellers who have seen various kinds of these animals in their native solitudes, give us surprising accounts of their force, their swiftness, their address, and their ferocity. This creature is extremely swift, endowed with extraordinary strength, and passes from tree to tree with prodigious celerity. His skin is all hairy, his eyes sunk in his head, his countenance stern, his face tanned, and all his lineaments, though exactly human, harsh and blackened by the sun. Their faces are broad, their noses flat, their ears without a tip, their skins are

more bright than that of a Mulatto, and they are covered on many parts of the body with long and tawny coloured hair. Their belly is large, their heels flat, and yet rising behind. They sometimes walk upright, and sometimes upon all fours, when they are fantastically disposed. Their chief residence is among the trees where they build huts or nests with broken branches.

THE GORILLA

In Africa this creature is even still more formidable. Battel calls him the Pongo, and assures us that in all his proportions he resembles a man, except that he is much larger, even to a gigantic state. His face resembles that of a man, the eyes deep sunk in the head, the hair on each side extremely long, the visage naked and without hair, as also the ears and the hands. The body is lightly covered, and scarcely differing from that of a man, except that there are no calves to the legs. Still, however, the animal is seen to walk upon his hind legs, and in an erect posture. He sleeps under trees, and builds himself a hut, which serves to protect him against the sun and the rains of the tropical climates, of which he is a native. Like the orang-utan, he lives only upon fruits, and is no way carnivorous. He cannot speak, although furnished with greater instinct than any other animal of the brute creation.

It is impossible to take any of these dreadful creatures alive, for they are so strong that ten men would not be a match for one of them. None of this kind, therefore, are taken except when very young, and these but rarely, when the female happens to leave them behind, for in general they keep clung to the breast, and adhere both with legs and arms. From the same traveller we learn, that when one of these animals dies, the rest cover the body with a quantity of leaves and branches. They sometimes also show mercy to the human kind. A boy, taken by one of these, and carried into the woods, continued there a whole year, without receiving any injury. From another traveller we learn, that these animals often attempt to surprise women as they go into the woods, and frequently keep them against their wills for the pleasure of their company, feeding them very plentifully all the time. He assures us that he knew a woman of Loango who had lived among these animals for three years. They grow from six to seven feet hight, and are of unequalled strength, and make use of clubs for their defence.

THE CHIMPANZEE

The animal next to these, and to be placed in the same class, is the Chimpanzee. This is much less than the former, being not above a foot and a half high, but walks erect, is without a tail, and is easily tamed.

Naturalists who have observed their form and manners at home, have been as much struck with their patient, pliant, imitative dispositions; with their appearance and conformation, so nearly human.

The chimpanzee is covered with hair of a coal black colour, more resembling human hair than that of brutes, being in different lengths, and as in the human species, it is also longest on the head, the upper lip, the chin, and the pubes. The face is like that of a man, the forehead larger, and the head round. The upper and lower jaw are not so prominent as in monkeys; but flat, like those of a man, as are the ears and teeth. The bending of the arms and legs are just the same as in a man; and, in short, the animal, at first view, presents a figure almost human.

In a closer survey the obvious differences are revealed in the flatness of the nose; the lowness of the forehead, and the lack of a prominent chin. The ears are proportionately too large; the eyes too close to each other; and the interval between the nose and mouth too great. The body and limbs differ in the thighs being too short, and the arms too long; in the thumb being too little, and the palm of the hand too narrow. The feet also are rather more like hands than feet; and the animal, if we may judge from the figure, bent too much upon its haunches.

Anatomically, a surprising similitude prevails in its internal conformation. It differs from man in the number of its ribs, having thirteen; whereas, in man, there are twelve. The vertebrae of the neck also are shorter, the bones of the pelvis narrower, the orbits of the eyes deeper, the kidneys rounder, the urinary and gall bladders longer and smaller, and the ureters of a different figure. Such are the principal distinctions between the internal parts of this animal and those of a man; in almost everything else they are entirely and exactly the same. Indeed, many parts are so much alike in conformation, that it excites wonder how they are productive of such few advantages. The tongue, and all the organs of the voice are the same, and yet the animal is dumb; the brain is formed in the same manner with that of a man, and yet the creature lacks reason: an evident proof (as Mr. Buffon finely observes) that no disposition of matter will give mind; and that the body, however nicely formed, is formed in vain, when there is not infused a soul to direct its operations.

In the palms of its hands are remarkable those lines which are usually taken notice of in palmistry; and, at the tips of the fingers, those spiral lines observed in man. The palms of the hands are as long as the soles of the feet; and the toes upon these as long as the fingers; the middle toe the longest of all, and the whole foot different to the human. The hind feet being thus formed as hands, the animal often uses them as such; now and then using its hands instead of feet. The breasts appear small and shrivelled, but exactly like those of a man: the navel also appears very fair, and in exact disposition, being neither harder nor more prominent than is usually seen in children.

Dr. Tyfon's chimpanzee was a gentle, fond, harmless creature. In its passage to England from Angola, those that it knew on shipboard it would embrace with the greatest tenderness, opening their bosoms, and clasping its hands about them. Monkeys of a lower species it held in utter aversion; it would always avoid the place where they were kept in the same vessel; and seemed to consider itself as a creature of higher extraction. After it was taken, and a little used to wearing clothes, it grew very fond of them; a part it would put on without any help, and the rest it would carry in its hands to some of the company, for their assistance. It would lie in a bed, place its head on the pillow, and pull the clothes upwards, as a man would do.

'I have seen it,' says Mr. Buffon, 'give its hand to show the company to the door: I have seen it sit at table, unfold its napkin, wipe its lips, make use of the spoon and the fork to carry the victuals to its mouth, pour out its drink into a glass, touch glasses when invited, take a cup and saucer and lay them on the table, put in sugar, pour out its tea, leave it to cool before drinking, and all this without any other instigation than the signs or the command of its master, and often of its own accord. It was gentle and inoffensive; it even approached strangers with respect, and came rather to receive caresses than to

CHIMPANZEE *Troglodytes niger*

Wörner pinx   Annedouche Sc.

offer injuries. It was particularly fond of sugared comfits, which everybody was ready to give it; and, as it had a defluxion upon the breast, so much sugar contributed to increase the disorder and shorten its life. It continued at Paris but one summer, and died in London. It ate indiscriminately of all things, but it preferred dry and ripe fruits to other aliments. It would drink wine, but in small quantities, and gladly left it for milk, tea, or any other sweet liquor. Such these animals appeared when brought into Europe.

THE GIBBON

Of this kind also is the Gibbon, so called by Buffon, or the Long Armed Ape, which is a very extraordinary and remarkable creature. It is of different sizes, being from four feet to two feet high. It walks erect, is without a tail, has a face resembling that of a man, with a circle of bushy hair all round the visage; its eyes are large and sunk in its head; its face tanned and its ears exactly proportioned. But that in which it chiefly differs from all others of the monkey tribe is the extraordinary length of its arms, which, when the animal stands erect, are long enough to reach the ground; so that it can walk upon all fours and yet keep its erect posture at the same time. This animal, next to the orang-utan and the chimpanzee, most nearly resembles mankind, not only in form, but in gentle manners and tractable disposition. It is a native of the East Indies, and particularly found along the coasts of Coromandel.

THE CYNOCEPHALUS

The last of the ape kind is the Cynocephalus, or the Magot of Buffon. This animal wants a tail, like the former, although there is a small protuberance at that part, which yet is rather formed by the skin than the bone. It differs also in having a large callous red rump. The face is prominent, and approaches more to that of quadrupeds than of man. The body is covered with a brownish hair, and yellow on the belly. It is about three feet and a half, or four feet high, and is a native of most parts of Africa and the East. As it recedes from man in its form, so also it appears different in its dispositions, being sullen, vicious, and intractable in every way; fierce, malicious, and ignorant.

THE BABOON

The Baboon, is from three to four feet high, very strongly built, with a thick body and limbs, and canine teeth, much longer than those of men. It has large callosities behind, which are quite naked and red. Its tail is crooked and thick, and about seven or eight inches long. Its snout is long and thick, and on each side of its cheeks it has a pouch, into which, when satiated with eating, it puts the remainder of its provisions. It is covered with long thick hair of a reddish brown colour, and pretty uniform over the

UAKARI *Cebus hypoleucus*

whole body. It walks more commonly upon all fours than upright, and its hands as well as its feet are armed with long sharp claws, instead of the broad round nails of the ape kind.

An animal thus made for strength, and furnished with dangerous weapons, is found in fact to be one of the most formidable of the savage race, in those countries where it is bred. From the Chevalier Forbin we learn that in Siam whole troops of these will often sally forth from their forests, and attack a village, when they know the men are engaged in their rice harvest. They are on such occasions actuated as well by desire as by hunger; and not only plunder the houses of whatever provisions they can find, but endeavour to force the women. These, however, as the Chevalier humourously relates, not at all liking either the manners of the figure of the paltry gallants, boldly stand on their defence, and with clubs, or whatever other arms they can provide, instead of answering their caresses, oblige their ugly suitors to retreat; not, however, before they have damaged or plundered everything eatable they can lay their hands on.

At the Cape of Good Hope they are less formidable, but to the best of their power equally mischievous. They are there under a sort of natural discipline, and go about whatever they undertake with surprising skill and regularity. When they set about robbing an orchard or a vineyard, for they are extremely fond of grapes, apples, and ripe fruit, they do not go singly to work, but in large companies, and with preconcerted deliberation. On these occasions, some of them enter the enclosure, while one is set to watch. The rest stand without the fence, and form a line reaching all the way from their fellows within to their rendezvous without, which is generally in some craggy mountain. Everything being thus disposed, the plunderers within the orchard throw the fruit to those that are without, as fast as they can gather it; or, if the wall or hedge be high, to those that sit on the top; and these hand the plunder to those next them on the other side. Thus the fruit is pitched from one to another all along the line, till it is safely deposited at their headquarters. They catch it as readily as the most skilful tennis player can a ball; and while the business is going forward, which they conduct with great expedition, a most profound silence is observed among them. Their sentinel, during this whole time, continues upon the watch, extremely anxious and attentive; but if he perceives anyone coming, he instantly sets up a loud cry, and at this signal the whole company scamper off. Nor yet are they at any time willing to leave the place empty handed; for if they are plundering a bed of melons, for instance, they go off with one in their mouths, one in their

hands, and one under their arm. If the pursuit is hot, they drop first that from under their arm, then that from their hand, and, if it be continued, they at last let fall that which they had hitherto kept in their mouths. The female brings forth usually but one at a time, which she carries in her arms, and in a peculiar manner clinging to her breast. As to the rest, these animals are not at all carnivorous; they principally feed upon fruits, roots, and corn, and generally keep together in companies. The internal parts are more unlike those of man than of quadrupeds, particularly the liver, which is like that of a dog divided into six lobes. The lungs are more divided, the guts in general are shorter, and the kidney rounder and flatter.

THE MANDRILL

The largest of the baboon kind is the Mandrill, a native of the Gold Coast; an ugly disgusting animal, with a tail shorter than the former, though of a much larger stature, being from four to five feet high. The muzzle is still longer than that of the preceeding, it is of a bluish colour, and strongly marked with wrinkles, which give it a frightful appearance.

THE WANDEROW

The Wanderow is a smaller baboon with the body less compact and muscular, and the hind parts seemingly more feeble. The tail is from seven to eight inches long; the muzzle is prominent as in the rest of this kind; but what particularly distinguishes it is a large long white head of hair, together with a monstrous white beard, coarse, rough and descending; the colour of the rest of the body being brown or black. In its savage state, it is equally fierce with the others; but, with a proper education, it seems more tractable than most of its kind, and is chiefly seen in the woods of Ceylon and Malabar.

THE MONKEY

There is scarce a country in the tropical climates that does not swarm with Monkeys, and scarce a forest that is not inhabited by a race of monkeys distinct from all others. Every different wood along the coasts of Africa may be considered as a separate colony of monkeys, differing from those of the next district in colour, in size, and malicious mischief. It is indeed remarkable that the monkey of two cantons are never found to mix with each other, but rigorou-

sly to observe a separation; each forest produces only its own; and these guard their limits from the intrusion of all strangers.

In general, monkeys of all kinds, being less than the baboon, are endued with less powers of doing mischief. Indeed, the ferocity of their nature seems to diminish with their size; and when taken wild in the woods, they are sooner tamed, and more easily taught to imitate man than the former. More gentle than the baboon, and less grave and sullen than the ape, they soon begin to exert all their sportive mimicries, and are easily restrained by correction.

In their native woods they are not less the pests of man than of other animals. The monkeys, says a traveller, are in possession of every forest where they reside, and may be considered as the masters of the place. Neither the tiger, nor the lion itself, will venture to dispute the dominion, since these, from the tops of trees, continually carry on an offensive war, and by their agility escape all possibility of pursuit. Nor have the birds less to fear from their continual depredations; for, as these harmless inhabitants of the wood usually build upon trees, the monkeys are for ever on the watch to find out and rob their nests; and such is their petulant delight in mischief, that they will fling their eggs against the ground when they lack appetite or inclination to devour them. Only the serpent ventures to oppose the monkey, and the larger snakes are often seen winding up the trees where the monkeys reside; and, when they happen to surprise them sleeping, swallow them whole before the little animals have time to make a defence. The monkeys in general inhabit the tops of the trees, and the serpents cling to the branches nearer the bottom; and in this manner they are forever seen near each other, like enemies in the same field of battle.

When a traveller enters among these woods, they consider him as an invader upon their dominions, and all join to repel the intrusion. At first they survey him with a kind of insolent curiosity. They jump from branch to branch, pursue him as he goes along, and make a loud chattering, to call the rest of their companions together. They then begin their hostilities by grinning, threatening, and flinging down the withered branches at him, which they break from the trees; they even take their excrements in their hands, and throw them at his head. Thus they attend him wherever he goes; jumping from tree to tree with such amazing swiftness, that the eye can scarce attend their motions. Although they take the most desperate leaps, they are seldom seen to come to the ground, for they easily fasten upon the branches that break their fall, and stick, either by their hands, feet, or tail, wherever they touch. If one of them happens to be wounded, the rest assemble round, and clap their fingers into the wound, as if they were desirous of founding its depth. If the blood flows in any quantity, some of them keep it shut up, while others get leaves, which they chew, and thrust into the opening: however extraordinary this may appear, it is asserted to be often seen, and to be strictly true. In this manner they wage a petulant, unequal war; and are often killed in numbers before they think proper to make a retreat. This they effect with the same precipitation with which they at first came together.

They do incredible damage, when they come in companies to lay waste a field of Indian corn or rice, or a plantation of sugar-canes. They carry off as much as they are able; and they destroy ten times more than they bear away. Their manner of plundering is pretty much like that of the baboons, in a garden. One of them stands sentinel upon a tree, while the rest are plundering, carefully and cautiously turning on every side, but particularly to that on which there is the greatest danger: in the meantime, the rest of the spoilers pursue their work with great silence and assiduity; they are not contented with the first blade of corn, or the first cane that they happen to lay their hands on: they pull up such as appear most alluring to the eye: they turn it round, examine, compare it with others, and if they find it to their mind, stick it under one of their shoulders. When in this manner they have got their load, they begin to think of retreating: but if it should happen that the owners of the field appear to interrupt their depredations, their faithful sentinel instantly gives notice, by crying out, *houp, houp, houp*; which the rest perfectly understand, and all at once throwing down the corn they hold in the left hands, scamper off upon three legs, carrying the remainder in the right. If they are still hotly pursued, they then are content to throw down their whole burden, and to take refuge among their woods, on the tops of which they remain in perfect security.

Were we to give faith to what some travellers

assure us, of the government, policies, and subordination of these animals, we might perhaps be taxed with credulity; but we have no reason to doubt that they are under a kind of discipline, which they exercise among each other. They are generally seen to keep together in companies, to march in exact order, and to obey the voice of some particular chieftain, remarkable for his size and gravity. One species of these, which Mr Buffon calls the Ouarine, and which are remarkable for the loudness and the distinctness of their voice, are still more so for the use to which they convert it. 'I have frequently been a witness,' says Morgrave, 'of their assemblies and deliberations. Every day, both morning and evening, the ouarines assemble in the woods to receive instructions. When all come together, one among the number takes the highest place on a tree, and makes a signal with his hand to the rest to sit round, in order to hearken. As soon as he sees them placed, he begins his discourse,

with so loud a voice, and yet in a manner so precipitate, that to hear him at a distance, one would think the whole company were crying out at the same time: however, during that time, one only is speaking; and all the rest observe the most profound silence. When this is done, he makes a sign with the hand for the rest to reply; and at that instant they raise their voices together, until by another signal of the hand they are enjoined silence. This they as readily obey; till, at last, the whole assembly breaks up, after hearing a repetition of the same preachment.'

The chief food of the monkey tribe is fruits, the buds of trees, or succulent roots and plants. They all, like man, seem fond of sweets, and particularly the pleasant juice of the palm-tree, and the sugar cane. With these, the fertile regions in which they are bred, seldom fail to supply them; but when it happens that these fail, or that more nourishing food becomes more agreeable, they eat insects and worms, and, sometimes, if near the coasts, descend to the sea-shore, where they eat oysters, crabs, and shellfish. Their manner of managing an oyster is extraordinary enough; but it is too well attested, to fail of our assent. As the oysters in the tropical climates are generally larger than with us, the monkeys, when they go to the sea-sides, pick up a stone, and clap it between the opening shells, this prevents them from closing; and the monkey then eats the fish at his ease. They often also draw crabs from the water, by

putting their tail to the hole where that animal takes refuge, and the crab fastening upon it, they withdraw it with a jerk, and thus pull their prey upon shore. This habit of laying traps for other animals, makes them very cautious of being entrapped themselves.

The monkey generally brings forth one at a time, and sometimes two. They are rarely found to breed when brought over into Europe; but of those that do, they exhibit a very striking picture of parental affection. The male and female are never tired of fondling their young ones. They instruct it with no little assiduity; and often severely correct it, if stubborn, or disinclined to profit by their example: they hand it from one to the other; and when the male had done showing his regard, the female takes her turn. When wild in the woods, the female, if she happens to have two, carries one on her back, and the other in her arms: that on her back clings very closely, clasping its hands round her neck, and its feet about her middle; when she wants to suckle it, she then alters their position; and that which has been fed given place to the other, which she takes in her arms. It often happens that she is unable to leap from one tree to another, when thus laden; and upon such occasions, their dexterity is very surprising. The whole family form a kind of chain, locking tail in tail, or hand in hand, and one of them holding the branch above, the rest swing down, balancing to and fro, like a pendulum, until the undermost is enabled to catch hold of the lower branches of some neighbouring tree. When the hold is fixed below, the monkey lets go that which was above, and thus comes undermost in turn; but, creeping up along the chain, attains the next branches, like the rest; and thus they all take possession of the tree, without ever coming to the ground.

THE OPOSSUM

The Opossum is a remarkable animal, about the size of a small cat, found in both North and South America. The head resembles that of a fox; it has fifty teeth in all; but two great ones in the midst, like those of a rat; the eyes are little, round, clear, lively, and placed upright; the ears are long, broad, and transparent, like those of the rat kind; its tail also increases the similitude, being round, long, a little hairy in the beginning, but quite naked towards the end. The forelegs are short, being about three inches long; while those behind are about four. The feet are like hands, each having five toes or fingers, with white crooked nails, and rather longer behind than

1 FOUR SPOTTED OPOSSUM *Didelphis opossum*
2 TINY OPOSSUM *Didelphis murina*

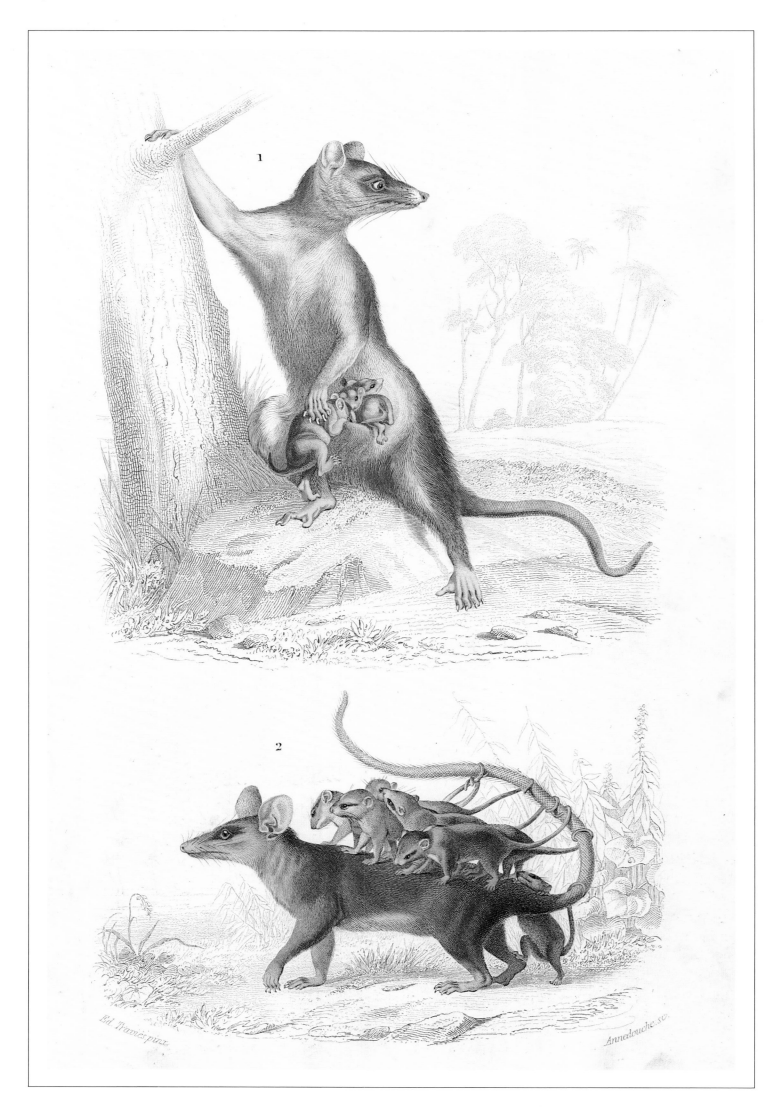

before. But it is particular in this animal, that the thumb on the hind legs lacks a nail; whereas the fingers are furnished with clawed nails as usual.

But that which distinguishes this animal from all others, and what has excited the wonder of mankind for more than two centuries, is the extraordinary conformation of its belly, as it is found to have a false womb, into which the young, when brought forth in the usual manner, creep, and continue for some days longer, to lodge and suckle securely. This pouch if we may so call it, being one of the most extraordinary things in natural history, requires a more minute description. Under the belly of the female is a kind of slit or opening, of about three inches long; this opening is composed of a skin, which makes a bag internally, which is covered on the inside with hair, and in this bag are the teats of the female; and into it the young, when brought forth, retire, either to suckle or to escape from danger. This bag has a power of opening and shutting, at the will of the animal; and this is performed by means of several muscles, and two bones, that are fitted for this purpose, and that are peculiar to this species of animal only. These two bones are placed before the *os pubis*, to which they are joined at the base, they are about two inches long, and grow smaller and smaller to their extremities. These support the muscles that serve to open the bag, and give them a fixture. To these muscles there are antagonists, that serve, in the same manner, to shut the bag; and this they perform so exactly, that in the living animal the opening can scarce be discerned, except when the sides are forcibly drawn asunder. The inside of this bag is furnished with glands, that exude a musky substance, which communicates to the flesh of the animal, and renders it unfit to be eaten. It is not to be supposed that this is the place where the young are conceived, as some have been led to imagine; for the opossum has another womb, like that of most animals, in which generation is performed in the ordinary manner. The bag we have been describing may rather be considered as a supplemental womb. In the real womb, the little animal is partly brought to perfection; in the ordinary one, it receives a kind of additional incubation; and acquires, at last, strength enough to follow the dam wherever she goes. We have many reasons to suppose that the young of this animal are all brought forth prematurely, or before they have acquired that degree of perfection, which is common in other quadrupeds. The little ones, when first produced, are in a manner half completed; and some travellers assert, that they are, at that time, not much larger than flies. We are assured also, that immediately on quitting the real womb, they creep into the false one; where they continue fixed to the teat, until they have strength sufficient to venture once more into the open air, and share the fatigues of the parent. Ulloa assures us, that he has found five of these little creatures hidden in the belly of the dam three days after she was dead, still alive, and all clinging to the teat with great avidity. It is probable, therefore, that upon their first entering the false womb, they seldom stir out from thence; but when more advanced, they venture forth several times in the day; and, at last, seldom make use of their retreat, except in cases of necessity or danger. Travellers are not agreed in their accounts of the time which these animals take to continue in the false womb; some assure us, they remain there for several weeks; and others, more precisely mention a month. During this period of strange gestation, there is no difficulty in opening the bag in which they are concealed; they may be reckoned, examined, and handled, without much inconvenience; for they keep fixed to the teat, and cling there as firm as if they made a part of the body of the animal that bears them. When they are grown stronger, they drop from the teat into the bag in which they are contained; and, at last, find their way out, in search of more copious subsistence. Still, however, the false belly serves them for a retreat; either when they want to sleep or to suckle, or when they are pursued by an enemy. The dam, on such occasions, opens her bag to receive them, which they enter,

The opossum, when on the ground, is a slow, helpless animal; the formation of its hands, are alone sufficient to show its incapacity of running with any degree of swiftness: but, to counterbalance this inconvenience, it climbs trees with great ease and expedition. It chiefly subsists upon birds; and hides among the leaves of the trees, to seize them by surprise. It often also hangs by the tail, which is long

and muscular; and in this situation, for hours together, with the head downwards, it keeps watching for its prey. If any lesser animal, which it is able to overcome, passes underneath, it drops upon it with deadly aim, and quickly devours it. By means of its tail, the opossum also slings from one tree to another, hunts insects, escapes its pursuers, and provides for its safety. It seems to be a creature that lives upon vegetables, as well as animal substances, roots, sugar-canes, the bark, and even the leaves of trees. It is easily tamed, but it is a disagreeable domestic, as well from its stupidity and figure as its scent, which, however fragrant in small quantities, fails not to be ungrateful when copiously supplied.

OTHER ANIMALS

THE ELEPHANT

In every respect the noblest quadruped in nature is the Elephant, not less remarkable for its size than its docility and understanding. All historians concur in giving it the character of the most sagacious animal next to man; and yet, were we to take our idea of its capacity from its outward appearance, we should be led to conceive very meanly of its abilities.

The elephant is seen from seven to no less than fifteen feet high and of all quadrupeds is the strongest, as well as the largest; and yet, in a state of nature, it is neither fierce nor formidable. Mild, peaceful, and brave, it never abuses its force for its own protection, or that of its community, but appears to be a social friendly creature, delighting to live along the sides of rivers, to keep in the deepest vales, and to refresh itself in the most shady forests and watery places. It cannot live far from water and fills its trunk with it either to cool that organ, or to divert itself by spurting it out like a fountain.

The elephant's chief food is of the vegetable kind, but with its broad and heavy feet it destroys much more than it devours; so that it is frequently obliged to change its quarters.

With a very awkward appearance, it nonetheless possesses all the senses in great perfection. Though the minuteness of its eyes may at first sight appear deformed, yet, when we come to examine them, they are seen to exhibit a variety of expression.

The elephant is not less remarkable for the excellence of its hearing. Its ears are extremely large, and greater in proportion than even those of an ass; they serve also to wipe its eyes. It appears delighted with music, and very readily learns to beat time, to move in measure, and even to join its voice to the sound of the drum and trumpet. This animal's sense of smelling is not only exquisite, but it is in a great measure pleased with the odours that delight mankind.

But it is in the sense of touching that this animal excels all others of the brute creation and perhaps even man himself. The organ of this sense lies wholly in the trunk, which is an instrument peculiar to this animal, and that serves it for all the purposes of a hand.

To the rest of the elephant's encumbrances may be added its enormous tusks, which are unserviceable for chewing and are only weapons of defence.

The hide of an elephant is as remarkable as any other part. It is not covered over with hair, as is the generality of quadrupeds, but is nearly bare.

It is not to be wondered at, that an animal furnished with so many various advantages both of strength, sagacity, and obedience, should be taken in to the service of man. We accordingly find that the elephant, from time immemorial, has been employed either for the purposes of labour, of war, or of ostentation; to increase the grandeur of eastern princes, or to extend their dominions.

The elephant alone has never been seen to breed; and though he has been reduced under the obedience of man for ages, the duration of pregnancy of the female still remains a secret. Aristotle, indeed, asserts that she goes two years with young; that she continues to suckle her young for three years, and that she brings forth but one at a time; but he does not inform us of the manner in which it was possible for him to have this information.

The elephant, when once tamed, becomes the most gentle and obedient of all animals. It soon conceives an attachment for the person that attends it, caresses him, obeys him, and seems to anticipate his desires. It perfectly distinguishes the tone of command from that of anger or approbation, and acts accordingly.

In Delhi, an elephant passing along the streets put his trunk into a tailor's shop, where several people were at work. One of the persons of the shop, desirous of some amusement, pricked the animal's trunk with his needle, and seemed highly delighted with this slight punishment. The elephant, however, passed on without any immediate signs of resentment; but coming to a puddle filled with dirty water, he filled his trunk, returned to the shop, and spurted the contents over the finery upon which the tailors were then employed.

THE RHINOCEROS

Next to the elephant, the Rhinoceros is the most powerful of animals. It is usually found twelve feet long, from the tip of the nose to the insertion of the tail; from six to seven feet high; and the circum-

ASIATIC ELEPHANT MALE, FEMALE (J. Stewart)

ference of its body is nearly equal to its length. It is, therefore, equal to the elephant in bulk; and if it appears much smaller to the eye, the reason is that its legs are much shorter. Its head is furnished with a horn, growing from the snout, sometimes three feet and a half long; and but for this, that part would have the appearance of the head of a hog; the upper lip, however, is much longer, ends in a point, is very pliable, and serves to collect food, delivering it into the mouth: the ears are large, erect, and pointed; the eyes are small and piercing; the skin is naked, rough, knotty, and, lying upon the body in folds, after a very peculiar fashion: there are two folds very remarkable; one above the shoulders, and another over the rump: the skin, which is of a dirty brown colour, is so thick as to turn the edge of a scimitar, and to resist a musket-ball: the belly hangs low; the legs are short, strong and thick, and the hooves divided into three parts, each pointing forward.

Such is the general outline of an animal that appears chiefly formidable from the horn growing from its snout; and formed rather for war, than with a propensity to engage. This horn grows from the solid bone, and so disposed, as to be managed to the greatest advantage. It is composed of the most solid substance; and pointed so as to inflict the most fatal wounds. The elephant, the boar, or the buffalo, are obliged to strike transversely with their weapons; but the rhinoceros employs all his force with every blow. Indeed, there is no force which this terrible animal has to apprehend: defended, on every side, by a thick, horny hide, which the claws of the lion or the tiger are unable to pierce, and armed before with a weapon that even the elephant does not choose to oppose.

The rhinoceros is a native of the deserts of Asia and Africa, and is usually found in those extensive forests, that are frequented by the elephant and the lion. As it subsists entirely upon vegetable food, it is peaceful and harmless among its fellows of the brute creation; but, though it never provokes combat, it equally disdains to fly. It is every way fitted for war, but rests content in the consciousness of its security. It is particularly fond of the prickly branches of trees, and is seen to feed upon such thorny shrubs as would be dangerous to other animals, either to gather, or to swallow. The prickly points of these, however, may only serve to give a poignant relish to this animal's palate.

There are some varieties in this animal, as in most others; some of them are found in Africa with a double horn, one growing above the other; this weapon, if considered in itself, is one of the strongest,

1 HIPPOPOTAMUS 2 INDIAN RHINOCEROS 3 MUCHOCO WHITE RHINOCEROS 4, 5 TWO HORNED AFRICAN RHINOCEROS 6 MALAY TAPIR (J. Stewart)

and most dangerous, that Nature furnishes to any part of the animal creation. The horn is entirely solid, formed of the hardest bony substance, growing from the upper maxilary bone. Many are the medicinal virtues that are ascribed to this horn, when taken in powder, but these qualities have been attributed to it, without any real foundation, and make only a small part of the many fables which this extraordinary animal has given rise to.

The rhinoceros which was shown at London in 1739, and described by Doctor Parsons, had been sent from Bengal. Though it was very young, not being above two years old, yet the charge of his carriage and food from India, cost near a thousand pounds. It was fed with rice, sugar, and hay; it was daily supplied with seven pounds of rice, mixed with three of sugar, divided into three portions; it was given great quantities of hay and grass, which it chiefly preferred; its drink was water, which it took in great quantities. It was of a gentle disposition, and permitted itself to be touched and handled by all visitors, never attempting mischief, except when abused, or when hungry; in such a case, there was no method of appeasing its fury, but by giving it something to eat. When angry, it would jump up against the walls of its room, with great violence; and, many efforts of escape, but seldom attempted to attack its keeper, and

was always submissive to his threats. It had a peculiar cry, somewhat a mixture between the grunting of a hog, and the bellowing of a calf.

THE HIPPOPOTAMUS

The Hippopotamus is an animal as large, and not less formidable than the rhinoceros; its legs are shorter, and its head rather more bulky; it is above seventeen feet long, from the extremity of the snout, to the insertion of the tail; above sixteen feet in circumference round the body, and above seven feet high; the head is near four feet long, and above nine feet in circumference. The jaws open about two feet wide, and the cutting teeth, of which it has four in each jaw, are above a foot long.

Its feet, in some measure, resemble those of the elephant, and are divided into four parts. The tail is short, flat, and pointed; the hide is amazingly thick, and though not impervious to weapons is impenetrable to the blow of a sabre; the body is covered over with a few scattered hairs, of a whitish colour. The whole figure of the animal is something between that of an ox and a hog, and its cry is something between the bellowing of the one, and the grunting of the other.

This animal, however, though so terribly furnished for war, seems no way disposed to make use of its prodigious strength against an equal enemy; it chiefly resides at the bottom of the great rivers and lakes of Africa; the Nile, the Niger, and the Zara; there it leads an indolent kind of life, and seems seldom disposed for action, except when excited by the calls of hunger. Upon such occasions, three or four of them are often seen at the bottom of a river, near some cataract, forming a kind of line, and seizing upon such fish as are forced down by the violence of the stream. In that element they pursue their prey with great swiftness and perserverance; they swim with much force, and remain at the bottom for thirty or forty minutes without rising to take breath. They traverse the bottom of the stream, as if walking upon land, and make a terrible devastation where they find plenty of prey. But it often

happens, that this animal's fishy food is not supplied in sufficient abundance, it is then forced to come up on land, where it is an awkward and unwieldy stranger; it moves but slowly, and, as it seldom forsakes the margin of the river, it sinks at every step it takes; sometimes, however, it is forced, by famine, up into the higher grounds, where it commits dreadful havoc among the plantations. It is extremely timorous upon land, unless wounded, when it becomes formidable to all that oppose it, overturning whatever it meets, and using all its strength, which it seemed not to have discovered before that dangerous occasion. It possesses the same inoffensive disposition in its favourite element, that it is found to have upon land; it is never found to attack the mariners in their boats, as they go up or down the stream; but should they inadvertently strike against it, or otherwise disturb its repose, there is much danger of its sending them, at once, to the bottom.

The female always comes upon land to bring forth, and it is supposed that she seldom produces above one at a time; upon this occasion, these animals are particularly timorous, and dread the approach of a terrestrial enemy; the instant the parent hears the slightest noise, it dashes into the stream, and the young one is seen to follow it with equal alacrity. These animals are found in great numbers, as they reproduce very fast, but this creature, which was once in such plenty at the mouth of the Nile, is now wholly unknown in Lower Egypt, and is nowhere to be found in that river, except above the cataracts.

THE CAMELOPARD OR GIRAFFE

Were we to be told of an animal so tall, that a man on horseback could with ease ride under its belly, without stooping, we should hardly give credit to the relation; yet, of this extraordinary size is the

HIPPOPOTAMUS *Hippopotamus amphibius*

Camelopard, an animal that inhabits the plains of Africa, and the accounts of which are so well ascertained, that we cannot deny our assent to their authority. It is no easy matter to form an adequate idea of this creature's size, and the oddity of its formation. It exhibits somewhat the slender shape of the deer, or the camel, but destitute of their symmetry, or their easy power of motion. The head somewhat resembles that of the deer, with two round horns, near a foot long; its neck resembles that of a horse; its legs and feet, those of the deer; but with this extraordinary difference, that the fore legs are near twice as long as the hind. As these creatures have been found eighteen feet high, and ten from the ground to the top of the shoulders, so allowing three feet for the depth of the body, seven feet remains, which is high enough to admit a man mounted upon a middle sized horse. The hind part, however, is much lower, so that when the animal appears standing and at rest, it has the appearance of a dog sitting, and this formation of its legs gives it an awkward and laborious motion; which, though swift, must be tiresome. For this reason, the camelopard is rarely found, and only finds refuge in the most internal regions of Africa.

No animal, either from its disposition, or its formation, seems less fitted for a state of natural hostility; its horns are blunt, and even knobbed at the ends; its teeth are made entirely for vegetable pasture; its skin is beautifully speckled with white spots, upon a brownish ground; it is timorous and harmless, and notwithstanding its great size, rather flies from, than resists the slightest enemy; it partakes very much of the nature of the camel, which it so nearly resembles; it lives entirely upon vegetation and when grazing, is obliged to spread its fore legs very wide, in order to reach its pasture; its motion is a kind of pace, two legs on each side moving at the same time, whereas in other animals they move transversely. It often lies down with its belly to the earth, and like the camel, has a callous substance upon its breast, which, when reposed, defends it from injury. This animal was known to the ancients, and has been rarely seen in Europe, but often seen tame at Grand Cairo, in Egypt. When ancient Rome was in its splendour, Pompey exhibited at one time, no less than ten, upon the theatre. It was the barbarous pleasure of the people, at that time, to watch the most terrible, and the most extraordinary animals in combat against each other. The lion, the lynx, the tiger, the elephant, the hippopotamus, were all let loose promiscuously, and were seen to inflict indiscriminate destruction.

THE CAMEL AND THE DROMEDARY

These names do not make two distinct kinds, but are only given to a variety of the same animal, which has subsisted since time immemorial. The principal difference by which these two races are distinguished, is that the camel has two bunches upon his back, whereas the dromedary has but one.

Of the two varieties, the Dromedary is by far the most numerous; the Camel being scarcely found, except in Turkey, and the countires of the Levant, while the other is found spread over all the Deserts of Arabia, the southern parts of Africa, Persia, Tartary, and a great part of the eastern Indies.

The camel is the most temperate of all animals, and it can continue to travel several days without drinking. In those vast deserts, where the earth is everywhere dry and sandy, where there are neither birds nor beasts, neither insects nor vegetables, where nothing is to be seen but hills of sand and heaps of bones, there the camel travels, without requiring either drink or pasture, and is often found six or seven days without any sustenance whatsoever. Its feet are formed for travelling upon land, and utterly unfit for moist or marshy places; the inhabitants, therefore, find a most useful assistant in this animal, where no other could subsist, and by its means, cross those deserts with safety, which would be unpassable by any other method of conveyance.

In Arabia, and those countries where the camel is turned to useful purposes, it is considered as a sacred animal, without whose help, the inhabitants could neither subsist, traffic, or travel; its milk makes a part of their nourishment; they feed upon its flesh particularly when young; they clothe themselves with its hair, which it is seen to moult regularly once a year, and if they fear an invading enemy, their camels serve them in flight, and in a single day, they are known to travel about a hundred miles. Thus, by means of the camel, an Arabian finds safety in his deserts; all the armies upon earth might be lost in the pursuit of a flying squadron of this country, mounted upon their camels, and taking refuge in solitudes where nothing interposes to stop their flight. Nothing can be more dreary than the aspect of these sandy plains, that seem entirely forsaken of life and vegetation: where nothing is presented but a sterile and dusty soil, some-

DROMEDARY *Camelus dromedarius*

times torn up by the winds, and moving in great waves along, which, when viewed from an eminence, resemble less the earth than the ocean; yet in this chasm of nature, by the help of the camel, the Arabian finds safety and subsistence. There are here and there found spots of verdure, where water and shrubs are in plenty, which, though remote from each other, are, in a manner, approximated by the labour and industry of the camel.

The camel is easily instructed in the methods of taking up and supporting his burden; their legs, a few days after they are produced, are bent under their belly; they are in this manner loaded, and taught to rise; their burden is every day thus increased, by insensible degrees, till the animal is capable of supporting a weight adequate to its force: the same care is taken in making them patient of hunger and thirst: while other animals receive their food at stated times, the camel is restrained for days together, and these intervals of famine are increased in proportion as the animal seems capable of sustaining them. By this method of education, they live five or six days without food or water; and their stomach is formed most admirably by nature, to fit them for long abstinence: besides the four stomachs, which all ruminating animals have, it has a fifth stomach, which serves as a reservoir, to hold a greater quantity of water than the animal has an immediate occasion for. It is of a sufficient capacity to contain a large quantity of water, where the fluid remains without corrupting, or without being adulterated by the other ailments: when the camel finds itself pressed with

thirst, it has here an easy resource for quenching it; it throws up a quantity of this water by a simple contraction of the muscles, into the other stomachs, and this serves to macerate its dry and simple food; in this manner, as it drinks but seldom, it takes in a large quantity at a time, and travellers, when straitened for water, have been often known to kill their camels for which they expected to find within them.

In Turkey, Persia, Arabia, Barbary, and Egypt, their whole commerce is carried on by means of camels, and no carriage is more speedy, and none less expensive in these countries. Merchants and travellers unite themselves into a body, furnished with camels, to secure themselves from the robbers that infest the countries in which they live. This assemblage is called a caravan, in which the numbers are sometimes known to amount to about ten thousand, and the number of camels is often greater than those of the men: each of these animals is loaded according to his strength, and he is so sensible of it himself, that when his burden is too great, he remains still upon his belly, the posture in which he is loaded, refusing to rise, till his burden be lessened or taken away. In general, the large camels are capable of carrying a thousand weight, and sometimes twelve hundred; the dromedary from six to seven. In these trading journeys, they travel slowly, their stages are generally regulated, and they seldom go above thirty miles a day. Every evening, when they arrive at a stage, or oasis, they are permitted to feed at liberty; they are

1 BACTRIAN CAMEL 2 DROMEDARY 3, 4 DROMEDARIES
CAPARISONED (J. Stewart)

then seen to eat as much in an hour, as will supply them for twenty-four, they seem to prefer the coarsest weeds to the softest pasture, the thistle, the nettle, the casia, and other prickly vegetables, are their favourite food; but their drivers take care to supply them with a kind of paste composition, which serves as a more permanent nourishment.

The humps upon the back grow large in proportion as the animal is well fed, and if examined they will be found composed of a substance not unlike the udder of a cow. As these animals have often gone the same track, they are said to know their way precisely, and to pursue their passage when their guides are utterly astray: when they come within a few miles of their baiting-place, in the evening, they sagaciously scent it at a distance, and increasing their speed, are often seen to trot, with vivacity to their stage.

The patience of this animal is most extraordinary; and its sufferings seem great, for when it is loaded, it sends forth most lamentable cries, but never resists the tyrant that oppresses it. At the slightest sign, it bends its knees and lies upon its belly, suffering itself to be loaded in this position; at another sign it rises with its load, and the driver getting upon its back, between the two panniers, which, like hampers, are placed upon each side, he encourages the camel to proceed with his voice and with a song. In this manner the creature proceeds contentedly forward, with a slow uneasy walk, of about four miles an hour, and when it comes to its stage, lies down to be unloaded, as before.

The inhabitants generally leave but one male to wait on ten females, the rest they castrate; and though they thus become weaker, they are more manageable and patient. The female receives the male in the same position as when these animals are loaded, she goes with young for about a year, and, like all other great animals, produces but one at a time. The camel's milk is abundant and nourishing, and mixed with water makes a principle part of the beverage of the Arabians. These animals begin to engender at three years of age, and they ordinarily live from thirty to forty years. The genital part of the male resembles that of the bull, but is placed pointing backwards, so that its urine seems to be ejected in the manner of the female. This, as well as the dung, and almost every part of this animal, is converted to some useful purpose by the keepers. Of the urine, salmoniac is made; and of the dung, litter for the horses, and fuel for fire. Thus, this animal alone comprises within itself, a variety of qualities, any one of which serves to render other quadrupeds absolutely necessary for the welfare of man; like the elephant, it is manageable and tame; like the horse, it gives the rider security; it carries greater burdens than the ox, or the mule, and its milk is furnished in as great abundance as that of the cow; the flesh of the young ones is supposed to be as delicate as veal; their hair is more beautiful, and more in request than wool; while of its very excrements, no part is useless.

THE LLAMA

The Llama is found chiefly in South America, upon those mountains, that stretch from New Spain to the Straits of Magellan. They inhabit the highest regions of the globe, and seem to require purer air than animals of a lower situation are found to enjoy. Peru seems to be the place where they are found in greatest plenty. In Mexico, they are introduced rather as curiosities than beasts of burden; but in Potosi, and other provinces of Peru, they make the chief riches of the Indians and Spaniards who rear them: their flesh is excellent food; their hair or rather wool, white, black but mostly brown, may be spun into beautiful clothing, and they are capable, in the most rugged and dangerous ways, of carrying burdens, not exceeding a hundred weight, with the greatest safety. It is true indeed that they go but slowly, and seldom above fifteen miles a day; their tread is heavy, but sure, they descend precipices, and find footing among the most craggy rocks where even men can scarce accompany them; they are, however, but feeble animals, and after four or five days labour, they are obliged to repose for a day or two. They are chiefly used in carrying the riches of the mines of Potosi, and we are told that there are about three hundred thousand of these animals in actual employ.

The llama resembles the camel not only in its natural mildness, but its aptitude for servitude, its moderation and patience. This animal is above three

feet high, and the neck is three feet long, the head is small and well proportioned, the eyes large, the nose long, the lips thick, the upper divided, and the lower a little depending; like all those animals that feed upon grass, it wants the upper cutting teeth; the ears are four inches long, and move with great agility; the tail, if but five inches long, is small, straight, and a little turned up at the end; it is cloven footed, like the ox, but it has a kind of spear-like appendage behind, which assists it in moving over precipices and rugged ways; the wool on the back is short, but long on the sides and the belly; it resembles the camel in the formation of the genital parts in the male, so that it

makes urine backwards; it couples also in the same manner, and though it finds much difficulty in the action, it is said to be much inclined to venery. A whole day is often passed, before this necessary business can be completed, which is spent in growling, quarrelling, and spitting at each other; they seldom produce above one at a time, and their age never extends above ten or twelve years at farthest.

Though the llama is no way comparable to the camel, either for size, strength, or perserverance, the South Americans find a substitute in it, with which they seem perfectly contented; it requires no care, nor expense in the attending or providing for its sustenance; it is supplied with a warm covering, and therefore does not require to be housed; satisfied with vegetables and grass, it needs neither corn nor hay to subsist; it is not less moderate in what it drinks, and exceeds even the camel in temperance. Indeed, of all the creatures, it seems to require water least, as it is supplied by nature with saliva in such large quantities, that it spits it out on every occasion: this saliva seems to be the only offensive weapon that the harmless creature has to testify its resentment. When overloaded, or fatigued, and driven beyond endurance, it falls on its belly, and pours out against him, a quantity of this fluid; which, though probably no way hurtful, the Indians are much afraid of. They say, that wherever it falls, it is of such an acrimonious nature, that it will either burn the skin, or cause very dangerous eruptions.

Such are these animals in their domestic state; but as they are found wild in very great numbers, they

ALPACA *Auchenia alpaca*

exhibit marks of great force and agility, in their state of nature. The stag is scarcely more swift, or the goat, or the chamois a better climber. All its shapes are more delicate and strong; its colour is tawny, and its wool is short; in their native forests, they are gregarious animals, and are often seen in flocks of two or three hundred at a time. When they perceive a stranger, they regard him at first with astonishment, without showing any fear or surprise; but shortly, as if by common consent, they snuff up the air, somewhat like horses, and at once, by a common flight take refuge on the tops of the mountains; they are fonder of the northern than the southern side of the Andes; they often climb above the snowy tracts of the mountain, and seem vigorous in proportion to the coldness of their situation. The wild llama is hunted for the sake of its fleece. If the dogs surprise one upon the plain, they are generally successful; but if once the llama obtains the rocky precipice of the mountain, the hunters are obliged to desist in their pursuit.

The llama seems to be the largest of the camel kind in South America; there are others, which are called guanacoes and pacos, that are smaller and weaker, but endued with the same nature, and formed pretty much in the same manner. They seem to bear the same proportions to each other, that the horse does to the ass, and are employed with the same degree of subordination. The wool, however, of the Alpaca, seems to be the most valuable, and it is formed into

stuffs, not inferior to silk, either in price or beauty. The natural colour of the paco, is that of a dried rose leaf; the manufacturers seldom give its wool any other dye, but form it into quilts and carpets, which exceed those from the Levant.

THE BEAR

Of the Bear, there are three different kinds, the Brown Bear of the Alps, the Black Bear of North America, which is smaller, and the great Polar Bear of Greenland, or White Bear. These, though different in their form, are no doubt of the same origin, and owe their chief variations to food and climate. They have all the same habitudes, being equally carnivorous, treacherous and cruel.

The brown bear, is properly an inhabitant of the temperate climates; the black inhabits the northern regions of Europe and America, while the great white bear takes refuge in the most icy climates, and lives where scarce any other animal can find subsistence.

The brown bear is not only savage but solitary; he takes refuge in the most unfrequented parts, and the most dangerous precipices of uninhabited mountains. It chooses its den in the most gloomy parts of the forest, in some cavern that has been hollowed by time, or in the hollow of some old enormous tree. There it retires alone, and passes some months of the winter without provisions, or without ever stirring abroad. However this animal is not entirely deprived

BROWN BEAR *Ursus arctos*

1 GRISLY BEAR 2 EUROPEAN BROWN BEAR 3 AMERICAN BLACK
BEAR 4 POLAR BEAR (J. Stewart)

of sensation like the bat, or the dormouse, but seems rather to subsist upon the exuberance of its former flesh, and only feels the calls of appetite, when the fat it had acquired in summer, begins to be entirely wasted away. In this manner, when the bear retires to its den, to hide for the winter, it is extremely fat, but at the end of forty or fifty days, when it comes forth to seek for fresh nourishment, it seems to have slept all its flesh away. It is a common report, that during this time, they live by sucking their paws, which is a vulgar error that scarce requires confutation. These solitary animals couple in autumn, but the time of gestation with the female is still unknown; the female takes great care to provide a proper retreat for her young, she secures them in the hollow of a rock, and provides a bed of hay in the warmest part of the den; she brings forth in winter, and the young ones begin to follow her in spring. The male and female, by no means inhabit the same den; they each have their separate retreat, and seldom are seen together but upon the accesses of genial desire.

The voice of the bear is a kind of growl, interrupted with rage, which is often capriciously exerted; and though this animal seems gentle and placid to its master, when tamed; yet it is still to be distrusted and managed with caution, as it is often treacherous and resentful without a cause.

This animal is capable of some degree of instruction. There are few but have seen it dance in awkward measures upon its hind feet, to the voice or the instrument of its leader; and it must be confessed that the dancer is often found to be the best performer of the two. I am told, that it is first taught to perform in this manner, by setting it upon hot plates of iron, and then playing to it, while in this uneasy situation.

The bear seems to be chiefly fond of honey which it seeks for in the hollow of trees.

The white Greenland bear differs greatly, both in figure and dimensions, growing to above three times the size. The brown bear is seldom above six feet long; the white bear is often known from twelve to thirteen. The brown bear is made rather strong and sturdy; like the mastiff; the Greenland bear, though covered with very long hair, and apparently bulky, is nevertheless more slender, both as to the head, neck, and body. In short, all the variations of its figure and its colour, seem to proceed from the coldness of the climate, where it resides, and the nature of the food it is supplied with.

The white bear, seems the only animal, that by being placed in the coldest climate, grows larger than those that live in the temperature zones. All other species of animated nature, diminish as they approach the poles, and seem contracted in their size, by the rigours of the ambient atmosphere, but the bear, being unmolested in these desolate climates, and meeting no animal, but what he can easily conquer, finding also a sufficient supply of fishy provisions, grows to an enormous size, and as the lion is the tyrant of an African forest, so the bear remains undisputed master of the icy mountains in the artic regions. When our mariners land upon those shores, in such parts as have not been frequented before, the white bears come down to view them with an awkward curiosity; they approach slowly, seeming undetermined whether to advance or retreat, and being naturally a timorous animal, they are only urged on by the conscious experience of their former

victories; however, when they are shot at, or wounded, they endeavour to fly, or finding that impracticable, they make a fierce and desperate resistance till they die. As they live upon fish and seals, their flesh is too strong for food, and the captors have nothing but the skin, to reward them for the dangers incurred in the engagement.

The number of these animals that are found about the North Pole, if we consider the scarcity thereof, of all other terrestrial creatures, is very amazing. They are not only seen on land, but on ice-floats, several leagues at sea. They are often transported in this manner to the very shores of Iceland, where all the natives are in arms to receive them. It happens, that when a Greenlander and his wife are paddling out at sea, by coming too near an ice-float, a white bear unexpectedly jumps into their boat, and if he does not overset it, sits calmly where he first came down, and like a passenger, suffers himself to be rowed along. It is probable the poor little Greenlander is not very fond of his new guest, however he makes a virtue of necessity, and hospitably rows him to shore.

As this animal lives chiefly upon fish, seals, and dead whales, it seldom removes far from the shore. When forced by hunger, it often ventures into the deep, swims after seals, and devours whatever it can seize.

THE BADGER

The Badger's legs are so short, that its belly seems to touch the ground; this however is but a deceitful appearance, as it is caused by the length of the hair, which is very long all over the body, and makes it seem much more bulky that it really is. It is a solitary slow moving animal, that finds refuge, remote from man, and digs itself a deep hole, with great assiduity. It seems to avoid the light, and seldom quits its retreat by day, only stealing out at night to find subsistence. It burrows in the ground very easily, its legs being short and strong, and its claws, stiff and horny. As it continues to bury itself, and throw the earth behind it, to a great distance, it thus forms to itself a winding hole, some six to seven feet deep and thirty feet in length, at the bottom of which it remains in safety. As the fox is not so expert at digging into the earth, it often takes possession of that which has been quitted by the badger, and some say, forces it from its retreat, by laying its excrements at the mouth of the badger's hole.

This animal, however, is not long in making itself a new habitation, from which it seldom ventures far, as it flies but slowly, and can find safety only in the strength of its retreat. When it is surprised by the dogs at some distance from its hole, it then combats with desperate resolution; it falls upon its back, defends itself on every side, and seldom dies unrevenged in the midst of its enemies.

The badger is an omnivorous animal living upon fruit, roots, beechmast, slugs, worms and small mammals. It sleeps the greatest part of its time, and thus without being a voracious feeder, it still keeps fat, particularly in winter, during hibernation. They always keep their earth very clean, and when the female brings forth, she makes a comfortable warm bed of hay, at the bottom of her lair for the reception of her young. She brings forth in summer, generally to the number of three or four, which she feeds at first with her milk, and afterwards with such petty prey as she can surprise. She seizes the young rabbits in their warren, robs birds' nests, finds out where the wild bees have laid up their honey, and brings all to her expecting brood.

The young ones when taken are easily tamed, but the old still continue savage and incorrigible; the former, after a short time, play with the dogs, follow their master about the house, but seem of all other animals the most fond of the fire. They often approach it so closely, that they singe themselves in a dangerous manner. They are sometimes also subject to the mange, and have a gland under their tail, which scents pretty strongly, to direct the male and female to one another during their solitary wanderings.

THE ANT-BEAR

There are many animals that live upon ants in Africa and America; the pangolin or scaly lizard of Guinea may be considered among this number; but there are a greater variety in America, which makes those minute insects their only subsistence.

Under the common name of Ant-Bear they have been classed by Mr. Buffon into the larger Tamandua, the smaller Tamandua, and the Ant-Eater. The longest of this kind is four feet long, from the tip of the snout to the insertion of the tail; their legs are short and armed with four strong claws; their tail is long and tufty, and the animal often throws it on its back like the squirrel. The second of this kind is not above eighteen inches long, the tail is without hair,

and it sweeps the ground as the animal moves. The ant-eater, which is the third variety, is still smaller than either of the former, as it is not above seven inches from the tip of the snout to the insertion of the tail. The two former are of a brown dusky colour, but this of a beautiful reddish, mixed with yellow; though they differ in figure, they all resemble each other in one peculiarity, which is the extreme slenderness of their snout, and the amazing length of their tongue.

The snout is produced in so disproportionate a manner, that the length of it makes near a quarter of the whole figure. A horse has one of the longest heads of any animal we know, and yet the ant-bear has one above twice as long, in proportion to its body. The snout of this animal is almost round and cylindrical; it is extremely slender, and is scarce thicker near the eyes than at its extremity. The mouth is very small, the nostrils are very close to each other, the eyes are little, in proportion to the length of the nose, the neck is short, the tongue is extremely long, slender, and

Left BADGER *Ursus meles*   TAPIR *Tapirus indicus*
Right **1** TWO-TOED ANT-EATER *Myrmecophaga didactyla*
2 GREAT ANT-EATER *Myrmecophaga jubata*

flattened on both sides; this it keeps generally doubled up in the mouth, and is the only instrument by which it finds subsistence; for the whole of this tribe are entirely without teeth, and find safety only in the remoteness and security of their retreat.

It may well be supposed that an animal so helpless as the ant-bear is, with legs too short to fit it for flight, and unprovided with teeth to give it a power of resistance, is neither numerous, nor often seen; its retreats are in the most barren and uncultivated parts of South America. It lives chiefly in the woods, and hides itself under the fallen leaves. It seldom ventures from its retreat, and the industry of an hour supplies it with sufficient food for several days together. Its manner of procuring its prey, is one of the most singular in all natural history; as its name implies, it lives entirely upon ants and insects; these, in the countries where it is bred, are found in the greatest abundance, and often build themselves hills, five or six feet high, where they live in community. When this animal approaches an ant-hill, it creeps slowly forward on its belly, taking every precaution to keep itself concealed, till it comes within a proper distance of the place where it intends to make a banquet; there, lying closely along at its length, it thrusts forth its round red tongue, which is often two feet long, across the path of these busy insects, and there lets it lie motionless for several minutes together. The ants of that country, some of which are half an inch long, considering it as a piece of flesh accidentally thrown before them, come forth and swarm upon it in great numbers, but wherever they touch, they stick; for this instrument is covered with a slimy fluid, which like bird-lime, entangles every creature that lights upon it. When therefore the ant-bear has found a sufficient number for one morsel, it instantly draws in the tongue, and devours them all in a moment; after which it still continues in its position, practising the same arts until its hunger is entirely appeased; it then retires to its hiding-place once more, where it continues in indolent existence, till again excited by the calls of hunger.

Such is the luxurious life of a creature, that seems of all others the most helpless and deformed. It finds safety in its hiding-places from its enemies, and an ample supply in some neighbouring ant-hill, for all its appetites. As it only tries to avoid its pursuers, it is seldom discovered by them; yet helpless as this animal is, when driven to an extremity, though without teeth, it will fight with its claws, with great obstinacy. With these arms alone, it has often been found to oppose the dog, and even the Jaguar. It throws itself upon its back, fastens upon its enemy with all its claws, sticks with great strength and perseverance, and even after killing its invader, which is sometimes the case, does not quit its hold, but remains fastened upon him with vindictive desperation.

THE RACOON

The Racoon, a native of America, is about the size of a small badger; its body is short and bulky; its fur is fine, long and thick, blackish at the surface, and grey towards the bottom; the nose is rather shorter, and more pointed than that of a fox; the eyes large and yellow, the teeth resembling those of a dog, the tail thick, but tapering towards a point, regularly marked with rings of black, and at least as long as the body; the fore-feet are much shorter than the hind, both armed with five sharp claws, with which, and his teeth, the animal makes a vigorous resistance. Like the squirrel, it makes use of its paws to hold its food while eating, but it differs from the monkey-kind, which use only one hand on those occasions, whereas the racoon and the squirrel use both; as wanting the thumb, their paws singly are unfit for grasping or holding; though this animal is short and bulky, it is however very active; its pointed claws enable it to climb trees with great facility; it runs on the trunk with the same swiftness that it moves upon the plain, and sports among the most extreme branches with great agility, security and ease; it moves forward chiefly by bounding, and though it proceeds in an oblique direction, it has speed enough most frequently to escape its pursuers.

When wild they are troublesome, feeding upon crops such as sugar cane and corn; in a state of tameness no animal is more harmless or amusing; they are capable of being instructed in various little amusing tricks. The racoon is playful and cleanly, and is very easily supported; it eats of everything that's given it, and if left to itself, no cat can be a better provider; it examines every corner, eats of all flesh, either boiled or raw, eggs, fruits or corn, insects themselves cannot escape it, and if left at liberty in a garden, it will feed upon snails, worms and beetles; but it has a particular fondness for sweets of every kind, and to be possessed of these in its wild state, it incurs every danger. Though it will eat its provisions dry, it will for choice dip them in water if it happens to be in the way; it has one particularity

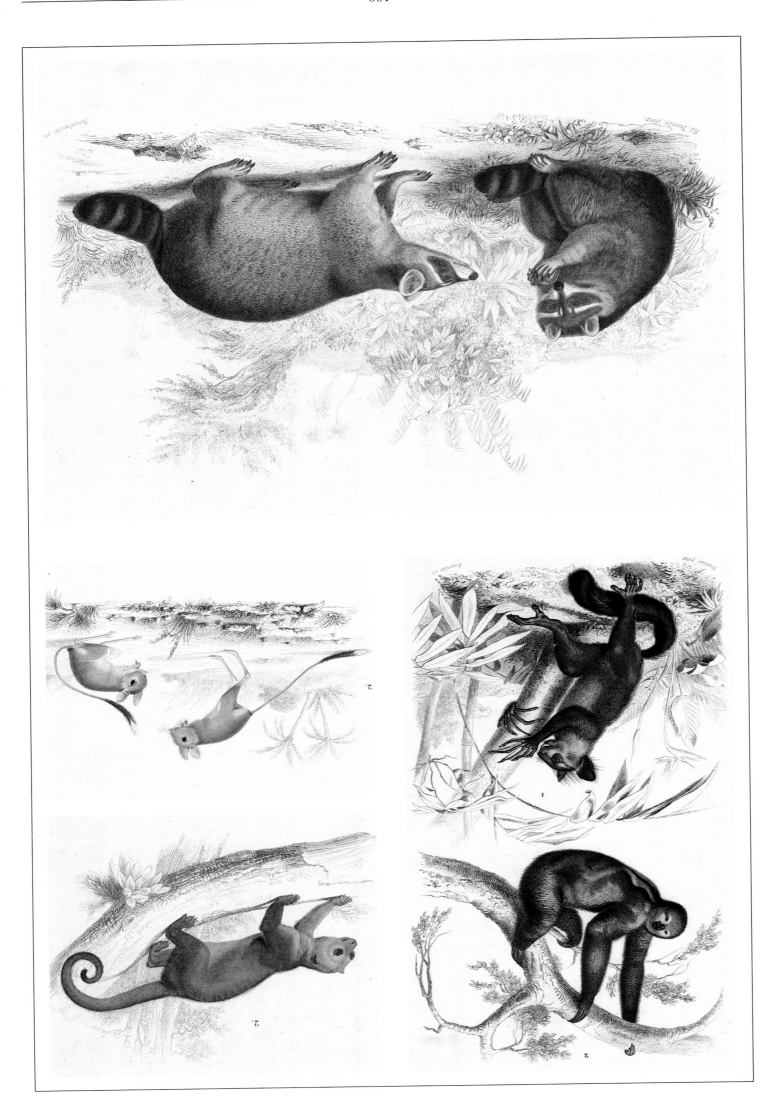

which few other animals have been found to possess, it drinks as well by lapping, like the dog, as by sucking like the horse.

THE SLOTH

Of the Sloth there are two different kinds, distinguished from each other by their claws; the one, which in its native country is called the unan, having only two claws upon each foot, and being without a tail; the other, which is called the ai, having a tail and three claws upon each foot. The unan has the snout longer, the ears more apparent, and the fur very different from the other. It differs also in the number of its ribs, this having forty-six, while the ai has but twenty-eight. Nature seems cramped and constrained in their helpless formation; other animals are often indolent from choice, these are slow from necessity; the ai, being rather more active than the unan, is of about the size of a badger. Its fur is coarse and staring, somewhat resembling dried grass; the tail very short, and scarce appearing; the mouth extending from ear to ear; the eye dull and heavy; the feet armed with three claws each, and made so short, and set on so awkwardly, that a few paces is often the journey of a week; but though the feet are short, they are still longer than its legs, and these proceed from the body in such an oblique direction, that the sole of the foot seldom touches the ground. When the animal therefore is compelled to make a step forward, it scrapes on the back of the nails along the surface, and wheeling the limbs circularly about, yet still touching the ground, it at length places its foot in a progressive position; the other three limbs are all brought about with the same difficulty; and thus it is seen to move, not above three feet in an hour. In fact, this poor creature seldom changes place but by constraint, and when impelled by the severest stings of hunger. The sloth lives entirely upon vegetable food, on the leaves, the fruit, and the flowers of trees, and often even on the very bark, when nothing else is left on the tree for its subsistence. Like all other ruminant animals, it has four stomachs; and these requiring a large share of provision to supply them, it generally strips a tree of all its verdure in less than a fortnight. Still however it keeps aloft, unwilling to descend, while anything remains that can serve it for food; it therefore falls to devouring the bark, and thus in a short time kills the tree upon which it found its support. Thus destitute of provisions above, and

Top Left PALE-THROATED SLOTH *Bradypus ustus*

AYE-AYE *Cheiromys madagascarienisis*

Top Right KINKAJOU *Potos caudivolvulus* GERBUA *Dipus gerboa*

Bottom RACOON *Procyon lotor*

crawling slowly from branch to branch, in hopes of finding something still left, it is at last obliged to encounter all the dangers that attend it below. Though it is formed by nature for climbing a tree with great pain and difficulty, yet it is utterly unable to descend; it therefore is obliged to drop from the branches to the ground, and as it is incapable of exerting itself to break the violence of its descent, it drops like a shapeless heavy mass, and feels no small shock in the fall. There, after remaining some time torpid, it prepares for a journey to some neighbouring tree; but this of all migrations is the most tedious, dangerous, and painful; it often takes a week in crawling to a tree not fifty yards distant; it moves with imperceptible slowness, and all motions seem to torture it. Every step it takes it sets forth a most plaintive, melancholy cry, which from some distant similitude to the human voice, excites a kind of disgust, mixed with pity. This plaintive sound seems its chief defence, few quadrupeds appear willing to interrupt its progress, either that the flesh is offensive, or that they are terrified at its cries. When at length they reach their destined tree, they mount it with much greater ease than when they moved upon the plain. They fall to with famished appetite, and as before, destroy the very source that supplies them. Like birds, they have but one common vent for the purposes of propagation, excrement, and urine. Like the tortoise, which they resemble, in the slowness of their motion, they continue to live some time after their nobler parts are wounded, or even taken away. They bear the marks of all those comely-formed animals, that like rude machines are not easily discomposed.

Its note, according to Kircher, is an ascending and descending hexachord, which it utters only by night; its look is so piteous, as to move compassion; it is also accompanied with tears, that dissuade everybody from injuring so wretched a being. Its abstinence from food is remarkably powerful; one that had fastened itself by its feet to a pole, and was so suspended cross two beams, remained forty days without meat, drink, or sleep; the strength of its feet is so great, that whatsoever it seizes on, cannot possibly be freed from its claws.

THE GERBUA

This animal as little resembles a quadruped, as that which has been described in a former chapter. If we should suppose a bird, divested of its feathers, and walking upon its legs, it might give us some idea of its figure. It has four feet indeed, but in running or resting, it never makes use of any but the hind. The number of legs, however, do not much contribute to any animal's speed; and the Gerbua, though properly speaking, furnished but with two, is one of the swiftest creatures in the world.

The gerbua is not above the size of a large rat, and its head is sloped somewhat in the manner of a rabbit, the teeth also are formed like those of the rat kind, there being two cutting teeth in each jaw; it has a very long tail, tufted at the end; the head, the back, and sides are covered with large ash-coloured soft hair; the breast and belly is whitish, but what most deserves our attention in the formation of this little animal, is the legs; the fore-legs are not an inch long, with four claws and a thumb upon each, while the hind-legs are two inches and a quarter, and exactly resemble those of a bird, there being but three toes, the middlemost of which is longest.

The gerbua is found in Egypt, Barbary, Palestine, and the deserts between Bufferah and Aleppo; its hind-legs, as was said before, are only used in running, while the fore-paws, like those of a squirrel, grasp its food, and in some measure perform the office of hands. It is often seen by travellers as they pass along the deserts, crossing their way, and jumping six or eight feet at every bound, and going so swiftly, that scarce any other quadruped is able to

BLACK-STRIPED WALLABY *Kangurus dorsalis*

overtake them. They are a lively, harmless race of animals, living entirely upon vegetables, and burrowing like rabbits in the ground. Mr. Pennant tells us of two that were lately brought to London, that burrowed almost through the brick wall of the room where they were kept; they came out of their hole at night for food, and when caught, were much fatter and slicker than when confined to their burrows. A variety of this animal is found also in Siberia and Circassia, and is most probably, common enough over all Asia. They are more expert diggers than even the rabbit itself; and when pursued for a long time, if they cannot escape by their swiftness, they try to make a hole instantly in the ground, in which they often bury themselves deep enough to find security before their pursuers come up. Their burrows, in some places, are so thick, as to be dangerous to travellers, the horses perpetually falling in them. It is a provident little animal, and lays up for the winter. It cuts grass in heaps of a foot square, which when dried, it carries into its burrow, therewith to serve it for food, or to keep its young warm during the rigours of the winter.

THE KANGAROO

But of all animals of this kind, that which was first discovered and described by Mr. Banks, is the most extraordinary. He calls it the Kangaroo; and though from its general outline, and the most striking peculiarities of its figure, it greatly resembles the gerbua, yet it entirely differs, if we consider its size,

RED KANGAROO *Kangurus laniger*

or those minute distinctions which direct the makers of systems in assorting the general ranks of nature.

The largest of the gerbua kind which are to be found in the ancient continent, do not exceed the size of a rabbit. The kangaroo of New Holland (Australia) where it is only to be found, is often known to weigh above sixty pounds, and must consequently be as large as a sheep. Although the skin of that which was stuffed and brought home by Mr. Banks, was not much above the size of a hare, yet it was greatly superior to any of the gerbua kind that have been hitherto known, and very different in many particulars. The snout of the gerbua, as has been said, is short and round, that of the new-discovered animal long and slender; the teeth also entirely differ; for as the gerbua has but two cutting teeth in each jaw, making four in all, this animal, besides its cutting teeth, has four canine teeth also; but what makes a more striking peculiarity, is the formation of its lower jaw, which, as the ingenious discoverer supposes, is divided into two parts, which open and shut like a pair of scissors, and cut grass, probably this animal's principal food. The head, neck, and shoulders are very small in proportion to the other parts of the body; the tail is nearly as long as the body, thick near the rump, and tapering towards the end, the skin is covered with a short fur, excepting the head and the ears, which bear a slight resemblance to those of the hare. We are not told, however, from the formation of its stomach, to what class of quadrupeds it belongs, from its eating grass, which it has been seen to do, one would be apt to rank it among the ruminant animals, but from the canine teeth which it is found to have, we may on the other hand suppose it to bear some relation to the carnivorous. Upon the whole, however, it can be classed with none more properly, than with animals of the gerbua kind, as its hind legs are so much longer than the fore; it moves also precisely in the same manner, taking great bounds of ten or twelve feet at a time, and thus sometimes escaping even the fleetest greyhound, with which Mr. Banks pursued it. One of them that was killed, proved to be good food; but a second, which weighed eighty-four pounds, and was not yet come to its full growth, was found to be much inferior.

Buffon, whose only errors were those of genius, clearly perceived that every continent, in its animal productions, presented the appearance of an especial creation; but he gave a universality to this proposition, of which it is not altogether susceptible. It is nevertheless true, even at the present day, within certain limits. A great number of the Asiatic animals are not found in Africa, and *vice versa*. The lemurs seem to exist only in Madagascar. America is peopled with a host of mammalia, exclusively peculiar to itself, and there are many more in Europe not to be found in the other quarters of the globe. The discovery of Australasia has given an additional support to this opinion of Buffon. The species of animals there discovered, have not only no affinity with those of the other continents, but in fact, belong for the most part to genera altogether different. Such are those mammalia which the natives of New Holland call kangaroo, and which offer to the observation of the naturalist, organic peculiarities perceivable in no

other animal, with the exception of one single species. It is in this tribe that for the first time we view the singular phenomenon of an animal using its tail as a third hind-leg in standing upright and in walking. The species we are now upon has received the name of Gigantic, because when named, it was supposed to be the largest of all that are known. These singular animals were among the first fruits which accrued to natural history from the discovery of New South Wales, a country which has since proved so fertile in new and remarkable forms both of the animals and vegetable creations. Their natural habits in a wild state are still, however, very imperfectly known. They appear to live in small herds, perhaps single families, which are said to submit to the guidance of the older males, and to inhabit, in preference, the neighbourhood of woods and thickets. They are, as might be inferred from the small size of their mouths and the peculiar character of their teeth, purely herbivorous, feeding chiefly upon grass and roots. Their flesh is eaten by the colonists, by whom it is said to be nutritious and savoury, an assertion which is confirmed by those who have partaken of it in England. In order to procure this they are frequently hunted in their native country; but the dogs who are employed in this service sometimes meet with dangerous wounds, not only from the blows of their powerful tail, which is their usual weapon of defence, but also from the claws of their hind-feet, with which they have been known to lacerate the bodies of their assailants in a shocking manner. But, unless when thus driven to

1 LORD DERBY'S KANGAROO 2 AROE KANGAROO 3 PARRY'S KANGAROO 4 WOOLLY KANGAROO 5 BRUSH TAILED KANGAROO 6 RAT-TAILED HYPSIPRYMNUS 7 RABBIT-EARED PERAMELES (J. Stewart)

make use of such powers of self-defence as they possess, they are perfectly harmless and even timid; and, when domesticated, are not in the least mischievous. In several collections in this country, they have become almost naturalized, and appear to be but little affected by the change of climate. When confined in a small enclosure, they uniformly make their path round its circuit, seldom crossing it or passing in any other direction except for the purpose of procuring their food. Their whole appearance, and especially their mode of progression, is singularly curious, and even to a certain extent ludicrous.

THE PANGOLIN

The Pangolin, which is a native of the torrid climates of the ancient continent, is, of all other animals, the best protected from external injury by Nature. It is about three or four feet long, or, taking in the tail, from six to eight. Like the lizard, it has a small head, a very long nose, a short thick neck, a long body, legs very short, and a tail extremely long, thick at the insertion, and terminating in a point. It has no teeth, but is armed with five toes on each foot, with long white claws. But what it is chiefly distinguished by is its scaly covering, which in some measure hides all the proportions of its body. These scales defend the animal on all parts, except the under part of the head and neck, under the shoulders, the breast, the belly, and the inner side of the legs; all which parts are covered with a smooth soft skin, without hair. Between the shells of this animal, at all the interstices, are seen hairs like bristles, brown at the extremity and yellow towards the root. The scales of this extraordinary creature are of different sizes and different forms, and stuck upon the body somewhat like the leaves of an artichoke. The largest are found near the tail, which is covered with them like the rest of the body. These are above three inches broad, and about two inches long, thick in the middle and sharp at the edges, and terminated in a roundish point. They are extremely hard, and their substance resembles that of horn. They are convex on the outside and a little concave on the inner; one edge sticks in the skin, while the other laps over that immediately behind it. Those that cover the tail conform to the shape of that part, being of a dusky brown colour, and so hard, when the animal has acquired its full growth, as to turn a musket-ball.

Thus armed, this animal fears nothing from the efforts of all other creatures, except man. The instant it perceives the approach of an enemy, it rolls itself up like the hedgehog, and presents no part but the cutting edges of its scales to the assailant. Its long tail, which, at first view, might be thought easily separable, serves still more to increase the animal's security. This is lapped round the rest of the body, and, being defended with shells even more cutting than any other part, the creature continues in perfect security.

Incapable of being carnivorous, since it has no teeth, nor of subsisting on vegetables, which require much chewing, it lives entirely upon insects, for which Nature has fitted it in a very extraordinary manner. As it has a long nose, so it may naturally be supposed to have a long tongue, but, to increase its length still more, it is doubled in the mouth, so that when extended it is shot out to above a quarter of a yard beyond the tip of the nose. This tongue is round, extremely red, and covered with an unctuous and slimy liquor, which gives it a shining hue. When the pangolin, therefore, approaches an ant hill, for these are the insects on which it chiefly feeds, it lies down near it, concealing as much as possible the place of its retreat, and stretching out its long tongue among the ants, keeps it for some time quite immoveable. These little animals, allured by its appearance, and the unctuous substance with which it is smeared, instantly gather upon it in great numbers; and when

the pangolin supposes a sufficiency, it quickly withdraws the tongue, and swallows them at once.

The pangolin chiefly keeps in the most obscure parts of the forest, and digs itself a retreat in the clefts of rocks, where it brings forth its young, alive and perfectly formed, so that it is but rarely met with, and continues a solitary species, and an extraordinary instance of the variety of Nature.

THE ARMADILLO OR TATOU

The Armadillo is chiefly an inhabitant of South America; a peaceful harmless creature, incapable of offending any other quadruped, and furnished with a peculiar covering for its own defence. The pangolin seems an inactive helpless being, indebted for safety more to its patience than its power; but the armadillo is still more exposed and helpless. The pangolin is furnished with an armour that wounds while it resists, and that is never attacked with impunity; but the armadillo is obliged to submit to every insult, without any power of danger, and is consequently liable to more various persecutions.

This animal being covered, like a tortoise, with a shell, or rather a number of shells, its other proportions are not easily discerned. It appears, at first view,

1 ARMADILLO *Dasypus sexcintus* **2** PANGOLIN *Manis crassicaudata*

a round misshapen mass, with a long head, and a very large tail sticking out at either end, as if not of a piece with the rest of the body. It is of different sizes, from a foot to three feet long, and covered with a shell divided into several pieces, that lap over each other like the plates in a coat of armour, or in the tail of a lobster.

The confirmation of this natural coat of mail; affords one of the most striking curiosities in natural history. This shell, which in every respect resembles a bony substance, covers the head, the neck, the back, the sides, the rump, and the tail to the very point. The only parts to which it does not extend are, the throat, the breast, and the belly, which are covered with a white soft skin, somewhat resembling that of a fowl stripped of its feathers. If these naked parts are observed with attention, they will be found covered with the rudiments of shells, of the same substance with those which cover the back. The skin, even in the parts that are softest, seems to have a tendency to ossify; but a complete ossification takes place only on those parts which have the least friction and are the most exposed to the weather. The shell, which covers the upper part of the body, differs from that of the tortoise, in being composed of more pieces than one, which lie in bands over the body, and, as in the tail of the lobster, slide over each other, and are connected by a yellow membrane in the same manner. By this means the animal has a motion in its back, and the armour gives way to its necessary inflexions. These bands are of various numbers and sizes, and from them these animals have been distinguished into various kinds. In general, however, there are two large pieces that cover, one the shoulders and the other the rump. In the back, between these, the bands are placed in different numbers, that lap over each other, and give play to the whole. Besides their opening cross-ways, they also open down along the back, so that the animal can move in every direction.

Nature has given the armadillo the same method of protecting itself as the hedgehog or the pangolin. The instant it perceives itself attacked, it withdraws the head under its shells, and lets nothing be seen but the tip of the nose; if the danger increases, the animal's precautions increase in proportion; it then tucks up its feet under its belly, unites its two extremities together, while the tail seems as a band to strengthen the connection,; and it thus becomes like a ball, a little flattish on each side.

This animal is a native only of South America and is an inoffensive harmless creature, unless it finds the way into a garden, where it does a great deal of mischief, by eating the melons, the potatoes, and other vegetables. The motion of the armadillo seems to be a swift walk, but they can neither run, leap, nor climb trees; so that, if found in an open place, they have no method of escaping from their pursuers. Their only resource in such an extremity is to make towards their hole as fast as they can; or, if this be impracticable, to make a new hole before the enemy arrives. For this they require but a very few moments advantage; for the mole itself does not burrow swifter than they can. For this purpose, they are furnished with claws extremely large, strong, and crooked, and usually four upon each foot.

There are scarce any of these that do not root the ground, like a hog, in search of such roots as make a principal part of their food. They live also upon melons and other succulent vegetables, and all will eat flesh when they can get it. They frequent water and watery places, where they feed upon worms, small fish, and water insects. It is pretended that there is a kind of friendship between them and the rattlesnake, that they live peaceably and commodiously together, and are frequently found in the same hole. This, however, may be a friendship of necessity to the armadillo; the rattlesnake takes possession of its retreats, which neither are willing to quit while each is incapable of injuring the other.

THE BAT

The Bat in scarce any particular resembles the bird, except in its power of sustaining itself in the air. It brings forth its young alive; it suckles them; its mouth is furnished with teeth; its lungs are formed like those of quadrupeds; its intestines, and its skeleton, have a complete resemblance, and even are, in some measure, seen to resemble those of mankind.

The bat most common in England, is about the size of a mouse, nearly two inches and a half long. The membranes that are usually called wings, are, properly speaking, an extension of the skin all round the body, except the head, which, when the animal flies, is kept stretched on every side, by the four interior toes of the fore feet, which are enormously long, and serve like masts that keep the canvass of a sail spread, and regulate its motions. The first toe is quite loose, and serves as a heel when the bat walks, or as a hook, when it would adhere to anything. The hind feet are disengaged from the surrounding skin, and divided into five toes, somewhat resembling those of a mouse. The skin by which it flies is of a dusky colour. The body is covered with a short fur, of a mouse colour, tinged with red. The eyes are very small; the ears like those of a mouse.

1 COMMON LONG-EARED BAT *Plecotus auritus*
2 YELLOW-WINGED BAT *Megaderma frons*

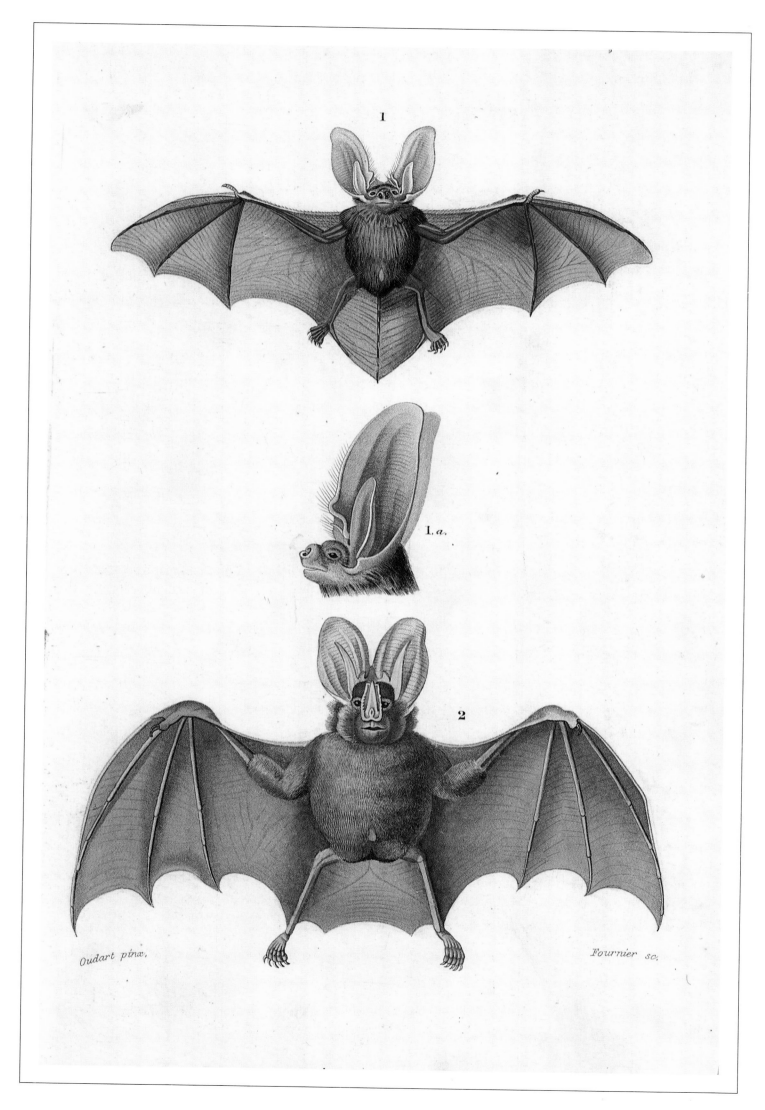

1

1.a.

2

Oudart pinx.

Fournier sc.

This species of the bat is very common in England. It makes its first appearance early in summer, and begins its flight in the dusk of the evening. It principally frequents the sides of woods, glades, and shady walks; and is frequently observed to skim along the surface of pieces of water. It pursues gnats, moths, and nocturnal insects of every kind. It feeds upon these; but will not refuse meat, whenever finds it. Its flight is a laborious, irregular movement; and if it happens to be interrupted in its course, it cannot readily prepare for a second elevation, so that if it strikes against any object, and falls to the ground, it is usually taken. It appears only in the most pleasant evenings, when its prey is generally abroad, and flies in pursuit with its mouth open. At other times it continues in its retreat: the chink of a ruined building, or the hollow of a tree. Thus this little animal, even in summer, sleeps the greatest part of its time, never venturing out by day, nor in rainy weather; never hunting except at night, and then returning to its hole. But its short life is still more abridged by continuing in a torpid state during the winter. At the approach of the cold season, the bat prepares for its state of lifeless inactivity, and seems rather to choose a place where it may continue safe from interruption, warmly or conveniently lodged. For this reason it is usually seen hanging by its hooked claws to the roofs of caves, regardless of the eternal damp. The bat seems the only animal that will venture to remain in these frightful subterranean abodes, where it continues in a torpid state, unaffected by every change of the weather. Such of this kind as are not provident enough to procure themselves a deep retreat, where

FRUIT BAT *Pteropus edwarsu*

the cold and heat seldom vary, are sometimes exposed to great inconveniences, for the weather often becomes so mild in the midst of winter as to warm them prematurely into life, and to allure them from their holes in quest of food. These have seldom strength to return; but, having exhausted themselves in a vain pursuit, after insects which are not to be found, are destroyed by the owl, or any other animal that follows such petty prey.

The bat couples and brings forth in summer, generally from two to five at a time. The female has but two nipples, and those forward on the breast, as in the human kind.

From Linnaeus we learn, that the female makes no nest for her young, as most birds and quadrupeds are known to do. She is barely content with the first hole she meets, where sticking herself by her hooks against the sides of her apartment, she permits her young to hang at the nipple, and in this manner to continue for the first or second day. When, after some time, the dam begins to grow hungry, and finds a necessity of stirring abroad, she takes her little ones and sticks them to the wall, there they immoveably cling, and patiently await her return.

Thus far this animal seems closely allied to the quadruped race. Its similitude to that of birds is less striking. As Nature has furnished birds with extremely strong pectoral muscles, to move the wings, and direct their flight, so has it also furnished this animal. As birds also have their legs weak, and unfit for the purposes of motion, the bat has its legs fashioned in the same manner, and is never seen to walk, or to push itself forward with its hind legs. The toes of the fore legs, extend the web like a membrane that lies between them; and this, which is extremely thin, serves to lift the little body into the air: in this manner, much swifter than that of birds, the animal continues, and directs its flight. However, the great labour required in flying, soon fatigues it; for, unlike birds, which continue for days together upon the wing, the bat is tired in less than an hour, and then returns to its hole, satisfied with its supply, to enjoy the darkness of its retreat.

The varieties of this animal, especially in the British Isles are few; and the differences scarce worth enumeration. Naturalists mention the Long-eared Bat, much less than that generally seen, and with much longer ears; the Horse-shoe Bat, with an odd protuberance round its upper lip, somewhat in the form of a horse-shoe; the Rhinoceros Bat, with a horn growing from the nose, similar to that animal whence it has the name. These, with several others, whose varieties are too numerous, and differences too minute for a detail, are all incapable of injuring mankind, and not sufficiently numerous to incommode him. But there is a larger race of bats, found in the East and West Indies.

Of foreign bats, the largest we have any certain accounts of, is the Great Bat of Madagascar. This formidable creature is near four feet broad, when the wings are extended; and a foot long. It resembles our bat in the form of its wings, in its manner of flying, and in its internal conformation. It differs from it in its enormous size; in its colour, which is red, like that of a fox; in its head and nose also, which resemble those of that animal, and which have induced some to call it the flying fox. It differs also in the number of its teeth; and in having a claw on the fore foot, which is wanting in ours. This formidable creature is found in India, Asia and Africa. When they repose, they stick themselves to the tops of the tallest trees, and hang with their heads downward. But when they are in motion, nothing can be more formidable: they are seen in clouds, darkening the air, as well by day as by night, destroying the ripe fruits of the country. They devour, indiscriminately, fruits, flesh, and insects, and drink the juice of the palm tree: they are heard at night with a horrible din; but at the approach of day, they usually begin to retire. The ancients seem to have taken their idea of harpies from these fierce and voracious creatures, as they both concur in many parts of the description, being equally deformed, greedy, uncleanly, and cruel.

E. Travies pinx.

Fournier sc.

BOOK II

BIRDS

THE OSTRICH, CASSOWARY AND DODO

THE OSTRICH

The Ostrich is a native only of the torrid regions of Africa and is the largest of all birds. Some of those that have been brought into England are above seven feet high. The head and bill somewhat resemble those of a duck; and the neck may be likened to that of a swan, but that it is much longer; the legs and thighs resemble those of a hen; though its whole appearance bears a strong resemblance to that of a camel. The head and neck are above three feet long. From the top of the head to the rump, when the neck is stretched out in a right line, it is six feet long, and the tail is about a foot more. One of the wings, without the feathers, is a foot and a half; and being stretched out, with the feathers, is three feet.

The plumage is much alike in all; that is, generally black and white. The greatest feathers are at the extremities of the wings and tail, and the largest are generally white. There are no feathers on the sides, nor yet on the thighs, nor under the wings. The lower part of the neck, about half way, is covered with still smaller feathers than those on the belly and back; and those, like the former, also are of different colours.

Ostrich feathers are almost all as soft as down, being utterly unfit to serve the animal for flying, and still less adapted to be a proper defence against external injury.

The neck seems to be more slender in proportion to that of other birds, from its not being furnished with feathers. The skin in this part is of a livid flesh colour, which some improperly would have to be

PEACOCK *Pavo cristatus*

blue. The bill is short and pointed, and two inches and a half at the beginning. The external form of the eye is like that of a man, the upper eyelid being adorned with eyelashes which are longer than those on the lid below.

What are called the legs of birds in this are covered before with large scales. The end of the foot is cloven, and has two very large toes. These toes are of unequal sizes. The largest, which is on the inside, is seven inches long, including the claw, which is near three fourths of an inch in length, and almost as broad. The other toe is but four inches long, and is without a claw.

The ostrich has two distinct stomachs. The first, which is lowermost, in its natural situation somewhat resembles the crop in other birds; but it is considerably larger than the other stomach, and is furnished with strong muscular fibres. The second stomach, or gizzard, has outwardly the shape of the stomach of a man; and upon opening is always found filled with a variety of discordant substances; hay, grass, barley, beans, bones, and stones, some of which exceed in size a pullet's egg.

The Arabians assert that the ostrich never drinks; and the place of its habitation seems to confirm the assertion. In these formidable regions, ostriches are seen in large flocks, which to the distant spectator appear like a regiment of cavalry, and have often alarmed a whole caravan. There is no desert, however barren, but is capable of supplying these animals with provision. The ostrich is of all other animals the most voracious. It will devour leather, grass, hair, iron, stones, or anything that is given. Those substances which the coats of the stomach cannot soften, pass whole; so that glass, stones, or iron, are excluded in the form in which they were devoured.

In their native deserts, however, it is probable they live chiefly upon vegetables, where they lead an inoffensive and social life; the male assorting with the female with connubial fidelity. They are said to be very much inclined to venery; and the make of the parts in both sexes seems to confirm the report. It is probable also they copulate, like other birds, by compression; and they lay very large eggs, some of them being above five inches in diameter, and weighing above fifteen pounds. These eggs have a very hard shell, somewhat resembling those of the crocodile.

These birds are very prolific, and lay generally from forty to fifty eggs at one clutch. It has been commonly reported that the female deposits them in the sand; and, covering them up, leaves them to be hatched by the heat of the climate, and then permits the young to shift for themselves. Very little of this however is true: no bird has a stronger affection for her young than the ostrich, nor none watches her eggs with greater assiduity.

The beauty of their plumage, particularly the long feathers that compose the wings and tail, is the chief reason that man has been so active in pursuing this harmless bird to its deserts, and hunting it with no small degree of expense and labour. The ancients used those plumes in their helmets; the ladies of the east make them an ornament in their dress; and among us, our undertakers and our fine gentlemen still make use of them to decorate their hearses and their hats.

Beside the value of their plumage, some of the savage nations of Africa, hunt them also for their flesh; which they consider as a delicacy. Even among the Europeans now, the eggs of the ostrich are said to be well tasted, and extremely nourishing; but they are too scarce to be fed upon, although a single egg be a sufficient entertainment for eight men.

Of all known animals that make use of their legs in running, the ostrich is by far the swiftest: upon observing himself pursued, he begins to run at first but gently; either insensible of his danger, or sure of escaping. In this situation he somewhat resembles a man at full speed; his wings, like two arms, keep working with a motion correspondent to that of his legs; and his speed would very soon snatch him from the view of his pursuers, but, unfortunately for the silly creature, instead of going off in a direct line, he takes his course in circles; while the hunters keep him thus employed, still follow for two or three days together. At last, spent with fatigue and famine, and finding all power of escape impossible, he endeavours to hide himself from those enemies he cannot avoid, and covers his head in the sand, or the first thicket he meets.

It is not for their feathers alone that they are prized in the domestic states; they are often ridden upon, and used as horses. Posterity may avail themselves of this creature's abilities; and riding upon an ostrich may one day become the favourite, as it most certainly is the swiftest mode of conveyance.

OSTRICH *Struthio camelus*

THE CASSOWARY

The Cassowary is a bird which was first brought into Europe by the Dutch, from Java, in the East–Indies, in which part of the world it is only to be found. Next to the ostrich, it is the largest and the heaviest of the feathered species.

The cassowary, though not so large as the former, yet appears more bulky to the eye. It is five feet and a half high, from the point of the bill to the extremity of the claws. The wing is so small, that it does not appear; it being hid under the feathers of the back. In other birds, a part of the feathers serve for flight, and are different from those that serve for merely covering; but in the cassowary, all the feathers are of the same kind, and outwardly of the same colour. They are generally double; having two long shafts, which grow out of a short one, which is fixed in the skin. There are feathers on the head and neck; but they are so short, and thinly sown, that the bird's skin appears naked, except towards the hind part of the head, where they are a little longer. The feathers which adorn the rump, are extremely thick; but do not differ, in other respects, from the rest, excepting their being longer.

The part, however, which most distinguishes this animal is the head; which, though small, like that of an ostrich, does not fail to inspire some degree of

CASSOWARY *Casuarius galeatus*

terror. It is bare of feathers, and is in a manner armed with a helmet of horny substance, that covers it from the root of the bill to near half the head backwards. This helmet is black before and yellow behind. Its substance is very hard, being formed by the elevation of the bone of the skull; and it consists of several plates, one over another, like the horn of an ox. To the peculiar oddity of this natural armour may be added the colour of the eye in this animal, which is a bright yellow, and the globe being above an inch and a half in diameter, give it an air equally fierce and extraordinary. At the bottom of the upper eyelid, there is a row of small hairs, over which there is another row of black hair, which look pretty much like an eyebrow. The lower eyelid, which is the largest of the two, is furnished also with plenty of black hair. The sides of the head, about the eye and ear, being destitute of any covering, are blue, except the middle of the lower eyelid, which is white. The part of the bill which answers to the upper jaw in other animals, is very hard at the edges; above is of a greyish brown, except a green spot on each side. As the beak admits a very wide opening, this contributes not a little to the bird's menacing appearance. The neck is of a violet colour, inclining to that of slate; and it is red behind in several places, but chiefly in the middle. The skin which covers the forepart of the breast, on which this bird leans and rests, is hard, callous, and without feathers. The thighs and legs are covered with feathers, and are extremely thick, strong, straight, and covered with scales of several

shapes. The toes are likewise covered with scales, and are but three in number; for that which should be behind is wanting.

The internal parts are equally remarkable. The cassowary unites with the double stomach of animals that live upon vegetables, the short intestines of those that live upon flesh. Upon the whole, it has the head of a warrior, the eye of a lion, the defence of a porcupine, and the swiftness of a courser.

Thus formed for a life of hostility, for terrifying others, and for its own defence, it might be expected that the cassowary was one of the most fierce and terrible animals of the creation. But nothing is so opposite to its natural character, nothing so different from the life it is contented to lead. It never attacks others; and instead of the bill, when attacked, it rather makes use of its legs, and kicks like a horse, or runs against its pursuer, beats him down, and treads him to the ground.

The same degree of voraciousness which we perceived in the ostrich, obtains as strongly here. The cassowary swallows everything that comes within the capacity of its gullet. The Dutch assert that it can devour not only glass, iron, and stones, but even live and burning coals, without testifying the smallest fear, or feeling the least injury.

The cassowary's eggs are of a grey ash colour, inclining to green. They are marked with a number of little tubercles of a deep green, and the shell is not very thick. The largest of these is found to be fifteen inches round one way, and about twelve the other.

The southern parts of the most eastern Indies seems to be the natural climate of the cassowary. His domain, if we may so call it, begins where that of the ostrich terminates. But the cassowary, that is the inhabitant of a more peopled and polished region, is growing scarcer every day. It is thus, that in proportion as man multiplies, all the savage and noxious animals fly before him: at his approach they quit their ancient habitations, and encounter all the dangers of famine, to avoid the oppressions of an unrelenting destroyer.

THE DODO

Mankind has generally made swiftness the attribute of birds; but the Dodo has no title to this distinction. Instead of conveying the idea of swiftness by its appearance, it seems to strike the imagination as a thing the most unwieldly and inactive of all Nature. Its body is massive, almost round, and covered with grey feathers; it is just barely supported upon two short thick legs like pillars, while its head and neck rise from it in a manner truly grotesque.

The neck, thick and puckered, is joined to the head, which consists of two great jaws, that open far behind the eyes, which are large, black and prominent; so that the animal when it gapes seems to be all mouth. The bill therefore is of an extraordinary length, not flat and broad, but thick, and of a bluish white, sharp at the end, and each piece crooked in opposite directions. From all this results a stupid physiognomy; which is still more increased by a bordering of feathers round the root of the beak, and which give the appearance of a hood or cowl. Bulk, which in other animals implies strength, in this only contributes to inactivity. The dodo seems weighed

down by its own heaviness, and has scarce strength to urge itself forward. It seems an unresisting thing, equally incapable of flight or defence. It is furnished with wings, covered with soft ash-coloured feathers, but they are too short to assist it in flying. It is furnished with a tail, with a few small curled feathers; but this tail is disproportioned and displaced. Its legs are too short for running, and its body too fat to be strong. One would take it for a tortoise that had supplied itself with the feathers of a bird.

This bird is a native of the Isle of France; and the Dutch, who first discovered it there, called it in their language the *nauseous bird*, as well from its disgusting figure as from the bad taste of its flesh. However, succeeding observers contradict this first report, and assert that its flesh is good and wholesome eating. It is a silly simple bird, as may very well be supposed from its figure, and is very easily caught. Three or four dodos are enough to dine a hundred men.

RAPACIOUS BIRDS

THE EAGLE

The Golden Eagle is the largest and the noblest of all those birds that have received the name of Eagle. It weighs above twelve pounds. Its length is three feet; the extent of its wings, seven feet four inches; the bill is three inches long, and of a deep blue colour; and the eye of a hazel colour. The sight and sense of smelling are very acute. The head and neck are clothed with narrow sharp pointed feathers, and of a deep brown colour, bordered with tawny. The whole body, above as well as beneath, is of a dark brown; and the feathers of the back are finely clouded with a deeper shade of the same. The legs are yellow, short, and very strong, being three inches in circumference, and feathered to the very feet. The toes are covered with large scales, and armed with the most formidable claws, the middle of which are two inches long.

Somewhat smaller than this terrible bird are the Ring Tailed Eagle, the Common Eagle, the Bald Eagle, the White Eagle, the Rough-Footed Eagle, the Erne, the Black Eagle, the Osprey, the Sea Eagle, and the Crowned Eagle. These, and others that might be added, form different shades in this fierce family; but have all the same rapacity, the same general form, the same habits, and the same manner of bringing up their young.

In general, these birds are found in mountainous and ill-peopled countries, and breed among the loftiest cliffs. They choose those places which are remotest from man, upon whose possessions they but seldom make their depredations, being contented rather to follow the wild game in the forest than to risk their safety to satisfy their hunger. However hungry they may be, they never stoop to carrion; and when satiated, they never return to the same carcas, but leave it for other animals, more rapacious and less delicate than they.

Of all animals the eagle flies highest; and from thence the ancients have given him the epithet of *the bird of Heaven*. He never pursues but in sight; and when he has seized his prey, he stoops from his height, as if to examine its weight, always laying it on the ground before he carries it off. As his wing is very powerful, yet, as he has but little suppleness in the joints of the leg, he finds it difficult to rise when down; however, if not instantly pursued, he finds no difficulty in carrying off geese and cranes. He also carries away hares, lambs, and kids; and often destroys fawns and calves, to drink their blood. Infants themselves, when left unattended, have been destroyed by these rapacious creatures; which prob-ably gave rise to the fable of Ganymede's being snatched up by an eagle to heaven.

The nest of the eagle is usually built in the most inaccessible cliff of the rock, and often shielded from the weather by some jutting crag that hangs over it. Sometimes, however, it is wholly exposed to the winds, for the nest is flat, though built with great labour. It is said that the same nest serves the eagle during life; and indeed the pains bestowed in forming it seems to argue as much. Eagles are remarkable for their longevity, and for their power of sustaining a long absence from food. One of this species, which has now been nine years in the possession of Mr. Owen Holland, of Conway, lived thirty-two years with the gentleman who made him a present of it; but what its age was when the latter received it from Ireland, is unknown. The same bird also furnishes a proof of the truth of the other remark; having once, through the neglect of servants, endured hunger and for thirst twenty-one days, without any sustenance whatever.

Such are the general characteristics and habitudes of the eagle; however, in some these habitudes differ, as the Sea Eagle and the Osprey live chiefly upon fish, and consequently build their nests on the sea-shore, and by the sides of rivers, on the ground among reeds; and often lay three or four eggs. They catch their prey, which is chiefly fish, by darting down upon them from above.

THE BALD EAGLE

Nor is the Bald Eagle, which is an inhabitant of North Carolina, less remarkable for habits peculiar to itself. These birds breed in that country all the year round. When the eaglets are just covered with down, the female eagle lays again. These eggs are left to be hatched by the warmth of the young ones that continue in the nest; so that the flight of one brood makes room for the next. These birds will often steal young pigs, and carry them alive to the

nest, which is composed of twigs, sticks and rubbish: it is large enough to fill the body of a cart; and is commonly full of bones half eaten, and putrid flesh, the stench of which is intolerable.

THE CONDOR

If size and strength, combined with rapidity of flight and rapacity, deserve pre-eminence, no bird can be put in competition with the Condor. The beak is so strong as to pierce the body of a cow and they do not even abstain from man himself: but fortunately there are but few of the species; for if they had been plenty, every order of animals must have carried on an unsuccessful war against them.

We have a circumstantial account of this amazing bird, by P. Feuillée, the only traveller who has accurately described it. "In the valley of Ilo in Peru, I discovered a condor, perched on a high rock before me: I approached within gun-shot and fired; but, as my piece was only charged with swan-shot, the lead was not able sufficiently to pierce the bird's feathers. I perceived, however, by its manner of flying, that it was wounded, and it was with a good deal of difficulty that it flew to another rock, about five hundred yards distant on the sea-shore. I therefore charged again with ball, and hit the bird under the throat, which made it mine. I accordingly ran up to seize it; but, even in death it was terrible, and defended itself upon its back, with its claws extended against me, so that I scarce knew how to lay hold of it, but I at last dragged it down from the rock, and with the assistance of one of the seamen, I carried it to my tent. The wings of this bird, which I measured very exactly, were twelve feet three inches from tip to tip. The great feathers, that were of a beautiful shining black, were two feet four inches long. The thickness of the beak was proportionable to the rest of the body; the length about four inches; the point hooked downwards, and white at its extremity; and the other part was of a jet black. A short down, of a brown colour, covered the head; the eyes were black, and surrounded with a circle of reddish brown. The feathers, on the breast, neck and wings, were of a light brown; those on the back were rather darker. Its thighs were covered with brown feathers to the knee. The thigh bone was ten inches long; the leg five inches: the toes were three before, and one behind: that behind was an inch and a half. These birds usually keep in the mountains, where they find their prey: they never descend to the sea-shore, but in the rainy season; for as they are very sensible of cold,

IMPERIAL EAGLE *Aquila heliaca*

they go there for greater warmth. Though these mountains are situated in the torrid zone, the cold is often very severe; for a great part of the year they are covered with snow, but particularly in winter. The little nourishment which these birds find on the sea-coast, except when the tempest drives in some great fish, obliges the condor to continue there but a short time. They usually come to the coast at the approach of evening; stay there all night, and fly back in the morning."

It is doubted whether this animal be proper to America only, or whether it may not have been described by the naturalists of other countries. It is supposed, that the great bird called the Roc, described by Arabian writers, and so much exaggerated by fable, is but a species of the condor. The great bird of Tarnaffar, in the East Indies, that is larger than the eagle, as well as the vulture of Senegal, that carries off children, are probably no other than the bird we have been describing. In the deserts of Pochomac, where it is chiefly seen, men seldom venture to travel. Those wild regions are very sufficient of themselves to inspire a secret horror: the mountains rendered still more terrible by the condor, the only bird that ventures to make its residence in those deserted situations.

THE VULTURE

The Vulture is indelicately voracious; and seldom attacks living animals when it can be supplied with the dead; putrefaction and stench, instead of deterring, only serves to allure it.

Vultures may be easily distinguished by the nakedness of their heads and necks, which are without feathers, and only covered with a very slight down, or a few scattered hairs. Their eyes are prominent; and their claws are shorter than those of the eagle. Their attitude is not so upright, and their flight more difficult and heavy.

The Golden Vulture seems to be the foremost of the kind; and is in many things like the golden eagle, but larger in every proportion. From the end of the beak, to that of the tail, it is four feet and a half; and to the claws end, forty-five inches. The length of the upper mandible is almost seven inches; and the tail twenty-seven in length. The lower part of the neck, breast and belly, are of a red colour; but on the tail it is more faint, and deeper near the head. The feathers are black on the back; and on the wings and tail, of a yellowish brown. Others of the kind differ from this in colour and dimensions; but they are all strongly marked by their naked heads, and beaks straight in the beginning, but hooking at the point.

They are still more strongly marked by their nature, which, as has been observed, is cruel, unclean, and indolent. Their sense of smelling, however, is amazingly great; and Nature, for this purpose, has given them two large apertures or nostrils without, and an extensive olfactory membrane within. Their intestines are formed differently from those of the eagle kind; for they partake more of the formation of such birds as live upon grain. They have both a crop and a stomach; which may be regarded as a kind of gizzard, from the extreme thickness of the muscles of which it is composed. In fact, they seem adapted inwardly, not only for being carnivorous, but to eat corn, or whatsoever of that kind comes in their way.

This bird, which is common in many parts of Europe, and well known on the western continent, is totally unknown in England. In Egypt, Arabia, and many other kingdoms of Africa and Asia, vultures are found in great abundance. The inside down of their wing is converted into a very warm and comfortable kind of fur, and is commonly sold in the Asiatic markets.

Indeed, in Egypt, this bird seems to be of singular service. There are great flocks of them in the neighbourhood of Grand Cairo, which no person is permitted to destroy. The service they render the inhabitants, is the devouring all the carrion and filth of that great city; which might otherwise tend to corrupt and putrify the air.

In America, they lead a life somewhat similar. Wherever the hunters, who there only pursue beasts for the skins, are found to go, these birds are seen to pursue them. They keep hovering at a little distance; and when they see the beast flayed and abandoned, they call out to each other, swoop down upon the carcass, and, in an instant, pick its bones as bare and clean as if they had been scraped by a knife.

The sloth, the filth, and the voraciousness of these birds, almost exceed credibility. In Brazil, where they are found in great abundance, when they light upon a carcass, which they have liberty to tear at their ease, they so gorge themselves, that they are unable to fly; but keep hopping along when they are pursued.

THE FALCON

Falconry, that is now so much disused among us, was the principal amusement of our ancestors. A person of rank scarce stirred out without his hawk on his hand; which in old paintings is the criterion of nobility.

Falcons which have been taken into the service of man, are endowed with natural powers that the other kinds are not possessed of. From the length of their wings, they are swifter to pursue their game and they have an attachment to their feeder, and consequently a docility which the baser birds are strangers to. The Falcon Gentil and the Peregrine Falcon are somewhat about the size of a Raven. The peregrine is stronger in the shoulder, has a larger eye, his beak is stronger, his legs longer, and the toes better divided.

Next in size to these is the Lanner, a bird now very little known in Europe; then follows the Sacre, the legs of which are of a bluish colour, and serve to distinguish that bird; to them succeeds the Hobby, used for smaller game, for chasing larks, and stooping at quails. The Kestrel was trained for the same purposes; and lastly the Merlin; which though the smallest of all the hawk or falcon kind, and not much larger than a thrush, yet displays a degree of courage that renders him formidable even to birds ten times his size. He has often been known to kill a partridge or a quail at a single pounce from above.

In order to train up a falcon, the master begins by clapping on straps upon his legs, which are called jesses, to which there is fastened a ring with the owner's name, by which, in case he should be lost, the finder may know where to bring him back. To these also are added little bells, which serve to mark the place where he is, if lost in the chase. He is always carried on the fist, and is allowed no sleep. Thus, by hunger, watching, and fatigue, he has to submit to having his head covered by a hood which covers his eyes. These privations continue often for three days and nights without ceasing and make him lose all idea of liberty, and bring down his natural wildness. His master judges of his being tamed when he permits his head to be covered without resistance, and when uncovered he seizes the meat before him contentedly.

When the first lessons have succeeded, and the bird shows signs of docility, he is carried out, the head is uncovered, and, by flattering him with food at different times, he is taught to jump on the fist, and to continue there. When confirmed in this habit, it is then thought time to make him acquainted with the lure. This lure is a thing stuffed like a bird and on this lure they always take care to give him his food. The

KING VULTURE *Sarcoramphus papa*

Traviés pinx.   Fournier sc.

Left RED-FOOTED FALCON *Falco rufipes*

Right SPARROWHAWK *Falco nisus*

use of this lure is to coax him back when he has flown in the air, which it sometimes fails to do; and it is always requisite to assist it by the voice and the signs of the master. By this method of instruction, a hawk may be taught to fly at any game whatsoever; but falconers have chiefly confined their pursuit only to such animals as yield them profit by the capture or pleasure in the pursuit. The hare, the partridge, and the quail, repay the trouble of taking them; but the most delightful sport is the falcon's pursuit of the heron, the kite, or the wood-lark.

THE BUTCHER-BIRD

The Greater Butcher-Bird is about as large as a thrush; its bill is black, an inch long, and hooked at the end. This together with its carnivorous appetites, ranks it among the rapacious birds.

Indeed, its habits seem entirely to correspond with its conformation, as it is found to live as well upon flesh as upon insects, and thus to partake in some measure of a double nature. However, its appetite for flesh is the most prevalent; and it never takes the

former when it can obtain the latter.

It is wonderful to see with what intrepidity this little creature goes to war with the magpie, the crow, and the kestrel, all above four times bigger than itself, and that sometimes prey upon flesh in the same manner. It not only fights upon the defensive, but often comes to the attack, and always with advantage, particularly when the male and female unite to protect their young.

Small birds are its usual food. It seizes them by the throat, and strangles them in an instant. When it has thus killed the bird or insect, it is asserted by the best authority, that it fixes them upon some neighbouring thorn, and, when thus spitted, pulls them to pieces with its bill.

During summer, such of them as constantly reside in England remain among the mountainous parts of the country; but in winter they descend into the plains and nearer human habitations. The larger kind make their nests on the highest trees, while the lesser build in bushes in the fields and hedgerows. They

Left **1** GREAT CONDOR *Vultur gryphus*
2 EAGLE OWL *Bubo europeus*
Right **1** BARN OWL *Strix flammea*
2 NIGHTJAR *Caprimulgus europeus*

both lay about six eggs, of a white colour, but encircled at the bigger end with a ring of brownish red. The nest on the outside is composed of white moss, interwoven with long grass; within, it is well lined with wool, and is usually fixed among the forking branches of a tree. The female feeds her

young with caterpillars and other insects while very young; but soon after accustoms them to flesh, which the male procures with surprising industry. Their nature also is very differnt from other birds of prey in their parental care; for, so far from driving out their

young from the nest to shift for themselves, they keep them with care and even when adult they do not forsake them, but the whole brood live in one family together.

THE OWL

All birds of the Owl kind may be considered as nocturnal robbers, who, unfitted for taking their prey while it is light, surprise it at those hours of rest when it is in the least expectation of an enemy.

All birds of the owl kind have one common mark, by which they are distinguished from others; their eyes are formed for seeing better in the dark, than in the broad glare of sunshine. In these birds the pupil is capable of opening very wide, or shutting very close.

But though owls are dazzled by too bright a daylight, yet they do not see best in the darkest nights, as some have been apt to imagine. It is in the dusk of the evening, or the grey of the morning, that they are best fitted for seeing; as those seasons when there is neither too much light, nor too little. It is then that they issue from their retreats, to hunt or to surprise their prey, which is usually attended with great success. The common White or Barn Owl, sees with such exquisite acuteness in the dark, that though the barn has been shut at night, and the light thus totally excluded, yet it perceives the smallest mouse that peeps from its hole: on the contrary, the Brown Horn Owl is often seen to prowl along the hedges by day, like the sparrow-hawk; and sometimes with good success.

All birds of the owl kind may be divided into two sorts; those that have horns, and those without. These horns are nothing more than two or three feathers that stand up on each side of the head over the ear, and give this animal a kind of horned appearance. Of the horned kind is the Great Horned Owl, which at first view appears as large as an eagle. When he comes to be observed more closely, however, he will be found much less. His legs, body, wings and tail, are shorter; his head much larger and thicker; his horns rise above two inches and a half high, and which he can erect or depress at pleasure: his eyes are large and transparent, encircled with an orange-coloured iris: his ears are large and deep, and it would appear that no animal is possessed with a more exquisite sense of hearing: his plumage is of a reddish brown, marked on the back with black and yellow spots, and yellow only upon the belly.

Next to this is the Common Horned Owl, of a much smaller size than the former, and with horns much shorter. As the great owl was five feet from the tip of one wing to the other, this is but three. The horns are but about an inch long, variegated with black and yellow.

To these succeeds the tribe without horns. The Howlet, which is the largest of this kind, with dusky plumes, and black eyes; the Screech Owl, of a smaller size, with blue eyes, and plumage of an iron grey; the White Owl, about as large as the former, with yellow eyes and whitish plumage; the Great Brown Owl, less than the former, with brown plumage and a brown beak; and lastly, the Little Brown Barn Owl, with yellowish coloured eyes, and an orange-coloured bill. To this catalogue might be added others of foreign denominations, which differ but little from our own,

if we except the Harsang, or Great Hudson's Bay Owl which is the largest of all the nocturnal tribe, and as white as the snows of the country of which he is a native.

These birds are not by any means silent; they all have an hideous note; which, while pursuing their prey, is seldom heard; but may be considered rather as a call to courtship. There is something always terrifying in this call, which is often heard in the silence of midnight, and breaks the general pause with a horrid variation. Indeed, the prejudices of mankind are united with their sensations to make the cry of the owl disagreeable. The screech-owl's voice was always considered among the people, as a presage of some sad calamity that was soon to ensue.

The usual place where the great horned owl breeds is in the cavern of a rock, the hollow of a tree, or the turret of some ruined castle. Its nest is near three feet in diameter, and composed of sticks, bound together by the fibrous roots of trees, and lined with leaves on the inside. It lays about three eggs, which are larger than those of a hen, and of a colour somewhat resembling the bird itself. The young ones are very voracious, and the parents not less expert at satisfying the call of hunger. The other owls in general build near the place where they chiefly prey.

BIRDS OF THE POULTRY KIND

THE COCK

Of all other birds, the Cock seems to be the oldest companion of mankind, to have been first reclaimed from the forest, and taken to supply the accidental failure of the luxuries or necessities of life. The tail, which makes such a beautiful figure in the generality of these birds, is yet found entirely wanting in others; and not only the tail but the rump also. The toes, which are usually four in all animals of the poultry kind, yet in a species of the cock are found to amount to five.

The cock is found in the islands of the Indian Ocean, and in the woods on the coasts of Malabar, in his ancient state of independence. In his wild condition, his plumage is black and yellow, and his comb and wattles yellow and purple.

No animal in the world has greater courage than the cock when opposed to one of his own species. In China, India, the Philipine Islands, and all over the east, cock-fighting is the sport and amusement even of kings and princes. With us it is declining every day; and it is to be hoped it will in time become only the pastime of the vulgar.

The extraordinary courage in the cock is thought to proceed from his being the most salacious of all other birds whatsoever. A single cock suffices for ten or a dozen hens; and it is said of him that he is the only animal whose spirits are not abated by indulgence. But then he soon grows old; the radical moisture is exhausted; and in three or four years he becomes utterly unfit for the purposes of impregnation. Hens also, as they for the greatest part of the year daily lay eggs, cannot suffice for so many births, but for the most part after three years become effete and barren: for when they have exhausted all their feed-eggs, of which they had but a certain quantity from the beginning, they must necessarily cease to lay.

The hen seldom hatches a brood of chickens above once a season. The number of eggs a domestic hen will lay in the year are above two hundred, provided she be well fed and supplied with water and liberty. It matters not much whether she be trodden by the cock or no; she will continue to lay, although all the eggs of this kind can never by hatching be brought to produce a living animal.

The cock, from his salaciousness, is allowed to be a short lived animal; but how long these birds live, if left to themselves, is not yet well ascertained by any historian. As they are kept only for profit, and in a few years become unfit for generation, there are few that, from mere motives of curiosity, will make the

DOMESTIC JUNGLEFOWL *Gallus domesticus*

tedious experiment of maintaining a proper number till they die. It is probable that this may be ten years or so. They are subject to some disorders, and as for poisons, they are injured by elderberries; of which they are not a little fond.

THE PEACOCK

The Peacock, by the common people of Italy, is said to have the plumage of an angel, the voice of a devil, and the guts of a thief. In fact, each of these qualities mark pretty well the nature of this extraordinary bird. When it appears with its tail expanded, there is none of the feathered creation can vie with it for beauty; yet the horrid scream of its voice serves to abate the pleasure we find from viewing it; and still more, its insatiable gluttony and spirit of depredation make it one of the most noxious domestics that man has taken under his protection.

Our first peacocks were brought from the East Indies; and we are assured, that they are still found in vast flocks, in a wild state, in the islands of Java and Ceylon. So beautiful a bird, and one esteemed such a delicacy at the tables of the luxurious, could not be permitted to continue long at liberty in its distant retreats. So early as the days of Solomon, we find in his navies, among the articles imported from the East, apes and peacocks.

Whatever there may be of delicacy in the flesh of a young peacock, it is certain an old one is very indifferent eating. Its fame for delicacy, however, did

not continue very long; for we find, in the times of Francis the First, that it was a custom to serve up peacocks to the tables of the great, with an intention not be eaten, but only to be seen. Their manner was to strip off the skin; and then preparing the body with the warmest spices, they covered it up again in its former skin, with all its plumage in full display, and no way injured by the preparation.

Like other birds of the poultry kind, the peacock feeds upon corn; but its chief predilection is for barley. But as it is a very proud and fickle bird, there is scarce any food that it will not at times covet and pursue. Insects and tender plants are often eagerly sought at a time that it has a sufficiency of its natural food provided more nearly. In the indulgence of these capricious pursuits, walls cannot easily confine it; it strips the tops of houses of their tiles or thatch, it lays waste the labours of the gardener, roots up his choicest seeds, and nips his favourite flowers in the bud. Thus its beauty but ill recompenses for the mischief it occasions; and many of the more homely looking fowls are very deservedly preferred before it.

Nor, is the peacock less a debauchee in its affections, than a glutton in its appetities. He is still more salacious than even the cock; and though not possessed of the same vigour, yet burns with more immoderate desire. He requires five females at least to attend him; and if there be not a sufficient number, he will even run upon and tread the sitting hen. For this reason, the peahen endeavours, as much as she can, to hide her nest from the male, as he would otherwise disturb her sitting, and break her eggs.

The peahen seldom lays above five or six eggs in this climate before she sits. This bird lives about twenty years; and not till its third year has it that beautiful variegated plumage that adorns its tail.

There are varieties of this bird, some of which are white, others crested: that which is called the Peacock of Tibet, is the most beautiful of the feathered creation, containing in its plumage all the most vivid colours, red, blue, yellow, and green, disposed in an almost artificial order, as if merely to please the eye of the beholder.

THE TURKEY

The domestic Turkey, when young, is one of the most delicate of all birds; yet, in its wild state, it is found in great plenty in the forests of Canada, that are covered with snow above the three parts of the year. In their natural woods, they are found much larger than in their state of domestic captivity. They

PHEASANT *Phasianus colchicus*

are much more beautiful also, their feathers being of a dark grey, bordered at the edges with a bright gold colour. These the savages of the country weave into cloaks to adorn their persons, and fashion into fans and umbrellas.

In their captive state turkeys do not appear to be possessed of much intelligence. They seem a stupid, vain, querulous tribe, apt enough to quarrel among themselves, yet without any weapons to do each other an injury. Everybody knows the strange antipathy the turkeycock has to a red colour; how he bristles and, with his peculiar gobbling sound, flies to attack it.

But though so furious among themselves, they are weak and cowardly against other animals, though far less powerful than they. The cock often makes the turkey keep at a distance, but, with the insolence of a bully, he pursues any thing that seems to fear him, particularly lap-dogs and children, against both which he seems to have a peculiar aversion. On such occasions, after he has made them scamper, he returns to his female train, displays his plumage around, struts about the yard, and gobbles out a note

GOLDEN PHEASANT *Phasianus pictus*

of self-approbation.

The female seems of a milder, gentler disposition. Rather querulous than bold, she hunts about in quest of grain, and pursuit of insects, being particularly delighted with the eggs of ants and caterpillars. She lays eighteen or twenty eggs, larger than those of a hen, whitish, but marked with spots resembling the freckles of the face. Her young are extremely tender at first, and must be carefully fed with curd chopped with dock leaves; but as they grow older, they become more hardy, and follow the mother to considerable distances, in pursuit of insect food, which they prefer to any other. On these occasions, however, the female, though so large and, as it would seem, so powerful a bird, gives them but very little protection against the attacks of any rapacious animal that comes in her way. She rather warns her young to shift for themselves, than prepares to defend them.

When once grown up, turkeys are very hardy birds, and feed themselves at very little expense to the farmer. Those of Norfolk are said to be the largest of this kingdom, weighing from twenty to thirty pounds. There are places, however, in the East Indies, where they are known only in their domestic state, in which they grow to the weight of sixty pounds.

THE PHEASANT

It would surprise a sportsman to be told that the Pheasant which he finds wild in the woods, in the remotest parts of the kingdom, and in forests, which

can scarce be said to have an owner, is a foreign bird, and was at first artificially propagated amongst us. They were brought into Europe from the banks of the Phasis, a river of Colchis, in Asia Minor; and from whence they still retain their name.

Next to the peacock, they are the most beautiful of birds, as well for the vivid colour of their plumes as for their happy mixtures and variety.

In fact, nothing can satisfy the eye with a greater variety and richness of ornament than this beautiful creature. The iris of the eyes is yellow; and the eyes themselves are surrounded with a scarlet colour, sprinkled with small specks of black. On the fore-part of the head there are blackish feathers mixed with a shining purple. The top of the head and the upper part of the neck are tinged with a darkish green that shines like silk. In some, the top of the head is of a shining blue, and the head itself, as well as the upper part of the neck, appears sometimes blue and some-times green, as it is differently placed to the eye of the spectator. The feathers of the breast, the shoulders, the middle of the back, and the sides under the wings, have a blackish ground, with edges tinged of an exquisite colour, which appears sometimes black and sometimes purple, according to the different lights it is placed in; under the purple there is a transverse streak of gold colour. The tail, from the middle feathers to the root, is about eighteen inches long; the legs, the feet and the toes, are of the colour of horn. There are black spurs on the legs, shorter than those of a cock; there is a membrane that connects two of the toes together; and the male is much more beauti-ful than the female.

This bird, though so beautiful to the eye, is not less delicate when served up to the table. Its flesh is considered as the greatest delicacy; and when the old physicians spoke of the wholesomeness of any viands, they made their comparison with the flesh of the pheasant. However, notwithstanding all these perfections to tempt the curosity or the palate, the pheasant has multiplied in its wild state; and, as if disdaining the protection of man, has left him to take shelter in the thickest woods and the remotest forests. All others of the domestic kind, the cock, the turkey, or the pintada, when once reclaimed, have still con-tinued in their domestic state, and persevered in the habits and appetites of willing slavery. But the pheas-ant, though taken from its native warm retreats, where the woods supply variety of food and the warm sun suits its tender constitution, has still con-tinued its attachment to native freedom; and now wild among us, makes the most envied ornament of our parks and forests, where he feeds upon acorns and berries, and the scanty produce of our chilling climate.

However, it has been the aim of late to take these birds once more from the woods, and to keep them in places fitted for their reception. Like all others of the poultry kind, they have no great sagacity, and suffer themselves easily to be taken. At night they roost upon the highest trees of the wood; and by day they come down into the lower brakes and bushes, where their food is chiefly found. They generally make a kind of flapping noise when they are with the females; and this often apprises the sportsman of their retreats. But of all birds they are shot most easily, as they always make a whirring noise when they rise, by which they alarm the gunner, and being a large mark, and flying very slow, there is scarce any missing them.

In the natural state the female makes her nest of dry grass and leaves. The young ones are very difficult to rear; and they must be supplied with ants-eggs, which is the food the old one leads them to gather when wild in the woods. When they become adults, they very well can shift for themselves, but they are particularly fond of oats and barley.

Of the pheasants, as of all other domestic fowl, there are many varieties. There are White Pheasants, Crested Pheasants, Spotted Pheasants; but of all others, the Golden Pheasant of China is the most beautiful. It is a doubt whether the peacock itself can bear the comparison.

THE PINTADA OR GUINEA-HEN

This is a very remarkable bird, and in some measure unites the characteristics of the pheasant and the turkey. It has the fine delicate shape of the one, and the bare head of the other. To be more particular, it is about the size of a common hen; but as it is supported on longer legs it looks much larger. It has a round back, with a tail turned downwards like a partridge. The head is covered with a kind of helmet, and the whole plumage is black or dark grey, speckled with white spots. It has wattles under the bill which gives it a very peculiar air, while its restless gait and odd chuckling sound distinguish it suffici-ently from all other birds.

Left HIMALAYAN MONAL *Lophophorus refulgens*
Right GREAT ARGUS *Phasianus argus*

It is well known all over Europe, the nations that border on the Mediterranean had it from those parts of Africa which lay nearest. Accordingly we find it in different countries called by different names, from the place whence they had it. They are by some called the Barbary-hen; by others, the Tamis bird; and by others, the bird of Numidia. We have given it the name of that part of Africa from whence probably it was first brought.

In many parts of their native contry, they are seen in vast flocks together, feeding their young, and leading them in quest of food. All their habits are like those of the poultrykind, and they agree in every other respect, except that the male and female are so much alike, that they can hardly be distinguished asunder. Their eggs, like their bodies, are speckled; in our climate, they lay but five or six in a season; but they are far more prolific in their sultry regions at home. They are kept among us rather for show than use, as their flesh is not much esteemed, and as they give a good deal of trouble in the rearing.

THE BUSTARD

The Bustard is the largest land-bird that is a native of Britain. It was once much more numerous than it is at present; but the increased cultivation of the country, and the extreme delicacy of its flesh, has greatly thinned the species; so that a time may come when it may be doubted whether ever so large a bird was bred among us. It inhabits only the open and extensive plain, where its food lies in abundance, and whence every invader may be seen at a distance.

The bustard is much larger than the turkey, the male generally weighing from twenty-five to twenty-seven pounds. The neck is a foot long, and the legs a foot and a half. The wings are not proportionable to the rest of the body, being but four feet from the tip of one to the other; for which reason the bird flies with great difficulty. The head and neck of the male are ash-coloured; the back is barred transversely with black and rust colour. The greater quill feathers are black; the belly white; and the tail, which consists of twenty feathers, is marked with broad black bars.

Like all other birds of the poultry kind, they

change their mates at the season of incubation, which is about the latter end of summer. They separate in pairs if there be a sufficiency of females for the males; but when this happens to be otherwise, the males fight until one of them falls.

They make their nests upon the ground, only just scraping a hole in the earth, and sometimes lining it

with a little long grass or straw. There they lay two eggs only, almost of the size of a goose egg, of a pale olive brown, marked with spots of a darker colour. They hatch for about five weeks, and the young ones run about as soon as they are out of the shell.

The bustards assemble in flocks in the month of October, and keep together till April. In winter, as their food becomes more scarce, they support themselves indiscriminately, by feeding on moles, mice, and even little birds, when they can seize them. For want of other food, they are contented to live upon turnip leaves and such like succulent vegetables. They usually live fifteen years, and are incapable of being propagated in a domestic state, as they probably want that food which best agrees with their appetite.

THE GROUSE AND ITS AFFINITIES

The Woodcock, the Black Cock, the Grouse, and the Ptarmigan – These are all birds of a similar nature, and chiefly found in heathy mountains and piny forests, at a distance from mankind.

The woodcock is sometimes of the size of a turkey, and often weighs near fourteen pounds; the black cock, of which the male is all over black, though the female is of the colour of a partridge, is about the size of a hen, and, like the former, is only found in the highlands of Scotland; the grouse is about half as large again as a partridge, and its colour much like that of a woodcock, but redder; the ptarmigan is still smaller and is of a pale brown or ash-colour. They are all distinguishable from other birds of the poultry kind, by a naked skin, of a scarlet colour, above the eyes, in the place and of the figure of eye-brows. While the woodcock is seldom seen, except on the inaccessible parts of heathy mountains, or in the midst of piny forests, the grouse is found, in great

numbers, in the neighbourhood of cornfields, where there is heath to afford retreat and shelter. Their food too somewhat differs: while the smaller kind lives upon heath blossoms, cranberries and corn, the larger feeds upon the cones of the pine-tree. In other respects, the manners of these birds are the same; being both equally simple in their diet, and licentious in their amours.

At the earliest return of spring these birds begin to feel the genial influence of the season. During the month of March, the approaches of courtship are begun, and do not desist till the trees have all their leaves, and the forest is in full bloom. The mating cry of these birds is a kind of loud explosion, which is instantly followed by a noise like the whetting of a scythe, which ceases and commences alternatively for about an hour.

The female hearing it replies, approaches, and places herself under the tree, from whence the cock descends to impregnate her.

The female is much smaller than her mate, and entirely unlike him in plumage, so that she might be mistaken for a bird of anther species: she seldom lays more than six or seven eggs, which are white, and marked with yellow, of the size of a common hen's egg: she generally lays them in a dry place and a mossy ground, and hatches them without the company of the cock. When she is obliged, during the time of incubation, to leave the eggs in quest of food, she covers them up so artfully, with moss or dry leaves, that it is extremely difficult to discover them.

As soon as the young ones are hatched, they are seen running with extreme agility after the mother, though sometimes they are not entirely disengaged from the shell. The hen leads them forward, for the first time, into the woods, shews them ant's eggs, and the wild mountain-berries, which, while young, are their only food. As they grow older, their appetites grow stronger, and they then feed upon the tops of heather and the cones of the pine-tree.

From top to bottom Left GREAT CURASSOW *Crax rubra* WESTERN TRAGOPAN *Tragopan hastingsii* HEMIPODE *Ortygis tachydromus* SANDGROUSE *Pterocles sctarius*
Right VALLEY QUAIL *Perdix californica* LUZON'S BLEEDING HEART *Columba cruenta* BOHEMIAN WAXWING *Bombycilla garrula* REGENT BOWER-BIRD *Sericulus chrysocephalus*

THE PARTRIDGE

The Partridge may be particularly considered as belonging to the sportsman. It is a bird which even our laws have taken under protection; and, like a peacock or a hen, may be ranked as a private property.

In England, it is a favourite delicacy at the tables of the rich; and the desire of keeping it to themselves, has induced them to make laws for its preservation, no way harmonizing with the general spirit of English legislation.

They feed everywhere; upon every man's ground; and no man can say, these birds are fed only by me. Those birds which are nourished by all, belong to all; nor can any one man, or any set of men, lay claim to them, when still continuing in a state of nature.

Of partridges there are two kinds; the grey and the red. The red partridge is the largest of the two, and often perches upon trees; the grey, with which we are best acquainted in England, is most prolific, and always keeps on the ground.

The partridge seems to be a bird well known all over the world, as it is found in every country, and in every climate; as well in the frozen regions about the pole, as the torrid tracts under the equator. It even seems to adapt itself to the nature of the climate where it resides. In Greenland, the partridge, which is brown in summer, as soon as the icy winter sets in, begins to take a covering suited to the season: it is then clothed with a warm down beneath; and its outward plumage assumes the colour of the snows amongst which it seeks its food. Thus it is doubly fitted for the place, by the warmth and the colour of its plumage; the one to defend it from the cold, the other to prevent its being noticed by the enemy. Those of Barakonda, on the other hand, are longer legged, much swifter of foot, and choose the highest rocks and precipices to reside in.

Their cunning and instincts seem superior to other birds. Whenever a dog or other formidable animal approaches their nest, the female uses every means to draw him away. She keeps just before him, pretends to be incapable of flying, just hops up and then falls down before him, but never goes off so far as to discourage her pursuer. At length, when she has drawn him entirely away from their secret treasure, she at once takes wing, and fairly leaves him to gaze after her in despair.

There are several methods of taking them, as is well known; that by which they are taken in a net, with a setting dog, is the most pleasant, as well as the most secure. The dog, as everybody knows, is trained to this exercise, by a long course of education: a partridge is shown him, and he is then ordered to lie down; he is brought into the field, and when the sportsman perceives where the covey lies, he orders his dog to crouch: at length the dog, from habit, crouches wherever he approaches a covey; and this is the signal which the sportsman receives for unfolding and covering the birds with his net. A covey thus caught, is sometimes fed in a place proper for their reception; but they can never be thoroughly tamed, like the rest of our domestic poultry.

THE QUAIL

The last of the poultry kind that I shall mention is the Quail; a bird much smaller than any of the former, being not above half the size of a partridge. The feathers of the head are black, edged with rusty brown; the breast is of a pale yellowish red, spotted with black; the feathers on the back are marked with lines of pale yellow, and the legs are of a pale hue. Except in the colours thus described, and the size, it every way resembles a partridge in shape; and, except that it is a bird of passage, in its habits and nature, we should be surprised that a bird so apparently ill qualified for migration, should take such extensive journeys.

For instance, in England, they fly from the inland countries, to those bordering on the sea, and continue there all the winter. If frost or snow drive them out of the stubble fields or marshes, they then retreat to the sea side, shelter themselves among the weeds, and live upon what is thrown up from the sea upon shore. So that what has been said of their long flights is probably not so well founded as is generally supposed.

Quails are easily caught by a call: the fowler, early in the morning, having spread his net, hides himself under it, among the corn; he then imitates the voice of the female, with his quail-pipe, which the cock hearing, approaches with the utmost assiduity; when he has got under the net, the fowler then discovers himself, and terrifies the quail, who attempting to get away, entangles himself the more in the net, and is taken. The quail may thus very well serve to illustrate the old adage, that every passion, carried to an inordinate excess, will at last lead to ruin.

BIRDS OF THE PIE KIND

THE RAVEN

The Raven is a bird found in every region of the world: strong and hardy, he is uninfluenced by the changes of the weather; and when other birds seem numbed with cold, or pining with famine, the raven is active and healthy, busily employed in prowling for prey, or sporting in the coldest atmosphere. As the heats at the line do not oppress him, so he bears the cold of the polar countries with equal indifference. He is sometimes indeed seen milk white; and this may probably be the effect of the rigorous climates of the north. It is most likely that this change is wrought upon him as upon most other animals in that part of the world, where their robes, particularly in winter, assume the colour of the country they inhabit. As in old age, when the natural heat decays, the hair grows grey, and at last white, so among these animals the cold of the climate may produce a similar languishment of colour, and may shut up those pores that conveyed the tincturing fluids to the extremest parts of the body.

However this may be, white ravens are often shown amongst us, which, I have heard some say, are rendered thus by art; and this we could readily suppose if they were as easily changed in their colour as they are altered in their habits and dispositions. A raven may be reclaimed to almost every purpose to which birds can be converted. He may be trained up for fowling like a hawk; he may be taught to fetch and carry like a spaniel; he may be taught to speak like a parrot; but the most extraordinary of all is, that he can be taught to sing like a man. I have heard a raven sing the Black Joke with great distinctness, truth, and humour.

Indeed, when the raven is taken as a domestic, he has many qualities that render him extremely amusing. Busy, inquisitive, and impudent, he goes everywhere, affronts and drives off the dogs, plays his pranks on the poultry, and is particularly assiduous in cultivating the good will of the cook-maid, who seems to be the favourite of the family. But then, with the amusing qualities of a favourite, he often also has the vices and defects. He is a glutton by nature, and a thief by habit. He does not confine himself to petty depredations on the pantry or the larder; he soars at more magnificent plunder; at spoils that he can neither exhibit nor enjoy; but which, like a miser, he rests satisfied with having the satisfaction of sometimes visiting and contemplating in secret. A piece of money, a tea-spoon, or a ring, are always tempting baits to his avarice; these he will slyly seize upon, and if not watched will carry to his favourite hole.

Notwithstanding the injury these birds do in picking out the eyes of sheep and lambs, when they find them sick and helpless, a vulgar respect is paid them as being the birds that fed the prophet Elijah in the wilderness. This prepossession in favour of the raven is of very ancient date, as the Romans themselves, who thought the bird ominous, paid it from motives of fear the most profound veneration. Hesiod asserts that a raven will live nine times as long as a man; but though this is fabulous, it is certain that some of them have been known to live near a hundred years. This animal seems possessed of those qualities that generally produce longevity, a good appetite and in great exercise. In clear weather, the ravens fly in pairs to a great height, making a deep loud noise different from that of their usual croaking.

THE ROOK

The Rook, as is well known, builds in woods and forests in the neighbourhood of man, and sometimes makes choice of groves in the very midst of cities for the place of their retreat and security. In these they establish a kind of legal constitution, by which all intruders are excluded from coming to live among them, and none suffered to build but acknowledged natives of the place. At the commencement of spring, the rookery, which during the continuance of winter seemed to have been deserted, or only guarded by about five or six, like old soldiers in a garrison, now begins to be once more frequented; and in a short time all the bustle and hurry of business is fairly commenced.

They keep together in pairs; and when the offices of courtship are over, they prepare for making their nests and laying. The old inhabitants of the place are all already provided; the nest which served them for years before, with a little trimming and dressing will serve very well again; the difficulty of nesting lies only upon the young ones who have no nest, and must therefore get up one as well as they can. But not only the materials are wanting, but also the place in which to fix it. Every part of a tree will not do for this purpose, as some branches may not be sufficiently forked; others may not be sufficiently strong; and still others may be too much exposed to the rockings of the wind. The male and female upon this occasion are, for some days, seen examining all the trees of the grove very attentively; and when they have fixed upon a branch that seems fit for their purpose, they continue to sit upon and observe it very sedulously for two or three days longer. The place being thus determined upon, they begin to gather the materials for their nest; such as sticks and fibrous roots, which they regularly dispose in the most substantial manner. It often happens that the young couple have made choice of a place too near the mansion of an older pair, who do not choose to be incommoded by such troublesome neighbours. A quarrel therefore instantly ensues; in which the old ones are always victorious.

The young couple, thus expelled, are obliged again to go through the fatigues of deliberating, examining, and choosing; and having taken care to keep their due distance, the nest begins again. Away they go, therefore, to pilfer as fast as they can; and wherever they see a nest unguarded, they take care to rob it of the very choicest sticks of which it is composed. But these thefts never go unpunished; and probably upon complaint being made there is a general punishment inflicted. I have seen eight or ten rooks come upon such occasions, and setting upon the new nest of the young couple all at once, tear it in pieces in a moment.

THE MAGPIE

The Magpie is the chief of this kind with us, and is too well known to need a description. Indeed, were its other accomplishments equal to its beauty, few birds could be put in competition. Its black, its white, its green and purple, with the rich and gilded combination of the glosses on its tail, are as fine as any that adorn the most beautiful of the feathered tribe. But it has too many of the qualities of a beau, to depreciate these natural perfections: vain, restless, loud, and quarrelsome, it is an unwelcome intruder everywhere; and never misses an opportunity, when it finds one, of doing mischief.

They often are seen perched upon the back of an ox or a sheep, pecking up the insects to be found there, chattering and tormenting the poor animal at the same time, and stretching out their necks for combat, if the beast turns its head backward to reprehend them. They seek out also the nests of birds; and, if the parent escapes, the eggs make up for the deficiency:

the thrush and the blackbird are but too frequently robbed by this assassin, and this in some measure causes their scarcity.

No food seems to come amiss to this bird; it shares with ravens in their carrion, with rooks in their grain, and with the cuckoo in bird's eggs: but it seems possessed of a providence seldom usual with gluttons; for when it is satisfied for the present, it lays up the remainder of the feast for another occasion. It will even in a tame state hide its food when it has done eating, and after a time return to the secret hoard with renewed appetite and vociferation.

In all its habits it discovers a degree of instinct unusual to other birds. Its nest is not less remarkable for the manner in which it is composed than for the place the magpie takes to build it in. The nest is usually placed conspicuous enough, either in the middle of some hawthorn bush or on the top of some high tree. The place, however, is always found difficult of access; for the tree pitched upon usually grows in some thick hedgerow, fenced by brambles at the root; or sometimes one of the higher bushes is fixed upon for the purpose.

The body of the nest is composed of hawthorn branches; the thorns sticking outward, but well united together by their mutual insertions. Within, it is lined wth fibrous roots, wool, and long grass, and then nicely plastered all round with mud and clay. The body of the nest being thus made firm and commodious, the next work is to make the canopy which is to defend it above. This is composed of the sharpest thorns wove together in such a manner as to deny all entrance except at the door, which is just large enough to permit egress and regress to the owners. In this fortress the male and female hatch and bring up their brood with security, sheltered from all attacks but those of the climbing schoolboy, who often finds his torn and bloody hands too dear a price for the eggs or the young ones. The magpie lays six or seven eggs, of a pale green colour, spotted with brown.

Everybody knows what a passion the magpie has for shining substances and such toys as some of us put a value upon. A whole family has been alarmed at the loss of a ring; every servant has been accused, and every creature in the house, conscious of their own innocence, suspected each other, when, to the utter surprise of all, it has been found in the nest of a tame magpie or a jackdaw that nobody had ever thought of.

In the wild or in the cage it has the same noisy, mischievous habits and being more cunning, so it is also a more docile bird than any other taken into keeping. Those who are desirous of teaching it to speak, have a foolish custom of cutting its tongue, which only puts the poor animal to pain, without improving its speech in the smallest degree. Its speaking is sometimes very distinct; but its sounds are too thin and sharp to be an exact imitation of the human voice, which the hoarse raven and parrot can counterfeit more exactly.

THE JAY

The Jay is one of the most beautiful of the British birds. The forehead is white, streaked with black; the head is covered with very long feathers, which it can erect into a crest at pleasure; the whole neck, back, breast and belly, are of a faint purple,

dashed with grey; the wings are most beautifully barred with a lovely blue, black and white; the tail is black, and the feet of a pale brown. Like the magpie, it feeds upon fruits, will kill small birds, and is extremely docile.

THE TOUCAN

Of this extraordinary bird there are four or five varieties. I will only describe the Red-Beaked Toucan; as the figure of this bird makes the principal part of its history. It has a large head to support its monstrous bill: this bill, from the angles of the mouth to its point, is six inches and a half; and its breadth, in the thickest part, is a little more than two. Its thickness near the head, is one inch and a quarter; and it is a little rounded both on the upper and underside. The upper part of the bill is of a bright yellow with a stripe on each side of a fine scarlet colour; as is also the lower bill, except at the base, which is purple. Between the head and the bill there is a black line of separation all round the base of the bill. Round the eyes, on each side of the head, is a space of bluish skin, void of feathers, above which the head is black. The hind part of the neck, the back, wings, tail, belly and thighs, are black. The underside of the head, throat, and the beginning of the breast, are white. Between the white on the breast, and the black on the belly, is a space of red feathers, in the form of a new

moon, with its horns upwards. The legs, feet and claws, are of an ash-colour; and the toes stand like those of parrots, two before, and two behind.

It is reported, by travellers, that this bird, though furnished with so formidable a beak, is harmless and gentle, being so easily made tame, as to sit and hatch its young in houses. It feeds chiefly upon pepper, which it devours very greedily, gorging itself in such a manner, that it voids it crude and unconcocted. This, however, is no objection to the natives from using it again; they even prefer it before that pepper which is fresh gathered from the tree: and seem persuaded that the strength and heat of the pepper is qualified by the bird, and that all its noxious qualities are thus exhausted.

Whatever the truth of this report, nothing is more certain than that the toucan lives only upon a vegetable diet; and in a domestic state, to which it is frequently brought in the warm countries where it is bred, it is seen to prefer such food to all other.

There is no bird secures its young better from external injury than the toucan. It has not only birds, men, and serpents to guard against, but a numerous tribe of monkey, still more prying, mischievous, and hungry than all the rest. The toucan, however, scoops out its nest into the hollow of some tree, leaving only a hole large enough to go in and out at. There it sits, with its great beak, guarding the entrance; and if the monkey ventures to offer a visit of curiosity, the toucan gives him such a welcome, that he presently thinks proper to pack off, and is glad to escape to safety.

This bird is only found in the warm climates of South America, where it is in great request, both for the delicacy of its flesh, which is tender and nourishing and for the beauty of its plumage, particularly the feathers of the breast. The skin of this part the Indians pluck off, and, when dry, glue to their cheeks; and this they consider as an irresistible addition to their beauty.

THE WOODPECKER

The Green Wood-spite or Woodpecker, is called the Rain-Fowl in some parts of the country; because, when it makes a greater noise than ordinary, it is supposed to foretell rain. It is about the size of a jay; the throat, breast and belly are of a pale greenish colour; and the back, neck and covert feathers of the wings are green. But the tongue of this little animal makes its most distinguished characteristic, as it serves for its support and defence. As was said above, the woodpecker feeds upon insects; and particularly on those which are lodged in the body of hollow or of

rotting trees. The tongue is its instrument for killing and procuring this food; which cannot be found in great plenty. This is round, ending in a stiff, sharp, bony tip, dentated on both sides, like the beard of an arrow; and this it can dart out three or four inches from the bill, and draw in again at pleasure. Its prey is thus transfixed, and drawn into the bill, which, when swallowed, the dart is again launched at fresh game.

Such is the instrument with which this bird is provided; and this is the manner in which this instrument is employed. When a woodpecker, by its natural sagacity, finds out a rotten hollow tree, where there are worms, ant's eggs, or insects, it immediately prepares for its operations. Resting by its strong claws, and leaning on the thick feathers of its tail, it begins to bore with its sharp strong beak, until it discloses the whole internal habitation. Upon this, either through pleasure at the sight of its prey, or with a desire to alarm the insect colony, it sends forth a loud cry, which throws terror and confusion into the whole insect tribe. They creep hither and thither, seeking for safety; while the bird luxuriously feasts upon them at leisure, darting its tongue with unerring certainty, and devouring the whole brood.

As the woodpecker is obliged to make holes in trees to procure food so it is also to make cavities still larger to form its nest and to lay in.

The woodpecker takes no care to line its nest with feathers or straw; its eggs are deposited in the hole, without anything to keep them warm, except the heat of the parent's body. Their number is generally five or six; always white, oblong, and of a middle size. Boys sometimes have thrust in their hands with certain hopes of plucking out a bird's egg; but, to their great mortification have had their fingers bitten by a bat at the bottom.

THE BIRD OF PARADISE

This bird, which for beauty exceeds almost all other kinds, is a native of the Molucca Islands. It appears to the eye as large as a pigeon, though in

TOUCAN *Ramphastos maximus*

reality the body is not much greater than that of a thrush. The tail, which is about six inches, is as long as the body; the wings are large compared with the bird's other dimensions. The head, the throat and the neck are of a pale gold colour. The base of the bill is surrounded by black feathers, as also the side of the head and throat, as soft as velvet. The hind part of the head is of a shining green, mixed with gold. The body and wings are chiefly covered with beautiful brown, purple and gold feathers. The uppermost part of the tail feathers are of a pale yellow, and those under them white and longer than the former; for which reason the hind part of the tail appears to be all white. But what chiefly excites curiosity are, the two long naked feathers which spring from the upper part of the rump above the tail, and which are usually about three feet long. These are bearded only at the beginning and the end; the whole shaft above two feet nine inches, being of a deep black, while the feathered extremity is of a changeable colour.

The natives, who make a trade of killing and selling these birds to the Europeans, generally conceal themselves in the trees where they resort, and having covered themselves up from sight in a bower made of the branches, they shoot at the birds with reedy arrows. When they have taken a number of these birds, their usual method is to gut them and cut off their legs; they then run a hot iron into the body, which dries up the internal moisture; and filling the cavity with salts and spices, they sell them to the Europeans for an ornament.

THE CUCKOO

This singular bird, which is somewhat less than a pigeon, shaped like a magpie, and of a greyish colour, is distinguished from all other birds, by its round prominent nostrils. Having disappeared all the winter, it announces itself in our country early in the spring, by its well known call. From the cheerful voice of this bird the farmer may be instructed in the real advancement of the year. The fallibility of human calendars is but too well known; but from this bird's note the husbandman may be taught when to sow his most useful seeds, and do such work as depends upon a certain temperature of the air. These feathered guides come to us heaven-taught, and point out the true commencement of the season.

The Cuckoo begins at first feebly, and at very distant intervals, to give its call, which, as the summer advances, improves both in its frequency and loudness. This is an invitation to courtship, and used only by the male, who sits generally perched upon some dead tree, or bare bough, and repeats his song, which he loses as soon as the warm season is over. His note is pleasant though uniform; and, from an association of ideas, seldom occurs to the memory without reminding us of the sweets of summer.

Nothing is more certain than that the female makes no nest of her own. She repairs for that purpose to the nest of some other bird, generally the water-wagtail or hedge sparrow, and, having devoured the eggs of the owner, lays her own in their place. She usually lays but one, which is speckled, and of the size of a blackbird's. This the fond foolish bird hatches with great assiduity, and, when excluded, finds no difference in the great ill-looking changeling from her own. To supply this voracious creature, the credulous nurse toils with unusual labour, not knowing that she is feeding up an enemy to her race, and one of the most destructive robbers of her future progeny.

The young are fed on flesh and insects and as they swallow rather than peck they have to be fed until they are as big as the mother.

The cuckoo, when fledged and fitted for flight, follows its supposed parent but for a little time; its appetites for insect food increasing, as it finds no great chance for a supply in imitating its little instructor, it parts good friends, the step-child seldom offering any violence to its nurse.

Such are the manners of this bird while it continues to reside, or to be seen amongst us. But early, at the approach of winter, it totally disappears, and its passage can be traced to no other country.

Of this bird there are many kinds in various parts of the world, not only differing in their colours but their size, but what analogy they bear to our English cuckoo I will not take upon me to determine.

THE PARROT

The Parrot is the best known among us of all foreign birds, as it unites the greatest beauty with the greatest docility. Its voice also is more like a man's than that of any other, and is of the true pitch and capable of a number of modulations that even some of our orators might wish in vain to imitate.

The ease with which this bird is taught to speak, and the great number of words which it is capable of repeating, are no less surprising. We are assured, by a grave writer, that one of these was taught to repeat a whole sonnet from Petrarch; and I have seen a parrot, belonging to a distiller, who had suffered pretty largely in his business from an informer who lived opposite him. This bird was taught to pronounce the ninth commandment, *Thou shalt not bear false witness against thy neighbour*, with a very clear, loud, articulate voice. The bird was generally placed in its cage against the informer's house, and delighted the whole neighbourhood with its persevering exhortations.

Another story of a parrot which is not so dull as those usually brought up when this bird's facility of talking runs as follows. "A parrot belonging to King Henry the Seventh, who then resided at Westminster, in his palace by the river Thames, had learned to talk many words from the passengers, as they happened to take water. One day, sporting on its perch, the poor bird fell into the water, at the same time crying out, as loud as he could, *A boat, twenty pound for a boat*. A waterman, who happened to be near, hearing the cry, made to the place where the parrot was floating, and taking him up restored him to the king. As it seems the bird was a favourite, the man insisted that he ought to have a reward rather equal to his services than his trouble; and, as the parrot had cried twenty pounds, he said the king was bound in honour to grant it. The king at last agreed to leave it to the parrot's own determination, which the bird hearing, cried out, *Give the knave a groat*."

The forests of the East and West Indies swarm with parrots. The naturalists tell us that there are at least forty-seven varieties, perhaps as many as ninety-five though those who usually bring these birds to this country are content to make three or four distinctions, to which they give names. The large kind, which are of the size of a raven, are called Macaws; the next size are simply called Parrots; those which are entirely white are called Lories; and the lesser size of all are called Parakeets.

Their toes are contrived in a singular manner, which appears when they walk or climb, and when they are eating. For the first purpose they stretch, two of their toes forward and two backward; but when they take their food, and bring it to their mouths with their foot, they dexterously and nimbly turn the greater hind toe forward, so as to take a firmer grasp of the nut or the fruit they are going to feed on, standing all the while upon the other leg.

The bill is fashioned with still greater peculiarities; for the upperpart, as well as the lower, are both moveable. In most other birds the upper part is

From top to bottom Left SCARLET MACAW *Aracanga* GREATER SPOTTED WOODPECKER *Picus major* GREAT BIRD OF PARADISE *Paradisea apoda* Right SAFFRON-HEADED PARROT *Psittacus carolinensis* EASTERN ROSELLA *Psittacus eximius* QUETZAL *Trogon pavoninus*

connected, and makes one piece with the skull; but in the parrot the upper part is connected to the one of the head by a strong membrane, placed on each side, that lifts and depresses it at pleasure. By this contrivance they can open their bills the wider; which is not a little useful, as the upper beak is so hooked and so over-hanging, that, if the lower only had motion, they could scarce gape sufficiently to take any thing in for their nourishment.

The parrot, though common enough in Europe, will not, however, breed here. The climate is too cold for its warm constitution; and though it bears our winter when arrived at maturity, yet it always seems sensible of its rigour, and loses both its spirit and appetite during the colder part of the season. It then becomes torpid and inactive, and seems quite changed from that bustling loquacious animal which it appeared in its native forests, where it is almost ever upon the wing. Notwithstanding, the parrot lives even with us a considerable time, if it be properly attended to; and indeed, it must be owned, that it employs but too great a part of some peoples' attention.

Parrots have usually the same disorders with other birds; and they have one or two peculiar to their kind. They are sometimes struck by a kind of apoplectic blow, by which they fall from their perches, and for a while seem ready to expire. The other is the growing of the beak, which becomes so very much hooked as to deprive them of the power of eating. These infirmities, however, do not hinder them from being long-lived; for a parrot well kept will live five or six and twenty years.

THE PIGEON

The tame Pigeon, and all its beautiful varieties, derive their origin from one species, the Stock-Dove only, the English name, implying its being the flock or item from whence the other domestic kinds have been propagated. This bird, in its natural state, is of a deep bluish ash colour; the breast dashed with a fine changeable green and purple; its wings marked

with two black bars; the back white, and the tail barred near the end with black. These are the colours of the pigeon in a state of nature; and from these simple tints has man by art propagated a variety that words cannot describe, nor even fancy suggest.

However, Nature still perseveres in her great outline; and though the form, colour, and even the fecundity of these birds may be altered by art, yet their natural manners and inclinations continue still the same.

THE STOCK-DOVE

The Stock-Dove, in its native woods, differs from the Ring-Dove, a bird that has never been reclaimed, by its breeding in the holes of rocks and the hollows of trees. All other birds of the pigeon-kind build like rooks, in the topmost branches of the forest, and choose their habitation as remote as possible from man.

The Dove-House pigeon, as is well known, breeds every month; but then it is necessary to supply it with food when the weather is severe, or the fields are covered with snow. Upon other occasions, it may be left to provide for itself; and it generally repays the owner for his protection. The pigeon lays two white eggs, which most usually produce young ones of different sexes. For the laying of each egg, it is necessary to have a particular congress with the male; and the egg is usually deposited in the afternoon. When the eggs are thus laid, the female in the space of fifteen days, not including the three days during which she is employed in laying, continues to hatch, relieved at intervals by the male. The turns are usually regulated with great exactness.

The young ones when hatched require no food for the three first days, only wanting to be kept warm, which is an employment the female takes entirely upon herself. During this period, she never stirs out, except for a few minutes to take a little food. From this they are fed for eight or ten days, with corn or grain of different kinds, which the old ones gather in the fields, and keep treasured up in their crops, from whence they throw it up again into the mouths of their young ones who very greedily demand it.

THE CARRIER PIGEON

It is from a species of the stock-dove that those pigeons whch are called Carriers, and are used to convey letters, are produced. These are easily distinguished from all others by their eyes, which are compassed about with a broad circle of naked white skin, and by being of a dark blue or blackish colour. It is from their attachment to their native place, and particularly where they have brought up their young, that these birds are employed in several countries as the most expeditious carriers. They are first brought from the place where they were bred and whither it is intended to send them back with information. The letter is tied under the bird's wing, and it is then let loose to return. The little animal no sooner finds itself at liberty, than its passion for its native spot directs all its motions. It is seen, upon these occasions, flying directly into the clouds to an amazing height; and then, with the greatest certainty and exactness, directing itself by some surprising instinct towards home, which lies sometimes at many miles distance, bringing its message to those to whom it is directed. By what marks they discover the place, by what chart they are guided in the right way, is to us utterly unknown; certain it is, that in the space of an hour and a half they perform a journey of forty miles; which is a degree of dispatch three times greater than the fleetest quadruped can perform.

THE TURTLE DOVE

The fidelity of the Turtle Dove is proverbial, and makes the usual comparison of such poets as are content to repeat what others have said before them.

The turtle dove is a smaller, but a much shyer, bird than any of the former. It may easily be distinguished from the rest by the iris of the eye, which is of a fine yellow, and by a beautiful crimson circle that encom-

CROWNED PIGEON *Columba coronata*

passes the eye-lids. The fidelity of these birds is noted; and a pair being put in a cage, if one dies, the other will not survive it. The turtle dove is a bird of passage, and few or none remain in our northern

climates in winter, They fly in flocks when they come to breed here in summer, and delight in open, mountainous, sandy countries. But they build their nests in the midst of woods, and choose the most retired situations for incubation. They feed upon all sorts of grain, but are fondest of millet-feed.

To this short list might be added a long catalogue of foreign pigeons, of which we know little more than the plumage and the names: indeed, the variety of their plumage is as beautiful as the names by which they are known are harsh and dissonant. The Ocotzimtzcan, for instance, is one of the most splendid tenants of the Mexican forests; but few, I believe, would desire to learn the name, only to be informed that it is covered with purple, green, and yellow plumage. To describe such birds, the historian's pen is not half such an useful implement as the painter's pencil.

BIRDS OF THE SPARROW KIND

THE SPARROW

As they are the favourites of man, so they are chiefly seen near him. These birds seldom resort to the thicker parts of the wood; they keep near its edges, in the neighbourhood of cultivated fields; in the hedgerows of farmgrounds; and even in the yard, mixing with the poultry.

It must be owned, indeed, that their living near man is not due to affection on their part, as they approach inhabited grounds merely because their chief provision is to be found there. In the depth of

the desert, or the gloom of the forest, there is no grain to be picked up; none of these tender buds that are so grateful to their appetites; insects, themselves, that make so great a part of their food, are not found there in abundance; their natures being unsuited to the moisture of the place.

There is still another reason for these little birds avoiding the depths of the forest; which is that their most formidable enemies reside there. The greater birds, like robbers, choose the most dreary solitudes for their retreats; and, if they do not find they make a desert all around them. The small birds fly from their tyranny, and take protection in the vicinity of man, where they know their more unmerciful foes will not venture to pursue them.

THE THRUSH

The Missel-Thrush is distinguished from all other thrushes by its superior size, being much larger than any of them. It differs scarcely in any other

respect from the common thrush, except that the spots on the breast are larger. It builds its nest in bushes, or on the side of some tree, as all of this kind are found to do, and lays four or five eggs in a season. Its song is very fine, which it begins in spring, sitting

on the summit of a high tree. It is the largest bird of all the feathered tribe that has music in its voice; the note of all greater birds being either screaming, chattering, or croaking. It feeds on insects, holly, and mistletoe-berries; and sometimes sends forth a very disagreeable scream when frighted or disturbed.

THE BLACKBIRD

The Blackbird, which in cold countries, and particularly upon the Alps, is sometimes seen all over white, is a beautiful bird, whistling all the spring and summer-time with a note at a distance the most pleasing of all the grove. It is the deepest toned warbler of the woods; but it is rather unpleasant in a cage, being loud and deafening. It lays four or five bluish eggs, in a nest usually built at the stump of some old hawthorn, well plastered on the inside with clay, straw, and hair.

Pleasing, however, as this bird may be, the blue-bird is in every respect far superior. This beautiful animal entirely resembles a blackbird in all but its blue colour. It lives in the highest parts of the Alps, and even there chooses the most craggy rocks and the most frightful precipices for its residence. As it is rarely caught, it is in high estimation even in the countries where it breeds, but still more valuable when carried from home. It not only whistles in the most delightful manner, but speaks with an articulate distinct voice. It is so docile, and observes all things with such diligence, that, though waked at midnight by any of the family, it will speak and whistle at the word of command. Its colour, about the beginning of winter, from blue becomes black, which changes to its original hue in the first approaches of spring. It makes its nest in deep holes, in very high and inaccessible solitudes, and removes it not only from the accesses of man, but also hides it with surprising cunning from the chamois, and other wild beasts that might annoy its young.

THE FIELD-FARE

The Field-Fare and the Red-Wing make but a short stay in this country. With us they are insipid tuneless birds, flying in flocks, and excessively watchful to preserve the general safety. All their season of music and pleasure is employed in the more

From top to bottom Left FLYCATCHERS *Muscicapa chrysomela* *Muscicapa miniata* BLUE TIT *Parus coeruleus* ORANGE ORIOLE *Ramphocelus ignescens* Right ROYAL FLYCATCHER *Muscicapa regia* LYRE BIRD *Maenura lyra* EUROPEAN WRYNECK *Yunx torquilla* HOOPEE *Upapa epops*

northern climates, where they sing most delightfully, perched among the forests of maples, with which those countries abound. They build their nests in hedges; and lay six bluish green eggs spotted with black.

THE STARLING

The Starling, distinguishable from the rest of this tribe by the glossy green of its feathers, in some lights, and the purple in others, breeds in hollow trees, eaves of houses, towers, ruins, cliffs, and often in high rocks over the sea. It lays four or five eggs of a pale greenish ash-colour, and makes its nest of straw, small fibres of roots, and such like. Its voice is rougher than the rest of this kind; but what it wants in the melody of its note, it compensates by the facility with which it is taught to speak. In winter these birds assemble in vast flocks, and feed upon worms and insects. At the approach of spring, they assemble in fields, as if in consultation together, and for three or four days seem to take no nourishment: the greater part leave the country; the rest breed here and bring up their young.

THE MOCKING BIRD

This valuable bird does not seem to vie with the feathered inhabitants of America in the beauty of its plumage, content with qualifications that endear it to mankind much more. It is but a plain bird to the eye, about the size of a thrush, of a white and grey colour, and a reddish bill. It is possessed not only of its own natural notes which are musical and solemn, but it can assume the tone of every other animal in the wood, from the wolf to the raven. It seems even to enjoy leading them astray. It will at one time allure the lesser birds with the call of their males, and then terrify them when they have come near with the screams of the eagle. There is no bird in the forest that it cannot mimic; and there is none that it has not at times deceived by its call. But the mocking bird is ever surest to please when it is most itself. At those times it usually frequents the houses of the American planters: and, sitting all night on the chimney-pot, pours forth the sweetest and the most various notes of any bird whatever. It would seem, if accounts be true, that the deficiency of most other song-birds in that country is made up by this bird alone. They often build their nests in the fruit trees about houses, feed upon berries and other fruits, and are easily rendered domestic.

THE NIGHTINGALE

The Nightingale is not only famous among the moderns for its singing, but almost every one of the ancients who undertook to describe beautiful nature, has contributed to raise its reputation. "The nightingale," says Pliny, "that, for fifteen days and nights hid in the thickest shades, continues her note without intermission deserves our attention and wonder. How surprising that so great a voice can reside in so small a body! Such perserverance in so minute an animal! With what a musical propriety are the sounds it produces modulated! The note at one time drawn out with a long breath, now stealing off into a different cadence, now interrupted by a break, then changing into a new note by an unexpected transition, now seeming to renew the same strain, then deceiving expectation! She sometimes seems to murmur within herself; full, sharp, swift, drawing, trembling; now at the top, the middle, and the bottom of the scale! In short, in that little bill seems to reside all the melody which man has vainly laboured to bring from a variety of musical instruments. Some even seem to be possessed of a different song from the rest, and contend with each other with great ardour."

These most famous of the feathered tribe visit England in the beginning of April, and leave us in August. They are found in some of the southern parts of the country, being totally unknown in Scotland, Ireland, or North Wales. They frequent thick hedges and low coppices, and generally keep in the middle of the bush, so that they are rarely seen. They begin their song in the evening, and generally continue it for the whole night. For weeks together, if undisturbed, they sit upon the same tree; and Shakespeare rightly describes the nightingale sitting nightly in the same place, which I have frequently observed she seldom parts from.

In the beginning of May, the nightingale prepares to make its nest, which is formed of the leaves of trees, straw and moss. The nest being very eagerly fought after, is as cunningly secreted; so that but very few of them are found by the boys when they go upon these pursuits. It is built at the bottom of hedges, where the bushes are thickest and best covered. While the female continues sitting, the male at a good distance, but always within hearing, cheers the patient hour with his voice, and, by the short interruption of his song, often gives her warning of approaching danger. She lays four or five eggs; of which but a few, in our cold climate, come to maturity.

The delicacy, or rather the fame, of this bird's music, has induced many to capture it to procure its song. Its song, however, in captivity is not so very alluring; and the tyranny of taking it from those hedges where only it is most pleasing, still more depreciates its imprisoned efforts.

THE ROBIN

There is a little bird, rather celebrated for its affection to mankind than its singing, which however, in our climate, has the sweetest note of all others. The reader already perceives that I mean the Red-breast, the well known friend of man, that is found in every hedge, and makes it vocal. The note of other birds is louder, and their inflections more capricious; but this bird's voice is soft, tender, and well supported; and the more to be valued as we enjoy it the greatest part of the winter. If the nightingale's song has been compared to the fiddle, the red-breast's voice has all the delicacy of the flute.

The red-breast, during the spring, haunts the wood, the grove, and the garden; it retires to the thickest and shadiest hedgerows to breed in. But in winter it seems to become more domestic, and often to claim protection from man. The red-breast continues with us the year round, and endeavours to support the famine of winter by chirping round the warm habitations of mankind, by coming into those shelters where the rigour of the season is artificially expelled, and where insects themselves are found in greater numbers, attracted by the same cause.

This bird breeds differently in different places: in some countries, its nest is usually found in the crevice of some mossy bank, or at the foot of a hawthorn in hedgerows; in others it chooses the thickest coverts, and hides its nest with oak leaves. The eggs are from four to five, of a dull white, with reddish streaks.

THE LARK

The Lark, whether the Sky-Lark, the Wood, or the Tit-Lark, are louder in their song than either the nightingale or the robin. Nothing can be more pleasing than to see the lark warbling upon the wing;

raising its note as it soars until it seems lost in the immense heights above us; the note continuing, the bird itself unseen; to see it then descending with a swell as it comes from the clouds, yet sinking by degrees as it approaches its nest, the spot where all its affections are centered; the spot that has prompted all this joy.

The lark builds its nest upon the ground, beneath some turf that serves to hide and shelter it. The female lays four or five eggs of a dusky hue in colour, somewhat like those of a plover. It is while she is sitting that the male thus usually entertains her with his singing; and while he is risen to an imperceptible height, yet he still has his loved partner in his eye, nor once loses sight of the nest either while he ascends or is descending. This harmony continues several months, beginning early in the spring on pairing. In winter they assemble in flocks, when their song forsakes them and the bird-catchers destroy them in great numbers for the tables of the luxurious.

THE WREN

The Wren is admired for the loudness of its note, compared to the little body from whence it issues. It must be confessed that this disproportion between the voice of a bird and its size, in some measure demands our wonder.

THE CANARY

The Canary-bird is now become so common and has continued so long in a domestic state, that its native habits, as well as its native country, seem almost forgotten. Though, by the name, it appears

that these birds came originally from the Canary Islands, yet we have it only from Germany, where they are bred up in great numbers, and sold into different parts of Europe. At what period they were brought into Europe is not well known; but it is certain that about a century ago they were sold at very high prices, and kept only for the amusement of the great. They have since been multiplied in great abundance; and their price is diminished in proportion to their plenty.

In its native islands, a region equally noted for the beauty of its landscapes and the harmony of its groves, the canary-bird is of a dusky grey colour, and so different from those usually seen in Europe, that some have even doubted whether it be of the same species. With us, they have that variety of colouring usual in all domestic birds; some white, some mottled, some beautifully shaded with green; but they are more esteemed for their note than their beauty, having a high piercing pipe, as indeed all those of the finch tribe have, continuing for some time in one breath without intermission, then raising it higher and higher by degrees, with great variety.

It is this that has rendered the canary-bird next to the nightingale the most celebrated songster; and, as it is more easily reared than any of the soft billed birds, and continues its song throughout the year, it is the most common in our houses.

Canary-birds sometimes breed all the year round; but they most usually begin to pair in April, and to breed in June and August. Those are said to be the best breeders that are produced between the English and the French.

Towards the latter end of March, a cock and a hen should be put together in a small cage, where they will peck at each other in the beginning, but will soon become thoroughly reconciled. The room where they are kept to breed should be so situated as to let the birds have the benefit of the morning sun, and the windows should be of wire, not glass, that they may enjoy the benefit of the air. The floor of the room should be kept clean, and sometimes there should be dry gravel or sand sifted upon it. There should also be two windows, one at each end, and several perches at proper distances for the birds to settle on, as they fly backwards and forwards. A tree in the middle of the room would be most convenient to divert the birds, and sometimes to serve for building their nest upon.

While the birds are pairing it is usual to feed them

From top to bottom Left SUPERB TANAGER *Tangara tatao* BLUE-HEADED TANAGER *Tangara cyanocephala* SIBERIA RUBYTHROAT *Lusciola calliope* DESERT WHEATEAR *Saxicola stapazina*
Right WHITE BELLIED DRONGO *Edolius coerulescens* SHORE LARK *Alauda alpestris* RICHARD'S PIPIT *Anthus richardii*

with soft meat; that is, bread, maw-feed, a little scalded rapeseed, and near a third part of an egg. The room should be furnished with stuff for making their nests, such as fine hay, wool, cotton, and hair. These materials should be thoroughly dry, and then mixed and tied together in such a manner that the birds may readily pull out what they want. This should be hung in a proper part of the room, and the male will take his turn in building the nest, sitting upon the eggs, and feeding the young. They are generally two or three days in building their nests; the hen commonly lays five eggs; and in the space of fourteen days the young will be hatched.

THE SWALLOW

In the Swallow tribe is to be found the Goat Sucker, which may be styled a nocturnal swallow: it is the largest of this kind, and is known by its tail, which is not forked, like that of the Common Swallow. It begins its flight at evening, and makes a loud singular noise, like the whirr of a spinning-wheel. To this tribe also belongs the House-Swallow, which is too well known to need a description and the Martin, inferior in size to the former, and the tail much less forked; it differs also in its nest, which is covered at top, while that of the house-swallow is open; and the Swift, rather larger than the house-swallow, with all the toes standing forward; in which it differs from the rest of its kind. All these resemble each other so strongly, that it is not without difficulty the smaller kinds are known asunder.

These are all known by their very large mouths, which, when they fly, are always kept open; they are not less remarkable for their short slender feet, which scarce are able to support the weight of their bodies; their wings are of immoderate extent for their bulk; their plumage is glossed with a rich purple; and their note is a slight twittering, which they seldom exert but on the wing.

This peculiar conformation seems attended with a similar peculiarity of manners. Their food is insects, which they always pursue flying. For this reason, during fine weather, when the insects are most likely to be abroad, the swallows are for ever upon the wing, and seen pursuing their prey with amazing swiftness and agility.

It sometimes happens that a rainy season, by

repelling the insects, stints the swallow in its food; the poor bird is then seen slowly skimming along the surface of the ground, and often resting after a flight of a few minutes. In general, however, it keeps on the wing, and moving with a rapidity that nothing can escape. When the weather promises to be fair, the insect tribe feel the genial influence, and make bolder flights; at which time the swallow follows them in their aerial journeys, and often rises to imperceptible heights in the pursuit. When the weather is likely to be foul, the insects feel the first notices of it; and from the swallow's following low we are often apprised of the approaching change.

The nest is built with great industry and art; particularly by the common swallow, which builds it on the tops of chimneys. The martin sticks it to the eaves of houses. The goat-sucker, as we are told, builds it on the bare ground. This nest is built with mud from some neighbouring brook, well tempered with the bill, moistened with water for the better adhesion; and still further kept firm, by long grass and fibres: within it is lined with goose feathers, which are ever the warmest and the neatest. The martin covers its nests at top, and has a door to enter at; the swallow leaves hers quite open.

The swallow usually lays from five to six eggs, of a white colour, speckled with red; and sometimes breeds twice a year. When the young brood are hatched, the swallow supplies them very plentifully, the first brood particularly, when she finds herself capable of producing two broods in a year. This happens when the parents come early, when the season is peculiarly mild, and when they begin to pair soon. Sometimes they find a difficulty in rearing even a single nest, particularly when the weather has been severe. By this accident, this important task is sometimes deferred to the middle of September.

At the latter end of September they leave us; and for a few days previous to their departure, assemble, in vast flocks, on house-tops, as if deliberating on the fatiguing journey that lies before them. This is no slight undertaking, as their flight is directed to Congo, Senegal; and along the whole Morocco shore. There are some, however, left behind in this general expedition, that do not part till eight or ten days after the rest. These are chiefly the latter weakly broods which are not yet in a condition to set out. They are sometimes even too feeble to venture, till the setting in of winter; while their parents vainly exhort them to efforts which instinct assures them they are incapable of performing. Thus it often happens, that the wretched little families, being compelled to stay, perish the first cold weather that comes; while the tender parents share the fate of their offspring, and die with their new-fledged brood.

THE HUMMING-BIRD

Of this charming little animal, there are six or seven varieties. A European could never have supposed a bird existing so very small, and yet completely furnished out with a bill, feather, wings, and intestines, exactly resembling those of the largest kind. A bird not so big as the end of one's little finger, would probably be supposed to be a creature of imagination, were it not seen in infinite numbers, and as frequent as butterflies in a summer's day, sporting in the fields of America, from flower to flower and extracting their sweets with its little bill.

The smallest Humming-Bird is about the size of a hazel-nut. The feathers on its wings and tail are black; but those on its body, and under its wings, are of a greenish brown, with a fine red cast or gloss, which no silk or velvet can imitate. It has a small crest on its head, green at the bottom, and as it were gilded at the top; and which sparkles on the sun like a little star in the middle of its forehead. The bill is black, straight, slender, and of the length of a small pin. The larger humming-bird is near half as big as the common wren, and without a crest on its head; but to make amends, it is covered, from the throat halfway down the belly, with changeable crimson coloured feathers, that, in different lights, change to a variety of beautiful colours, much like an opal. The heads of both are small, with very little round eyes as black as jet.

It is inconceivable how much these add to the high finishing and beauty of a rich luxurious western landscape. As soon as the sun is risen, the humming-birds, of different kinds, are seen fluttering about the flowers, without ever lighting upon them. Their wings are in such rapid motion, that it is impossible to discern their colours, except by their glittering. They are never still, but continually in motion, visiting flower after flower, and extracting its honey as if with a kiss. For this purpose they are furnished with a forky tongue, that enters the cup of the flower and extracts its nectared tribute. Upon this alone they subsist. The rapid motion of their wings brings out an humming sound, from whence they have their name; for whatever divides the air swiftly, must thus produce a murmur.

The nests of these birds are not less curious than the rest: they are suspended in the air, at the point of the twigs of an orange, a pomegranate, or a citron-tree. The female is the architect, while the male goes in

From top to bottom Left RED-CHEEKED CORDON BLEU *Fringilla bengalus* JAVA SPARROW *Loxia oryzivora* WALLCREEPER *Tichodroma phoenicoptera* NUTHATCH *Sitta europea*
Right COLLIE'S MAGPIE-JAY *Pica colliei* WHISKERED TREESWIFT *Cypselus mystaceus* TANAGER *Xanthornus aurantius*

quest of materials; such as cotton, fine moss, and the fibres of vegetables. Of these materials a nest is composed, of about the size of a hen's egg cut in two, admirably contrived, and warmly lined with cotton. They lay two eggs at a time, and never more, about the size of small peas, and as white as snow, with here and there a yellow speck. The male and the female sit upon the nest by turns; but the female takes to herself the greatest share. She seldoms quits the nest, except a few minutes in the morning and evening, when the dew is upon the flowers and their honey in perfection. During this short interval, the male takes her place. The time of incubation continues twelve days; at the end of which the young ones appear, much about the size of a blue-bottle fly. They are at first bare; by degrees they are covered with down; and, at last, feathers succeed, but less beautiful at first than those of the old ones.

These birds, on the continent of America, continue to flutter the year round, as their food, which is the honey of flowers, never forsakes them in those warm latitudes where they are found. But it is otherwise in the islands of the Antilles, where, when the winter season approaches, they retire, and, as some say, continue in a torpid state during the severity of that season. In Surinam and Jamaica, where they constantly have flowers, these beautiful birds are never known to disappear.

BIRDS OF THE CRANE KIND

THE CRANE

The Crane is exactly three feet four inches from the tip to the tail and four feet from the head to the toe. It is a tall, slender bird with a long neck and long legs. The top of the head is covered with black bristles, and the back of it is bald and red, which sufficiently distinguishes this bird from the stork, to which it is very nearly allied in size and figure. The plumage, in general, is ash-coloured; and there are two large tufts of feathers, that spring from the pinion of each wing. These bear a resemblance to hair, and are finely curled at the ends, which the bird has a power of erecting and depressing at pleasure.

The crane is a very social bird, and they are seldom seen alone. Their usual method of flying or sitting, is in flocks of fifty or sixty together; and while a part feed, the rest stand like sentinels upon duty. The fable of their supporting their aged parents, may have arisen from their strict connubial affection; and as for their fighting with the pygmies, it may not be improbable but that they have boldly withstood the invasions of monkeys coming to rob their nests; for,

in this case, as the crane lives upon vegetables, it is not probable that it would be the first aggressor.

However this be, the crane is a wandering sociable bird, and is known in every country of Europe except in England. As they are birds of passage, they are seen to depart and return regularly at those seasons when their provision invites or repels them. They generally leave Europe about the latter end of autumn, and return in the beginning of summer. In the inland parts of the continent, they are seen crossing the country, in flocks of fifty or a hundred, making from the northern regions towards the south. In these migrations, however, they are not so resolutely bent upon going forward, but that if a field of corn offers in their way, they will stop a while to feed upon it: on such occasions they do incredible damage, chiefly in the night; and the farmer, who lay down in joyful expectation, rises in the morning to see his fields laid entirely waste, by an enemy whose march is too swift for his vengeance to overtake.

In these journeys it is amazing to conceive the heights to which they ascend, when they fly. Their note is the loudest of all other birds; and that is often heard in the clouds, when the bird itself is entirely unseen. As it is light for its size, and spreads a large expanse of wing, it is capable of floating, at the greatest height, where the air is lightest; and as it secures its safety, and is entirely out of the reach of man, it flies in tracts which would be too fatiguing for any other bird to move forward in.

It is an animal easily tamed, and, has a particular affection for man. This quality, however, is not sufficient to guard it from being made the victim of his fierce amusements. The female, which is easily distinguished from the male, by not being bald behind as he is, never lays above two eggs at a time; being like those of a goose, but of a bluish colour. The young ones are soon fit to fly, and then the parents forsake them to shift for themselves; but, before this time, they are led forth to the places where their food is most easily found. Though yet unfledged, they run with such swiftness that a man cannot easily overtake them. We are told, that as they grow old, their plumage becomes darker; and it is said that one man kept one tame for above forty years.

THE STORK

The Stork is a silent bird and produces no other noise than the clacking of its under beak against the upper.

Storks are birds of passage but it is hard to say whence they come or whither they go. When they withdraw from Europe, they all assemble on a particular day, and never leave one of their company behind them. They take their flight in the night; which is the reason the way they go has never been observed. They generally return into Europe in the middle of March, and make their nests on the tops of chimneys and houses as well as high trees. The females lay from two to four eggs, of the size and colour of those of geese; and the male and female sit upon them by turns. They are a month in hatching; and when their young are hatched, they are particularly solicitous for their safety.

As the food of these birds consists in a great measure of frogs and snakes, it is not to be wondered at that different nations have paid a particular veneration. The Dutch are very solicitous for the preservation of the stork in every part of their republic. This bird seems to have taken refuge among their towns; and builds on the tops of their houses without any molestation. There it is seen resting familiarly in their streets, and protected as well by the laws as the favour of the people. They have even got an opinion that it will only live in a republic, but it is not in republics alone that the stork is seen to reside, as there are few towns on the continent, in low marshy situations, but have the stork as an inmate among them; as much in the despotic princedoms of Germany as the little republics of Italy.

THE BALEARIC CRANE

No bird presents to the eye a more whimsical figure than this bird, which we must be content to call the Balearic Crane. It is pretty nearly of the shape and size of the ordinary crane, with long legs and a long neck, like others of the kind; but the bill is shorter, and the colour of the feathers of a dark greenish grey. The head and throat form the most striking part of this bird's figure. On the head is seen standing up, a thick round crest, made of bristles, spreading every way, and resembling rays standing out in different directions. The longest of these rays are about three inches and a half; and they are all topped with a kind of black tassel, which give them a beautiful appearance. The sides of the head and cheeks are bare, whitish, and edged with red, while underneath the throat hangs a kind of bag or wattle, like that of a cock, but not divided into two. To give this odd composition a higher finishing, the eye is large and staring; the pupil black and big, surrounded with a gold-coloured iris that completes the bird's very singular appearance.

This bird comes from the coast of Africa and the Cape de Verd Islands. As it runs, it stretches out its wings, and goes very swiftly, otherwise its usual motion is very slow. In their domestic state they walk very deliberately among other poultry, and suffer themselves to be approached by every spectator. They never roost in houses but about night: when they are disposed to go to rest, they search out some high wall, on which they perch in the manner of a peacock. Indeed, they do so much resemble that bird in manners and disposition, that some have described them by the name of the sea-peacock. But, though their voice and roosting be similar, their food, which is entirely upon greens, vegetables, and barley, seems to make some difference.

THE ANHIMA

A most extraordinary bird is called the Anhima, a native of Brazil. This is a water-fowl of the rapacious kind, and bigger than a swan. The head, which is small for the size of the body, bears a black bill, which is not above two inches long; but what distinguishes it in particular is a horn growing from the forehead as long as the bill, and bending forward like that of the fabulous unicorn of the ancients. This horn is not much thicker than a crow-quill, as round as if it were turned in a lathe, and of an ivory colour. But this is not the only instrument of battle this formidable bird carries; it seems to be armed at all points for at the fore-part of each wing, at the second joint, spring two straight triangular spurs, about as thick as one's little finger. The claws also are long and sharp; the colour is black and white; and they cry terribly loud, sounding something like *Vyhoo Vyhoo*. They are never found alone, but always in pairs; the cock and hen prowl together; and their fidelity is said to be such, that when one dies, the other never departs from the carcase, but dies with its companion.

THE DEMOISELLE CRANE

The peculiar gestures and contortions of this bird, the proper name of which is the Numidian Crane, are extremely singular; and the French, who are skilled in the arts of elegant gesticulation, consider all its motions as lady-like and graceful. Our English sailors however, who have not entered so deeply into the dancing art, think, that while thus in motion, the bird cuts but a very ridiculous figure. It stoops, rises, lifts one wing, then another, turns around, falls forward, then back again; all which highly diverts our seamen; not imagining, perhaps that all these contortions are but the awkward expression not of

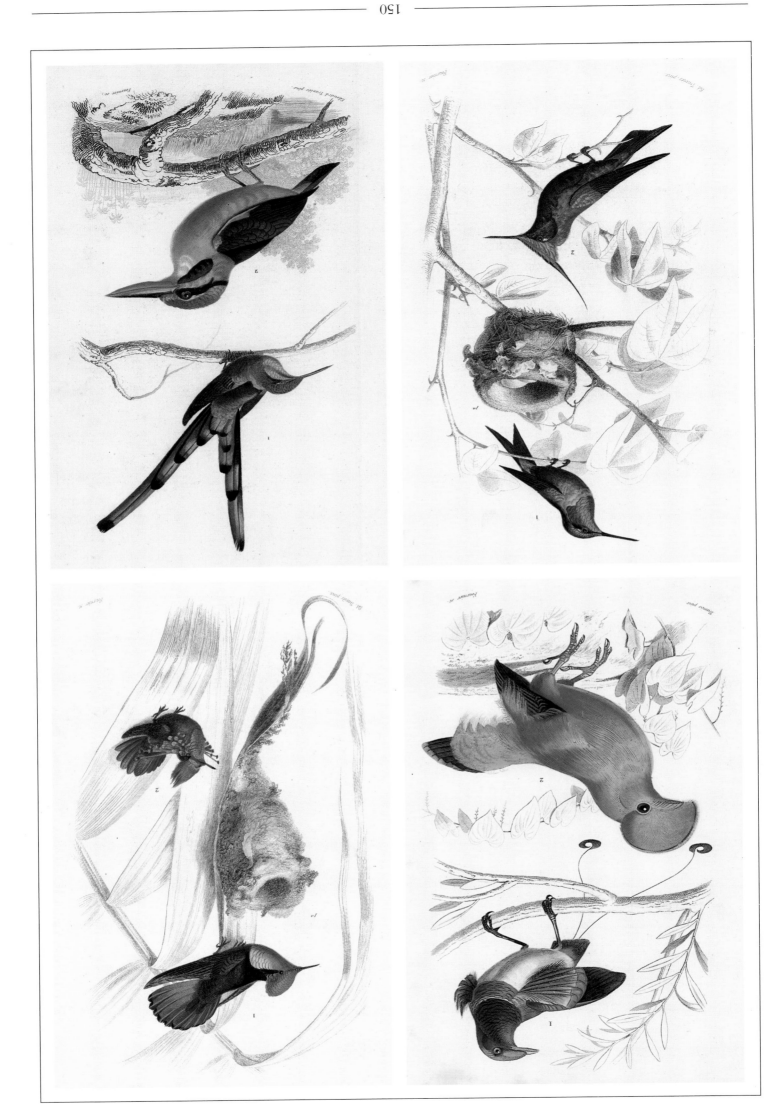

the poor animal's pleasures but its fears.

It is a very scarce bird; the plumage is of a leaden grey; but it is distinguished by fine white feathers, consisting of long fibres, which fall from the back of the head, about four inches long; while the fore-part of the neck is adorned with black feathers, composed of very fine, soft and long fibres, that hang down upon the stomach, and give the bird a very graceful appearance.

THE HERON

Of the Heron tribe there are not less than forty-seven sorts, all differing in their size, figure, and plumage; and with talents adapted to their place of residence, or their peculiar pursuits. But, how various soever the heron kind may be in their colours or their bills, they all seem possessed of the same manners, and have but one character of cowardice and rapacity, indolence, yet insatiable hunger.

The common heron is remarkably light, in proportion to its bulk, scarce weighing three pounds and a half, yet it expands a breadth of wing which is five feet from tip to tip. Its bill is very long, being five inches from the point to the base; its claws are long, sharp, and the middlemost toothed like a saw. Yet, thus armed as it appears for war, it is indolent and cowardly, and even flies at the approach of a sparrow-hawk. It was once the amusement of the great to pursue this timorous creature with the falcon; and heron-hawking was so favourite a diversion among our ancestors, that laws were enacted for the preservation of the species; and the person who destroyed their eggs was liable to a penalty of twenty shillings for each offence.

At present, however, the defects of the ill-judged policy of our ancestors is felt by their posterity; for, as the amusement of hawking has given place to the

more useful method of stocking fish-ponds, the heron is now become a most formidable enemy. Of all other birds, this commits the greatest devastation in fresh waters; and there is scarce a fish, though never so large, that he will not strike at and wound, though unable to carry it away. But the smaller fry are his chief subsistence; these, pursued by their larger fellows of the deep, are obliged to take refuge in shallow waters, where they find the heron a still more formidable enemy. His method is to wade as far as he can go into the water, and there patiently wait the approach of his prey, which when it comes within sight, he darts upon but with inevitable aim. In this manner he is found to destroy more in a week than an otter in three months.

In general, he is seen taking his gloomy stand by the lake side, as if meditating mischief, motionless and gorged with plunder. His usual attitude on this occasion is to sink his long neck between his shoulders, and keep his head turned on one side, as if eyeing the pool more intently. When the call of hunger returns, the toil of an hour or two is generally sufficient to fill his capacious stomach; and he retires long before night to his retreat in the woods. Early in the morning, however, he is seen assiduous at his usual occupation.

Though this bird lives chiefly among pools and marshes, yet its nest is built on the tops of the highest trees, and sometimes on cliffs hanging over the sea. They are never in flocks when they fish, committing their depredations in solitude and silence; but in making their nests they love each other's society; and they are seen, like rooks, building in company with flocks of their kind. Their nests are made of sticks and lined with wool; and the female lays four large eggs of a pale green colour.

The French seem to have availed themselves of the indolence of this bird in making its nest, and they actually provide a place with materials fitted for their nestling, which they call heronries. The heron, which with us is totally unfit for the table, is more sought for in France, where the flesh of the young ones is in particular estimation. To obtain this, the natives raise up high sheds along some filthy stream; and furnishing them with materials for the herons to nestle with, these birds build and breed there in great abundance. As soon as the young ones are supposed to be fit, the owner of the heronry comes, as we do into a pigeon-house, and carries off such as are proper for eating, and these are sold for a very good price to the neighbouring gentry. It was formerly much esteemed as a food in England, and made a favourite dish at great tables. It was then said that the flesh of a heron was a dish for a king; at present, nothing about the house will touch it but a cat.

THE BITTERN

Those who have walked in an evening by the sedgy sides of unfrequented rivers, must remember a variety of notes from different water-fowl: of all those sounds, there is none so dismally hollow as the booming of the Bittern. It is impossible for words to give those who have not heard its evening call an adequate idea of its solemnity. It is like the interrupted bellowing of a bull, but hollower and louder, and is heard at a mile's distance, as if issuing from some formidable being that resided at the bottom of the waters.

The bird, however, that produces this terrifying sound is not so big as a heron, with a weaker bill which is not above four inches long. It differs from the heron chiefly in its colour, which is in general of a palish yellow, spotted and barred with black. Its wind-pipe is fitted to produce the sound for which it is remarkable; the lower part of it dividing into the lungs supplied with a thin loose membrane, that can be filled with a large body of air and exploded at pleasure. These bellowing explosions are chiefly heard from the beginning of spring to the end of autumn; and, however awful they may seem to us, are the calls to courtship, or of connubial felicity.

From the loudness and solemnity of the note, many have been led to suppose that the bird made use of external instruments to produce it, and that so small a body could never eject such a quantity of tone. The common people are of opinion, that it thrusts its bill into a reed that serves as a pipe for swelling the note above its natural pitch; while others imagine that the bittern puts its head under water, and then violently blowing produces its boomings. The fact is that the bird is sufficiently provided by Nature for this call; and it is often heard where there are neither reeds nor waters to assist its sonorous invitations.

The bittern is a retired timorous animal, concealing itself in the midst of reeds and marshy places, and living upon frogs, insects, and vegetables. The bittern lays its nest in a sedgy margin, or amidst a tuft of rushes. It lays seven or eight eggs and three days after they are hatched it leads its little ones to their food. The bittern is plump and fleshy, as it feeds upon vegetables when more nourishing food is wanting.

It cannot be, therefore, from its voracious appetites, but its hollow boom, that the bittern is held in such detestation by the vulgar. I remember in the place where I was a boy with what terror this bird's note affected the whole village; they considered it as the presage of some sad event; and generally found or made one to succeed it.

THE SPOONBILL

The European Spoonbill or shoveler is of about the bulk of a crane; but as the one is above four feet high, the other is not more than three feet three inches. The common colour of those in Europe, is a dirty white; but those of America are of a beautiful rose colour, or a delightful crimson. Beauty of plumage seems to be the prerogative of all the birds of that continent; and we here see the most splendid tints bestowed on a bird, whose figure is sufficient to destroy the effects of its colouring, for its bill is so oddly fashioned, and its eyes so stupidly staring, that its fine feathers only tend to add splendour to deformity. The bill, which in this bird is so very particular, is about seven inches long, and running out broad at the end, as its name justly serves to denote; it is there about an inch and a half wide. This strangely fashioned instrument, in some is black; in others of a light grey; and in those of America, it is of a red colour, like the rest of the body. All round the upper beak there runs a kind of rim, with which it covers that beneath; and as for the rest, its cheeks, and its throat, are without feathers, and covered with a black skin.

Nature, when she made the bill of this bird so very broad, seems rather to have sported with its form, than to aim at any final cause for which to adapt it.

The shoveler chiefly feeds upon frogs, toads and serpents; of which, particularly at the Cape of Good Hope, they destroy great numbers. The inhabitants of that country hold them is as much esteem as the ancient Egyptians did the ibis: the shoveler runs tamely about their houses; and they are content with its society, as a useful though a homely companion. They are never killed; and indeed they are good for nothing when they are dead, for the flesh is unfit to be eaten.

THE FLAMINGO

The Flamingo is the most remarkable of all the crane kind, the tallest, bulkiest, and the most beautiful. The body, which is of a beautiful scarlet, is no bigger than that of a swan, but its legs and neck are of such an extraordinary length, that when it stands erect it is six feet six inches high. Its wings, extended, are five feet six inches from tip to tip; and it is four feet eight inches from tip to tail. The head is round and small, with a large bill, seven inches long, partly red, partly black, and crooked like a bow. The legs and thighs, which are not much thicker than a man's finger, are about two feet eight inches high; and its neck near three feet long. The feet are not furnished with sharp claws, as in others of the crane kind; but feeble, and united by membranes, as in those of the goose. Of what use these membranes are does not appear, as the bird is never seen swimming, its legs and thighs being sufficient for bearing it into those depths where it seeks for prey.

Left **1** CROWNED CRANE *Ardea pavonia* **2** MADAGASCAR CRESTED IBIS *Ibis cristata* Right **1** PHEASANT-TAILED JACANA *Parra sinensis* **2** ANHIMA OR HORNED SCREAMER *Palamedea cornuta*

This extraordinary bird is now chiefly found in America, but was once known on all the coasts of Europe.

When the Europeans first came to America, and coasted down along the African shores, they found the flamingoes on several shores on either continent, gentle and no way distrustful of mankind. They had long been used to security, in the extensive solitudes they had chosen, and knew no enemies, but those they could very well evade or oppose. The Africans and the native Americans, were possessed but of few destructive arts for killing them at a distance; and when the bird perceived the arrow, it well knew how to avoid it. But it was otherwise when the Europeans first came among them: the sailors, not considering that the dread of fire-arms was totally unknown in that part of the world, gave the flamingo the character of a foolish bird, that suffered itself to be approached and shot at. When the fowler had killed one, the rest of the flock, far from attempting to fly, only regarded the fall of their companion in a kind of fixed astonishment: another and another shot was discharged; and thus the fowler often levelled the whole flock, before one of them began to think of escaping.

But at present it is very different in that part of the world; and the flamingo is not only one of the scarcest but of the shyest birds in the world, and the most difficult of approach. They chiefly keep near the most deserted and inhospitable shores; near salt-water lakes and swampy islands. They come down to the banks of rivers by day; and often retire to the inland, mountainous parts of the country at the approach of night. Their rank, however, is broken when they seek for food; but they always appoint one of the number as a watch, whose only employment is to observe and give notice of danger, while the rest are feeding.

The Roman emperors considered the tongue of the flamingo as the highest luxury; and we have an account of one of them, who procured fifteen hundred flamingoes' tongues to be served up in a single dish. The tongue of this bird, which is so much sought after, is a good deal larger than that of any other bird whatever. The bill of the flamingo is like a large black box, of an irregular figure, and filled with a tongue which is black and gristly; but what peculiar flavour it may possess, I leave to be determined by such as understand good eating better than I do.

The young are sometimes caught; and suffer themselves to be carried home, and are tamed very easily. In five or six days they become familiar, eat out of the hand, and drink a surprising quantity of sea-water. But though they are easily rendered domestic, they are not reared without the greatest difficulty; for they generally pine away, for want of natural supplies and die in a short time. While they are yet young, their colours are very different from those lovely tints they acquire with age. In their first year they are covered with plumage of a white colour, mixed with grey; in the second year the whole body is white, with here and there a slight tint of scarlet; and the great covert feathers of the wings are black: the third year the bird acquires all its beauty; the plumage of the whole body is scarlet, except some of the feathers in the wings, that still retain their sable hue. Of these beautiful plumes, the savages make various ornaments, and the bird is sometimes skinned by the Europeans, to make muffs. But these have diminished in their price, since we have obtained the art of dying feathers of the brightest scarlet.

THE AVOCET

The Avocet is chiefly found in Italy, and now and then comes over into England. It is about the size of a pigeon, is a pretty upright bird, and has extremely long legs for its size. But the most extraordinary part of its figure, and that by which it may be distinguished from all others of the feathered tribe, is the bill, which turns up like a hook, in an opposite direction to that of the hawk or the parrot. This extraordinary bill is black, flat, sharp, and flexible at the end, and about three inches and a half long. From the avocet being bare a long way above the knee, it appears that it lives and wades in the waters. It has a chirping, pert note, as we are told; but with its other habits we are entirely unacquainted. I have placed it, from its slender figure, among the cranes; although it is web-footed, like the duck.

THE MOOR-HEN

The Moor-Hen weighs but fifteen ounces; the coot twenty four. The bald part of the forehead in the coot is black; in the moor-hen it is of a beautiful pink colour. The toes of the moor-hen are edged with a straight membrane; those of the coot have it scalloped and broader.

The differences in the figure are but slight; and those in their manner of living still less. The moor-hen whose wings are short, is obliged to reside entirely near those places where her food lies: compelled by her natural imperfections, as well perhaps as by inclination, she never leaves the side of the pond or the river in which she seeks for provision. Where the stream is bordered with sedges, or the pond edged with shrubby trees, the moor-hen is generally a resident there: she seeks her food along the grassy banks; and often along the surface of the water. With Shakespeare's Edgar, she drinks the green mantle of the standing pool; or, at least, seems to prefer those places where it is seen. Whether she makes pond-weed her food, or hunts among it for water insects, which are found there in great abundance, is not certain. She builds her nest upon low trees and shrubs, of sticks and fibres, by the water side. Her eggs are sharp at one end, white, with a tincture of green spotted with red. She lays twice or thrice in a summer; her young ones swim the moment they leave the egg, pursue their parent, and imitate all her manners. She rears, in this manner, two or three broods in a season; and when the young are grown up, she drives them off to shift for themselves.

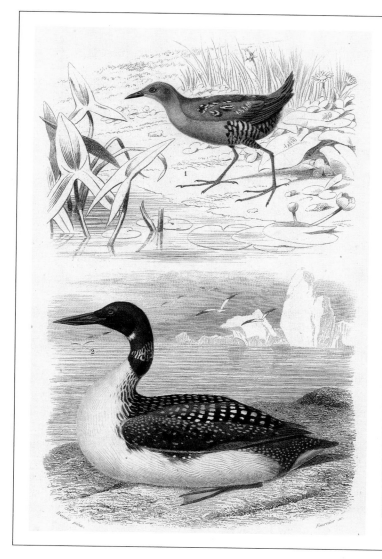

Left **1** WATERHEN *Gallinula baillonii*
2 GREAT NORTHERN DIVER *Colymbus glacialis*
Right **1** BLACK-HEADED PLOVER *Pluvianus melanocephalus*
2 WOODCOCK *Scolopax rusticola*

THE COOT

As the Coot is a larger bird, it is always seen in larger streams, and more remote from mankind. The coot keeps in rivers, and among rushy margined lakes. It there makes a nest of such weeds as the stream supplies, and lays them among the reeds, floating on the surface, and rising and falling with the water. The reeds among which it is built keep it fast; so that it is seldom washed into the middle of the stream. But if this happens, which is sometimes the case, the bird sits in her nest, like a mariner in his boat, and steers with her legs her cargo into the nearest harbour: there, having attained her port, she continues to sit in great tranquility, regardless of the impetuosity of the current; and though the water penetrates her nest, she hatches her eggs in that wet condition.

THE GREBE

The Grebe is much larger than the coot, and its plumage white and black: it differs also entirely in the shortness of its legs, which are made for swimming, and not walking: in fact, they are from the knee upward hid in the belly of the bird, and have consequently very little motion. By this mark, and by the scalloped fringe of the toes, may this bird be easily distinguished from all others.

As they are thus, from the shortness of their wings, ill formed for flying, and from the uncommon shortness of their legs, utterly unfitted for walking, they seldom leave the water, and chiefly frequent those broad shallow pools where their faculty of swimming can be turned to the greatest advantage, in fishing and seeking their prey.

They are chiefly, in England, seen to frequent the meres of Shropshire and Cheshire; where they breed among reeds and flags, in a floating nest, kept steady

by the weeds of the margin. The female is said to be a careful nurse of its young, being observed to feed them most assiduously with small eels; and when the little brood is tired, the mother will carry them, either on her back or under her wings. This bird preys upon fish, and is almost perpetually diving. It does not show much more than the head above water; and is very difficult to be shot, as it darts down on the appearance of the least danger. It is never seen on land; and, though disturbed ever so often, will not leave that lake where alone, by diving and swimming, it can find food and security.

OF WATER-FOWL

THE PELICAN

The Pelican of Africa is much larger in the body than a swan, and somewhat of the same shape and colour. Its four toes are all webbed together; and its neck in some measure resembles that of a swan: but that singularity in which it differs from all other birds is in the bill and the great pouch underneath, which are wonderful, and demand a distinct description. This enormous bill is fifteen inches from the point to the opening of the mouth, which is a good way behind the eyes. At the base the bill is somewhat greenish, but varies towards the end, being of a reddish blue. It is very thick in the beginning, but tapers off to the end, where it hooks downwards. The under beak is still more extraordinary; for to the lower edges of it hang a bag, reaching the whole length of the bill to the neck, which is said to be capable of containing fifteen quarts of water. This bag the bird has a power of wrinkling upwards. The skin of which it is formed will then be seen of a bluish ash-colour, with many fibres and veins running over its surface. It is not covered with feathers, but a short downy substance as smooth and as soft as satin, and is attached all along the under edges of the beak, to be fixed backward to the neck of the bird by proper ligaments, and reaches near half way down. The first thing the pelican does in fishing is to fill up the bag; and then it returns to digest its burden at leisure. When the bill is opened to its widest extent, a person may run his head into the bird's mouth, and conceal it in this monstrous pounch, thus adapted for very singular purposes. Yet this is nothing to what one man assures us, who avers that a man has been seen to hide his whole leg, boot and all, in the monstrous jaws of one of these animals.

Left PURPLE HERON *Ardea purpurea*

This is the bird of which so many fabulous accounts have been propagated; such as its feeding its young with its own blood, and its carrying a provision of water for them in its great reservoir in the desert. But the absurdity of the first account answers itself; and as for the latter, the pelican uses its bag for very different purposes than that of filling it with water.

The pelican has strong wings, furnished with thick plumage of an ash-colour, as are the rest of the feathers over the whole body. Its eyes are very small, when compared to the size of its head; there is a sadness in its countenance, and its whole air is melancholy. It is dull and reluctant in its motions, and slow of flight; and when it rises to fly, performs it with difficulty and labour. Nothing, as it would seem, but the spur of necessity, could make these birds change their situation, or induce them to ascend into the air: but they must either starve or fly.

They often spend a great part of the day, except such times as they are fishing, sitting in dismal solemnity, and, as it would seem, half asleep. Their attitude is, with the head resting upon their great bag, and that resting upon their breast. There they remain without motion, or once changing their situation, till the calls of hunger break their repose, and till they find it indispensibly necessary to fill their beak for a fresh meal. Thus their life is spent between sleeping and eating; and they are as foul as they are voracious, as they are every moment voiding excrements in heaps as large as one's fist.

It seems, however, that they are but disagreeable and useless domestics; their gluttony can scarcely be satisfied; their flesh smells very rancid; and tastes a thousand times worse than it smells. The native Americans kill vast numbers; not to eat, for they are not fit even for the banquet of a savage; but to convert their large bags into purses and tobacco-pouches. They bestow no small pains in dressing the skin with salt and ashes, rubbing it well with oil, and then forming it to their purpose. It thus becomes so soft and pliant, that the Spanish women sometimes adorn it with gold and embroidery to make workbags.

THE ALBATROSS

Though this is one of the largest and most formidable birds of Africa and America, yet we have but few accounts to enlighten us in its history. Its body is rather larger than that of the pelican; and its wings when extended ten feet from tip to tip. The bill, which is six inches long, is yellowish, and terminates in a crooked point. The top of the head is of a bright brown; the back is of a dirty deep spotted brown; and the belly and under the wings is white; the toes, which are webbed, are of a flesh colour.

This bird is an inhabitant of the tropical climates, and also beyond them as far as the Straits of Magellan in the South Seas. It is one of the most fierce and formidable of the aquatic tribe, not only living upon fish, but also such small water-fowl as it can take by surprise. It preys, as all the gull-kind do, upon the wing; and chiefly pursues the flying-fish, that are forced from the sea by the dolphins. The ocean in that part of the world presents a very different appearance from the seas with which we are surrounded. In our seas we see nothing but a dreary expanse, ruffled by winds, and seemingly forsaken by every class of animated nature. But the tropical seas, and the distant southern latitudes beyond them, are all alive with birds and fishes, pursuing and pursued. Every various species of the gull-kind are there seen hovering on the wing, at a thousand miles distance from the shore.

It is certain that few birds float upon the air with more ease than the albatross, or support themselves a longer time in that element. They seem never to feel the accesses of fatigue; but night and day upon the wing are always prowling, yet always emaciated and hungry.

THE CORMORANT

The Cormorant is about the size of a large Muscovy duck, and may be distinguished from all other birds of this kind, by its four toes being united by membranes together; and by the middle toe being toothed or notched, like a saw, to assist it in holding its filthy prey. The head and neck of this bird are of a sooty blackness; and the body thick and heavy, more inclining in figure to that of the goose than the gull. The bill is straight, till near the end, where the upper beak bends into a hook.

But notwithstanding the seeming heaviness of its make, there are few birds more powerfully predaceous. As soon as the winter approaches, they are seen dispersed along the sea-shore, and ascending up the mouths of fresh-water rivers, carrying destruction to all the finny tribe. They are most remarkably voracious and their appetite is for ever craving, and never satisfied. This gnawing sensation may probably be increased by the great quantity of small worms that fill their intestines, and which their unceasing gluttony contributes to engender.

The cormorant is the best fisher of all birds; and though fat and heavy with the quantity it devours, is nevertheless generally upon the wing. The great activity with which it pursues, and from a vast height drops down to dive after, its prey, offers one of the most amusing spectacles to those who stand upon a cliff on the shore. This large bird is seldom seen in the air, but where there are fish below; but then the fish must be near the surface. If they are at a depth beyond what the impetus of its flight makes the cormorant capable of diving to, they certainly escape him; for this bird cannot move so fast under water, as the fish can swim. It seldom, however, makes an unsuccessful dip; and is often seen rising heavily, with a fish larger than it can readily devour. It sometimes also happens, that the cormorant has caught the fish by the tail; and consequently the fins prevent its being easily swallowed in that position. In this case, the bird is seen to toss its prey above its head and very dexterously to catch it, when descending, by the proper end, and so swallow it with ease.

THE GANNET

The Gannet is of the size of a tame goose, but its wings much longer, being six feet over. The bill is six inches long, straight almost to the point, where it inclines down, and the sides are irregularly jagged, that it may hold its prey with greater security. It is chiefly white in colour and from the corner of the mouth is a narrow slip of black bare skin, that extends to the hind part of the head; beneath the skin is another that, like the pouch of the pelican, is dilatable, and of size sufficient to contain five or six entire herrings, which in the breeding season it carries at once to its mate or its young.

These birds, which subsist entirely upon fish, chiefly resort to those uninhabited islands where their food is found in plenty, and men seldom come to disturb them. The islands to the north of Scotland, the Skelig islands of the coasts of Kerry in Ireland, and those that lie in the North Sea off Norway, abound with them. But it is on the Bass Island, in the Firth of Edinburgh, where they are seen in the greatest abundance.

They are not less frequent upon the rocks of St. Kilda. We are told that the inhabitants of that small

CRESTED PELICAN *Pelecanus crispus*

island consume annually near twenty-three thousand young birds of this species, besides an amazing quantity of their eggs. On these they principally subsist throughout the year; and from the number of these visitants, make an estimate of their plenty for the season. They preserve both the eggs and fowls in small pyramidal stone buildings, covering them with turf-ashes, to prevent the evaporation of their moisture.

The gannet is a bird of passage. In winter it seeks the more southern coasts of Cornwall, hovering over the shoals of herrings and pilchards that then come down from the northern seas: its first appearance in the northern islands, is in the beginning of spring; and it continues to breed till the end of summer. But, in general, its motions are determined by the migrations of the immense shoals of herrings that come pouring down at that season through the British Channel, and supply all Europe as well as this bird with their spoil. The gannet assiduously attends the shoal on their passage, keeps with them in their whole circuit round our island, and shares with our fishermen this exhaustless banquet.

These birds breed but once a year, and lay but one egg, which being taken away, they lay another; if that is also taken, then a third; but never more for that season. Their egg is white, and rather less than that of the common goose; and their nest large, composed of such substances as are found floating on the surface of the sea. The young birds, during the first year, differ greatly in colour from the old ones; being of a dusky hue, speckled with numerous triangular white spots; and at that time resembling the colours of the speckled diver.

The Bass Island, where they chiefly breed, belongs to one proprietor; so that care is taken never to fright away the birds when laying, or to shoot them upon the wing. By that means, they are so confident as to alight and feed their young ones close beside you.

THE GULL

The Gull, and all its varieties, is very well known in every part of the kingdom. It is seen with a slow sailing flight hovering over rivers to prey upon the smaller kinds of fish; it is seen following the ploughman in fallow fields to pick up insects; and where living animal food does not offer, it has even been known to eat carrion and whatever else of the kind that offers. Gulls are found in great plenty in every place; but it is chiefly round our boldest rockiest shores that they are seen in the greatest abundance; it is there that the gull breeds and brings up its young; it is there that millions of them are heard screaming with discordant notes for months together.

Those who have been much upon the coasts of Britain know that there are two different kinds of shores; those which slant down to the water with a gentle declivity, and those which rise with a precipitate boldness, and seem set as a bulwark to repel the force of the invading deeps. It is to such shores as these that the whole tribe of the gull kind resort, as the rocks offer them a retreat for their young, and the sea a sufficient supply. It is in the cavities of these rocks, of which the shore is composed, that the vast variety of sea fowls retire to breed in safety. The waves beneath, that continually beat at the base, often wear the shore, so that the cliff seems to jut out over the water, while the raging of the sea makes the place inaccessible from below. These are the situations to which sea-fowl chiefly resort, and bring up their young in undisturbed security.

The contemplation of a cliff thus covered with hatching birds affords a very agreeable entertainment; and as they sit upon the ledges of the rocks, one above another, with their white breasts forward, the whole group has not unaptly been compared to an apothecary's shop.

These birds, like all others of the rapacious kind, lay but few eggs; and hence, in many places, their number is daily seen to diminish. Most of the kind are fishy tasting, with black stringy flesh; yet the young ones are better food: and of these the poor inhabitants of our northern islands make their wretched banquets. They have been long used to no other food; and even salted gull can be relished by those who know no better.

THE PENGUIN

The gulls are long winged, swift flyers, that hover over the most extensive seas, and dart down upon such fish as approach too near the surface. The Penguin kind are but ill fitted for flight, and still less for walking. Their wings are much shorter, more scantily furnished with quills and the whole pinion placed too forward, to be usefully employed. For this reason, the largest of the penguin kind, that have a thick, heavy body to raise, cannot fly at all. Their wings serve them rather as paddles to help them forward, when they attempt to move swiftly; and in a manner walk along the surface of the water. Even the smaller kinds seldom fly by choice; they flutter their wings without making way; and though they have but a small weight of body to sustain, yet they seldom venture to quit the water where they are provided with food and protection.

As the wings of the penguin tribe are unfitted for flight, their legs are still more awkwardly adapted for walking. This whole tribe have all above the knee hid within the belly; and nothing appears but two short legs, or feet, as some would call them, that seem stuck under the rump, and upon which the animal is very awkwardly supported. They seem, when sitting or attempting to walk, like a dog that has been taught to sit up, or to move to a minuet. Their short legs drive the body in progression from side to side; and were they not assisted by their wings, they could scarcely move faster than a tortoise.

This awkward position of the legs, which so unqualifies them for living upon land, adapts them admirably for a residence in water. In that, the legs placed behind the moving body, pushes it forward with greater velocity; and these birds, like Indian canoes, are the swiftest in the water, by having their paddles in the rear. Our sailors, for this reason, give these birds the very homely, but expressive, name of Arse-feet.

Nor are they less qualified for diving than swimming. By ever so little inclining their bodies forward, they lose their centre of gravity; and every stroke from their feet only tends to sink them the faster. In this manner they continue fishing for some minutes, and then ascending, catch an instantaneous breath, to descend once more to renew their operations. Hence it is that these birds which are so defenceless, and so easily taken by land, are impregnable by water. That part of them which has been continually bathed in the water, is white; while their backs and wings are of different colours, according to the different species. They are also covered more warmly all over the body with feathers, than any other birds whatever: so that the sea seems entirely their element.

Of all this tribe, the Magellanic Penguin is the largest, and the most remarkable. In size it

CRESTED PENGUIN *Aptenodytes chrysocoma*

CAPE WANDERING ALBATROSS *Diomedea exulans*

Edouard Travies pinx.

Fournier sc.

1

2

approaches near that of a tame goose. It never flies, as its wings are very short, hanging uselessly down by the bird's sides. The upper part of the head, back and rump, are covered with stiff, black feathers; while the belly and breast, as is common with all of this kind, are of a snowy whiteness. The bill, which from the base to about half way is covered with wrinkles, is black, but marked crosswise with a stripe of yellow. They walk erect with their heads on high, their fin-like wings hanging down like arms; so that to see them at a distance, they look like so many children with white aprons.

THE PUFFIN

Words cannot easily describe the form of the bill of the Puffin, which differs so greatly from that of any other bird. Those who have seen the blade of a plough, may form some idea of the beak of this odd-looking animal. The bill is flat and is of a triangular figure, and ending in a sharp point; the upper part bent a little downward, where it is joined to the head: and a certain callous substance encompassing its base, as in parrots. It is of two colours; ash-coloured near the base, and red towards the point. It has three furrows or grooves impressed in it. The eyes are outlined with a protuberant skin, of a livid-colour; and they are grey.

The puffin like all the rest of this kind, has its legs thrown so far back, that it can hardly move without tumbling. This makes it rise with difficulty, and subject to many falls before it gets upon the wing; but as it is a small bird, not much bigger than a pigeon, when it once rises, it can continue its flight with great celerity.

Relying on its courage, and the strength of its bill, with which it bites most terribly, it either makes or finds a hole in the ground, where to lay and bring forth its young. All the winter these birds, like the rest, are absent from our shores; visiting regions too remote for discovery. At the latter end of March, or the beginning of April, come over a troop of their spies or harbingers, that stay two or three days, as it were to view and search out for their former situations, and see whether all be well. This done, they once more depart; and, about the beginning of May, return again with the whole army of their companions. But if the season happens to be stormy and tempestuous, and the sea troubled, the unfortunate voyagers undergo incredible hardships; and they are found, by hundreds, cast away upon the shores, lean and perished with famine.

Near the Isle of Anglesey, in an islet called Priestholm, their flocks may be compared, for multi-tude, to swarms of bees. In another islet, called the Isle of Man, a bird of this kind, but of a different species, is seen in great abundance. In both places, numbers of rabbits are found to breed; but the puffin, unwilling to be at the trouble of making a hole, when there is one ready made, dispossesses the rabbits, and it is not unlikely destroys their young. Whatever fish, or other food, they have procured in the day, by night begins to suffer a kind of half digestion, and is reduced to an oily matter, which is ejected from the stomach of the old ones into the mouth of the young. By this they are nourished, and become fat to an amazing degree.

Their flesh is said to be excessively rank, as they feed upon fish, especially sprats and sea-weed; however, when they are pickled and preserved with spices they are admired by those who are fond of high eating. We are told, that formerly their flesh was allowed by the church on Lenten days.

THE SWAN

No bird makes a more indifferent figure upon land, or a more beautiful one in the water, than the Swan. When it ascends from its favourite element, its motions are awkward, and its neck is stretched forward with an air of stupidity; but when it is seen smoothly sailing along the water, commanding a thousand graceful attitudes, moving at pleasure without the smallest effort there is not a more beautful figure in all nature. In the exhibition of its form, there are no broken or harsh lines; no constrained or catching motions; but the roundest contours, and the easiest transitions; the eye wanders over every part with insatiable pleasure, and every part takes a new grace with new motion.

This beautiful bird is as delicate in its appetites, as elegant in its form. Its chief food is corn, bread, herbs growing in the water, and roots and seeds, which are found near the margin. It prepares a nest in some retired part of the bank, and chiefly where there is an islet in the stream. This is composed of water-plants, long grass and sticks; and the male and female assist in forming it with great assiduity. The swan lays seven or eight eggs, white, much larger than those of a goose, with a hard, and sometimes a tuberous shell.

It sits near two months before its young are excluded; which are ash-coloured when they first leave the shell, and for some months after. It is not a little dangerous to approach the old ones, when their little family are feeding round them. Their fears, as well as their pride, seems to take the alarm; and they have sometimes been known to give a blow with their pinion, that has broken a man's leg or arm.

It is not till they are a twelve-month old that the young swans change their colour with their plumage. All the stages of this bird's approach to maturity are slow, and seem to mark its longevity. It is two months hatching; a year in growing to its proper size.

Swans were formerly held in such great esteem in England, that, by an act of Edward the Fourth, none, except the son of the king, was permitted to keep a swan, unless possessed of five marks a year. By a subsequent act, the punishment for taking their eggs was imprisonment for a year and a day, and a fine at the king's will. At present they are but little valued for the delicacy of their flesh; but many are still preserved for their beauty. We see multitudes on the Thames and Trent; but nowhere greater numbers than on the salt-water inlet of the sea near Abbotsberry, in Dorsetshire.

THE GOOSE

The wild Goose is supposed to breed in the northern parts of Europe; and, in the beginning of winter, to descend into more temperate regions. They are often seen flying at very great heights, in flocks from fifty to a hundred, and seldom resting by

day. Their cry is frequently heard when they are at an imperceptible distance above us; and this seems bandied from one to the other, as among hounds in the pursuit. Whether this be the note of mutual encouragement, or the necessary consequence of respiration, is doubtful; but they seldom exert it when they alight in these journeys.

Their flight is very regularly arranged: they either go in a line abreast, or in two lines, joining in an angle in the middle. I doubt whether the form of their flight be thus arranged to cut the air with greater ease, as is commonly believed; I am more apt to think it is to present a smaller mark to fowlers from below.

THE BARNACLE GOOSE

The Barnacle differs in some respects from the wild goose, being smaller with a black bill. It is scarce necessary to combat the idle error of this bird's being bred from a shell sticking to ship's bottoms; it is well known to be hatched from an egg, in the ordinary manner, and to differ in very few particulars from all the rest of its kind.

THE BRENT GOOSE

The Brent Goose is not bigger than a Muscovy duck, except that the body is longer. The head, neck, and upper part of the breast, are black; but about the middle of the neck, on each side, are two small spots or lines of white, which together appear like a ring.

THE TAME GOOSE

All geese are remarkable for their fecundity and the tame Goose is the most fruitful. Having less to fear from its enemies, leading a securer and a more plentiful life, its prolific powers increase in proportion to its ease; and though the wild goose seldom lays above eight eggs, the tame goose is often seen to lay above twenty. The female hatches her eggs with great assiduity; while the gander visits her twice or thrice a day, and sometimes drives her off to take her place, where he sits with great state and composure.

But beyond that of all animals is his pride when the young are hatched: he seems then to consider himself as a champion not only obliged to defend his young, but also to keep off the suspicion of danger; he pursues dogs and men that never attempt to molest him; and, though the most harmless thing alive, is then the most petulant and provoking. When, in this manner, he has pursued the calf or the mastiff, to whose contempt alone he is indebted for safety, he returns to his female and her brood in triumph, clapping his wings, screaming, and showing all the marks of conscious superiority. It is probable, however, these arts succeed in raising his importance among the tribe where they are displayed; and it is probable there is not a more respectable animal on earth to a goose than a gander!

A young goose is generally reckoned very good

eating; yet the feathers of this bird still farther increase its value. I feel my obligations to this animal every word I write; for, however deficient a man's head may be, his pen is nimble enough upon every occasion: it is happy indeed for us, that it requires no great effort to put it in motion. But the feathers of this bird are still as valuable in another capacity, as they make the softest and the warmest beds to sleep on.

As feathers are a very valuable commodity, great numbers of geese are kept tame in the fens in Lincolnshire, which are plucked once or twice a year. These make a considerable article of commerce. The feathers of Somersetshire are most in esteem; those of Ireland are reckoned the worst. The best method of curing feathers, is to lay them in a room in an open exposure to the sun, and, when dried, to put them into bags, and beat them well with poles to get the dust off. But, after all, nothing will prevent, for a time, the heavy smell which arises from the putrefaction of the oil contained in every feather; no exposure will draw this off, how long soever it be continued; they must be lain upon, which is the only remedy: and for this reason, old feathers are much more valuable than new.

THE DUCK

The tame Duck is the most easily reared of all our domestic animals. The very instincts of the young ones direct them to their favourite element; and though they are conducted by a hen, yet they despise the admonitions of their leader.

The duck seems to be a heedless, inattentive mother; she frequently leaves her eggs till they spoil, and even seems to forget that she is entrusted with the charge: she is equally regardless of them when hatched; she leads them to the pond, and thinks she has sufficiently provided for her offspring when she has shown them the water. For this reason it is usual to lay duck eggs under a hen because she hatches them better than the original parent would have done and guards them with greater assiduity.

THE WILD DUCK

The Wild Duck differs, in many respects, from the tame; and in them there is still greater variety than among the domestic kinds. Of the tame duck there are not less than ten different sorts; and of the wild, above twenty. The most obvious distinction between wild and tame ducks is in the colour of their feet; those of the tame duck being black; those of the wild duck yellow. The difference between wild ducks among each other, arises as well from their size as the nature of the place they feed in. Sea-ducks, which feed in the salt-water, and dive much, have a broad bill, bending upwards, a large hind toe, and a long blunt tail. Pond-ducks, which feed in plashes, have a straight and narrow bill, a small hind toe, and a sharp pointed train. The former are called, by our decoy-men, foreign ducks; the latter are supposed to be natives of England. In this tribe, we may rank, as natives of our own European dominions, the Eider Duck, which is double the size of a common duck, with a black bill; the Velvet Duck, not so large, and with a yellow bill; the Scoter, with a knob at the base of a yellow bill; the Tufted Duck, adorned with a thick crest; the Scaup Duck, less than the common duck, with the bill of a greyish blue colour; the

Golden Eye, with a large white spot at the corners of the mouth, resembling an eye; the Sheldrake, with the bill of a bright red, and swelling into a knob; the Mallard, which is the stock from whence our tame breed has probably been produced; the Pintail, with the two middle feathers of the tail three inches longer than the rest; the Pochard, with the head and neck of a bright bay; the Widgeon, with a lead-coloured bill, and the plumage of the back marked with narrow black and white undulated lines, but best known by its whistling sound: lastly, the Teal, which is the smallest of this kind, with the bill black, the head and upper part of the neck of a bright bay.

All these live in the manner of our domestic ducks, keeping together in flocks in the winter, and flying in pairs in summer, bringing up their young by the water-side, and leading them to their food as soon as out of the shell. Their nests are usually built among heath or rushes, nor far from the water; and they lay twelve, fourteen, or more eggs before they sit: yet this is not always their method; the dangers they continually encounter from their ground situation, sometimes oblige them to change their manner of building; and their awkward nests are often seen exalted on the tops of trees. This must be a very great labour to perform, as the duck's bill is but ill-formed for building a nest, and giving the materials of which it is composed a sufficient stability to stand the weather. The nest, whether high or low, is generally composed of particular materials. The longest grass, mixed with heath, and lined within with the bird's own feathers, usually go to the composition: however, in proportion as the climate is colder, the nest is more artificially made, and more warmly lined. In the Arctic regions, nothing can exceed the great care all of this kind take to protect their eggs from the intenseness of the weather. While the gull and the penguin kind seem to disregard the severest cold, the duck, in those regions, forms itself a hole to lay in, shelters the approach, lines it with a layer of long grass and clay, within that another of moss, and lastly, a warm coat of feathers or down.

The eider duck of Iceland is particularly remarkable for the warmth of its nest. This bird, which, as was said, is above twice as large as the common duck, and resides in the colder climates, lays from six to eight eggs, making her nest among the rocks or the plants along the sea-shore. The external materials of the nest are such as are in common with the rest of the kind; but the inside lining, on which the eggs are immediately deposited, is at once the softest, warmest, and the lightest substance with which we are acquainted. This is no other that the inside down which covers the breast of the bird in the breeding-season. This the female plucks off with her bill, and furnishes the inside of her nest with a tapestry more valuable than the most skilful artists can produce. The natives watch the place where she begins to build, and, suffering her to lay, take away both the eggs and the nest. The duck, however, not discouraged by the first disappointment, builds and lays in the same place a second time; and this they in the same manner take away: the third time she builds, but the drake must supply the down from his breast to line the nest with: and, if this be robbed, they both forsake the place, and breed there no more. This down the natives take care to separate from the dirt and moss with which it is mixed; and, though no people stand in more need of a warm covering than themselves, yet their necessities compel them to sell it to the more indolent and luxurious inhabitants of the south for brandy and tobacco.

As they possess the faculties of flying and swimming, so they are in general birds of passage, and it is most probable perform their journeys across the ocean as well on the water as in the air. Those that migrate to this country, on the approach of winter, are seldom found so well tasted or so fat as the fowls that continue with us the year round: their flesh is often lean, and still oftener fishy; which flavour it has probably contracted in the journey, as their food in the lakes of Lapland, from whence they descend, is generally of the insect kind.

MANDARIN *Anas galericulata*

As soon as they arrive among us, they are generally seen flying in flocks to make a survey of those lakes where they intend to take up their residence for the winter. In the choice of these they have two objects in view; to be near their food, and yet remote from interruption. Their chief aim is to choose some lake in the neighbourhood of a marsh where there is at the same time cover, foods and where insects are found in greatest abundance. Lakes, therefore, with a marsh on one side and a wood on the other, are seldom without vast quantities of wild fowl; and where a couple are seen at any time, that is a sufficient inducement to bring hundreds of others. The ducks flying in the air are often lured down from their heights by the loud voice of the mallard from below. Nature seems to have furnished this bird with very particular faculties for calling. The wind pipe, where it begins to enter the lungs, opens into a kind of bony cavity, where the sound is reflected as in a musical instrument, and is heard a great way off. To this call all the stragglers resort; and in a week or a fortnight's time, a lake that before as quite naked is black with water-fowl, that have left their Lapland retreats to keep company with our ducks who never stirred from home.

They generally choose that part of the lake where they are inaccessible to the aproach of the fowler, in which they all appear huddled together, extremely busy and very loud. What it is that can employ them all the day is not easy to guess. There is no food for them at the place where they sit and cabal thus, as they choose the middle of the lake; and as for courtship, the season for that is not yet come; so that it is wonderful what can so busly keep them occupied. Not one of them seems a moment at rest. Now pursuing one another, now screaming, then all up at

once, then down again; the whole seems one strange scene of bustle with nothing to do.

They frequently go off on a more private manner by night to feed in the adjacent meadows and ditches, which they dare not venture to approach by day. In these nocturnal adventures they are often taken; for, though a timorous bird, yet they are easily deceived, and every springe seems to succeed in taking them. But the greatest quantities are taken in decoys; which, though well known near London, are yet untried in the remoter parts of the country.

WADING BIRDS

I will group into one general category of sea-birds those that are the more eminent or the most whimsical, which will naturally stand forward on the canvas.

In this group we find an extensive tribe of native birds with their varieties and affinities. In this list is exhibited the Curlew, a bird about the size of a duck with a bill about four inches long; The Godwit, about the size of a pigeon, the bill four inches: the Greenshank, longer legged: the Redshank, differing in the colour of its feet from the former: the Snipe, with a bill three inches.

Then with shorter bills; The Ruff, with a collar of feathers round the neck of the male; the Knot, the Sandpiper, the Sanderling, the Dunlin, and the Stint. To conclude; with bills very short, The Lapwing, the Green Plover, the Grey Plover, the Dottrel, the Turnstone and the Sea Lark. These, with their affinities, are properly natives or visitants of Britain; and are dispersed along our shores, rivers and watery grounds.

All these birds possess many marks in common; though some have peculiarities that deserve regard. All these birds are bare of feathers above the knee, or above the heel as some naturalists choose to express it. The nudity in that part, is partly natural, and partly produced by all birds of this kind habitually wading in water. The older the bird, the barer are its thighs; yet even then the young ones have not the same downy covering reaching so low as the birds of any other class. Such a covering there would rather be prejudicial, as being continually liable to get wet in the water.

As these birds are usually employed rather in running than in flying, and as their food lies entirely upon the ground, and not on trees, or in the air, so they run with great swiftness for their size, and the length of their legs assists their velocity. But as, in seeking their food, they are often obliged to change their station; so also are they equally swift of wing, and traverse immense tracts of country without much fatigue.

It has been thought by some, that a part of this class lived upon an oily slime, found in the bottoms of ditches and of weedy pools. But later discoveries have shown that, in these places, they hunt for caterpillars and worms. From hence, therefore, we may generally assert that all birds of this class live upon animals of one kind or another. The long billed birds suck up worms and insects from the bottom; those furnished with shorter bills, pick up such insects as lie nearer the surface of the meadow, or among the sands on the seashore.

Thus the curlew and the snipe, are ever seen in plashy brakes, and under covered hedges, assiduously employed in seeking out insects in their worm state; and it seems, from their fatness, that they find a plentiful supply. Nature, indeed, has furnished them with very convenient instruments for procuring their food. Their bills are made sufficiently long for searching; but still more, they are endowed with an exquisite sensibility at the point, for feeling their provision. They are furnished with no less than three pair of nerves, equal almost to the optic nerves in thickness; which pass from the roof of the mouth, and run along the upper bill to the point.

Nor are those birds with shorter bills, and destitute of such convenient instruments, without a proper provision made for their subsistence. The lapwing, the sandpiper, and the redshank, run with surprising rapidity along the surface of the marsh, or the seashore, quarter their ground with great dexterity, and leave nothing of the insect kind that happens to lie on the surface. These, however, are neither so fat nor so delicate as the former; as they are obliged to toil more for a subsistence, they are easily satisfied with whatever offers; and their flesh often contracts a flavour from what has been their latest, or their principal, food.

Most of the birds formerly described, have stated seasons for feeding and rest. These birds, seem at all hours employed: they are seldom at rest by day; and during the whole night season, every meadow and marsh resounds with their different calls, to courtship or to food.

As all of this kind live entirely in waters, and among watery places, they seem provided by Nature with a warmth of constitution to fit them for that cold element. They reside, by choice, in the coldest climates; and as other birds migrate here in our summer, their migrations hither are mostly in the winter. Even those that reside among us the whole season, retire in summer to the tops of our bleakest mountains; where they breed, and bring down their young, when the cold weather sets in.

Most of them, however, migrate, and retire to the polar regions; as those that remain behind in the mountains, and keep with us during summer, bear no proportion to the quantity which in winter haunt our marshes and low grounds.

In general, during summer, this whole class either choose the coldest countries to retire to, or the coldest and the moistest part of ours to breed in. The curlew, the snipe, the godwit, the grey plover, the green, and the long legged plover, the knot and the turnstone, are rather the guests than the natives of this island. They visit us in the beginning of winter, and forsake us in the spring. They then retire to the mountains of Sweden, Poland, Prussia, and Lapland, to breed. Our country, during the summer season, becomes uninhabitable to them. The ground parched up by the heat; the springs dried away, and the vermicular insects already upon the wing; they have no means of subsisting. Their weak and delicately pointed bills are unfit to dig into a resisting soil; and their prey is departed, though they were able to reach its retreats. Thus that season when Nature is said to teem with life, and to put on her gayest liveries, is to them an interval of sterility and famine.

Such are our visitants. With regard to those which keep with us continually, and breed here, they are neither so delicate in their food, nor perhaps so warm in their constitutions. The lapwing, the ruff, the redshank, the sandpiper, the Norfolk plover, and the sea lark, breed in this country and, for the most part, reside here. In summer they frequent such marshes as are not dried up in any part of the year; the Essex hundreds, and the fens of Lincolnshire. There, in solitudes formed by surrounding marshes, they breed and bring up their young. In winter they come down from their retreats, rendered uninhabitable by the flooding of the waters; and seek their food about our ditches and marshy meadow-grounds. Yet even of this class, all are wanderers upon some occasions; and take wing to the northern climates, to breed and find subsistence. This happens when the fenny countries are not sufficiently watered to defend their retreats.

In nestling, and, bringing up their young, one method takes place universally. As they all run and

The place these birds chiefly choose to breed in, is in some island surrounded with sedgy moors, where men seldom resort; and in such situations I have often seen the ground so strewed with eggs and nests, that one could scarce take a step, without treading upon some of them. As soon as a stranger intrudes upon these retreats, the whole colony is up, and a hundred different screams are heard from every quarter. The arts of the lapwing to allure men or dogs from her nest, are perfectly amusing. When she perceives the enemy approaching, she never waits till they arrive at her nest, but as near them as she dares to venture, she then rises with a loud screaming before them, seeming as if she were just flushed from hatching; while she is then probably a hundred yards from the nest. Thus she flies, with great clamour and anxiety, whining and screaming round the invaders, striking at them with her wings, and fluttering as if she were wounded. To add to the deceit, she appears still more clamorous, as more remote from the nest. If she sees them very near, she then seems to be quite unconcerned, and her cries cease, while her terrors are really augmenting. If there be dogs, she flies heavily at a little distance before them, as if maimed, still vocifer-

ous and still bold, but never offering to move towards the quarter where her treasure is deposited.

As the young of this class are soon hatched, so, when excluded, they quickly arrive at maturity. They run about after the mother as soon as they leave the egg. They come to their adult state long before winter; and then flock together, till the breeding season returns, which for a while dissolves their society.

As the flesh of almost all these birds is in high estimation, so many methods have been contrived for taking them. That used in taking the ruff, seems to be the most advantageous; and it may not be amiss to describe it. The ruff, which is the name of the male, the reeve that of the female, is taken in nets about forty yards long, and seven or eight feet high. The nets in which these are taken, are supported by sticks, at an angle of near forty-five degrees, and placed either on dry ground, or in very shallow water, not remote from reeds: among these the fowler conceals himself, till the birds, enticed by a stale or stuffed bird, come under the nets: he then, by pulling a

1 BLACK-HEADED GULL *Larus ridibundus*
2 BLACK SKIMMER *Rhynchops nigra*

feed upon the ground, so they are all found to nestle there. The number of eggs generally to be seen in every nest, is from two to four; never under, and very seldom exceeding. The nest is made without any art; but the eggs are either laid in some little depression of the earth, or on a few bents and long grass, that scarcely preserve them from the moisture below. Yet such is the heat of the body of these birds, that their time of incubation is shorter than with any others of the same size.

In their seasons of courtship, they pair as other birds; but not without violent contests between the males, for the choice of the female. The lapwing and the plover are often seen to fight among themselves; but there is one little bird of this tribe, called the ruff, that has got the epithet of the fighter, merely from its great perseverance and animosity on these occasions. In the beginning of spring, when these birds arrive among our marshes, they are observed to engage with desperate fury against each other; it is then that the fowlers, seeing them intent on mutual destruction, spread their nets over them, and take them in great numbers.

string, lets them fall, and they are taken; as are godwits, knots and grey plover, also in the same manner. When these birds are brought from under the net, they are not killed immediately, but fattened for the table, with bread and milk, hemp-feed, and sometimes boiled wheat; but if expedition be wanted, sugar is added, which will make them a lump of fat in a fortnight's time.

THE KINGFISHER

The Kingfisher is rather larger than a swallow; its shape is clumsy; the legs disproportionately small, and the bill disproportionately long; it is two inches from the base to the tip; the upper beak black and the lower yellow; but the colours of this bird atone for its inelegant form; the crown of the head and the coverts of the wings are of a deep blackish green, spotted with bright azure; the back and tail are of the most resplendent azure; the whole under-side of the body is orange-coloured; a broad mark of the same passes from the bill beyond the eyes; beyond that is a large white spot: the tail is short, and consists of twelve feathers of a rich deep blue; the feet are of a reddish yellow, and the three joints of the outmost toe adhere to the middle toe, while the inner toe adheres only by one.

From the small size, the slender short legs, and the beautiful colours of this bird, no person would be led to suppose it one of the most rapacious little animals that skims the deep. Yet it is for ever on the wing, and feeds on fish, which it takes in surprising quantities, when we consider its size and figure. It chiefly frequents the banks of rivers, and takes its prey balancing itself at a certain distance above the water for a considerable space, then darting into the deep, and seizing the fish with inevitable certainty. While it remains suspended in the air, in a bright day, the plumage exhibits a beautiful variety of the most dazzling and brilliant colours.

The kingfisher is contented to make its nest on the banks of rivers, in such situations as not to be affected by the rising of the stream. When it has found a place for its purpose, it hollows out with its bill a hole about a yard deep; or if it finds the deserted hole of a rat, or one caused by the root of a tree decaying, it takes quiet possession. This hole it enlarges at the bottom to a good size; and, lining it with the down of the willow, lays its eggs there without any further preparation.

In these holes, which, from the remains of fish brought there, are very foetid, the kingfisher is often found with from five eggs to nine. There the female continues to hatch even though disturbed; and though the nest be robbed, she will again return and lay there.

As the ancients have had their fables concerning this bird, so have the modern vulgar. It is an opinion generally received among them that the flesh of the kingfisher will not corrupt, and that it will even banish all vermin. This has no better foundation than that which is said of its always pointing, when hung up dead, with its breast to the north. The only truth which can be affirmed of this bird when killed, is that its flesh is utterly unfit to be eaten; while its beautiful plumage preserves its lustre longer than that of any other bird we know.

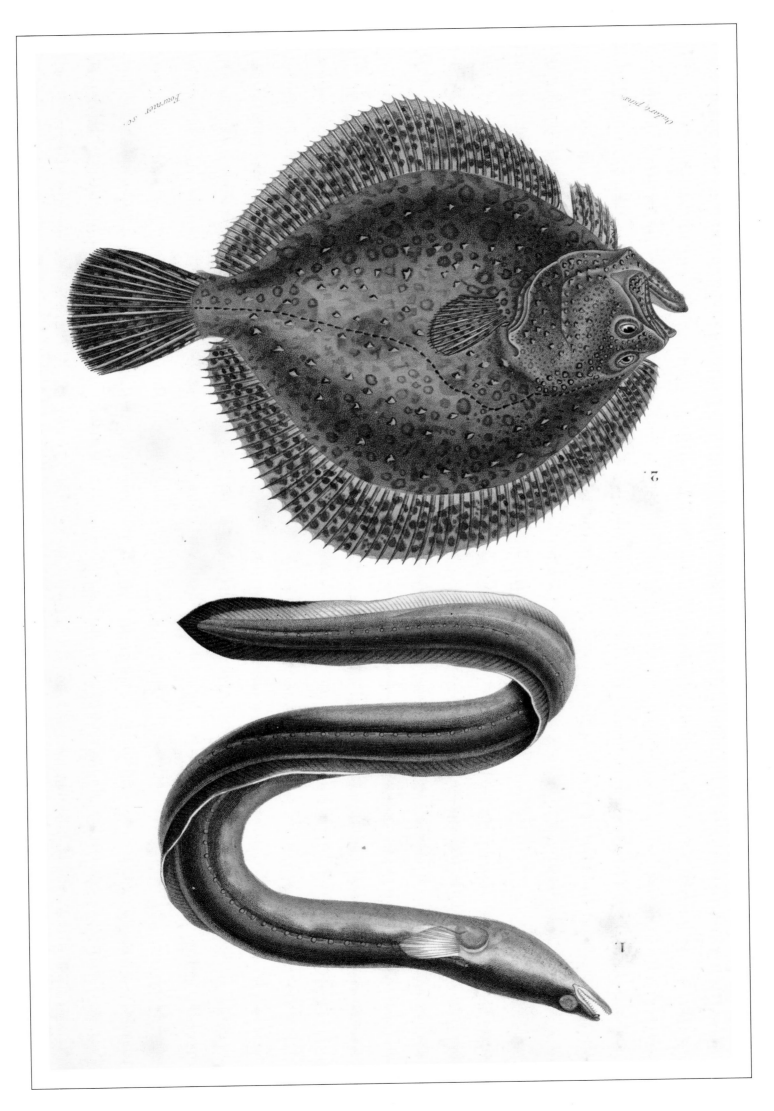

BOOK III

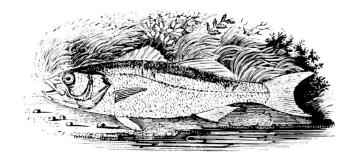

FISH

CETACEOUS FISH

THE WHALE

The northern seas were once the region to which the greatest of these animals resorted; but so great has been the slaughter of whales for more than two ages, that they begin to grow thinner every day; and those that are found there, seem, from their size, not come to their full dimensions. The greatest whales resort to places where they have the least disturbance; to those seas that are on the opposite side of the globe, near the South Pole. In that part of the world, there are still to be seen whales that are above a hundred and sixty feet long; and perhaps even longer might be found in those latitudes near the South Pole, to which we have as not yet ventured.

Taking the whale, however, at the ordinary size of eighty feet long and twenty feet high, what an enormous animated mass must it appear to the spectator! With what amazement must it strike him, to behold so great a creature gambolling in the deep, with the ease and agility of the smallest animal, and making its way with incredible swiftness! These large animals are obliged to show themselves in order to take breath; but who knows the size of those that are fitted to remain for ever under water; and that have been increasing in magnitude for centuries? To believe all that has been said of the sea-serpent, or the Kraken, would be credulity; to reject the possibility of their existence, would be presumption.

The Whale is the largest animal of which we have certain information. There are no less than seven different kinds; all distinguished from each other by their external figure, or internal conformation. The

1 EEL *Anguilla europea*

2 TURBOT *Passer maximus*

Great Greenland Whale, without a back-fin, and black on the back; the Iceland Whale, without a back-fin, and whitish on the back; the New England Whale, with a hump on the back; the Whale with six humps on the back; the Fin-fish, with a fin on the back near the tail; the Pike-headed Whale, and the Round-lipped Whale. All these differ from each other in figure, as their names obviously imply. The history of all of them may be comprised under that of the Great Common Greenland Whale, with which we are best acquainted.

It is a large heavy animal, and the head alone makes a third of its bulk. It is usually found from sixty to seventy feet long. The fins on each side are from five to eight feet, composed of bones and muscles and sufficiently strong to give the great mass of body which they move, speed and activity. The tail, which lies flat on the water, is about twenty-four feet broad,

and, when the fish lies on one side, its blow is tremendous. The skin is smooth and black, and, in some places, marbled with white and yellow; which, running over the surface, has a very beautiful effect. This marbling is particularly observable in the fins and the tail. In the figures which are thus drawn by Nature, fancy often forms the pictures of trees, landscapes and houses.

The whale makes use only of the tail to advance itself forward in the water. This serves as a great oar to push its mass along; and it is surprising to see with

what force and celerity its enormous bulk cuts through the ocean.

The outward or scarf skin of the whale is no thicker than parchment; but this removed, the real skin appears, of about an inch thick, and covering the fat or blubber that lies beneath: this is from eight to twelve inches in thickness; and is, when the fish is in health, of a beautiful yellow. The muscles lie beneath; and these, like the flesh of quadrupeds, are very red and tough.

The cleft of the mouth is above twenty feet long, which is near one third of the animal's whole length; and the upper jaw is furnished with barbs, that lie, like the pipes of an organ, the greatest in the middle, and the smallest to the sides. The tongue is almost immovably fixed to the lower jaw, seeming one great lump of fat. The eyes are not larger than those of an ox and are placed towards the back of the head, being the most convenient situation for enabling them to see both before and behind; as also to see over them, where their food is principally found. They are guarded by eyelids and eyelashes, as in quadrupeds; they seem to be very sharp-sighted.

Nor is their sense of hearing in less perfection; for they are warned, at great distances, of any danger preparing against them. It would seem as if Nature had designedly given them these advantages, as they multiply little, in order to continue their kind.

The whale has two spout holes or nostrils, one on each side of the head before the eyes, and crooked, somewhat like the holes on the belly of a violin. From these holes this animal blows the water very fiercely, and with such a noise that it roars like a hollow wind, and may be heard at three miles distance. When

RIGHT WHALE *Balaena mysticetus*

wounded, it then blows more fiercely than ever, so that it sounds like the roaring of the sea in a great storm.

As these animals resemble quadrupeds in confomation, so they bear a strong resemblance in some of their appetites and manners, The female joins with the male, as is asserted, *more humano*, and once in two years feels the accesses of desire.

The whale goes with young nine or ten months, and is then fatter than usual, particularly when near the time of bringing forth. It is said that the embryo, when first perceptible, is about seventeen inches long, and white; but the cub, when excluded, is black, and about ten feet long. She generally produces one young one, and never above two. When she suckles her young, she throws herself on one side on the surface of the sea, and the young one attaches itself to the teat. The breasts are two; generally hid within the belly; but she can produce them at pleasure so as to stand forward a foot and a half, or two feet; and the teats are like those of a cow. The breasts are white; in others, speckled.

The young ones continue at the breast for a year; during which time, they are called by the sailors, *short heads*. They are then extremely fat, and yield above fifty barrels of blubber. The mother, at the same time, is equally lean and emaciated. At the age of two years they are called *stunts*, as they do not thrive much immediately after quitting the breast: they then yield scarce above twenty, or twenty-four, barrels of blubber: from that time forward they are called *skull-fish*, and their age is wholly unknown.

RORQUAL *Balanoptera rorqual*

THE NARWHAL

The Narwhal or Sea-unicorn is not so large as the whale, not being above sixty feet long. Its body is slenderer than that of the whale, and its fat not in so great abundance. But this great animal is sufficiently distinguished from all others of the deep by its tooth or teeth, which stand pointing directly forward from the upper jaw, and are from nine to fourteen feet long. This terrible weapon is generally found single; and some are of opinion that the animal is furnished but with one by Nature.

Yet, notwithstanding all these appointments for combat, these long and pointed tusks, amazing strength, and unmatchable celerity, the narwhal is one of the most harmless and peaceful inhabitants of

the ocean. It is seen constantly and inoffensively sporting among the other great monsters of the deep, no way attempting to injure them, but pleased in their company.

The tooth of the narwhal was once ascribed to a very different animal from that which really bore it. Among other fossil substances they were sometimes dug up and were thought to be the horns of unicorns, an animal resembling a horse, and with one straight horn darting forward from the middle of its forehead.

These teeth were, therefore, considered as a strong testimony in favour of that historian's veracity, and were shown among the most precious remains of antiquity. Even for some time after the narwhal was known, the deceit was continued, as those who were possessed of a tooth sold it to great advantage. But at present they are too well known to deceive any, and are only shown for what they really are; their curiosity increasing in proportion to their weight and their size.

THE CACHALOT

There are no less than seven distinctions among whales, so also there are the same number of distinctions in the tribe we are describing. The Cachalot with two fins and a black back; the cachalot with two fins and a whitish back; that with a spout in the neck; that with the spout in the snout; that with three fins and sharp pointed teeth; that with three fins and sharp edged teeth; and lastly, the cachalot with three fins and slatted teeth.

This tribe is not of such enormous size as the whale, properly so called, not being above sixty feet long and sixteen feet high. In consequence of their being more slender, they are much more active than the common whale; they remain a longer time at the bottom; and afford a smaller quantity of oil.

The cachalot is the most sought after by man, as it contains two very precious drugs, spermateci and ambergris. The use of these, either for the purposes of luxury or medicine, is so universal, that the capture of this animal, that alone supplies them, turns

out to very great advantage, particularly since the art has been found out of converting all the oil of this animal into that substance called spermaceti.

This is performed by boiling it with potash, and hardening it in the manner of soap. Candles are now made of it, which are substituted for wax, and sold much cheaper.

As to the ambergris which is sometimes found in this whale, it was long considered as a substance found floating on the surface of the sea; however the ambergris is found in the place where the seminal vessels are usually situated in other animals. It is found in a bag of three or four feet long, in round lumps, from one to twenty pounds weight, floating in a fluid rather thinner than oil, and of a yellowish colour. These balls of ambergris are not found in all fishes of this kind, but chiefly in the oldest and the strongest. The uses of this medicine for the purposes of luxury and as a perfume are well known; though upon some subjects ignorance is preferable to information!

THE DOLPHIN

What could induce the ancients to a predilection in favour of the Dolphin, is not easy to account for. Historians and philosophers seem to have contended who should invent the greatest number of fables concerning them. The dolphin was celebrated in the earliest time for its fondness to the human race, and was distinguished by the epithets of the boy-

DOLPHIN *Delphinius delphis*

loving and philanthropist. Scarce an accident could happen at sea but the dolphin offered himself to convey the unfortunate to shore. The musician flung into the sea by pirates, the boy taking an airing into the midst of the sea, and returning again in safety, were obliged to the dolphin for its services. The figure of these animals is far from prejudicing us in their favour; their extreme rapacity tends still less to endear them. These fishes are regarded even by the vulgar in a very different light; their boundings, springs, and frolics in the water have taught the mariners to prepare for a storm.

THE PORPOISE

The Porpoise is found in vast numbers in all parts of the sea that surrounds this kingdom. They are sometimes noxious to seamen, when they sail in small vessels. In some places they almost darken the water as they rise to take breath, and particularly before bad weather are much agitated, swimming against the wind, and tumbling about with unusual violence.

Whether these motions be the gambols of pleasure, or the agitations of terror, is not well known. It is most probable that they dread those seasons of turbulence, when the lesser fishes shrink to the bottom, and their prey no longer offers in sufficient abundance. In times of fairer weather, they are seen herding together, and pursuing shoals of various fish with great impetuosity.

We have often seen them taken in the Thames at London, both above the bridges and below them. It is curious enough to observe with what activity they

avoid their pursuers, and what little time they require to fetch breath above the water.

The inhabitants of Norway prepare from the eggs found in the body of this fish, a kind of caviar, which is said to be very delicate sauce, or good when even eaten with bread. There is a fishery for porpoises along the western isles of Scotland during the summer season, when they abound on that shore; and this branch of industry turns to good advantage.

CARTILAGINOUS FISH

THE SHARK

As the Shark is formidable in his appearance, so is he also dreadful, from his courage and activity. No fish can swim as fast as he; none so constantly employed in swimming, he outstrips the swiftest ships, plays round them, darts out before them, returns, seems to gaze at the passengers, and all the while does not seem to exhibit the smallest symptom of an effort to proceed. Such amazing powers, with such great appetites for destruction, would quickly unpeople even the ocean, but providentially the shark's upper jaw projects so far above the lower, that he is obliged to turn on one side (not on his back, as is generally supposed) to seize his prey. As this takes some small time to perform, the animal pursued seizes that opportunity to make its escape.

Still, however, the depredations he commits are frequent and formidable. The shark is the dread of

sailors in all hot climates; where, like a greedy robber, he attends the ships, in expectation of what may drop over board. A man who unfortunately falls into the sea at such a time, is sure to perish, without mercy. A sailor that was bathing in the Mediterra-

nean, near Antibes, in the year 1744, while he was swimming about fifty yards from the ship, perceived a monstrous fish making towards him, and surveying him on every side, as fish are often seen to look round a bait. The poor man, struck with terror at its approach, cried out to his companions in the vessel to take him on board. They accordingly threw him a rope with the utmost expedition, and were drawing him up by the ship's side, when the shark darted after him from the deep, and snapped off his leg.

Such is the frightful rapacity of this animal; nothing that has life is rejected. But it seems to have a peculiar enmity to man: when once it has tasted human flesh, it never desists from haunting those places where it expects the return of its prey. It is even asserted, that along the coasts of Africa, where these animals are found in great abundance, numbers of the natives, who are obliged to frequent the waters, are seized and devoured by them every year. The people of these coasts are firmly of the opinion, that the shark loves the black man's flesh in preference to the white; and that when men of different colours are in the water together, it always makes a choice of the former.

THE RAY

The flat fish creep in security along the bottom of the sea and seize everything that comes in their way; neither the hardest shells nor the sharpest spines give protection to the animals that bear them; their

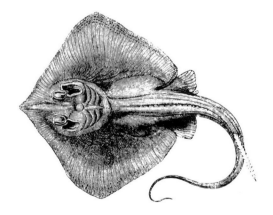

insatiable hunger is such, that they devour all; and the force of their stomach is so great, that it easily digests them.

All fish of the Ray kind are broad, cartilaginous, swimming flat on the water, and having spines on different parts of their body, or at the tail. They all have their eyes and mouth placed quite under the body, with apertures for breathing either about or near them. They all have teeth, or a rough bone, which answers the same purpose. Their bowels are very wide towards the mouth, and go on diminishing to the tail. The tail is very differently shaped from that of other fishes; and at first sight more resembling that of a quadruped, being narrow, and ending either in a bunch or a point. But what they are chiefly distinguished by is their spines or prickles, which the different species have on different parts of their body.

The ray generally chooses for its retreat such parts of the sea as have a black muddy bottom; the large ones keep at greater depths; but the smaller approach the shores, and feed upon whatever living animals they can surprise, or whatever putrid substances they meet with. As they are ravenous, they easily take the bait, yet will not touch it if it be taken up and kept a day or two out of water.

The Rough Ray inflicts but slight wounds with the prickles with which its whole body is furnished. To the ignorant it seems harmless, and a man would at first sight venture to take it in his hand, without any apprehensions; but he soon finds, that there is not a single part of its body that is not armed with spines; and that there is no way of seizing the animal, but by the little fin at the end of the tail.

THE TORPEDO

The body of this fish is almost circular, and thicker than others of the ray kind; the skin is soft, smooth, and of a yellowish colour, marked, as all the kind, with large annular spots; the eyes very small, the tail tapering to a point; and the weight of the fish from a quarter to fifteen pounds. To all outward appearance, it is furnished with no extraordinary powers; it has no muscles formed for particularly great exertions; no internal conformation perceptibly differing from the rest of its kind: yet such is that unaccountable power it possesses, that, the instant it is touched, it numbs not only the hand and arm, but sometimes also the whole body. The shock received, by all accounts, most resembles the stroke of an electrical machine, sudden, tingling, and painful. It is said that to avoid the shock, the whole secret is to keep in the breath. Upon trial this method answered. When the breath was held in, the torpedo was harmless, but with only a slight breath the shock was again felt.

THE LAMPREY

The Lamprey much resembles an eel in its general appearance, but is of a lighter colour; and rather a clumsier make. It differs however in the mouth, which is round, and placed rather obliquely below the end of the nose. The animal has a hole on the top of the head through which it spouts water. There are seven holes on each side for respiration; and the fins are formed rather by a lengthening out of the skin, than any set of bones or spines for that purpose. As the mouth is formed resembling that of a leech, so it has a property resembling that animal of sticking close to and sucking any body it is applied to. It is extraordinary the power they have of adhering to stones; which they do so firmly as not to be drawn off without some difficulty. We are told of one that

weighed but three pound; and yet it stuck so firmly to a stone of twelve pounds, that it remained suspended at its mouth, from which it was separated with no small difficulty.

From some peculiarity of formation, this animal swims generally with its body as near as possible to the surface; and it might easily be drowned by being kept by force for any time under water. I am very apt to suspect, that two red glands tissued with nerves, lying towards the back of the head, are no other than the lungs of this animal. The absolute necessity it is under of breathing in the air, convinces me that it must have lungs, though I do not know of any anatomist that has described them.

One story we are told of this fish with which I will conclude its history. A senator of Rome was famous for the delicacy of his lampreys. All the celebrated epicures of Rome were loud in his praises: no man's fish had such a flavour, was so nicely fed, or so exactly pickled. Augustus, hearing so much of this man's entertainments, desired to be his guest; and soon found that fame had been just to his merits; the man had indeed very fine lampreys, and of an exquisite flavour. The emperor was desirous of knowing the method by which he fed his fish to so fine a relish; and the glutton, making no secret of his art, informed him that his way was to throw into his ponds such of his slaves as had at any time displeased him. Augustus, we are told, was not much pleased with his recipe; and instantly ordered all his ponds to be filled up. The story would have ended better if he had ordered the owner to be flung in also.

THE STURGEON

The Sturgeon, with a form as terrible and a body as large as a shark, is harmless, incapable and unwilling to injure others. It flies from the smallest fishes, and generally falls a victim to its own timidity.

The sturgeon in its general form resembles a freshwater pike. The nose is long; the mouth is situated beneath, being small, and without jaw-bones or teeth. But, though it is so harmless and ill provided for war, the body is formidable enough in appearance. It is long, pentagonal, and covered with five rows of large bony knobs, one row on the back and two on each side, and a number of fins to give it greater expedition. Of this fish there are three kinds; the Common Sturgeon, the Caviar Sturgeon, and the Huso or Isinglass fish. The first is the sturgeon, the flesh of which is sent pickled into all parts of Europe. The second is the fish from the roe of which that noted delicacy called caviar is made; and the third, besides supplying the caviar, furnishes also the valuable commodity of isinglass. They all grow to a very great size, and some of them have been found about eighteen feet long.

The sturgeon is never caught by a bait in the ordinary manner of fishing, but always in nets. From the description given above of its mouth, it is not to be supposed that the sturgeon would swallow any hook capable of holding so large a bulk and so strong a swimmer. In fact, it never attempts to seize any of the finny tribe, but lives by rooting at the bottom of the sea, where it makes insects and sea-plants its

whole subsistence. That it lives upon no large animals is obvious to all those who cut it open, where nothing is found in its stomach but a kind of slimy substance, which has induced some to think it lives only upon water and air. From hence there is a German proverb, which is applied to a man extremely temperate, when they say he is as moderate as a sturgeon.

A very great trade is carried on with the roe of the sturgeon, preserved in a particular manner, and called Caviar. This is much more in request in other countries of Europe than with us. Though formerly even in England it was very much in request at the politest tables, it is at present sunk entirely into disuse. It is still, however, a considerable merchandise among the Turks, Greeks, and Venetians. Caviar somewhat resembles soft soap in consistence; but it is

of a brown, uniform colour, and is eaten as cheese with bread.

The Huso or Isinglass Fish furnishes a still more valuable commodity. It is for the commodity it furnishes that it is chiefly taken. Isinglass is of a whitish substance, inclining to yellow, done up into rolls, and so exported for use. It is very well known as serviceable not only in medicine, but many arts. The varnisher, the wine-merchant, and even the clothier know its uses; and very great sums are yearly expended upon this single article of commerce.

This valuable commodity is principally furnished from Russia, where they prepare great quantities surprisingly cheap.

THE SUN FISH

The Sun Fish sometimes grows to a very large size; one taken near Plymouth was five hundredweight. In form it resembles a bream, or some deep fish cut off in the middle: the mouth is very small, and contains in each jaw two broad teeth, with sharp edges: the colour of the back is dusky and dappled, and the belly is of a silvery white. When boiled, it has been observed to turn to a glutinous jelly, and would most probably serve for all the purposes of isinglass, were it found in sufficient plenty.

THE FISHING FROG

The Fishing Frog in shape very much resembles a tadpole or young frog, but then a tadpole of enormous size, for it grows to above five feet long, and its mouth is sometimes a yard wide. Nothing can exceed its deformity. The head is much bigger than the whole body; the under jaw projects beyond the upper, and both are armed with rows of slender, sharp teeth: the palate and the tongue are furnished with teeth in like manner; the eyes are placed on the top of the head, and are encompassed with prickles: immediately above the nose are two long beards or filaments, small in the beginning, but thicker at the end, and round: these, as it is said, answer a very singular purpose; for being made somewhat resembling a fishing-line, it is asserted, that the animal converts them to the purposes of fishing. With these extended, the fishing frog hides in muddy waters, and leaves nothing but the beards to be seen; the curiosity of the smaller fish bring them to view these filaments, and their hunger induces them to seize the bait; upon which the animal in ambush instantly draws in its filaments with the little fish that had taken the bait, and devours it without mercy.

SWIMMING CRAB Lupa pelagica

which are eight, four on either side. Like the lobster, it is a bold voracious animal; and such an enmity do crabs bear each other, that those who carry them for sale to market, often tie their claws with strings to prevent their fighting and maiming themselves by the way. In short, it resembles the lobster in everything but the amazing bulk of its body compared to the size of its head, and the length of its intestines, which have many convolutions.

As the crab, however, is found upon land as well as in the water, the peculiarity of its situation produces a difference in its habitudes, which it is proper to

describe. The Land Crab is found in some of the warmer regions of Europe, and in great abundance in all the tropical climates in Africa and America. They are of various kinds, and endued with various properties, some being healthful, delicious, and nourishing food; others, poisonous or malignant to the last degree; some are not above half an inch broad, others are found a foot or over; some are of a dirty brown, and others beautifully mottled. That animal called the Violet Crab of the Caribbee Islands, is the most noted both for its shape, the delicacy of its flesh, and the singularity of its manners.

THE TORTOISE

All Tortoises, in their external form, pretty much resemble each other; their outward covering being composed of two great shells, the one laid upon the other, and only touching at the edges: however, when we come to look closer, we shall find that the upper shell is composed of no less than thirteen pieces, which are laid flat upon the ribs, like the tiles of a house, by which the shell is kept arched and supported. The shells both above and below that, which seem, to an inattentive observer, to make each but one piece, are bound together at the edges by very strong and hard ligaments, yet with some small share of motion. There are two holes at either edge of this vaulted body; one for a very small head, shoulders and arms, to peep through; the other at the opposite edge, for the feet and the tail. These shells the animal is never disengaged from; and they serve for its defence against every creature but man.

The tortoise has but a small head, with no teeth; having only two bony ridges in the place, serrated and hard. These serve to gather and grind its food; and such is the amazing strength of the jaws, that it is impossible to open them where they once have fastened. The legs, though short, are inconceivably

From Top to Bottom

Left LOBSTER *Homarus vulgaris*

PRAWN *Palemon ornatum*

Right MANTIS SHRIMP *Squilla maculata*

COCONUT CRAB *Birgus latro*

190

strong; and torpid as the tortoise may appear, it has been known to carry five men standing upon its back, with apparent ease and unconcern. Its manner of going forward is by moving its legs one after the other; and the claws with which the toes are furnished sink into the ground like the nails of an iron-shod wheel, and thus assist its progression. Land tortoises, in some parts of India, grow to a very great magnitude; though probably not, as the ancients affirm, big enough for a single shell to serve for the covering of a house.

But if the different kinds of tortoises are not sufficiently distinguished by their figure, they are very obviously distinguishable by their methods of living. The Land Tortoise lives in holes dug in the mountains, or near marshy lakes; the Sea Turtle in

cavities of rocks, and extensive pastures at the bottom of the sea. The tortoise makes use of its feet to walk with, and burrow in the ground; the turtle chiefly uses its feet in swimming, or creeping at the bottom. Its head, the animal can put out and hide at pleasure under the great penthouse of its shell: there it can remain secure from all attacks; there, defended on every side, it can fatigue the patience of the most formidable animal of the forest, that makes use only of natural strength to destroy it. As the tortoise lives wholly upon vegetable food, it never seeks the encounter; yet, if any of the smaller animals attempt to invade its repose, they are sure to suffer. The tortoise, impregnably defended, is furnished with such a strength of jaw, that, though armed only with bony plates instead of teeth, wherever it fastens, it infallibly keeps its hold, until it has taken out the piece.

Though peaceable in itself, it is formed for war in another respect, for it seems almost endued with immortality. Tortoises are commonly known to exceed eighty years old; and there was one kept in the Archbishop of Canterbury's garden, at Lambeth, that was remembered above a hundred and twenty. It was at last killed by the severity of a frost, from which it had not sufficiently defended itself in its winter retreat, which was a heap of sand, at the bottom of the garden.

THE TURTLE

The Turtle as it is now called, is generally found larger than the tortoise. This element is possessed with the property of increasing the magnitude of those animals, which are common to the land and the ocean. It is of different magnitudes, according to its different kinds; some turtles being not above fifty pound weight, and some above eight hundred.

The Great Mediterranean Turtle is the largest of the turtle kind with which we are acquainted. It is found from five to eight feet long, and from six to nine hundred pounds weight. But, unluckily, its utility bears no proportion to its size as it is unfit for food, and sometimes poison to those who eat it. One, most probably of this kind, was caught about thirty years ago near Scarborough, and a good deal of company was invited to feast upon it: a gentleman, who was one of the guests, told the company that it was a mediterranean turtle, and not wholesome; but a person who was willing to satisfy his appetite at the risk of his life, ate of it: he was seized with a violent vomiting and purging; but his constitution overpowered the malignity of the poison.

THE GREEN TURTLE

But of all animals of the tortoise kind, the Green Turtle is the most noted, and the most valuable. The delicacy of its flesh, and its nutritive qualities, together with the property of being easily digested, were, for above a century, known only to our seamen and the inhabitants of the coasts where they were taken. It was not till by slow degrees the distinction came to be made between such as were poisonous and such as were wholesome. The flesh of turtle is become a branch of commerce; and therefore ships are provided with conveniences for supplying them with water and provision, to bring them over in health from Jamaica and other West India islands. This, however, is not always effected; for though they are very vivacious, and scarce require any provision upon the voyage, yet, by the working of the ship and their beating against the sides of the boat that contains them, they become battered and lean; so that to eat this animal in the highest perfection, instead of bringing the turtle to the epicure, he ought to be transported to the turtle.

This animal seldom comes from the sea but to

Right **1** GREEK TORTOISE *Testudo mauritanica*
2 BOX TORTOISE *Cistudo vulgaris*
Left **1** SOFT-SHELLED TORTOISE *Gymnopus spiniferus*
2 GREEN TURTLE *Chelonia mydas*

deposit its eggs, and now and then to sport in fresh water. Its chief food is a submarine plant, that covers the bottom of several parts of the sea not far from the shore. There the turtles are seen, when the weather is fair, feeding in great numbers like flocks of sheep, several fathoms deep upon the verdant carpet below. At other times they go to the mouths of rivers, as they seem to find gratification in fresh water. After some time thus employed, they seek their former stations; and when done feeding, they generally float with their heads above water, unless they are alarmed by the approach of hunters or birds of prey, in which case they suddenly plunge to the bottom. They often seek their provision among the rocks, feeding upon moss and seaweed; and it is probable will not disdain to prey upon insects and other small animals, as they are very fond of flesh when taken and fed for the table.

THE GARDEN SNAIL

We must now see what the Snail has peculiar to itself. The first striking peculiarity is that the animal has got its eyes on the points of its largest horns. When the snail is in motion, four horns are distinctly seen; but the two uppermost and longest deserve peculiar consideration, both on account of the various motions with which they are endued, as well as their having their eyes fixed at the extreme ends of them. These appear like two blackish points at their ends. The eyes the animal can direct to different objects at pleasure, by a regular motion out of the body; and sometimes it hides them, by a very swift contraction into the belly. Under the small horns is the animal's mouth; and though it may appear too soft a substance to be furnished with teeth, yet it has not less than eight of them, with which it devours leaves, and other substances, seemingly harder than itself.

But what is most surprising in the formation of this animal, are the parts that serve for generation. Every snail is at once male and female; and while it impregnates another, is itself impregnated in turn. The vessels supplying the fluid for this purpose, are placed chiefly in the forepart of the neck, and extend themselves over the body; but the male and female organs of generation, are always found united, and growing together.

For some days before coition, the snails gather together, and lie quiet near each other, eating very little in the mean time; but they settle their bodies in such a posture, that the neck and head are placed upright. In the meantime, the apertures on the side of the neck being greatly dilated, two organs, resembling intestines, are seen issuing from them, which some have thought to be the instruments of generation. Beside the protrusion of these, each animal is possessed of another peculiarity; for, from the same aperture, they launch forth a kind of dart at each other, which is pretty hard, barbed, and ending in a very sharp point. They then softly approach still nearer, and apply their bodies one to the other, as closely as the palms and fingers of the hands, when grasped together. At that time the horns are seen variously moving in all directions; and this sometimes for three days together.

At the expiration of eighteen days, the snails produce their eggs, at the opening of the neck, and hide them in the earth with the greatest solicitude and industry. These eggs are in great numbers, round, white, and covered with a soft shell: they are also stuck to each other by an imperceptible slime, like a bunch of grapes, of about the size of a small pea.

Sheltered in a hole from the weather, defended in its shell by a cover, it sleeps during the winter; and, for six or seven months, continues without food or motion, until the genial call of spring breaks its slumber and excites its activity.

THE FRESH WATER SNAIL

The Fresh Water Snail, is peculiarly furnished with a contrivance by Nature for rising to the surface, or sinking to the bottom. The manner in which this is performed is by opening and shutting the orifice on the right side of the neck, which is furnished with muscles for that purpose. By dilating this it rises; by compressing it, the animal sinks to the bottom. In this manner does the fresh water snail dive or swim, by properly managing the air contained in its body.

THE SEA SNAIL

The Sea Snail can sink to the depth of fifteen fathoms. They generally go every morning by break of day to this fatiguing employment, taking the land wind to waft them out to sea, and returning with the sea-breeze at night. The owners of the pearl fishing boats of the Indian Ocean usually hire the divers, and the rest of the boats crew, as we do our labourers, at so much a day. All the oysters are brought on shore, where they are laid in a great heap till the pearl fishery is over, which continues during

the months of November and December. When opportunity serves, they then examine every oyster, and it is accidental whether the capture turns out advantageous. Indeed no human being can wish well to a commerce, which thus chains such a number of fellow creatures to the bottom, to pluck up a glittering mouldering pebble.

All animals of the snail kind, as was observed before, are hermaphrodites; each containing the instruments of generation double. But some of the sea kinds copulate in a different manner from those of the garden. The one impregnates the other; but, from the position of the parts, is incapable of being impregnated by the same in turn. For this reason it is necessary for a third to be admitted as a partner in this operation: so that, while one impregnates that before it, another does the same office by this; which is itself impregnated by a fourth.

But this is not the only difference between land and sea snails. Many of the latter entirely want horns; and none of them have above two. Indeed, if the horns of snails be furnished with eyes, and if, as some are willing to think, the length of the horn, like the tube of a telescope, assists vision, these animals, that chiefly reside in the gloomy bottom of the deep, can have no great occasion for them. Eyes would be unnecessary to creatures whose food is usually concealed in the darkest places; and who, possessed of very little motion, are obliged to grope for what they subsist on.

Those that have seen the shells of sea snails, need not be told that the animal which produces them is larger than those of the same denomination upon land. The sea seems to have the property of enlarging the magnitude of all its inhabitants; and the same proportion that a trout bears to a shark, is often seen to obtain between a shell bred upon the land, and one

Top Left **1** SEA SNAIL *Strombus variabilis*

2 PERUVIAN ROCK SHELL *Concholepas peruvianus*

3 POLYNESIAN DRUPA SHELL *Ricinula digitata*

4 *Monoceros crassilabrum*

5 MARTINI'S TIBIA SHELL *Rostellaria curvirostris*

6 BLUE-STRIPED HELMET SHELL *Cassis undata*

7 INDO-PACIFIC PEACH PURPURID *Purpura persica*

Bottom Left **1 2** *Bulimus mendorensis* **3 4** *Bulimus signatus*

5 6 *Bulimus pudicus* **7 8** *Bulimus pantagruelinus* **9 10** *Bulimus exesus*

11 12 *Pupa chrysalis* Top Right LAND SNAILS **1 2** *Helix epistylium*

3 4 *Helix vittata* **5 6** *Helix sinuata* **7 8** *Helix polychroa*

9 10 *Helix pyramidella* **11 12 13** *Helix listeriana*

14 15 16 *Helix polygirata*

Bottom Right **1** SEA HARE *Aplysia punctata* **2 3** *Sigaretus haliotoideus*

4 5 CARIBBEAN MOON SHELL *Natica canrena* **6 7 8** STRIPED BUBBLE SHELL *Bulla aplustre* **9** MEDITERRANEAN UMBRELLA SHELL *Umbrella mediterranea*

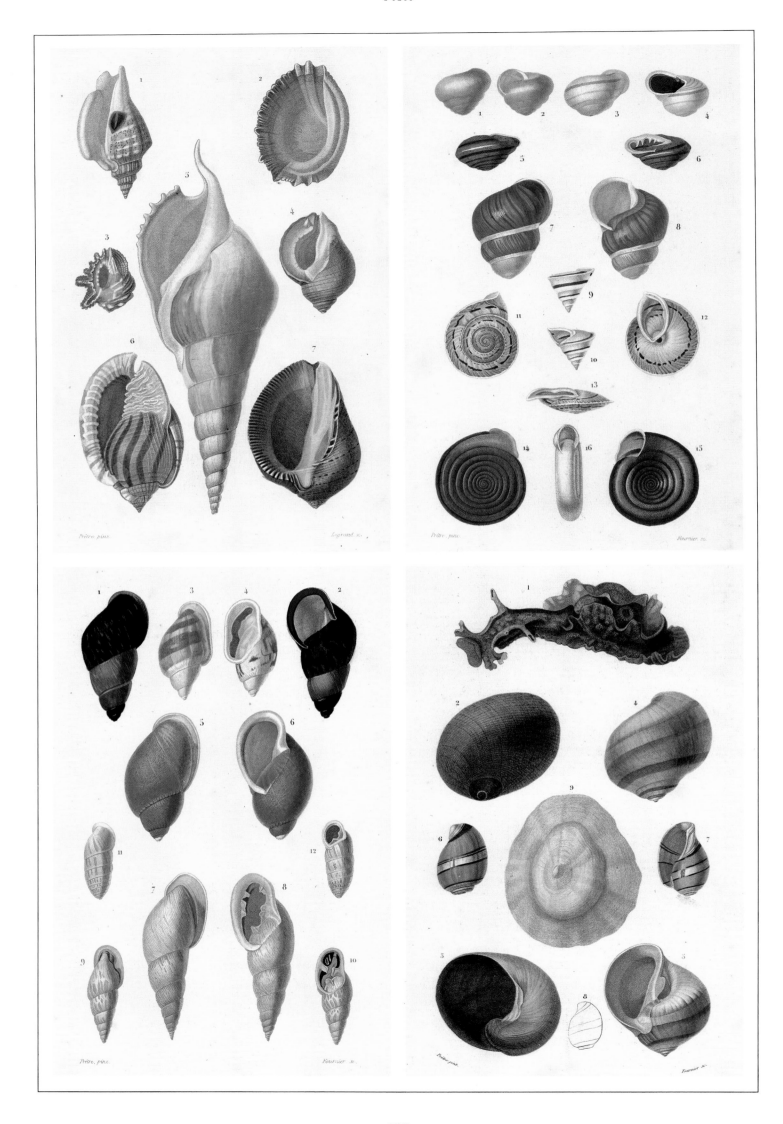

bred in the ocean. Its convolutions are more numerous. The garden snail has but five turns at the most; in the sea snail the convolutions are sometimes seen amounting to ten. Beside this thick shell, many of them are also furnished with a lid, which covers the mouth of the shell, and which opens and shuts at the animal's pleasure. When the creature hunts for food, it opens its box, gropes or swims about; and, when satisfied, drops its lid and sinks to the bottom.

THE NAUTILUS

Of all sea snails, that which is most frequently seen swimming upon the surface, and whose shell is the thinnest and most easily pierced, is the Nautilus. Whether, upon these occasions, it is employed in escaping its numerous enemies at the bottom, or seeking for food at the surface, I will not venture to decide. It seems most probable, that the former is the cause of its frequently appearing; for, upon opening the stomach, it is found to contain chiefly that food which it finds at the bottom. This animal's industry, therefore, may be owing to its fears; and all those arts of sailing, which it has taught mankind, may have been originally the product of necessity. But the nautilus is too famous not to demand a more ample description.

Although there be several species of the nautilus, yet they all may be divided into two: the one with a white shell, as thin as paper, which it often is seen to quit, and again to resume; the other with a thicker shell, sometimes of a beautiful mother-of-pearl colour, and that quits its shell but rarely. This shell outwardly resembles that of a large snail, but is generally six or eight inches across: within, it is divided into forty partitions, that communicate with each other by doors, if I may so call them, through which one could not thrust a goose quill: almost the whole internal part of the shell is filled by the animal; the body of which, like its habitation, is divided into as many parts as there are chambers in its shell: all the parts of its body communicate with each other, through the doors or openings, by a long blood vessel, which runs from the head to the tail: thus the body of the animal, if taken out of the shell, may be likened to a number of soft bits of flesh, of which there are forty, threaded upon a string. From this extraordinary conformation, one would not be apt to suppose that the nautilus sometimes quitted its shell, and returned to it again; yet nothing, though seem-ingly more impossible, is more certain. The manner by which it contrives to disengage every part of its body from so intricate a habitation; by which it makes a substance, to appearance as thick as one's wrist, pass through forty doors, each of which would scarcely admit a goose-quill, is not yet discovered: but the fact is certain; for the animal is often found without its shell; and the shell more frequently destitute of the animal. It is most probable, that it has a power of making the substance of one section of its body remove up into that which is next; and thus, by multiplied removals, it gets free.

But this, though very strange, is not the peculiarity for which the nautilus has been the most distinguished. Its spreading the thin oar, and catching the flying gale, to use the poet's description of it, has chiefly excited human curiosity. These animals, particularly those of the white, light kind, are chiefly found in the Mediterranean; and scarce any who have failed on that sea, but must often have seen them. When the sea is calm, they are observed floating on the surface; some spreading their little sail; some rowing with their feet, as if for life and death; and others still, floating upon their mouths, like a ship with the keel upward.

THE MUSSEL

The Mussel, as is well known, whether belonging to fresh or salt water, consists of two equal shells, joined at the back by a strong muscular ligament that answers all the purposes of a hinge. By the elastic contraction of these, the animal can open its shells at pleasure, about a quarter of an inch from each other. The fish is fixed to either shell by four tendons, by means of which it shuts them close, and keeps its body firm from being crushed by any shock against the walls of its own habitation. It is furnished, like all other animals of this kind, with vital organs, though these are situated in a very extraordinary manner. It has a mouth furnished with two fleshy lips; its intestine begins at the bottom of the mouth, passes through the brain, and makes a number of circumvolutions through the liver; on leaving this organ, it goes on straight into the heart, which it penetrates, and ends in the anus, near which the lungs are placed, and through which it breathes, like those of the snail kind; and in this manner its languid circulation is carried on.

Prêtre pinx.

Fournier sc.

But the organs of generation are what most deserve to excite our curiosity. These consist in each mussel of two ovaries, which are the female part of its furniture, and of two seminal vessels resembling what are found in the male. Each ovary and each seminal vessel has its own proper canal; by the ovary canal the eggs descend to the anus; and there also the seminal canals send their fluids to impregnate them. By this contrivance, one single animal suffices for the double purposes of generation; and the eggs are excluded and impregnated by itself alone.

As the mussel is thus furnished with a kind of self creating power, there are few places where it breeds that it is not found in great abundance. They produce in great numbers, as all bivalved shellfish are found to do. The fecundity of the snail kind is trifling in comparison to the fertility of these. Indeed it may be asserted as a general rule in nature, that the more helpless and contemptible the animal, the more prolific it is always found. Thus all creatures that are incapable of resisting their destroyers have nothing but their quick multiplication, for the continuation of their existence.

The multitude of these animals in some places is very great; but, from their defenceless state, the number of their destroyers are in equal proportion. The crab, the crayfish, and many other animals, are seen to devour them; but the trochus is their most formidable enemy. When their shells are found deserted, if we then observe closely, it is most probable we shall find that the trochus has been at work in piercing them. There is scarce one of them without a hole in it; and this probably was the avenue by which the enemy entered to destroy the inhabitant.

THE OYSTER

From the mussel the Oyster differs very little, except in the thickness of its shell, and its greater imbecility. The oyster, like the mussel, is formed with organs of life and respiration; with intestines which are very voluminous, a liver, lungs, and heart. Like the mussel it is self-impregnated; and the shell, which the animal soon acquires, serves it for its future habitation. Like the mussel it opens its shell to receive the influx of water; and like that animal is strongly attached to its shells both above and below.

But it differs in many particulars. In the first place its shells are not equal, the one being cupped, the other flat; upon the cupped shell it is always seen to rest; for if it lay upon the flat side it would then lose all its water. It differs also in the thickness of its shells, which are so strongly lined and defended, that no animal will attempt to pierce them. But though the oyster be secured from the attacks of the small reptiles at the bottom, yet it often serves as an object to which they are attached. Pipe-worms and other little animals fix their habitation to the oyster's sides, and in this manner continue to live in security. Among the number of these is a little red worm, that is often found upon the shell; which some, from never seeing oysters copulate, erroneously supposed to be the male by which their spawn was impregnated.

The oyster differs also from the mussel in being utterly unable to change its situation. The mussel is capable of erecting itself on an edge, and going forward with a slow laborious motion. The oyster is wholly passive, and endeavours by all its powers to rest fixed to one spot at the bottom. Rocks, stones, pieces of timber, or seaweeds, all seem proper to give it a fixture, and to secure it against the agitation of the waves. Nothing is so common in the rivers of the tropical climates as to see oysters growing even amidst the branches of the forest. Many trees which grow along the banks of the stream often bend their branches into the water, and particularly the mangrove, which chiefly delights in a moist situation. To these the oysters hang in clusters, like apples upon the most fertile tree; and in proportion the weight of the fish sinks the plant into the water, where it still continues growing, the number of oysters increase, and hang upon the branches. Thus there is nothing that these shellfish will not stick to; they are often even found to stick to each other. This is effected by means of a glue proper to themselves, which, when it cements, the joining is as hard as the shell, and is as difficultly broken. The joining substance, however, is not always of glue; but the animal grows to the rocks, somewhat like the mussel, by threads; although these are only seen to take root in the shell, and not, as in the mussel, to spring from the body of the fish itself.

It is particularly in this class of shellfish that pearls are found in greatest abundance; and it is in the internal parts of those shells that are of a shining silvery colour that these gems are usually generated; but the pearl is also found to breed as well in the mussel or the scallop as in the oyster.

SQUID *Histioteuthis bonelliana*
OCTOPUS *Octopus vulgaris*

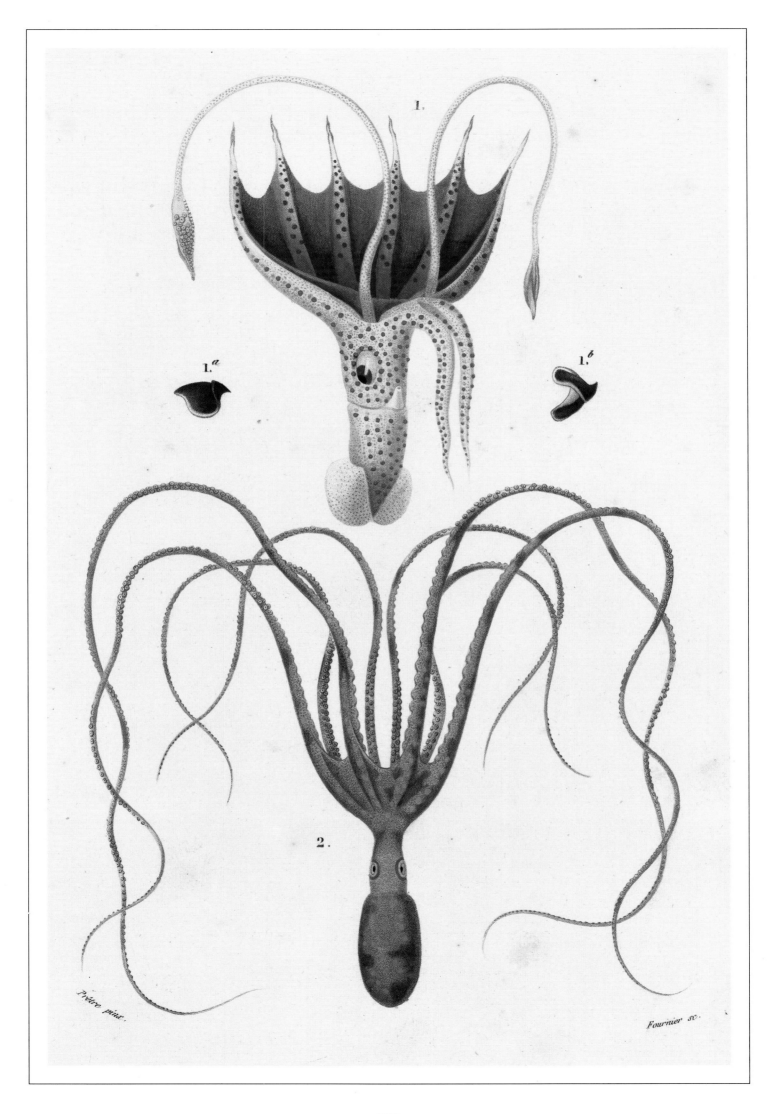

All oysters, and most shellfish are found to contain pearls; but that which particularly bears the name of the Pearl Oyster, has a large strong whitish shell, wrinkled and rough without, and within smooth and of a silver colour. From these the mother-of-pearl is taken, which is nothing more than the internal coats of the shell, resembling the pearl in colour and consistence. This is taken out and shaped into that variety of utensils which are found so beautiful; but the pearl itself is chiefly prized; being found but in few oysters, and generally adhering, sometimes making a print in the body of the shell, sometimes at large within the substance of the fish.

The oysters found along the coast of Coromandel are capable of furnishing a plentiful meal to eight or ten men; but it seems universally agreed that they are no way comparable to ours for delicacy or flavour.

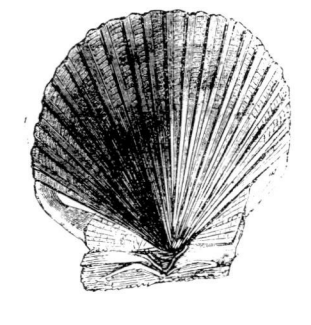

THE SCALLOP

The Scallop is particularly remarkable for its method of moving forward upon land, or swimming upon the surface of the water. When this animal finds itself deserted by the tide, it makes very remarkable efforts to regain the water, moving towards the sea in a most singular manner. It first gapes with its shell as widely as it can, the edges being often an inch asunder; then it shuts them with a jerk, and by this the whole animal rises five or six inches from the ground. It thus tumbles anyhow forward, and then renews the operation until it has attained its journey's end. When in the water it is capable of supporting itself upon the surface; and there opening and shutting its shells, it tumbles over and over, and makes its way with some celerity.

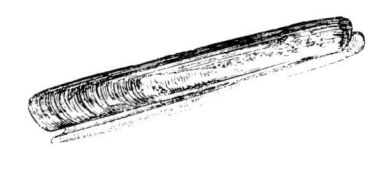

THE RAZOR SHELL

The Pivot or Razor Shell has a very different kind of motion. As the former moves laboriously and slowly forward, so the razor shell has only a power of

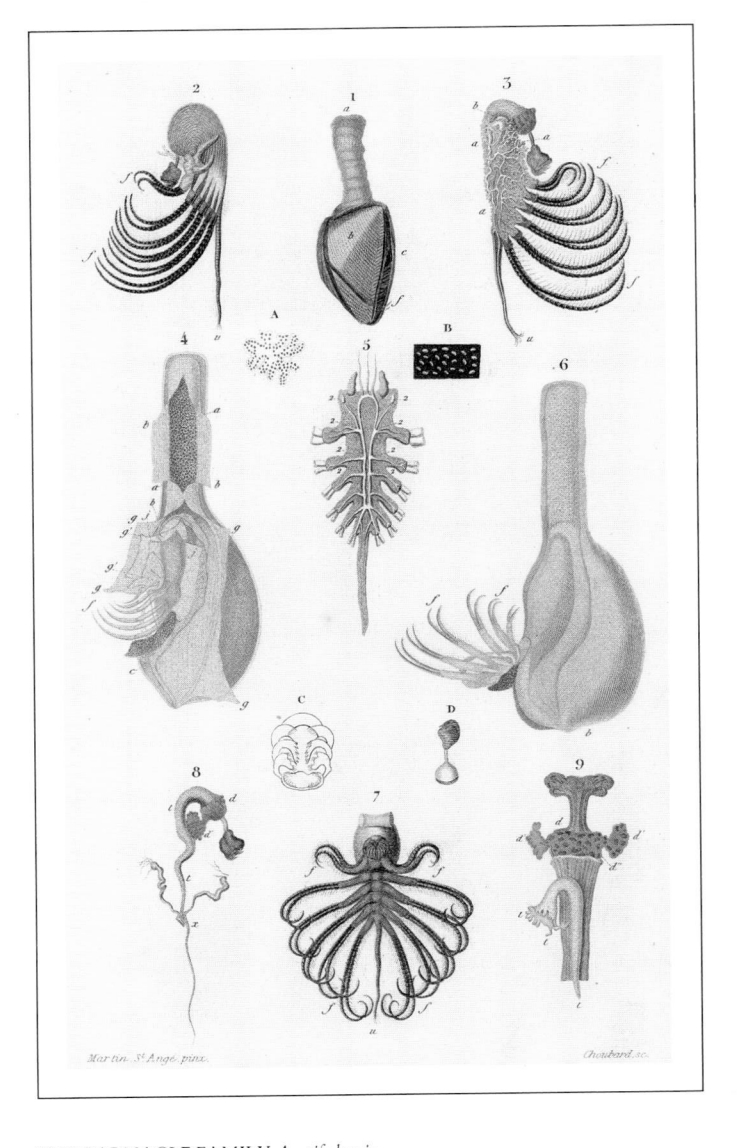

THE BARNACLE FAMILY *Anatifa larvis*

sinking, point downward. The shells of this animal resemble nothing so much as the haft of a razor; and by this form it is better enabled to dive into the soft sand at the bottom. All the motions of this little creature are confined to sinking or rising a foot downwards or upwards in the sand, for it never leaves the spot where first it was planted. From time to time it is seen to rise about halfway out of its hole; but if any way disturbed, it sinks perpendicularly down again. Just over the place where the razor buries itself, there is a small hole like a chimney, through which the animal breathes, or imbibes the seawater. Upon the desertion of the tide, these holes are easily distinguished by the fishermen who seek for it; and their method of enticing the razor up from the depth of its retreat is by sprinkling a little sea-salt upon the hole. This melting, no sooner reaches the razor below than it rises instantly straight upwards, and shows about half its length above the surface. This appearance however is instantaneous; and if the fisher does not seize the opportunity, the razor buries itself with great ease to its former depth. There it continues secure; no salt can allure it a second time; but it remains unmolested, unless the fisher will be at the trouble of digging it out sometimes two feet below the surface.

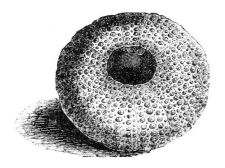

THE SEA URCHIN

At first glance, the Sea Urchin may be compared to the husk of a chestnut; being like it round, and with a number of bony prickles standing out on every side. If we could conceive a turnip stuck full of pins, and running upon these pins with some degree of swiftness, we should have some idea of this extraordinary creature. The mouth is placed downwards; the vent is above; the shell is a hollow vase, resembling a scooped apple; and this filled with a soft, muscular substance, through which the intestines wind from the bottom to the top. The mouth, which is placed undermost, is large and red, furnished with five sharp teeth, which are easily discerned. The jaws are strengthened by five small bones, in the centre of which is a small fleshy tongue; and from this the intestines make a winding of five spires, round the internal sides of the shell, ending at the top, where the excrements are excluded. But what makes the most extraordinary part of this animal's conformation, are its horns and its spines, that point from every part of the body, like the horns of a snail, and that serve at once as legs to move upon, as arms to feel with, and as instruments of capture and defence.

Some kinds of this animal are as good eating as the lobster; and its eggs, which are of a deep red, are considered as a very great delicacy. But of others the taste is but indifferent; and in all places, except the Mediterranean, they are little fought for, except as objects of curiosity.

Very different in motion, though not much different in shape from these, are the Acorn Shellfish, the Thumb-footed Shellfish, and the Imaginary Barnacle. These are fixed to one spot, and appear to vegetate from a stalk. Indeed, to an inattentive spectator, each actually seems to be a kind of fungus that grows in the deep, destitute of animal life as well as motion. But the enquirer will soon change his opinion, when he comes to observe this mushroom-like figure more minutely. He will then see that the animal residing within the shell has not only life, but

some degree of voraciousness; that it has a cover, by which it opens and shuts its shell at pleasure; that it has twelve long crooked arms, furnished with hair, which it thrusts forth for its prey; and eight smaller, which are generally kept in the shell. They are seen adhering to every substance that is to be met with in the ocean; rocks, roots of trees, ships' bottoms, whales, lobsters, and even crabs, like bunches of grapes clung to each other.

THE PHOLADES

Of all animals of the shelly tribe, the Pholades are the most wonderful. From their great powers of penetration, compared with their apparent imbecility, they justly excite the astonishment of the curious observer. These animals are found in different places; sometimes clothed in their proper shell, at the bottom of the water; sometimes concealed in lumps of marly earth; and sometimes lodged, shell and all, in the body of the hardest marble. In their proper shell they assume different figures; but, in general, they somewhat resemble a mussel, except that their shell is found actually composed of five or more pieces, the smaller valves serving to close up the openings left by the irregular meeting of the two principal shells. But their penetration into rocks, and their residence there, makes up the most wonderful part of their history.

Yet the pholades thus shut up, is not so solitary an animal as it would at first appear; for though it is immured in its hole without egress, though it is impossible for the animal, grown to a great size, to get out by the way it made in, yet many of this kind often meet in the heart of the rock, and, like miners in a siege, who sometimes cross each other's galleries, they frequently break in upon each other's retreats. Whether their thus meeting be the work of accident or of choice, few can take upon them to determine; certain it is, they are most commonly found in numbers in the same rock; and sometimes above twenty are discovered within a few inches of each other.

As to the rest, this animal is found in greatest numbers at Ancona, in Italy; it is found along the shores of Normandy and Poitou, in France; it is found also upon some of the coasts of Scotland: and, in general, is considered as a very great delicacy, at the tables of the luxurious.

BOOK IV

REPTILES

FROGS AND TOADS

THE FROG

The external figure of the Frog is too well known to need a description. Its power of taking large leaps is remarkably great, compared to the bulk of its body. It is the best swimmer of all four-footed animals; and Nature has finely adapted its parts for those ends, the arms being light and active, the legs and thighs long, and furnished with very strong muscles.

If we examine this animal internally, we shall find that it has a very little brain for its size; a very wide swallow; a stomach seemingly small, but capable of great distension. The heart in the frog, as in all other animals that are truly amphibious, has but one ventricle, so that the blood can circulate without the assistance of the lungs, while it keeps under water. The lungs resemble a number of small bladders joined together, like the cells of a honeycomb: they are connected to the back by muscles, and can be distended or exhausted at the animal's pleasure. The male has two testiculi lying near the kidneys; and the female has two ovaries, lying near the same place: but neither male or female have any of the external instruments of generation; the anus serving for that purpose in both.

The Common Brown Frog begins to couple early in the season, and as soon as the ice is thawed from the stagnating waters. The male is usually of a greyish brown colour; the female is more inclining to yellow, speckled with brown.

They couple only once a year; and then continue united sometimes for four days together. At this time

1 WIED'S CORAL SNAKE *Elaps corallinus*

2 COBRA *Naje hoje*

they both have their bellies greatly swollen; that of the female being filled with eggs: the male having the skin of the whole body distended with a limpid water, which is ejected in impregnation.

A single female produces from six to eleven hundred eggs at a time; and, in general, she throws them all out together by a single effort; though sometimes she is an hour in performing this task. While she is thus bringing forth, it may be observed, that the male acts the part of a midwife, and promotes the expulsion of the eggs by working with his thumbs, and compressing the female's body more closely.

When the spawn is emitted and impregnated by the male, it drops to the bottom, and there the white quickly and sensibly increases. The eggs, which during the first four hours suffer no perceptible change, begin then to enlarge and grow lighter; by which means they mount to the surface of the water.

At the end of eight hours, the white in which they swim grows thicker, the eggs lose their blackness, and as they increase in size, somewhat of their spherical form. The twenty-first day the egg is seen to open a little on the side, and the beginning of a tail to peep out, which becomes more and more distinct every day. The thirty-ninth day the little animal begins to have motion; it moves at intervals its tail; and it is perceived that the liquor in which it is circumfused, serves it for nourishment. The next day they acquire their tadpole form. In three days more they are perceived to have two little fringes, that serve as fins beneath the head; and these four days after assume a more perfect form. It is then also that they are seen to feed very greedily upon the pond-weed with which they are to be supplied; and, leaving their former food, on this they continue to subsist till they arrive at maturity. When they come to be ninety-two days old, two small feet are seen beginning to burgeon near the tail; and the head appears to be separate from the body. The next day, the legs are considerably enlarged; four days after they refuse all vegetable food; their mouth appears furnished with

teeth; and their hind legs are completely formed. In two days more the arms are completely produced; and now the frog is every way perfect, except that it still continues to carry the tail. In this state it continues for about six or eight hours; and then the tail dropping off by degrees, the animal appears in its most perfect form.

THE TOAD

The body of the Toad is broad; its back flat; covered with a dusky, pimpled hide; the belly is large and sagging; the pace laboured and crawling; its retreat gloomy and filthy; and its whole appearance calculated to excite disgust and horror.

A Mr. Ariscott relates some curious particulars relating to this animal. "Concerning the toad that lived for many years with us, and was so great a favourite, the greatest curiosity was its becoming so remarkably tame: it had frequented some steps before our hall door some years before my acquaintance commenced with it, and had been admired by my father for its size (being the largest I ever met with) who paid it a visit every evening. I knew it myself above thirty years; and by constantly feeding it, brought it to be so tame, that it always came to the candle and looked up, as if expecting to be taken up and brought upon the table, where I always fed it with insects of all sorts. It was fondest of flesh maggots, which I kept in bran; it would follow them, and when within a proper distance, would fix its eyes and remain motionless for near a quarter of a minute, as if preparing for the stroke, which was an instantaneous throwing its tongue at a great distance upon the insect, which stuck to the top by a glutinous matter. The motion is quicker than the eye can follow. I cannot say how long my father had been acquainted with the toad before I knew it; but when I

was first acquainted with it, he used to mention it as "the old toad I have known so many years". I can answer for thirty-six years. This old toad made its appearance as soon as the warm weather came; and I always concluded it retired to some dry bank, to repose till spring. When we new laid the steps, I had two holes made in the third step, each with a hollow of more than a yard long for it, in which I imagine it slept; as it came from thence at its first appearance. In respect to its end, had it not been for a tame raven, I make no doubt but it would have been now living. This bird, one day seeing it at the mouth of its hole, pulled it out, and, although I rescued it, pulled out one eye, and hurt it so, that notwithstanding its living a twelve-month, it never enjoyed itself, and had a difficulty of taking its food, missing the mark for want of its eye. Before that accident, it had all the appearance of perfect health."

There are several varieties of toads such as the Water and the Land Toad, which probably differ only in the ground-colour of their skin. In the first, it is more inclining to ash-colour, with brown spots; in the other, the colour is brown, approaching to black. The water toad is not so large as the other; but both equally breed in that element. The size of the toad with us is generally from two to four inches long; but, in the fenny countries of Europe, I have seen them much larger; and not less than a common crab when brought to table. But this is nothing to what they are found in some of the tropical climates, where travellers often, for the first time, mistake a toad for a tortoise. Their actual size is from six to seven inches; but there are some still larger, and as broad as a plate. Of these some are beautifully streaked and coloured; some studded over, as if with pearls; others bristled with horns or spines; some have the head distinct from the body, while others have it so sunk in, that the animal appears without a head. All these are found in the tropical climates, in great abundance; and particularly after a shower of rain. It is then that the streets seem entirely paved with them; they then crawl from their retreats, and go into all places, to enjoy their favourite moisture. With us the belief of its raining toads and frogs, has long been justly exploded, but it still is entertained in the tropical countries; and that not only by the savage natives, but the more refined settlers, who are apt enough to add the prejudices of other nations to their own.

From Top to Bottom
Left HARLEQUIN FROG *Pseudis merianae*
CASQUE-HEADED TREE FROG *Trachycephalus geographicus*
CLAWED TOAD *Dactylethra capensis* SURINAM TOAD *Pipa americana*
Right SHORT-HEADED FROG *Engystoma ovale* GREEN TOAD *Bufo viridis*
MUDPUPPY *Menobranchus lateralis* SIREN *Siren lacertina*

MIKAN'S COECILIAN *Siphonops annulatus*

THE PIPAL

The Pipal or Surinam Toad is in form more hideous than even the common toad. Nature seeming to have marked all those strange mannered animals with peculiar deformity. The body is flat and broad; the head small; the jaws, like those of a mole, are extended, and evidently formed for rooting in the ground: the skin of the neck forms a sort of wrinkled collar: the colour of the head is of a dark chestnut, and the eyes are small: the back, which is very broad, is of a lightish grey, and seems covered over with a number of small eyes, which are round, and placed at nearly equal distances. These eyes are very different

from what they seem; they are the animal's eggs, covered with their shells, and placed there for hatching. These eggs are buried deep in the skin, and only just appear in the beginning of incubation; but are very visible when the young animal is about to burst from its confinement. They are of a reddish, shining yellow colour; and the spaces between them are full of small warts, resembling pearls.

THE LIZARD KIND

THE CROCODILE

The Crocodile is an animal placed at a happy distance from the inhabitants of Europe, and formidable only in those regions where men are scarce, and arts are but little known. The crocodile that was once so terrible along the banks of the river Nile, is now neither so large, nor its numbers so great as formerly.

To look for this animal in all its natural terrors, grown to an enormous size, propagated in surprising numbers, and committing unceasing devastations, we must go to the uninhabited regions of Africa and America, to those immense rivers that roll through extensive and desolate kingdoms. Those that sail up the river Amazon, or the river Niger, well know how numerous and terrible those animals are in such parts of the world. In both these rivers, they are found from eighteen to twenty-seven feet long; and sometimes lying as close to each other, as a raft of timber upon one of our streams. There they indolently bask on the surface, no way disturbed at the approach of an enemy, since, from the repeated trials of their strength, they found none that they were not able to subdue.

This animal grows to great length, being sometimes found thirty feet long, from the tip of the snout to the end of the tail.

They are seen, in some places, lying for whole hours, and even days, stretched in the sun, and

motionless; so that one not used to them, might mistake them for trunks of trees, covered with a rough and dry bark; but the mistake would soon be fatal, if not prevented: for the torpid animal, at the near approach of any living thing, darts upon it with instant swiftness, and at once drags it down to the bottom. In the times of an inundation, they sometimes enter the cottages of the natives, where the dreadful visitant seizes the first animal it meets with. There have been several examples of their taking a man out of a canoe in the sight of his companions, without their being able to lend him any assistance.

The strength of every part of the crocodile is very great; and its arms, both offensive and defensive, irresistible. The back-bone is jointed in the firmest manner; the muscles of the fore and hind

1 ALLIGATOR *Alligator lucius*

2 GEKKO *Platydactylus muralis*

legs are vigorous and strong; and its whole form calculated for force. Its teeth are sharp, numerous and formidable; its claws are long and tenaceous; but its principal instrument of destruction is the tail: with a single blow of this it has often overturned a canoe, and seized upon the poor navigator.

Though not so powerful, yet it is very terrible even upon land. The crocodile seldom, except when pressed by hunger, or with a view of depositing its eggs, leaves the water. Its usual method is to float along upon the surface and seize whatever animals come within its reach; but when this method fails, it then goes closer to the bank.

Wherever the crocodile has reigned long unmolested, it is there fierce, bold, and dangerous;

wherever it has been harrassed by mankind, its retreats invaded, and its numbers destroyed, it is there timorous and inoffensive.

In some places, this animal, instead of being formidable, is not only inoffensive, but is cherished and admired. In the river San Domingo, the crocodiles are the most inoffensive animals in nature; the

children play with them, and ride about on their backs; they even beat them sometimes without receiving the smallest injury. It is true the inhabitants are very careful of this gentle breed, and consider them as harmless domestics.

The crocodile's flesh is at best very bad tough eating. The natives themselves cannot well digest the flesh, but then, a crocodile's egg is to them the most delicate morsel in the world.

THE SALAMANDER

The ancients have described a lizard that is bred from heat, that lives in the flames, and feeds upon fire as its proper nourishment. As they saw every other element, the air, the earth and water, inhabited, fancy was set to work to find or make an inhabitant in fire; and thus to people every part of nature. It will be needless to say that there is no such animal existing; and that, of all others, the modern Salamander has the greatest affinity to such an abode.

Whether the animal that now goes by the name of the salamander be the same with that described by Pliny, is a doubt with me; but this is not a place for the discussion. It is sufficient to observe that the modern salamander is an animal of the lizard kind, and under this name is comprehended a large tribe that all go by the same name. There have been not less than seven sorts of this animal described; and to have some idea of the peculiarity of their figure, if we suppose the tail of a lizard applied to the body of a frog, we shall not be far from precision.

The salamander, like the frog, has its eyes towards the back of the head; like the frog, its snout is round and not pointed, and its belly thick and swollen. The claws of its toes are short and feeble; its skin rough; and the tongue, unlike that of the smallest of the lizard kind in which it is long and forked, is short, and adhering to the under jaw.

But it is not in figure that this animal chiefly differs from the rest of the lizard tribe; for it seems to differ in nature and conformation. In nature it is unlike, being a heavy, torpid animal; whereas the lizard tribe are active, restless, and ever in motion: in conformation it is unlike, as the salamander is produced alive from the body of its parent, and is completely formed the moment of its exclusion. It differs from them also

in its general reputation of being venomous; however, no trials that have been hitherto made seem to confirm the truth of the report.

The salamander best known in Europe, is from eight to eleven inches long, usually black, spotted with yellow; and when taken in the hand, feeling cold to a great degree. The idle report of its being inconsumable in fire, has caused many of these poor animals to be burnt; but we cannot say as philosophical martyrs; since scarce any philosopher could think it necessary to make the experiment. When thrown into the fire, the animal is seen to burst with the heat of its situation, and to eject its fluids. We are gravely told, in the Philosophical Transactions, that this is a method the animal takes to extinguish the flames.

THE IGUANA

The Iguana, which deserves our notice, is about five feet long, and the body about as thick as one's thigh: the skin is covered with small scales, like those of a serpent; and the back is furnished with a row of prickles, that stand up, like the teeth of a saw: the eyes seem to be but half opened, except when the animal is angry, and then they appear large and sparkling: both the jaws are full of very sharp teeth, and the bite is dangerous though not venomous, for it never lets loose till it is killed. The male has a skin hanging under his throat, which reaches down to his breast; and, when displeased, he puffs it up like a bladder: he is one third larger and stronger than the female; though the strength of either avails them little towards their defence. The males are ash-coloured, and the females are green.

The flesh of these may be considered as the greatest delicacy of Africa and America; and the sportsmen of those climates go out to hunt the iguana, as we do in pursuit of the pheasant or the hare. In the beginning of the season, when the great floods of the tropical climates are past away, and vegetation starts into universal verdure, the sportsmen are seen, with a noose and a stick, wandering along the sides of the rivers, to take the iguana. This animal, though apparently formed for combat, is the most harmless creature of all the forest; it lives among the trees, or sports in the water, without ever offering to offend: there, having fed upon the flowers of the mahot, and the leaves of the mapou, that grow along the banks of the stream, it goes to repose upon the branches of the trees that hang over the water. Upon land the animal is swift of foot; but when once in possession of a tree, it seems conscious of the security of its situation, and never offers to stir. There the sportsman easily finds it, and as easily fastens his noose around its neck: if

1 LINNEAN IGUANA *Iguana tuberculata*
2 GREEN LIZARD *Lacerta viridis*

the head be placed in such a manner that the noose cannot readily be fastened, by hitting the animal a blow on the nose with the stick, it lifts the head, and offers it in some measure to the noose. In this manner, and also by the tail, the iguana is dragged from the trees, and killed by repeated blows on the head.

THE CHAMELEON

The head of a large Chameleon is almost two inches long; and from thence to the beginning of the tail, four and a half: the tail is five inches long, and the feet two and a half: the thickness of the body is different at different times; for sometimes, from the back to the belly, it is two inches, and sometimes but one; for it can blow itself up, and contract itself, at pleasure. The swelling and contraction is not only of the back and belly, but of the legs and tail.

These different tumours do not proceed from a dilatation of the breast in breathing, which rises and falls by turns; but are very irregular, and seem adopted merely from caprice. The chameleon is often seen, as it were, blown up for two hours together; and then it continues growing less and less insensibly; for the dilatation is always more quick and visible than the contraction. In this last state the animal

appears extremely lean; the spine of the back seems sharp, and all the ribs may be counted; likewise the tendons of the legs and arms may be seen very distinctly.

When the animal is removed into the sun, then comes the wonderful part of its history. At first it appears to suffer no change to colour, its greyish spots still continuing the same: but the whole surface soon seems to imbibe the rays of light; and the simple colouring of the body changes into a variety of beautiful hues. Wherever the light comes upon the body, it is of a tawny brown; but that part of the skin on which the sun does not shine, changes into several brighter colours, pale yellow, or vivid crimson; which form spots of the size of half one's finger: some of these descend from the spine half way down the back; and others appear on the sides, arms and tail.

Where the sun has done shining, the original grey colour returns by degrees, and covers all the body. Sometimes the animal becomes all over spotted with brown spots, of a greenish cast. When it is wrapped up in a white linen cloth for two or three minutes, the natural colour becomes much lighter; but not quite

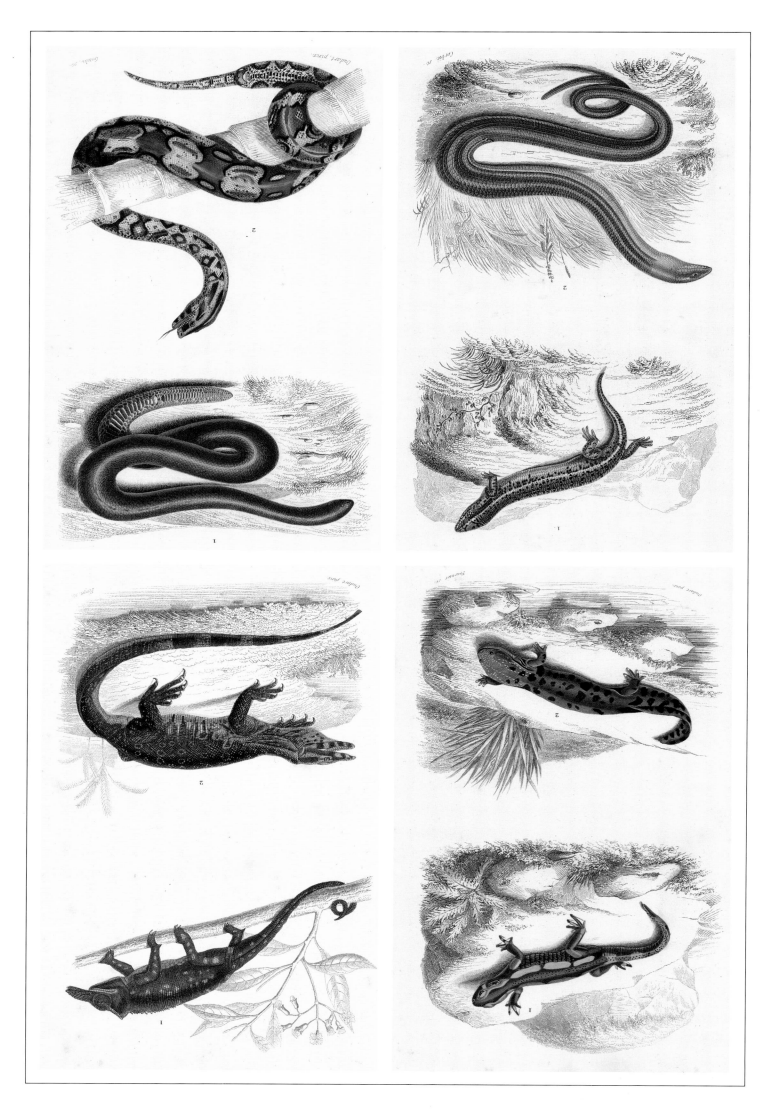

white, as some authors have pretended: however, from hence it must not be concluded that the chameleon assumes the colour of the objects which it approaches; this is entirely an error, and probably has taken its rise from the continual changes it appears to undergo.

THE FLYING LIZARD

The Flying Lizard of Java, perches upon fruit-trees, and feeds upon flies, ants, butterflies, and other small insects. It is a very harmless creature, and does no mischief in any respect. On the island of Java in the East Indies it has been seen flying swiftly from tree to tree.

The skin is painted with several beautiful colours: it is about a foot in length and has four feet, like the common lizards; but its head is flat and has a small hole in the middle; the wings are very thin and resemble those of a flying fish. About the neck are a sort of wattle, not unlike that of a cock, which gives it no disagreeable appearance.

THE CHALCIDIAN LIZARD

The Chalcidian Lizard of Aldrovandus, very improperly called the Seps, by modern historians, seems to be half-way between the lizard and the serpent race. It has four legs, like the lizard; but so short, as to be utterly unserviceable in walking: it has a long slender body like the serpent; and it is said to have the serpent's malignity also. The fore-legs are very near the head; the hind legs are placed far backward; but before and behind they seem rather useless incumbrances, than instruments serving to assist the animal in its motions, or in providing for its subsistence. These animals are found above three feet

From Top to Bottom Left SPOTTED SALAMANDER *Salamandra maculosa*
HELLBENDER *Menopoma alleghnensis* SKINK *Gongylus ocellatus* GLASS SNAKE *Pseudopus pallasii*
Right CHAMELEON *Chamaelo bifidus* MONITOR *Varanus bivittatus*
SAND BOA *Eryx duvaucelii* BOA CONSTRICTOR *Boa constrictor*

long, and thick in proportion, with a large head and pointed snout. The whole body is covered with scales; and the belly is white, mixed with blue. It has four crooked teeth; also a pointed tail, which, however, can inflict no wound. It is viviparous; fifteen young ones having been taken alive out of its belly. Upon the whole, it appears to bear a strong affinity to the viper; and, like that animal, its bite may be dangerous.

SERPENTS

THE VIPER

The Viper is the only creature in Great Britain from whose bite we have anything to fear. Vipers are found in many parts of Britain; but the dry, stony, and in particular the chalky, counties abound with them. This creature seldom grows to a greater length than two feet; though sometimes they are found above three. The ground colour of their bodies is a dirty yellow; that of the female is deeper. The back is marked the whole length with a series of rhomboid black spots, touching each other at the points; the sides with triangular ones, the belly entirely black. It is chiefly distinguished from the common black snake by the colour, which in the latter is more beautifully mottled, as well as by the head, which is thicker than the body; but particularly by the tail, which in the viper, though it ends in a point, does not run tapering to so great a length as in the other. When, therefore, other distinctions fail, the difference of the tail can be discerned at a single glance.

The viper differs from most other serpents in being much slower, as also in giving birth to young completely formed. The kindness of Providence seems exerted not only in diminishing the speed, but also the fertility, of this dangerous creature. They copulate in May, and are supposed to be about three months before they bring forth, and have seldom above eleven eggs at a time. These are of the size of a blackbird's eggs, and chained together in the womb like a string of beads. Each egg contains from one to four young ones; so that the whole of a brood may amount to about twenty or thirty. They continue in the womb till they come to such perfection as to be able to burst from the shell; and they are said by their own efforts to creep from their confinement into the open air, where they continue for several days without taking any food whatsoever.

The viper is capable of supporting very long abstinence, it being known that some have been kept

Mme Fournier. sc.

Oudart. pinx.

2

1

in a box six months without food; yet during the whole time they did not abate of their vivacity. They feed only a small part of the year, but never during their confinement; for if mice, their favourite diet, should at that time be thrown into their box, though they will kill, yet they will never eat, them. When at liberty, they remain torpid throughout the winter; yet, when confined, have never been observed to take their annual repose.

THE RATTLE SNAKE

The Rattlesnake lives in America, and in no part of the old world. Some are as thick as a man's leg, and six feet in length; but the most usual size is from four to five feet long. In most particulars it resembles the viper: like that animal, having a large head and a small neck, being of a dusky colour, and furnished with fangs that inflict the most terrible wounds. It differs, however, in having a large scale, which hangs also like a penthouse over each eye. The eye also is furnished with an inner eyelid that preserves it from dust; and its scales are of a considerable degree of hardness. They are of an orange, tawny, and blackish colour on the back; and of an ash colour on the belly; inclining to lead. The male may be readily distin-

guished from the female, by a black velvet spot on the head, and by the head being smaller and longer. But that which, besides their superior malignity, distinguishes them from all other animals, is their rattle, an instrument lodged in their tail, by which they make such a loud, rattling noise, when they move, that their approach may readily be perceived, and the danger avoided. This rattle, which is placed in the tail, somewhat resembles, when taken out of the body, the curb chain of a bridle: it is composed of several thin, hard hollow bones, linked to each other, and rattling upon the slightest motion.

As a gentleman in Virginia was walking in the fields for his amusement, he accidentally trod upon a rattlesnake, that had been lurking in a stony place; which, enraged by the pressure, reared up, bit his hand, and shook its rattles. The gentleman readily perceived that he was in the most dreadful danger;

1 RATTLESNAKE *Crotalus durissus*
2 HORNED CERASTES VIPER *Cerastes cornutus*

but unwilling to die unrevenged, he killed the snake, and carrying it home in his hand, threw it on the ground before his family, crying out, "I am killed, and there is my murderer!" His arm, which was beginning to swell, was tied up near the shoulder, the wound was annointed with oil, and every precaution taken to stop the infection. By the help of a very strong constitution he recovered, but not without feeling the most various and dreadful symptoms for several weeks together. His arm, below the ligature, appeared of several colours, with a writhing among the muscles, that, to his terrified imagination, appeared like the motions of the animal that had wounded him. A fever ensued, the loss of his hair, giddiness, drought, weakness, and nervous faintings: till, by slow degrees, a very strong habit over-powered the latent malignity of the poison.

THE COBRA

The Cobra di Capello, or Hooded Serpent, inflicts the most deadly and incurable wounds. Of this formidable creature there are five or six different kinds; but they are all equally dangerous, and their bite followed by speedy and certain death. It is from three to eight feet long, with two large fangs hanging out of the upper jaw. It has a broad neck, and a mark of dark brown on the forehead; which, when viewed frontwise, looks like a pair of spectacles, but behind, like the head of a cat. The eyes are fierce, and full of fire; the head is small, and the nose flat, though covered with very large scales, of a yellowish ash-colour; the skin is white, and the large tumour on the neck is flat, and covered with oblong, smooth scales. The bite of this animal is said to be incurable, the patient dying in about an hour after the wound; the whole frame being dissolved into one putrid mass of corruption.

THE BLACK SNAKE

The Black Snake is the largest of English serpents, sometimes exceeding four feet in length. The neck is slender; the middle of the body thick; the back and sides covered with small scales; the belly with oblong, narrow, transverse plates: the colour of the back and sides are of a dusky brown; the middle of the back marked with two rows of small black spots, running from the head to the tail; the plates on the belly are dusky; the scales on the sides are of a bluish white: the teeth are small and serrated, lying on each side of the jaw in two rows. The whole species is perfectly inoffensive; taking shelter in dunghills, and

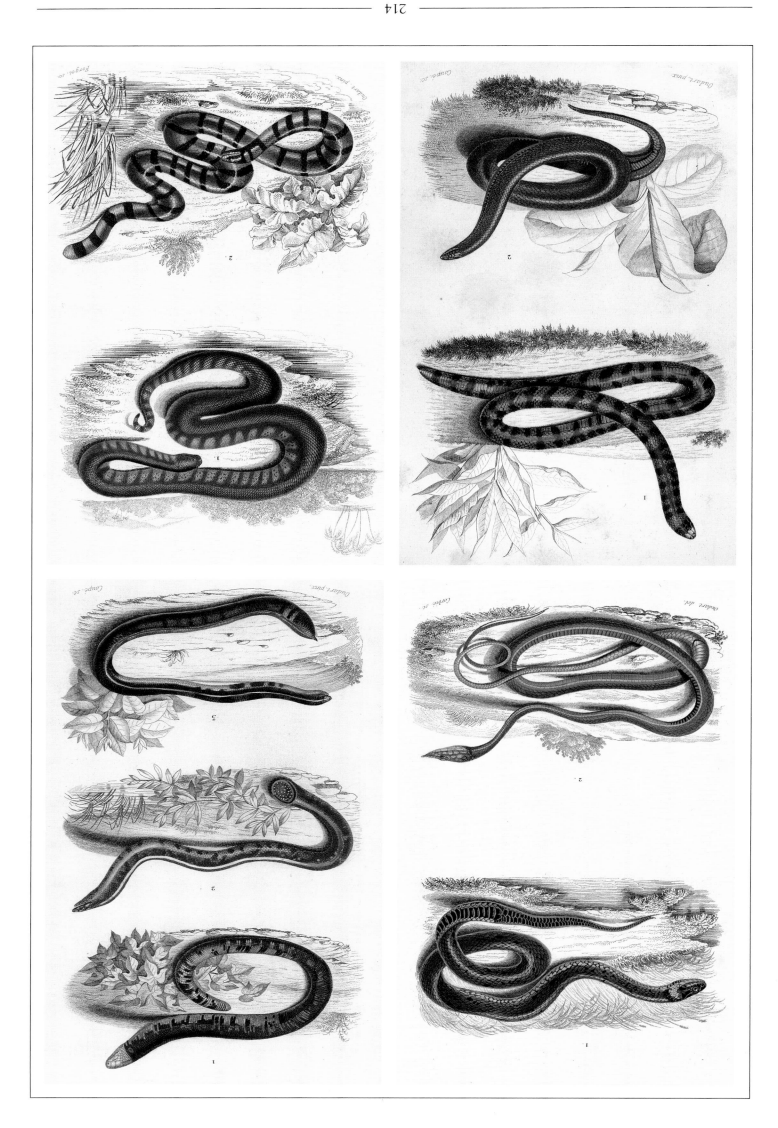

among bushes in moist places, from whence they seldom remove, unless in the midst of the day, in summer, when they are called out by the heat to bask themselves in the sun. If disturbed or attacked, they move away among the brambles with great swiftness; but if too closely pursued, they hiss and threaten, and thus render themselves formidable, though incapable of offending.

The black snake preys upon frogs, insects, worms, mice, and young birds; and considering the smallness of the neck, it is amazing how large an animal it will swallow. The black snake of Virginia, which is larger than ours and generally grows to six feet long, takes a prey proportionable to its size; partridges, chickens, and young ducks. It is generally found in the neighbourhood of the hen roost, and will devour the eggs even while the hen is sitting upon them: these it swallows whole; and often, after it has done the mischief, will coil itself round in the nest.

From Top to Bottom

Left GRASS SNAKE *Tropidonotus torquatus*

TREE SNAKE *Dryinus nasutus*

CYLINDER SNAKE *Tortrix scytale*

SMOOTH-BELLIED SNAKE *Homalosoma acretiventris*

Right BURROWING LIZARD *Amphisboena fuliginosa*

BLIND SNAKE *Typhlops lumbricalis*

Vropeltis philippinus

ELEPHANT WATER-SNAKE *Acrochordus javanicus*

SEA-SNAKE *Platurus fasciatus*

THE BLIND WORM

The Blind Worm is a harmless reptile, with a formidable appearance. The usual length of this species is eleven inches. The eyes are red; the head small, the neck still more slender: from that part the body grows suddenly, and continues of an equal bulk to the tail, which ends quite blunt: the colour of the back is cinereous, marked with very small lines, composed of minute black specks; the sides are of a reddish cast; the belly dusky, and marked like the back. The motion of this serpent is slow; from which, and from the smallness of the eyes, are derived its names; some calling it the Slow and some the Blind Worm. Like all the rest of the kind in our climates, they lie torpid during winter; and are sometimes found, in vast numbers, twisted together. This animal, like the former, is perfectly innocent; however, like the viper, it brings forth its young alive.

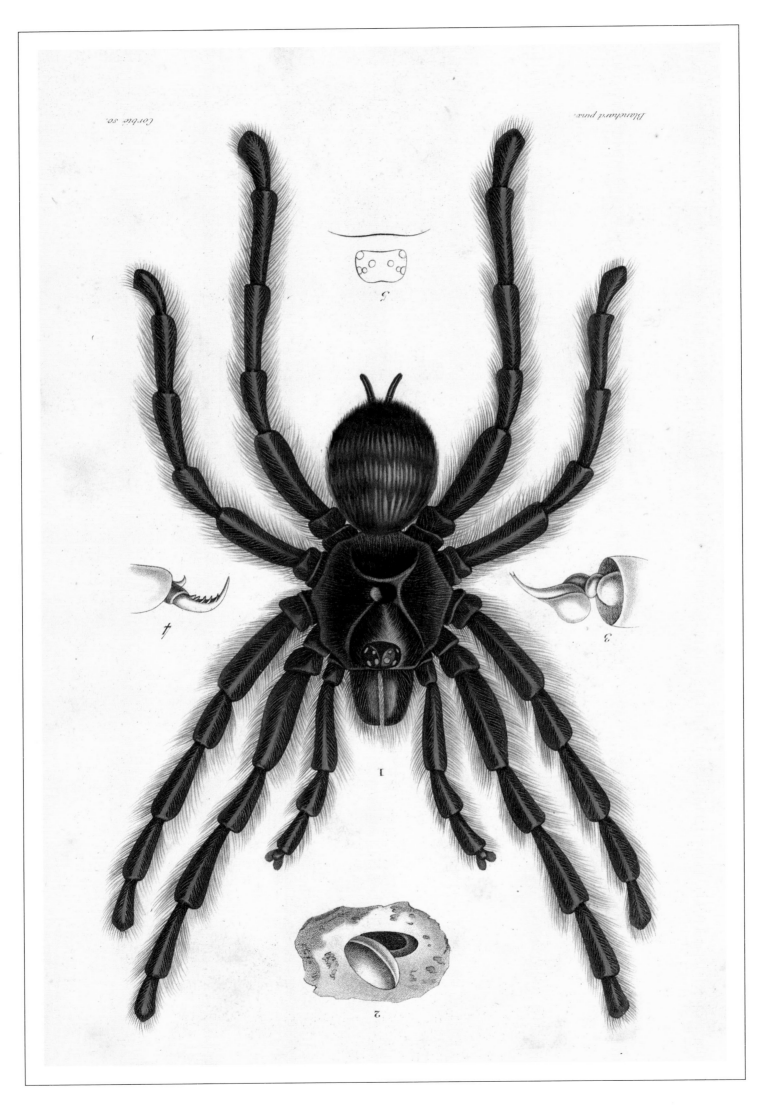

BOOK V

INSECTS

INSECTS OF THE FIRST ORDER

THE HOUSE SPIDER

When a House Spider proposes to begin a web, it first makes choice of some commodious spot, where there is an appearance of plunder and security. The animal then distils one little drop of its glutinous liquor, which is very tenacious, and then creeping up the wall, and joining its thread as it proceeds, it darts in a very surprising manner, as I have often seen, to the opposite place, where the other end of the web is to be fastened. The first thread thus formed, drawn tight, and fixed at each end, the spider then runs upon it backward and forward, still assiduously employed in doubling and strengthening it, as upon its force depends the strength and stability of the whole. The scaffolding thus completed, the spider makes a number of threads parallel to the first, in the same manner, and then crosses them with others; the clammy substance of which they are formed, serving to bind them, when newly made, to each other. The insect, after this operation, doubles and trebles the thread that borders its web, and secures the edges, so as to prevent the wind from blowing the work away. The edges being thus fortified, the retreat is next to be attended to; and this is formed like a funnel at the bottom of the web, where the little creature lies concealed. Still attentive to its web, the spider, from time to time, cleans away the dust that gathers round it, which might otherwise clog and incommode it: for this purpose, it gives the whole a shake with its legs; still, however, proportioning the blow so as not to endanger the fabric. It often happens also, that from the main web there are several threads extended at some distance on every side: these are, in some

BIRD-EATING SPIDER *Mygale avicularia*

measure, the outworks of the fortification, which, whenever touched from without, the spider prepares for attack or self-defence. If the insect impinging be a fly, it springs forward with great agility; if, on the contrary, it be the assault of an enemy stronger than itself, it keeps within its fortress, and never ventures out till the danger be over. Another advantage which the spider reaps from this contrivance of a cell or retreat behind the web, is, that it serves for a place where the creature can feast upon its game with all safety, and conceal the fragments of those carcasses which it has picked, without exposing to public view the least trace of barbarity, that might create a suspicion in any insects that their enemy was near.

THE GARDEN SPIDER

The Garden Spider spins a great quantity of thread, which floating in the air in various directions, happens from its glutinous quality, at last to stick to some object near it, a lofty plant or the branch of a tree. The spider only wants to have one end of the line fast, in order to secure and tighten the other. It accordingly draws the line when thus fixed, and then by passing and repassing upon it, strengthens the thread in such a manner as to answer all its intentions. The first cord being thus stretched, the

spider walks along a part of it, and there fastens another, and dropping from thence, fastens the thread to some solid body below, then climbs up again and begins a third, which it fastens by the same contrivance. When three threads are thus fixed, it

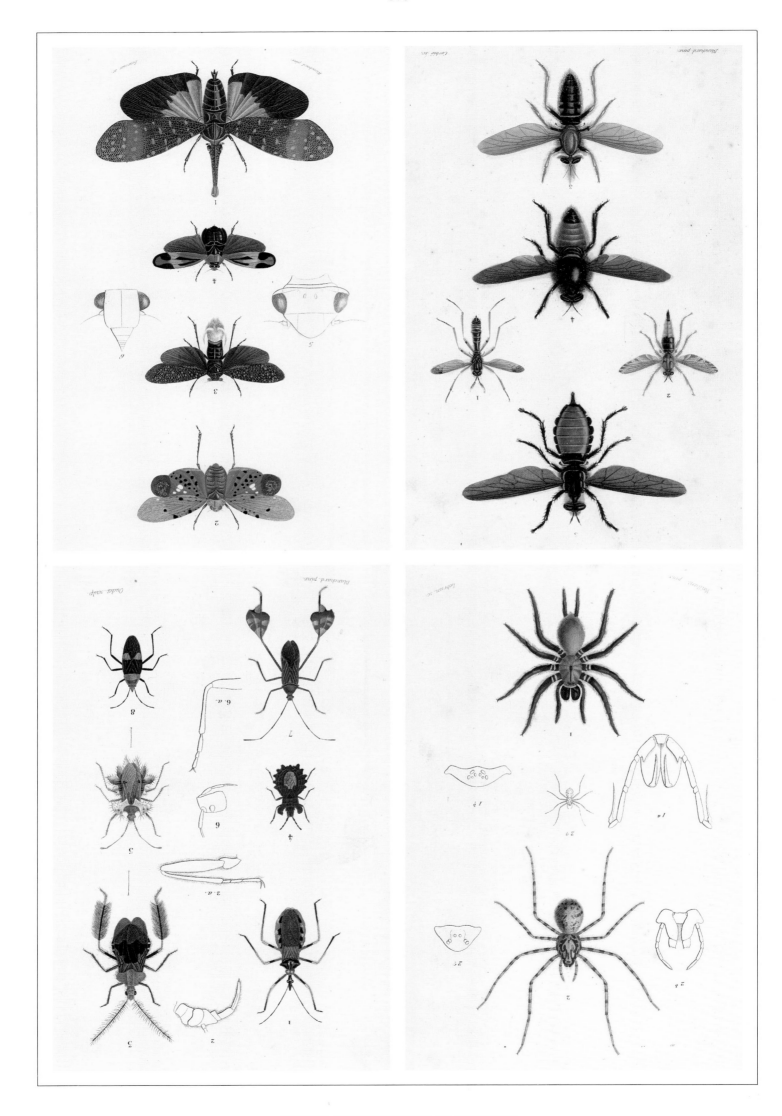

forms a square, or something that very nearly resembles one; and in this the animal is generally seen to reside.

THE TARANTULA

The Tarantula is the largest of the spider kind known in Europe, and is a native of Apulia in Italy. Its body is three quarters of an inch long, and about as thick as one's little finger; the colour is generally an olive brown, variegated with one that is more dusky; it has eight legs and eight eyes, like the rest, and nippers, which are sharp and serrated: between these and the forelegs, there are two little horns, or feelers, which it is observed to move very briskly when it approaches its prey. It is covered all over the body with a soft down; and propagates, as other spiders, by laying eggs. In the summer months, particularly in the dog days, the tarantula creeping among the corn, bites the mowers and harvesters; but in winter, it lurks in holes, and is seldom seen.

Thus far is true; but now the fable begins: for though the bite is attended with no dangerous symptoms, and will easily cure of itself, wonderful stories are reported concerning its virulence. The part which is bitten, as we are told, is soon after discoloured with a livid black, or yellowish circle, attended with an inflammation. At first the pain is scarcely felt; but a few hours after, come on a violent sickness, difficulty of breathing, fainting, and sometimes trembling. The person bit, after this does nothing but laugh, dance and skip about, putting himself into the most extravagant postures; and sometimes also is seized with a most frightful melancholy. At the return of the season in which he was bit, his madness begins again; and the patient always talks of the same things. Sometimes he fancies himself a shepherd; sometimes a king; appearing entirely out of his senses. These

troublesome symptoms sometimes return for several years successively, and at last terminate in death. But so dreadful a disorder, has it seems, not been left without a remedy; which is no other than a well played fiddle. For this purpose the medical musician plays a particular tune, famous for the cure, which he begins slow, and increases in quickness as he sees the patient affected. The patient no sooner hears the music, but he begins to dance; and continues so doing till he is all over in a sweat, which forces out the venom that appeared so dangerous. This dancing sometimes continues for three or four hours, before the patient is weary, and before the sweating is copious enough to cure the disorder. Such are the symptoms related of the tarantula poison; symptoms which some of the best and gravest physicians have credited, and attempted to account for. But the truth is, that the whole is an imposition of the peasants upon travellers who happen to pass through that part of the country, and who procure a trifle for suffering themselves to be bitten by the tarantula. Whenever they find a traveller willing to try the experiment, they readily offer themselves; and are sure to counterfeit the whole train of symptoms which music is supposed to remove. A friend of mine, who passed through that part of the country, had a trusty servant bitten, without ever administering the musical cure; the only symptoms were a slight inflammation, which was readily removed, and no other consequence ever attended the bite. It is thus that falsehoods prevail for a century or two; and mankind at last begins to wonder how it was possible to keep up the delusion so long.

THE FLEA

The history of those animals with which we are the best acquainted, are the first objects of our chiefest curiosity. There are few but are well informed of the agility and the blood-thirsty disposition of the Flea; of the caution with which it comes to the attack; and the readiness, with which it avoids the pursuit. This insect, which is not only the enemy of mankind, but of the dog, cat and several other animals, is found in every part of the world, but bites with greater severity in some countries than in others. Its numbers in Italy and France are much greater than in England; and yet its bite is much more troublesome here, than I have found it in any other place. It would seem that its force increased with the coldness of the climate; and though less prolific, that it became more predacious.

If the flea be examined with a microscope, it will be observed to have a small head, large eyes, and a

Top Left **1** FUNNEL WEB MYGALOMORPH *Mygale quoyi* **2** SPITTING SPIDER *Scytodes thoracica*

Top Right **1** ASSASSIN BUG *Reduvius amaenus* **3** FEATHER-LEGGED BUG *Holoptilus lemur* **4** LACE BUG *Dysodius lunulatus* **5** MEDITERRANEAN COREIDID BUG *Phyllomorpha algirica* **7** FOLIACEOUS BUG *Anisoscelis flavolineatus* **8** MADAGASCAN DAMSEL BUG *Astemma madagascariensis*

Bottom Left **1** ORNATE CRANE-FLY *Ctenophora flabellata* **2** ROBBER FLY *Asilus erabroniformis* **3** GIANT ROBBER FLY *Laphria gigas* **4** *Mallophore infernalis* **5** *Midas giganteus*

Bottom Right **1** FIRE BUG *Pyrophorus pyrrorhynchus* **2** PLANT BUG *Penthicodes picta* **3** PLANT BUG *Lystra pulverulenta* **4** FROG HOPPER *Cercopis farcata*

LANTERN BUG *Fulgora graciliceps*

roundish body. It has two feelers, or horns, which are short, and composed of four joints; and between these lies its trunk, which it buries in the skin, and through which it sucks the blood in large quantities. The body appears to be all over curiously adorned with a suit of polished armour, neatly jointed, beset with multitudes of sharp pins, almost like the quills of a porcupine. It has six legs, the joints of which are so adapted, that it can as it were, fold them up one within another; and when it leaps, they all spring out at once, whereby its whole strength is exerted, and the body raised above two hundred times its own diameter.

The young fleas are at first a sort of nits or eggs, which are round and smooth; and from these proceed white worms, of a shining pearl colour: in a fortnight's time they come to a tolerable size, and are very lively and active; but if they are touched at this time, they roll themselves up in a ball: soon after this they begin to creep and then they seek a place to lie hid in, where they spin a silken thread from their

mouth, and with this they enclose themselves in a small round bag or case, as white within as writing paper, but dirty without: in this they continue for a fortnight longer; after which they burst from their confinement perfectly formed, and armed with powers to disturb the peace of an emperor.

LANTERN BUG *Fulgora graciliceps*

THE LOUSE

In examining the human Louse with the microscope, its external deformity first strikes us with disgust: the shape of the fore part of the head is somewhat oblong; that of the hind part somewhat round: the skin is hard, and being stretched, transparent, with here and there several bristly hairs: in the fore part is a proboscis or sucker, which is seldom visible: on each side of the head are antennae, or horns, each divided into five joints, covered with bristly hair; and several white vessels are seen through these horns: behind these are the eyes, which seem to want those divisions observable in other insects, and appear encompassed with some few hairs: the neck is very short, and the breast is divided into three parts; on each side of which are placed six legs, consisting of six joints, covered also with bristly hairs: the ends of the legs are armed with two smaller and larger ruddy claws, serving those insects as a finger and thumb, by which they catch hold of such objects as they approach: the end of the body terminates in a cloven tail, while the sides are all over hairy; the whole resembling clear parchment, and, when roughly pressed, cracking with a noise. When the louse feeds, the blood is seen to rush, like a torrent, into the stomach; and its greediness is so great, that the excrements contained in the intestines are ejected at the same time, to make room for this new supply.

The louse has neither beak, teeth, nor any kind of mouth for the entrance into the gullet is absolutely

GIANT BORNEAN CICADA *Cicada speciosa*

closed. In the place of all these, it has a proboscis with which it pierces the skin, and sucks the human blood, taking that for food only.

If this animal be kept from food two or three days, and then placed upon the back of the hand, or any

soft part of the body, it will immediately seek for food; which it will the more readily find, if the hand be rubbed till it grows red.

There is scarce any animal that multiplies so fast as this unwelcome intruder. It has been pleasantly said, that a louse becomes a grandfather in the space of twenty-four hours.

THE BED BUG

By day it lurks, like a robber, in the most secret parts of the bed; takes the advantage of every chink and cranny, to make a secure lodgement; and contrives its habitation with so much art, that scarce any industry can discover its retreat. It seems to avoid the light with great cunning; and even if candles be kept burning, this formidable insect will not issue from its hiding-place. But when darkness promises security, it then issues from every corner of the bed, drops from the tester, crawls from behind the arras, and travels with great assiduity to the unhappy

patient, who vainly wishes for rest and refreshment

Nor are these insects less disagreeable from their nauseous stench, than their unceasing appetites. When they begin to crawl, the whole bed is infected with the smell, but if they are accidentally killed, then it is insupportable.

These are a part of the inconveniences that result from the persecution of these odious insects: but happily for Great Britain, they multiply less in these islands, than in any part of the continent. In France and Italy the beds, particularly in their inns, swarm with them; and every piece of furniture seems to afford them a retreat. They grow larger also with them than with us, and bite with more cruel appetite.

This animal, if examined minutely, appears to consist of three principal parts; the head, the corselet, and the belly. It has two brown eyes, that are very small and a little prominent, besides two feelers, with three joints: underneath these there is a crooked trunk, which is its instrument of torture, and which, when in motion lies close upon the breast. The breast is a kind of ring, in which are placed the first pair of legs. The belly consists of nine rings; under which are placed two pairs of legs more, making six in all. Each leg has three joints, which form the thigh, the leg, and the foot, which is armed with a crooked claw, like a hook. The body is smooth, except a few short hairs, that may be seen by the microscope, about the vent, and on the two last rings. Its motion is slow and unwieldy; yet its sight is so exquisite, that the instant it perceives the light, it generally makes good its retreat; and they are seldom caught, though the bed swarms with them.

THE WOOD LOUSE

The common Wood Louse is seldom above half an inch long, and a quarter of an inch broad. The colour is of a livid black, especially when found about dunghills, and on the ground; but those that are to be met with under tiles, and in drier places, are of the colour of the hair of an ass. It has fourteen feet, seven on each side; and they have only one joint each, which is scarcely perceivable. It has two short feelers, and the body is of an oval shape. When it is touched, it rolls itself up into a sort of a ball; and the sides, near the feet, are dentated, like a saw. It is often found among rotten timber, and on decayed trees: in winter

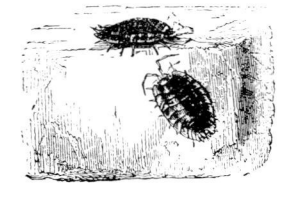

it lies hid in the crevices of walls and all sorts of buildings. The male is easily distinguishable from the female, being smaller, and more slender. The eggs they lay are white and shining, like seed pearls, and are very numerous: however, more properly speaking, although, when excluded, the young have all the appearance of an egg, yet they are alive, and, without throwing off any shell, stir and move about with great vivacity; so that this animal may properly be said to be viviparous.

THE WATER FLEA

These insects are of a blood red colour; and sometimes are seen in such multitudes on the surface of standing water, as to make it appear all over red, whence many fanciful people have thought the water to be turned into blood.

It is said that a celebrated professor of Leyden, was at first astonished by an appearance of this kind. Being once intent upon his studies, he heard a noise, of which, as it increased by degrees, he was desirous to know the cause. The maidservant attending to his summons, appeared quite petrified with fear, and told him, with a tremulous voice, that all the waters of Leyden were turned into blood. Upon this he went directly in a small boat to the place where the water was thus changed, and put some of the bloody water into a glass; but upon viewing it with attention, he observed, that it abounded with infinite numbers of these little red insects, which tinged the whole body of the fluid with that seemingly formidable colour.

THE SCORPION

The Scorpion is one of the largest of the insect tribe, and not less terrible from its size than its malignity. It resembles a lobster somewhat in shape, but is infinitely more hideous. There have been enumerated nine different kinds of this dangerous insect, chiefly distinguished by their colour: there being scorpions yellow, brown, and ash coloured; others that are the colour of rusty iron, green, pale yellow, black, claret colour, white, and grey.

There are four principal parts distinguishable in this animal; the head, the breast, the belly, and the tail. The scorpion's head seems, as it were, jointed to the breast; in the middle of which are seen two eyes; and a little more forward, two eyes more, placed in the fore part of the head: these eyes are so small, that they are scarcely perceivable; and it is probable the animal has but little occasion for seeing. The mouth is furnished with two jaws; the undermost is divided into two, and the parts notched into each other, which serves the animal as teeth, and with which it breaks its food, and thrusts it into its mouth: these the scorpion can at pleasure pull back into its mouth, so that no part of them can be seen. On each side of the head are two arms, each composed of four joints; the last of which is large, with strong muscles, and made in the manner of a lobster's claw. Below the breast are eight articulated legs, each divided into six joints; the two hindmost of which are each provided with two crooked claws, and here and there covered with hair. The belly is divided into seven little rings; from the lowest of which is continued a tail, composed of six joints, which are bristly, and formed like little globes, the last being armed with a crooked sting. This is that fatal instrument which renders this insect so formidable: it is long, pointed, hard and hollow; it is pierced near the base by two small holes, through which, when the animal stings, it ejects a drop of poison, which is white, caustic, and fatal. The reservoir in which this poison is kept, is in a small bladder near the tail, into which the venom is distilled by a peculiar apparatus. If this bladder be gently pressed, the venom will be seen issuing out through the two holes above-mentioned; so that it appears that when the animal stings, the bladder is pressed, and the venom issues through the two apertures into the wound.

There are few animals more formidable, or more truly mischievous than the scorpion. As it takes refuge in a small place, and is generally found sheltering in houses, so it cannot be otherwise than that it must frequently sting those among whom it resides.

IMPERIAL SCORPION *Scorpio buthus*

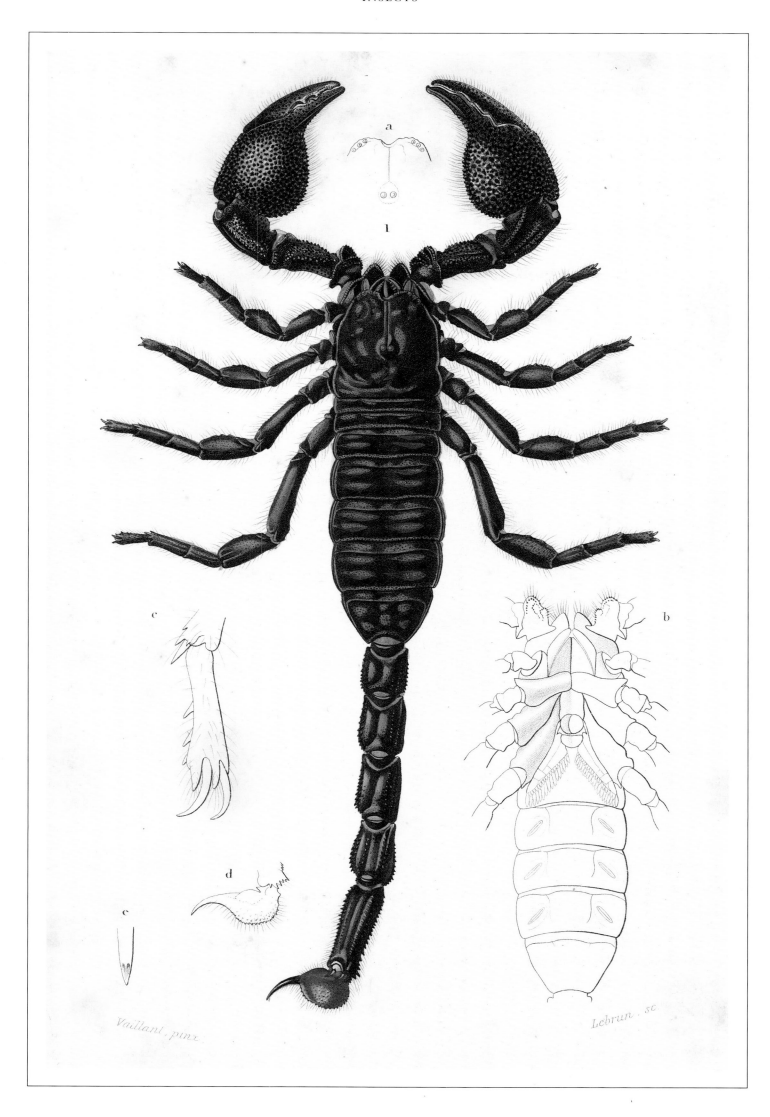

Vaillant. pinx

Lebrun . sc

In some of the towns of Italy, and in France, in the province of Languedoc, it is one of the greatest pests that torment mankind: but its malignity in Europe is trifling, when compared to what the natives of Africa, and the east, are known to experience. In Batavia, where they grow twelve inches long, there is no removing any piece of furniture, without the utmost danger of being stung by them. Along the Gold Coast, they are often found larger than a lobster, and their sting is inevitably fatal. In Europe,

however, they are by no means so large, so venomous, or so plentiful. The general size of this animal does not exceed two or three inches; and its sting is very seldom found to be fatal.

The fierce spirit of this animal is equally dangerous to its own species; for scorpions are the cruellest enemies to each other. One man put about a hundred of them together in the same glass; and they scarce came into contact, when they began to exert all their rage in mutual destruction: there was nothing to be seen but one universal carnage, without any distinction of age or sex; so that, in a few days, there remained only fourteen, which had killed and devoured all the rest.

THE LEECH

The Leech, from its uses in medicine, is one of those insects that man has taken care to provide; but of a great variety, one kind only is considered as serviceable. The Horse Leech, which is the largest of all, and grows to four inches in length, with a glossy black surface, is of no use, as it will not stick to the skin; the Snail Leech is but an inch in length; and though it will stick, is not large enough to extract a sufficient quantity of blood from the patient; the Broad Tailed Leech, which grows to an inch and a half in length, with the back raised into a sort of a ridge, will stick but on very few occasions: it is the Large Brown Leech, with a whitish belly, that is made use of in medicine, and whose history best merits our curiosity.

The leech has the general figure of a worm, and is about as long as one's middle finger. Its skin is composed of rings, by means of which it is possessed of its agility and swims in water. It contracts itself, when out of water, in such a manner, that when

touched it is not above an inch long. It has a small head, and a black skin, edged with a yellow line on each side, with some yellowish spots on the back. The belly also, which is of a reddish colour, is marked with whitish yellow spots. But the most remarkable part of this animal is the mouth, which is composed of two lips, that take whatever form the insect finds convenient. When at rest, the opening is usually triangular; and within it are placed three very sharp teeth, capable of piercing not only the human skin, but also that of a horse or an ox. Still deeper in the head, is discovered the tongue, which is composed of a strong fleshy substance, and which serves to assist the animal in sucking, when it has inflicted its triple wound; for no sooner is this voracious creature applied to the skin, than it buries its teeth therein, then closes its lips round the wounds which it has made; and thus, in the manner of a cupping-glass, extracts the blood as it flows to the different orifices.

When leeches are to be applied, the best way is to take them from the water in which they are contained about an hour before, for they thus become more voracious and fasten more readily. When saturated with blood, they generally fall off of themselves; but if it be thought necessary to take them from the wound, care should be used to pull them very gently, or even to sprinkle them with salt if they continue to adhere; for if they be plucked rudely away, it most frequently happens that they leave their teeth in the wound, which makes a very troublesome inflammation, and is often attended with danger. If they be slow in fixing to the part, they are often enticed by rubbing it with milk or blood, or water mixed with sugar. As salt is a poison to most insects, many people throw it upon the leech when it has dropped from the wound, by which means it disgorges the blood it has swallowed, and it is then kept for repeated application. They seldom, however, stick after this operation; and as the price is but small, fresh leeches should always be applied whenever such an application is thought necessary.

INSECTS OF THE SECOND ORDER

THE DRAGONFLY

Of all the flies which adorn or diversify the face of Nature, these are the most various and the most beautiful; they are of all colours, green, blue, crimson, scarlet, white; some unite a variety of the most vivid tints, and exhibit in one animal more different shades than are to be found in the rainbow. They are called, in different parts of the kingdom, by different names; but none can be at a loss to know them, as they are distinguished from all other flies by the length of their bodies, by the largeness of their eyes, and the beautiful transparency of their wings, which are four in number. They are seen in summer flying with great rapidity near every hedge, and by every running brook; they sometimes settle on the leaves of plants, and sometimes keep for hours together on the wing.

Dragonflies, though there are three or four different kinds, yet agree in the most striking parts of their history, and one account may serve for all. The largest sort are generally found from two to three inches long; their tail is forked; their body divided into eleven rings; their eyes are large, horny, and transparent, divided by a number of intersections; and their wings, that always lie flat when they are at

Left **1** CHINESE DEMOISELLE DAMSELFLY *Agrion chinensis*

2 BROAD-BODIED DRAGONFLY *Libellula hersilia*

Right **1** BUTTERFLY-LION *Ascalphus macaronius*

2 GIANT ANT-LION *Myrmeleon libelluloides*

3 BALKAN THREAD LACEWING *Nemoptera sinuta*

rest, are of a beautiful glossy transparency, sometimes shining like silver, and sometimes glistening like gold. Within the mouth are to be seen two teeth covered with a beautiful lip: with these the creatures bite fiercely when they are taken, but their bite is perfectly harmless as I have experienced more than once.

These insects, beautiful as they are, are produced from eggs, which are deposited in the water, where they remain for some time without showing life or motion. They are ejected by the female into the water in clusters, like a bunch of grapes, where they sink to the bottom by their natural weight, and continue in that state till the young ones find strength enough to break the shell, and to separate from each other. The form in which they first show life is that of a worm with six legs, bearing a strong resemblance to the dragon-fly in its winged state, except that the wings are yet concealed within a sheath peculiar to this animal. The rudiments of these appear in bunches on the back, within which the wings are folded up into each other, while all the colours and varieties of painting appear transparent through the skin. These animals, upon quitting the egg, still continue in the

water, where they creep and swim, but do not move swiftly. They have likewise a sharp sight, and immediately sink to the bottom if any one comes to the places wherein they live, or whenever they perceive the least uncommon object.

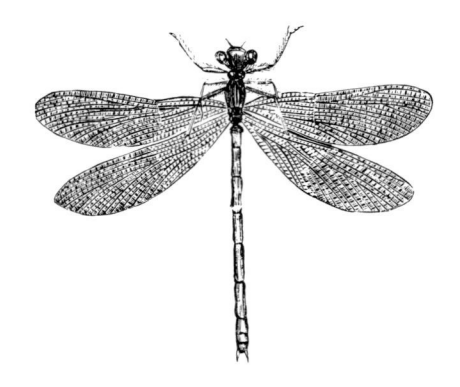

When these animals prepare to change from their reptile to their flying state, they then move out of the water to a dry place; as into grass, to pieces of wood, stone, or anything else they meet with. They there continue quite immoveable, as if meditating on the change they are to undergo. It is then observed, that the skin first opens on the head and back; and out of this opening they exhibit their real head and eyes, and at length their six legs. After this the enclosed creature creeps forward by degrees. During this time, the wings, which were moist and folded, begin by degrees to expand themselves. The body is likewise insensibly extended, until all the limbs have obtained their proper size and dimensions. The creature cannot at first make use of its new wings, and therefore is forced to stay in the same place until all its limbs are dried by the circumambient air.

No animal is more amply fitted for motion, subsistence and enjoyment. As it haunts and seeks after its food flying in the air, Nature has provided it with two large eyes, which make almost the whole head, and which resemble glittering mother of pearl. It has also four expansive silver-coloured wings, with which, as with oars, it can turn itself with prodigious velocity; and to assist these, it is furnished with a very long body, which, like a rudder, directs its motions. As the wings are long, and the legs short, they seldom walk, but are ever seen either resting or flying. For this reason, they always choose dry branches of trees or shrubs to remain on; and when they have refreshed themselves a little, they renew their flight. Thus they are seen adorning the summer with a profusion of beauty, lightly traversing the air in a thousand directions, and expanding the most beautiful colours to the sun. The garden, the forest, the hedges, and the rivulets, are animated by their sports; and there are few who have been brought up in the country who have not employed a part of their childhood in the pursuit.

THE GRASSHOPPER

The little Grasshopper that breeds in such plenty in every meadow, and that continues its chirping through the summer, is best known to us. This animal is of the colour of green leaves, except a line of brown which streaks the back, and two pale lines under the belly and behind the legs. It may be divided into the head, the thorax and the belly. The head is oblong, regarding the earth, and bearing some resemblance to that of a horse. Its mouth is covered by a kind of round buckler jutting over it, and armed with teeth of a brown colour, hooked at the points. Within the mouth is perceivable a large reddish tongue, and fixed to the lower jaw. The feelers or horns are very long, tapering off to a point; and the eyes are like two black specks, a little prominent. The thorax is elevated, narrow, armed above and below, by two serrated spines. The back is armed with a strong buckler, to which the muscles of the legs are firmly bound, and round these muscles are seen the vessels by which the animal breathes, as white as snow.

These insects are generally vocal in the midst of summer, and they are heard at sunsetting much louder than during the heats of the day. They are fed upon grass; and, if their belly be pressed, they will be seen to return the juices of the plants they have last fed upon. Though unwilling to fly, and slow in flight, particularly when the weather is moist or cool, they are sometimes seen to fly to considerable distances. If they are caught by one of the hind legs, they quickly disengage themselves from it, and leave the leg behind them. This prevents them from their chirping, for the sound is produced by rubbing their hind legs together. The loss of their leg also prevents

Top Left **1** BUSH CRICKET *Locusta sexpunctata*

3 FIELD CRICKET *Gryllus campestris*

4 MOLE CRICKET *Gryllotalpa nitidula*

Top Right TITAN STICK INSECT *Cyphocrana titan*

Bottom Left **1** CONE HEADED GRASSHOPPER *Truxalis miniata*

2 GRASSHOPPER *Acridium moestum*

4 HORNED GROUNDHOPPER *Tetrix lucifer*

Bottom Right **1** TWO-SPOTTED EARWIG *Forficula biguttata*

3 MADEIRA COCKROACH *Batta maderae*

5 PRAYING MANTIS *Mantis oratoria*

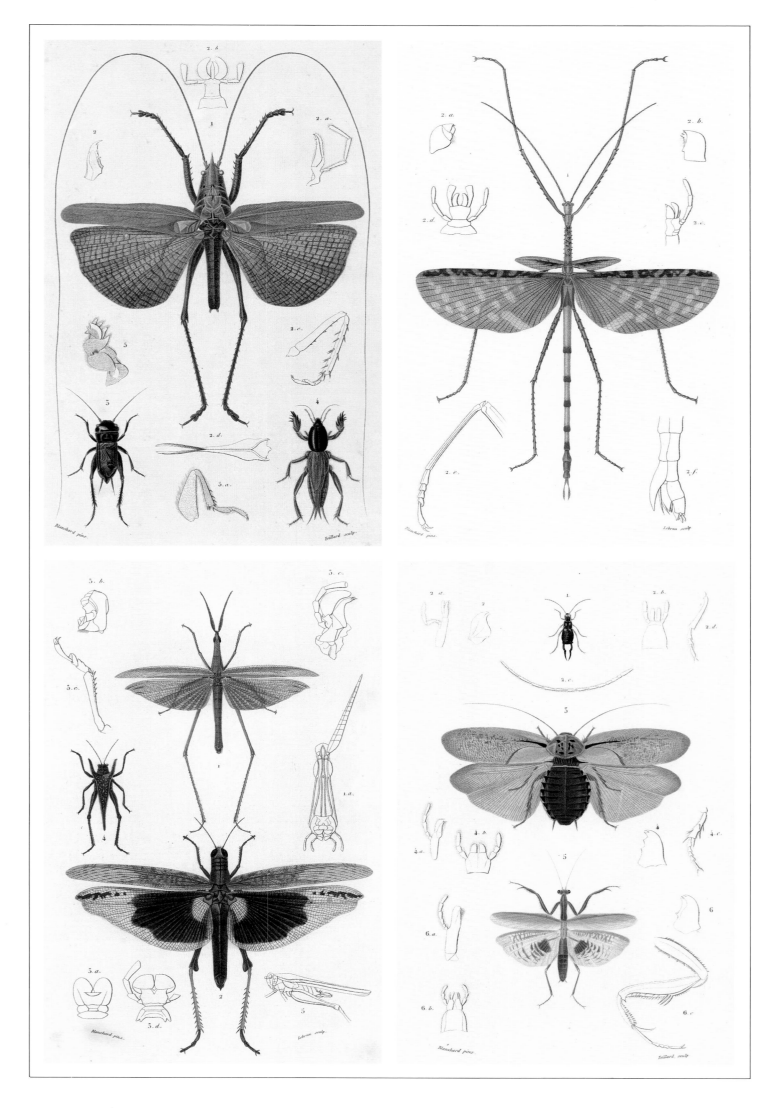

them from flying; for, being unable to lift themselves in the air, they have not room upon the ground for the proper expansion of their wings. If they be handled roughly, they will bite very fiercely; and when they fly, they make a noise with their wings. They generally keep in the plain, where the grass is luxuriant, and the ground rich and fertile: there they deposit their eggs, particularly in those cracks which are formed by the heat of the sun.

THE LOCUST

A swarm of Locusts, two or three miles long, and several yards deep, settle upon a field, and the consequences are frightful. The annals of every country are marked with the devastation which such a multitude of insects produces; and though they seldom visit Europe in such dangerous swarms as formerly, yet, in some of the southern kingdoms, they are still formidable. Those which have at uncertain intervals visited Europe, in our memory, are supposed to have come from Africa, and the animal is called the Great Brown Locust. It was seen in several parts of England in the year 1718, and many dreadful consequences were apprehended from its appearance. This insect is about three inches long; and has two horns or feelers, an inch in length. The head and horns are of a brownish colour; it is blue about the mouth, as also on the inside of the larger legs. The shield that covers the back is greenish; and the upper side of the body brown, spotted with black, and the underside purple. The upper wings are brown, with small dusky spots, with one larger at the tips; the under wings are more transparent, and of a light brown, tinctured with green, but there is a dark cloud of spots near the tips. This is that insect that has threatened us so often with its visitations; and that is so truly terrible in the countries where it is bred.

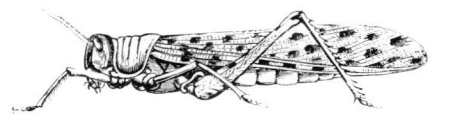

There is no animal in creation that multiplies so fast as these, if the sun be warm, and the soil in which their eggs are deposited be dry. Happily for us, the coldness of our climate, and the humidity of our soil, are no way favourable to their production; and as they are but the animals of a year, they visit us and perish.

The Scripture, which was written in a country where the locust made a distinguished feature in the picture of Nature, has given us several very striking images of this animal's numbers and rapacity. It compares an army, where the numbers are almost infinite, to a swarm of locusts: it describes them as rising out of the earth, where they are produced; as pursuing a settled march to destroy the fruits of the earth, and co-operate with divine indignation.

THE CRICKET

The Cricket is a very inoffensive and pretty animal. Though there be a species of this insect that lives entirely in the woods and fields, yet that with which we are best acquainted is the House Cricket, whose voice is so well known behind a country fire in a winter's evening. There is something so unusual in hearing a sound while we do not see the animal producing it, nor discover the place from whence it comes, that among the country people the chirping of the cricket is always held ominous; and whether it deserts the fireside, or pays an unexpected visit, the

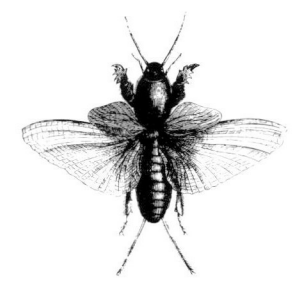

credulous peasantry always find something to be afraid of. In general, however, the killing of a cricket is considered as a most unlucky omen; and though their company is not much desired, yet no methods must be taken to remove them.

The cricket very much resembles the grasshopper in its shape, its manner of ruminating, its voice, its leaping, and methods of propagation. It differs in its colour, which is uniformly of a rusty brown; in its food, which is more various; and in its place of residence, which is most usually in the warmest chinks behind a country hearth. They are, in some measure, obliged to the bad masonry employed in making peasants houses for their retreats. The smallest chink serves to give them shelter; and where they once make their abode they are sure to propagate. They are of a most chilly nature, seldom leaving the fireside; and, if undisturbed, are seen to hop from their retreats to chirrup at the blaze in the chimney. The Wood Cricket is the most timorous animal in nature; but the Chimney Cricket, being used to noises, disregards not only those, but the appearance of people near it. There is a story of a woman who was very much incommoded by crickets, and tried, but in vain, every method of banishing them from her house. She at last accidentally succeeded, for having one day invited several guests to her house,

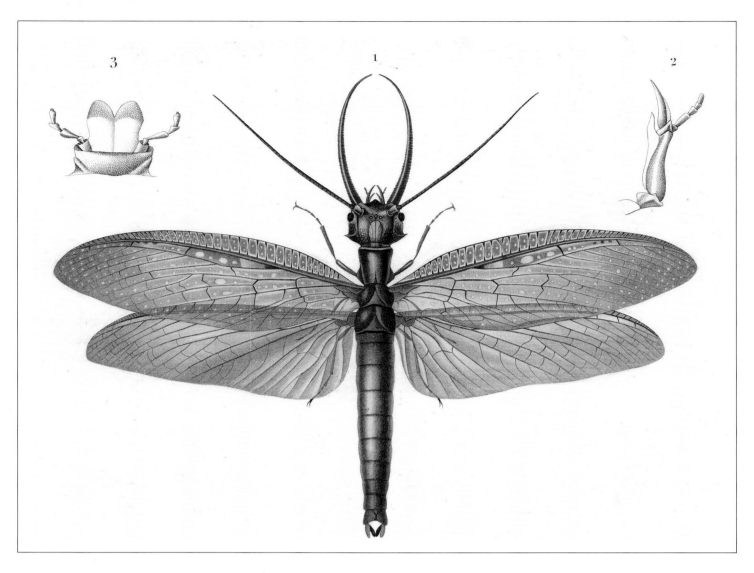

DOBSON FLY *Corydalis cornutus*

where there was a wedding, in order to increase the festivity of the entertainment, she procured drums and trumpets to entertain them. The noise of these was so much greater than what the little animals were used to, that they instantly forsook their situation, and were never heard in that mansion more.

THE EARWIG

This animal is so common, that it scarce needs a description: its swiftness in the reptile state is not less remarkable than its indefatigable velocity when upon the wing. That it must be very prolific, appears from its numbers; and that it is very harmless, every one's experience can readily testify. It is provided with six feet, and two feelers: the tail is forked; and with this it often attempts to defend itself against every assailant. But its attempts are only the threats of impotence; they draw down the resentment of powerful animals, but no way serve to defend it. The deformity of its figure, and its slender make, have also subjected it to an imputation, which, though entirely founded in prejudice, has more than once

procured its destruction. It is supposed, as the name imports, that it often enters into the ears of people sleeping, thus causing madness, from the intolerable pain, and, soon after, death itself. Indeed, the French name, which signifies the Ear-piercer, urges the calumny against this harmless insect, in very plain terms: yet nothing can be more unjust; the ear is already filled with a substance which prevents many insect from entering and besides, it is well lined and defended with membranes, which would keep out any little animal, even though the ear-wax were away. These reproaches, therefore, are entirely groundless: but it were well if the accusations which gardeners bring against the earwig, were as slightly

founded. There is nothing more certain than that it lives among flowers, and destroys them. When fruit also has been wounded by flies, the earwig generally comes in for a second feast, and sucks those juices which they first began to broach.

THE WATER SCORPION

We may also add the Water Scorpion, which is a large insect, being near an inch in length, and about half an inch in breadth. Its body is nearly oval, but very flat and thin; and its tail long and pointed. The head is small; and the feelers appear like legs, resembling the claws of a scorpion, but without sharp points. This insect is generally found in ponds; and is of all others the most tyrannical and rapacious. It destroys, like a wolf among sheep, twenty times as many as its hunger requires. One of these, when put into a basin of water, in which were thirty or forty worms of the libellula kind, each as large as itself, destroyed them all in a few minutes; getting on their backs, and piercing with its trunk through their body. These animals, however, though so formidable to others, are nevertheless themselves greatly overrun with a little kind of louse, about the size of a nit, which very probably repays the injury which the water scorpion inflicts upon others.

The water scorpions live in the water by day, out of which they rise in the dusk of the evening into the air, and so flying from place to place, often betake themselves, in quest of food, to other waters. The insect, before its wings are grown, remains in the place where it was produced; but when come to its state of perfection, sallies forth in search of a companion of the other sex, in order to continue its noxious posterity.

INSECTS OF THE THIRD ORDER

THE CATERPILLAR

Caterpillars may be easily distinguished from worms or maggots, by the number of their feet; and by their producing butterflies or moths. When the sun calls up vegetation, and vivifies the various eggs of insects, the caterpillars are the first that are seen, upon almost every vegetable and tree, eating its leaves, and preparing for a state of greater perfection. They have feet both before and behind; which not only enable them to move forward by a sort of steps made by their fore and hind parts, but also to climb up vegetables, and to stretch themselves out from the boughs and stalks, to reach their food, at a distance. All of this class have from eight feet at the least, to sixteen. Of these feet the six foremost are covered with a shiny gristle, and the hindmost feet are soft and flexible. The animal into which they are converted, is always a butterfly or a moth; and these are always distinguished from other flies, by having their wings covered over with a painted dust, which gives them such various beauty. The butterfly makes one of the principal ornaments of oriental poetry; but, in those countries, the insect is larger and more beautiful than with us.

The transmutations that caterpillars undergo, are more numerous than those of any other insect. When they are excluded from the egg, they assume the form of a small caterpillar, which feeds and grows larger every day, often changing its skin, but, still preserving its form. When the animal has come to a certain

magnitude in this state, it discontinues eating, makes itself a covering or husk, in which it remains wrapped up, seemingly without life or motion; and after having for some time continued in this state, it once more bursts its confinement, and comes forth a butterfly.

The butterfly is very careful in depositing its eggs in those places where they are likely to be hatched with the greatest safety and success. During winter, therefore, the greatest number of caterpillars are in an egg state; and in this lifeless situation, brave all the rigours and the humidity of the climate and still preserve the latent principles of life, which is more fully exerted at the approach of spring. When the insect has found force to break its shell, it always finds its favourite food provided in abundance before it.

But all caterpillars are not hatched from the egg in the beginning of spring; for many of them have subsisted during the winter in their aurelia state: in which, the animal is seemingly deprived of life and motion. In this state of insensibility, many of these insects continue during the winter; some enclosed in a kind of shell, which they have spun for themselves at

Top Left **1** RED-TIP BUTTERFLY *Anthocharis eupompe*

2 TROPICAL ORANGE TIP *Zegris eupheme*

3 CLEOPATRA BUTTERFLY *Rodocera cleopatra*

4 CLOUDED YELLOW *Colias palaeno*

Top Right **1** PANSY BUTTERFLY *Vanessa almana*

2 TIGER BUTTERFLY *Limenitis jadera*

3 RED-TIPPED ADMIRAL *Danais juventa*

4 CARDINAL BUTTERFLY *Argynnis pandora*

Bottom Left MADAGASCAN DAY-FLYING URANID MOTH *Urania riphaeus*

Bottom Right **1** MONARCH BUTTERFLY *Danais archippus*

2 PERUVIAN CRACKER BUTTERFLY *Peridromia amphinome*

3 DORIS BUTTERFLY *Heliconius doris*

the end of autumn; some concealed under the bark of trees; others in the chinks of old walls; and many buried underground. From all these, a variety of butterflies are seen to issue, in the beginning of spring, and adorn the earliest part of the year with their painted flutterings.

Some caterpillars do not make any change whatever at the approach of winter; but continue to live in their reptile state, through all the severity of the season. These choose themselves a retreat, where they may remain undisturbed and motionless for some months together. In general, caterpillars of this kind are found in great numbers together, enclosed in one common web, that covers them all, and serves to protect them from the injuries of the air.

Lastly, there are some of the caterpillar kind, whose butterflies live all the winter; and who, having fluttered about for some part of the latter end of autumn, seek for some retreat during the winter, in order to answer the ends of propagation, at the approach of spring. These are often found lifeless and motionless in the hollows of trees, or the clefts of timber; but, by being approached to the fire, they recover life and activity, and seem to anticipate the desires of spring.

The life of a caterpillar seems one continued succession of changes; and it is seen to throw off one skin only to assume another; which also is divested in its turn: and thus for eight or ten times successively. We must not, however, confound this changing of the skin with the great metamorphosis which it is after-

wards to undergo. The throwing off one skin, and assuming another, seems, in comparison, but a slight operation among these animals: this is but the work of a day; the other is the great adventure of their lives.

Preparatory to this important change, the caterpillar most usually quits the plant, or the tree on which it fed; or at least attaches itself to the stalk or the stem, more gladly than the leaves. It forsakes its food, and prepares, by fasting, to undergo its transmutation. Some of this tribe, at this period also, are seen entirely to change colour; and the vivacity of the tints in all, seem faded. The web or cone, with which some cover themselves, hides the aurelia contained within from the view; but in others, where it is more transparent, the caterpillar, when it has done spinning, strikes into it the claws of the two feet under the tail, and afterwards forces in the tail itself, by contracting those claws, and violently striking the feet one against the other. In this condition they remain one or two days; they then appear with their bodies bent into a bow, which they occasionally straighten: they make no use of their legs; but if they attempt to change place, do so by contortions. In proportion as their change into an aurelia approaches, their body becomes increasingly bent; while their extensions and convulsive contractions become more frequent. The hind end of the body is the part which the animal first disengages from its caterpillar skin; that part of the skin remains empty, while the body is drawn up

D'URVILLE'S BIRD-WING BUTTERFLY *Ornithoptera urvilliana*

contractedly towards the head. In the same manner they disengage themselves from the two succeeding rings; so that the animal is then lodged entirely in the fore-part of its caterpillar covering: that half which is abandoned, remains flacid and empty; while the fore-part, on the contrary, is swollen and distended. The animal still continues to heave and work as before, so that the skull is soon seen to burst into three pieces, and a longitudinal opening is made in the three first rings of the body, through which the insect thrusts forth its naked body, with strong efforts.

The caterpillar, thus stripped of its skin for the last time, has now become an aurelia; in which the parts of the future butterfly are all visible; but in so soft a state, that the smallest touch can discompose them. The animal is now helpless and motionless; only waiting for the assistance of the air to dry up the moisture on its surface, and supply it with a crust capable of resisting external injuries. Immediately after being stripped of its caterpillar skin, it is of a green colour, especially in those parts which are distended by an extraordinary afflux of animal moisture; but in ten or twelve hours after being thus exposed, its parts harden, the air forms its external covering into a firm crust, and in about twenty four hours, the aurelia may be handled without endan-

1 GREAT PEACOCK MOTH *Attacus pavonia major*
2 EMPEROR MOTH *Attacus pavonia minor*

gering the embryo butterfly. Such is the history of the little pod or cone that is found so common by every pathway, sticking to nettles, and sometimes shining like polished gold. From the beautiful and resplendent colour, with which it is thus sometimes adorned, some authors have called it a Chrysalis, implying a creature made of gold.

The aurelia, though it now bears a different external appearance, nevertheless contains within it all the parts of the butterfly in perfect formation; and lying each in a very orderly manner, though in the smallest compass.

The efforts which the butterfly makes to get free from its aurelia state, are by no means so violent as those which the insect had in changing from the caterpillar into the aurelia. When this operation begins, there seems to be a violent agitation in the humours contained within the little animal's body. Its fluids seem driven, by a hasty fermentation, through all the vessels, while it labours violently with its legs,

and makes several other violent struggles to get free. As all these motions concur with the growth of the insect's wings and body, it is impossible that the brittle skin which covers it should longer resist: it at length gives way, by bursting into four distinct and regular pieces.

The butterfly, to enjoy life, needs no other food but the dews of Heaven; and the honeyed juices which are distilled from every flower. The pageantry of princes cannot equal the ornaments with which it is invested; nor the rich colouring that embellishes its wings. The skies are the butterfly's proper habitation, and the air its element.

BUTTERFLIES AND MOTHS

The number of these beautiful animals is very great; and though Linnaeus has reckoned up above seven hundred and sixty different kinds, the catalogue is still very incomplete.

The wings of Butterflies are four in number; though the animal can fly with only two. They are, in their own substance, transparent; but owe their opacity to the beautiful dust with which they are

covered; and which has been likened, by some naturalists, to the feathers of birds; by others, to the scales of fishes. In fact, under a good microscope, we shall perceive it studded over with a variety of little grains of different dimensions and forms, generally supported upon a footstalk, regularly laid upon the whole surface. Nothing can exceed the beautiful and regular arrangement of these little substances; which thus serve to paint the butterfly's wing, like the tiles of a house. The wing itself is composed of several thick nerves, which render the construction very strong, though light; and though it be covered over with thousands of these scales or studs, its weight is very little increased by the number, enabling it to support itself a long while in air, although its flight is not very graceful. When flying to a considerable distance, it follows a haphazard path. Upon closer examination, however, it will be found that it flies thus irregularly in pursuit of its mate; and as dogs bait and quarter the ground in pursuit of their game, so these insects traverse the air, in quest of their mates, whom they can discover at more than a mile's distance.

The butterfly may be divided into three parts; the

head, the corselet, and the body.

The body is the hind part of the butterfly, and is composed of rings, which are generally concealed under long hair, with which that part of the animal is clothed. The corselet is more solid than the rest of the body, because the fore-wings, and the legs, are fixed therein. The legs are six in number, although four only are made use of by the animal; the two fore-legs being often concealed in the long hair of the body.

The eyes of butterflies have not all the same form; for in some they are large, in others small; in some they are the larger portion of a sphere, in others they are but a small part of it, and just appearing from the head. In all of them, however, the outward coat has a lustre, containing the various colours of the rainbow. When examined closely it has the appearance of a multiplying glass; having a great number of sides, or facets, in the manner of a brilliant cut diamond.

Butterflies, as well as most other flying insects, have two instruments, like horns, on their heads, which are commonly called feelers. They differ from the horns of greater animals, in being moveable at their base; and in having a great number of joints, by which means the insect is enabled to turn them in every direction. Those of butterflies are placed at the top of the head, pretty near the external edge of each eye.

The trunk or proboscis is placed exactly between the eyes; and when the animal is not employed in seeking its nourishment, it is rolled up, like a curl. A butterfly, when it is feeding, flies round some flower, and. settles upon it. The trunk is then uncurled, and thrust out either wholly or in part; and is employed in searching the flower to its very bottom, however deep. This search being repeated seven or eight times, the butterfly then passes to another; and continues to hover over those agreeable to its taste, like a bird over its prey. This trunk consists of two equal hollow tubes, nicely joined to each other, like the pipes of an organ.

Such is the figure and conformation of these beautiful insects, that cheer our walks, and give us the earliest intimations of summer. But it is not by day alone that they are seen fluttering wantonly from flower to flower, as the greatest number of them fly by night, and expand the most beautiful colouring, at those hours when there is no spectator. This tribe of insects has therefore been divided into Diurnal and Nocturnal Flies; or, more properly speaking, into Butterflies and Moths: the one only flying by day, the other most usually on the wing in the night. They

1 ARGENTINIAN SWALLOWTAIL *Papilio duponcheli*

2 EASTERN FESTOON *Thais cerisyi*

3 SMALL APOLLO *Parnassius phoebus*

Delarue pinx.

Lebrun sc.

may be easily distinguished from each other, by their horns or feelers: those of the butterfly being clubbed, or knobbed at the end; those of the moth, tapering finer and finer to a point. To express it technically; the feelers of butterflies are clavated; those of moths, are filiform.

The butterflies, as well as the moths, employ the short life assigned them, in a variety of enjoyments. Their whole time is spent either in quest of food, which every flower offers; or in pursuit of the female.

The general rule among insects is, that the female is larger than the male; and this obtains particularly in the tribe I am describing. The body of the male is smaller and slenderer; that of the female, more thick and oval.

But the females of many moths and butterflies seem to have assumed their airy form for no other reason but to fecundate their eggs, and lay them. They are not seen fluttering about in quest of food, or

a mate: all that passes, during their short lives, is a junction with the male of about half an hour; after which they deposit their eggs, and die, without taking any nourishment, or seeking any. It may be observed, however, that in all the females of this tribe, they are impregnated by the male by one aperture, and lay their eggs by another.

The eggs of female butterflies are disposed in the body like a bed of chaplets; which, when excluded, are usually oval, and of a whitish colour: some,

however, are quite round; and others flattened, like a turnip. The covering or shell of the egg, though solid, is thin and transparent; and in proportion as the caterpillar grows within the egg, the colours change, and are distributed differently. Each egg contains but one caterpillar; and it is requisite that this little animal, when excluded, should be near its peculiar provision. The butterfly, therefore, is careful to place her brood only upon those plants that afford good nourishment to its posterity. Though the little winged animal has been fed itself upon dew, or the honey of flowers, yet it makes choice for its young of a very different provision, and lays its eggs on the most unsavoury plants; the ragweed, the cabbage, or the nettle. Thus every butterfly chooses not the plant

Top Left **1** BRAZILIAN BROWN BUTTERFLY *Hoetera philocteles* **2** HORSFIELDS JAVANESE NYMPHALID BUTTERFLY *Hyades horsfieldii* **3** S. AMERICAN SKIPPER BUTTERFLY *Eudamus versicolor*

Top Right **1** GIANT STEM-BOORER MOTH *Castnia japyx* **2** NEW GUINEAN BEE-MIMIC MOTH *Cocytia urvillaei* **3** *Agarista picta*

Bottom Left **1** CLIFDEN NONPAREIL *Catocala fraxini* **2** TROPICAL FRUIT-PIERCER *Ophideres imperator* **3** *Agarais vitripennis*

Bottom Right **1** S. AFRICAN SWIFT MOTH *Hepialus venus* **2 3** TIGER MOTHS *Chelonia purpurea, Chelonia hebe*

Below **1** DEATH'S-HEAD HAWK-MOTH *Acherontia atropos* **2** SIX-SPOT BURNET MOTH *Zygaena filipenular* **3** CTENUCHID DAY FLYING MOTH *Syntomis phegra*

most grateful to it in its winged state; but such as it has fed upon in caterpillar form.

All the tribe of female moths lay their eggs a short time after they leave the aurelia; but there are many butterflies that flutter about the whole summer, and do not think of laying, till the winter begins to warn them of their approaching end; some even continue the whole winter in the hollows of trees, and do not provide for posterity until the beginning of April, when they leave their retreats, deposite their eggs, and die. Their eggs soon begin to feel the genial influence of the season: the little animals burst from them in their caterpillar state, to become aurelias, and butterflies in their turn; and thus to continue the round of nature.

THE SILKWORM

The Silkworm which only works for itself and has been made of the utmost service to man, furnishing him with a covering more beautiful than any other animal can supply, is a large caterpillar, of a whitish colour, with twelve feet, producing a butterfly of the moth kind. The cone on which it spins, is formed for covering it while it continues in the aurelia state; and several of these, properly wound off, and united together, form those strong and beautiful threads, which are woven into silk.

There are two methods of breeding silkworms; for they may be left to grow, and remain at liberty upon the trees where they are hatched; or they may be kept in a place built for that purpose, and fed every day with fresh leaves. The first method is used in China, and other hot countries; the other is used in those places where the animal has been artificially propagated, and still continues a stranger. In the warm climates, the silkworm proceeds from an egg, which has been glued by the parent moth upon proper parts of the mulberry-tree, and which remains in that situation during the winter. The manner in which they are situated and fixed to the tree, keeps them unaffected by the influence of the weather, so that those frosts which are severe enough to kill the tree, have no power to injure the silkworm.

The insect never proceeds from the egg till Nature has provided it a sufficient supply; and till the budding leaves are furnished, in sufficient abundance, for its support. When the leaves are put forth, the worms seem to feel the genial summons, and bursting from their little eggs, crawl upon the leaves, where they feed with a most voracious appetite. Thus they become larger by degrees; and after some months feeding, they lay, upon every leaf, small bundles, or cones of silk, which appear like so many golden apples, painted on a fine green ground. Such is the method of breeding them in the East; and without

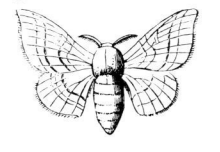

doubt it is best for the worms, and least troublesome for the feeder of them. But it is otherwise in our colder European climates, and to breed them in Europe, they must be sheltered and protected from every external injury.

For this purpose a well-insulated room with a South aspect is chosen. When the worms are hatched, some tender mulberry leaves are provided, and placed in the cloth or paper box in which the eggs were laid, and which are large enough to hold a great number.

There is another precaution of equal importance, which is to give them air, and open their chamber windows on sunny days. The place also must be kept as clean as possible; not only the several floors that are laid to receive their ordure, but the whole apartments in general. These things well observed, contribute greatly to their health and increase.

INSECTS OF THE FOURTH ORDER

THE BEE

The multitude of bees in one swarm all owe their origin to a single parent, the Queen-Bee. It is indeed surprising that a single insect shall, in one summer, give birth to above twenty thousand young; but, upon examining her body, the wonder will cease, as the number of eggs appearing, at one time, amounts to five thousand. This animal, whose existence is of such importance to her subjects, may easily be distinguished from the rest, by her size and the shape of her body. On her safety depends the whole welfare of the commonwealth; and the attentions paid her by all the rest of the swarm, evidently show the dependence her subjects have upon her security. If this insect be carefully observed, she will be seen at times attended with a numerous retinue of labouring bees marching from cell to cell, plunging the extremity of her body into many of them, and leaving a small egg in each.

There are three different kinds of bees in every

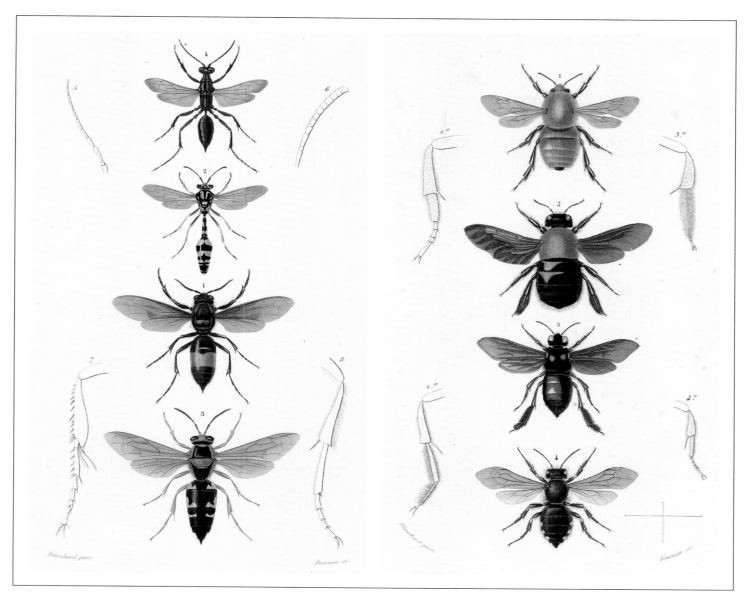

Left **1** *Vespa cincta*
2 POTTER WASP *Eumenes flavopictus*
3 DIGGER WASP *Stizus speciosus*
4 INDIAN HUNTING WASP *Chlorion lobatum*

Right **1** BUMBLE-BEE *Bombus dahlbomii*
2 *Acanthopus splendidus*
3 CARPENTER-BEE *Xylocopa trepida*
4 CUCKOO BEE *Melecta punctata*

hive. The bees which generally compose her train, are males, the Drones, generally not above a hundred in a hive of seven to eight thousand bees, which serve to impregnate her by turns. These are larger and blacker than the common bees; without stings, and without industry. They seem formed only to transmit a posterity; and to attend the queen, whenever she thinks proper to issue from the secret retreats of the hive, where she most usually resides. Upon the union of these two kinds depends all expectations of a future progeny; for the working bees which make up the greater number, are of no sex, and only labour for another offspring and continuing the breed, yet such is their attention to their queen, that if she happens to die, they will leave off working, and take no further care of posterity. If, however, another queen is, in this state of universal despair presented them, they immediately acknowledge her for sovereign, and

once more diligently apply to their labour.

In examining the structure of the common working bee, the first remarkable part that offers is the trunk, which serves to extract the honey from flowers. It is not formed, like that of other flies, in the manner of a tube, by which the fluid is to be sucked up; but like a besom, to sweep, or a tongue, to lick it away. The insect is furnished also with teeth, which serve it in making wax. This substance is gathered from flowers, like honey; it consists of that pollen dust or farina which contributes to the fecundation of plants, and is moulded into wax by the bee at leisure. Every bee, when it leaves the hive to collect this precious store, enters into the cup of the flower, particularly such as seem charged with the greatest quantities of this yellow farina. As the insect's body is covered over with hair, it rolls itself within the flower, and becomes quite covered with the dust, which it soon after brushes off with its two hind legs, and kneads into two little balls. In the thighs of the hind legs there are two cavities, edged with hair; and into these, as into a basket, the animal sticks its pellets. Thus employed, the bee flies from flower to flower, increasing its store, and adding to its stock of wax; until the ball, upon each thigh, becomes as big as a grain of pepper: by this time, having got a sufficient load, it returns, making the best of its way to the hive.

The belly of the bee is divided into six rings, which sometime shorten the body, by slipping one over the other. It contains within it, beside the intestines, the honey-bag, the venom-bag, and the sting. The honey-bag is as transparent as crystal, containing the honey that the bee has brushed from the flowers; of which the greater part is carried to the hive, and poured into the cells of the honey-comb; while the remainder serves for the bee's own nourishment: for, during summer, it never touches what has been laid up for winter. The sting, which serves to defend this creature from its enemies, is composed of three parts; the sheath, and two darts, which are extremely small and penetrating. Both the darts have several small points or barbs, like those of a fish-hook, which renders the sting more painful, and makes the darts rankle in the wound. Still, however, this instrument would be very slight, did not the bee poison the wound. The sheath, which has a sharp point, makes the first impression; which is followed by that of the darts, and then the venomous liquor is poured in. The sheath sometimes sticks so fast in the wound, that the animal is obliged to leave it behind; by which the bee soon after dies, and the wound is considerably enflamed. It might at first appear well for mankind, if the bee were without its sting; but, upon recollection, it will be found, that it would then have too many rivals in sharing its labours. A hundred other lazy animals, fond of honey, and hating labour, would intrude upon the sweets of the hive; and the treasure would be carried off, for want of armed guardians to protect it.

From examining the bee singly, we now come to consider it in society, as an animal not only subject to

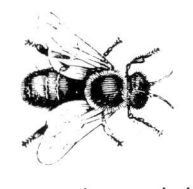 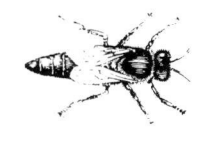

laws, but active, vigilant, laborious, and disinterested. All its provisions are laid up for the community; and all its arts in building a cell, designed for the benefit of posterity. The substance with which bees build their cells is wax; which is fashioned into convenient apartments for themselves and their young. When they begin to work in their hives, they divide themselves into four companies: one of which roves in the fields in search of materials; another employs itself in laying out the bottom and partitions of their cells; a third is employed in making the inside smooth from the corners and angles; and the fourth

company bring food for the rest, or relieve those who return with their respective burdens. But they are not kept constant to one employment; they often change the tasks assigned them; those that have been at work, being permitted to go abroad; and those that have been in the fields already, take their places. They seem even to have signs, by which they understand each other; for when any of them want food, it bends down its trunk to the bee from whom it is expected, which then opens its honey-bag, and lets some drops fall into the other's mouth, which is at that time opened to receive it. Their diligence and labour is so great, that, in a day's time, they are able to make cells, which lie upon each other numerous enough to contain three thousand bees.

THE ANT

The Common Ants of Europe, are of two or three different kinds; some red, some black, some with stings, and others without. Such as have stings, inflict their wounds in that manner; such as are unprovided with these weapons of defence, have a power of spurting, from their hind parts, an acid pungent liquor, which if it lights upon the skin, inflames and burns it like nettles.

The body of an ant is divided into, the head, breast and belly. In the head, the eyes are placed, which are entirely black, and under the eyes, there are two small horns or feelers, composed of twelve joints, all covered with a fine silky hair. The mouth is furnished with two crooked jaws, which project outwards, in each of which are seen incisors, that look like teeth. The breast is covered with a fine silky hair, from which project six legs, that are pretty stong and hairy, the extremities of each armed with two small claws, which the animal uses in climbing. The belly is more reddish than the rest of the body, which is of a brown chestnut colour, it is as shining as glass, and covered with extremely fine hair.

From such a formation, this animal seems bolder, and more active, for its size, than any other of the insect tribe, and fears not to attack a creature, often above ten times its own magnitude.

As soon as the winter is past, the ant hill, that before seemed a desert, now swarms with new life, and myriads of these insects awake from their annual lethargy, and prepare for the pleasures and fatigues of the season. For the first day they never leave the hill, which may be considered as their citadel, but run over every part of it, as if to examine its present situation, to observe what injuries it has sustained

GOLIATH BEETLE *Goliathus cacicus*

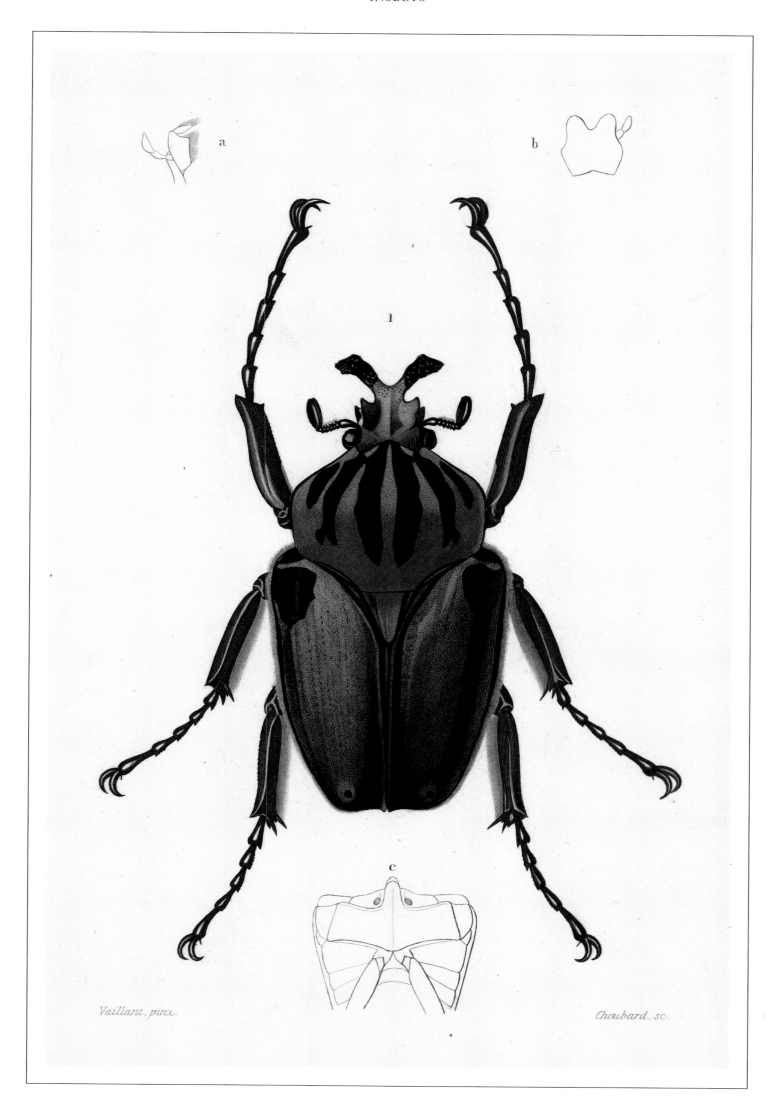

Vaillant, pinx.

Choubard, sc.

during the rigours of winter, and to mediate and settle the labours of the day ensuing.

At the first display of their forces, none but the wingless tribe, the working ants, appears, while those with wings, the males and females, remain at the bottom.

In eight or ten days after their first appearance, the labours of the hill are in some forwardness; the males and females are seen mixing with the working multitude, and pursued or pursuing each other. They seem no way to partake in the common drudgeries of the state; the males pursue the females with great assiduity, and they remain coupled for some time, while the males thus united, suffer themselves to be drawn along by the will of their partners.

In the meantime, the working body of the state take no part in their pleasures, they are seen diligently going from the ant-hill, in pursuit of food for themselves and their associates, and of proper materials for giving a comfortable retreat to their young, or safety to their habitation. In the fields of England, ant-hills are formed with but little apparent regularity. In the more southern provinces of Europe, they are constructed with wonderful contrivance, and offer a sight highly worthy of a naturalist's curiosity. These are generally formed in the neighbourhood of some large tree and a stream of water. The shape of the ant-hill is that of a sugar-loaf, about three feet high, composed of various substances; leaves, bits of wood, sand, earth, bits of gum, and grains of corn. These are all united into a compact body, perforated with galleries down to the bottom, and winding ways within the body of the structure.

The chief employment of the working ants, is in sustaining not only the idlers at home, but also finding a sufficiency of food for themselves. They live upon various provisions, as well of the vegetable as of the animal kind. Small insects they will kill and devour; sweets of all kinds, they are particularly fond of. They seldom, however, think of their community, till they themselves are first satiated. Having found a juicy fruit, they swallow what they can, and then tearing it in pieces, carry home their load. If they meet with an insect above their match, several of them will fall upon it at once, and having mangled it, each will carry off a part of the spoil. If they meet, in their excursions, anything that is too heavy for one to bear, and yet which they are unable to divide, several of them will endeavour to force it along; some dragging and others pushing. If any one of them happens to make a lucky discovery, it will immediately give advice to others, and then at once, the whole republic will put themselves in motion. If in these struggles, one of them happens to be killed, some kind survivor will carry him off to a great distance, to prevent the obstructions his body may give to the general spirit of industry.

But while they are thus employed in supporting the state, in feeding abroad, and carrying in provisions to those that continue at home, they are not unmindful of posterity. After a few days of fine weather, the female ants begin to lay their eggs, and those are as assiduously watched and protected by the working ants. They are carried as soon as laid, to the safest situation, at the bottom of their hill. Those white substances which we so plentifully find in every ant-hill, are not the eggs as newly laid. On the contrary, the ant's egg is so very small, that, though laid upon a black ground, it can scarcely be discerned. The little white bodies we see, are the young insects in their maggot state, long since freed from the egg, and often involved in a cone, which it has spun round itself, like a silkworm.

THE BEETLE

Of the Beetle there are various kinds; all, however, concurring in one common formation of having cases to their wings, which are the more necessary to those insects, as they often live under the surface of the earth, in holes, which they dig out by their own industry. These cases prevent the various injuries their real wings might sustain, by rubbing or crushing against the sides of their abode. These do not assist flight, yet keep the internal wings clean and even, and produce a loud buzzing noise, when the animal rises in the air.

If we examine the formation of all animals of the beetle kind, we shall find, as in shell-fish, that their bones are placed externally, and their muscles within. These muscles are formed very much like those of quadrupeds, and are endued with such surprising strength, that bulk for bulk, they are a thousand times stronger than those of a man. The strength of these muscles is of use in digging the animal's subterraneous abode, where it is most usually hatched, and to which it most frequently returns, even after it becomes a winged insect, capable of flying.

Top Left 1 ELEPHANT DUNG BEETLE *Copris isidis* 2 S. AMERICAN DUNG BEETLE *Phanaeus lancifer* 3 4 EGYPTIAN DUNG BEETLE *Ateuchus aegyptiorum* Top Right 1 RHINO BEETLE *Scarabaeus hyllus* 2 CHAFER BEETLE *Chrysophora macropa* Bottom Left 1 PEGOR BESS BEETLE *Passalus tridens* 2 STAG BEETLE *Lucanus cervus* 3 CHILEAN STAG BEETLE *Chiasognathus grantii* Bottom Right 1 C. AMERICAN TORTOISE BEETLE *Sagra boisduvalii* 2 FOUR SPOT LEAF BEETLE *Alurnus quadrimaculatus* 3 FROG BEETLE *Eugenysa grossa* 4 GIANT BRAZILIAN LEAF BEETLE *Eumolopus fulgidus* 5 BURRYING BEETLE *Doryphora punctatissima*

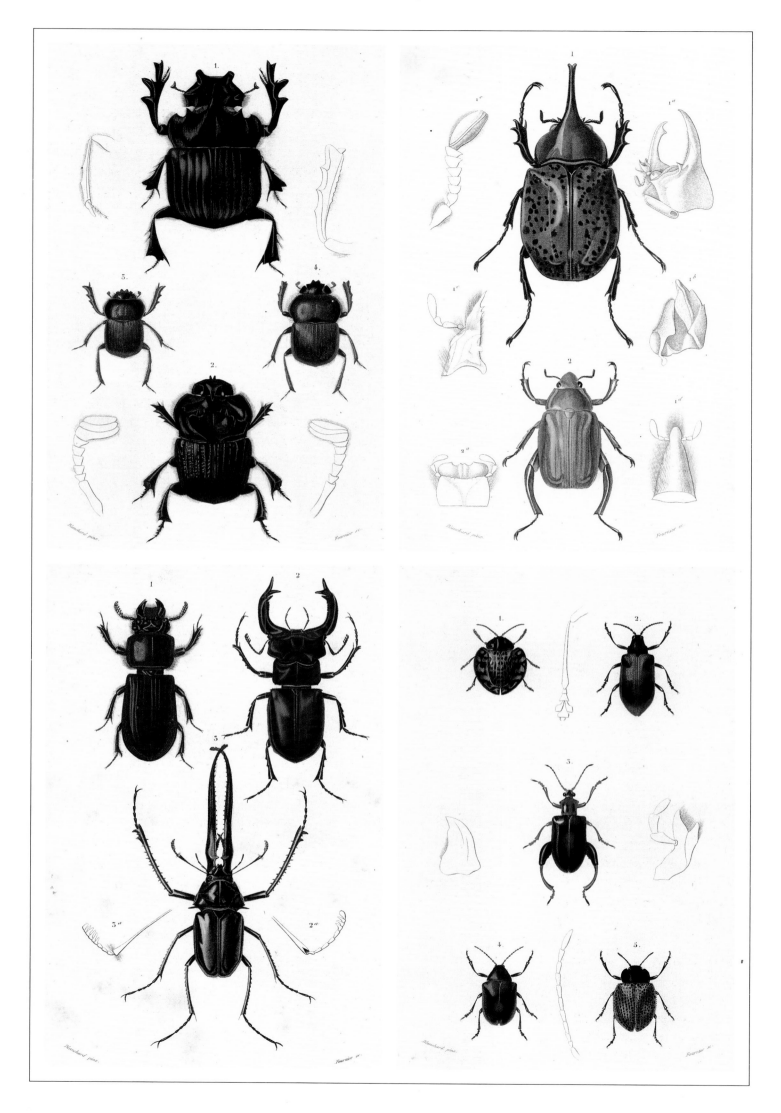

Beside the difference which results from the shape and colour of these animals, the size also makes a considerable one; some beetles being not larger than the head of a pin, while others, such as the elephant beetle, are as big as one's fist: But the greatest difference among them is, that some are produced in a month, and in a single season go through all the stages of their existence, while others take near four years to their production; and live as winged insects a year more.

The May-bug, or Dorr-Beetle, as some call it, has, like all the rest, a pair of cases to its wings, which are of a reddish brown colour, sprinkled with a whitish dust, which easily comes off. In some years their necks are seen covered with a red plate, and in others, with a black, these, however, are distinct sorts, and their difference is by no means accidental. The forelegs are very short, and the better calculated for burrowing in the ground, where this insect makes its

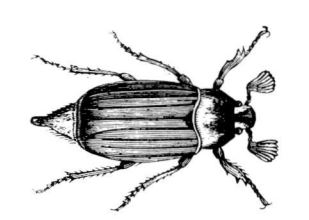

retreat. It is well known for its evening buzz to children; but still more formidably introduced to the acquaintance of husbandmen and gardeners, for in some seasons, it has been found to swarm in such numbers, as to eat up every vegetable production.

The two sexes in the may-bug are easily distinguished from each other, by the superior length of the tufts, at the end of the horns, in the male. They begin to copulate in summer, and at that season, they are seen joined together for a considerable time. The female being impregnated, quickly falls to boring a hole into the ground, where to deposit her burden. This is generally about half a foot deep, and in it she places her eggs, which are of an oblong shape, with great regularity, one by the other. They are of a bright yellow colour, and no way wrapped up in a common covering, as some have imagined. When the female is lightened of her burden, she again ascends from her hole, to live as before, upon leaves and vegetables, to buzz in the summer evening, and to lie hid, among the branches of trees, in the heat of the day.

In about three months these eggs hatch and a small grub or maggot crawls forth, and feeds upon the roots of whatever vegetable it happens to be nearest. In this manner these voracious creatures continue in the worm state, for more than three years, devouring the roots of every plant, they approach, and making their way under ground, in quest of food, with great

dispatch and facility. At length they grow to above the size of a walnut, being a great thick white maggot with a red head, which is seen most frequently in new turned earth, and which is so eagerly fought after by birds of every species. The body consists of twelve segments or joints, on each side of which there are nine breathing holes, and three red feet. The head is large, in proportion to the body, of a reddish colour, with a pincer before, and a semi-circular lip, with which it cuts the roots of plants, and sucks out their moisture. As this insect lives entirely underground, it has no occasion for eyes, and accordingly it is found to have none; but is furnished with two feelers, which, like the crutch of a blind man, serve to direct its motions.

That beetle which the Americans call the Tumble-Dung, is all over of a dusky black, rounder than those animals are generally found to be, and so strong, though not much larger than the common black beetle, that if one of them is put under a brass candlestick, it will cause it to move backwards and forwards, as if it were by an invisible hand, to the admiration of those who are not accustomed to the sight; but this strength is given it for much more useful purposes than those of exciting human curiosity, for there is no creature more laborious, either in seeking subsistence, or in providing a proper retreat for its young. They are endowed with sagacity to discover subsistence by their excellent smelling, which directs them in flights to excrements just fallen from man or beast, on which they instantly drop, and fall unanimously to work in forming round balls or pellets thereof, in the middle of which they lay an egg. These pellets, in September, they convey three

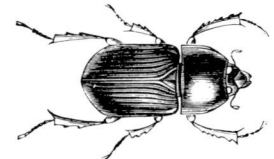

feet deep in the earth, where they lie till the approach of spring, when the eggs are hatched and burst their nests, and the insects find their way out of the earth. They assist each other with indefatigable industry, in rolling these globular pellets to the place where they are to be buried. This they are to perform with the tail foremost, by raising up their hind part, and shoving along the ball with their hind-feet. They are always accompanied with other beetles of a larger size, and of a more elegant structure and colour. The breast of these is covered with a shield of a crimson colour, and shining like metal; the head is of the like colour, mixed with green, and on the crown of the head stands a shining black horn, bended backwards. These are called the kings of the beetles, but for what reason is uncertain, since they partake of the same

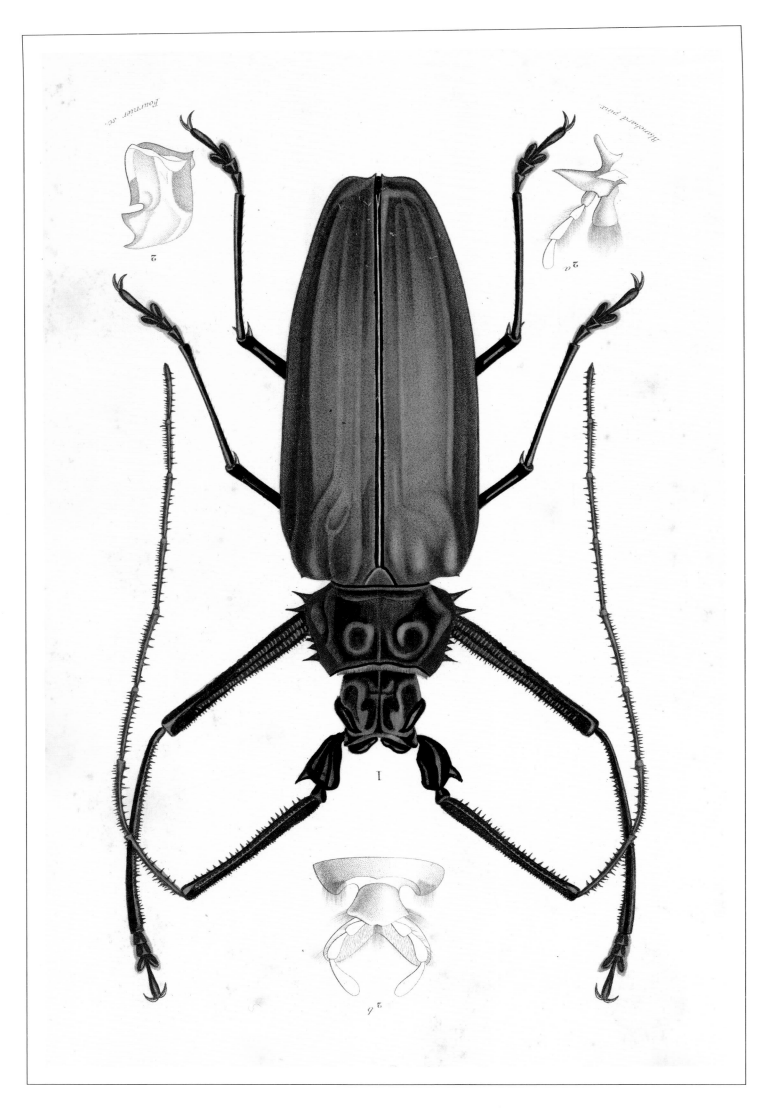

Fourvier sc.

Blanchard pinx.

2

2ᵃ

1

2ᵇ

dirty drudgery with the rest.

The Elephant-Beetle is the largest of this kind hitherto known, and is found in South America, particularly Guiana and Surinam, as well as about the river Orinoco. It is of a black colour, and the whole body is covered with a very hard shell, full as thick and as strong as that of a small crab. Its length, from the hind part to the eyes, is almost four inches, and from the same part to the end of the proboscis, or trunk, four inches and three quarters. The transverse diameter of the body is two inches and a quarter, and the breadth of each elytron, or case for the wings, is an inch and three tenths. The antennae or feelers, are quite horny; for which reason the proboscis or trunk is moveable at its insertion into the head, and seems to supply the place of feelers. The horns are eight tenths of an inch long, and terminate in points. The proboscis is an inch and a quarter long, and turns upwards, making a crooked line, terminating in two horns, each of which is near a quarter of an inch long; but they are not perforated at the end like the proboscis of other insects. About four tenths of an inch above the head, onr that side next the body, is a prominence, or small horn, which if the rest of the trunk were away, would cause this part to resemble the horn of a rhinoceros. There is indeed a beetle so called, but then the horns or trunk have no fork at the end, though the lower horn resembles this. The feet are all forked at the end, but not like lobsters' claws.

To this class we may also refer the Glow-Worm, that little animal which makes such a distinguished figure in the descriptions of our poets. No two insects can differ more than the male and female of this species from each other. The male is in every respect a beetle, having cases to its wings, and rising in the air at pleasure; the female, on the contrary has none, but is entirely a creeping insect, and is obliged to wait the approaches of her capricious companion. The body of the female has eleven joints, with a shield breast-plate, the shape of which is oval; the head is placed over this, and is very small, and the three last joints of her body are of a yellowish colour; but what distinguishes it from all other animals, at least in this part of the world, is the shining light which it emits by night, and which is supposed by some philosophers, to be an emanation which she sends forth to allure the male to her company. Most travellers who have gone through sandy countries, must well remember the little shining sparks with which the ditches are studed on each side of the road. If incited by curiousity to approach more nearly, he will find the light sent forth by the glow-worm; if he should keep the little animal for some time, its light continues to grow paler, and at last appears totally extinct: The manner in which this light is produced has hitherto continued inexplic-

able; it is probable the little animal is supplied with some electrical powers, so that by rubbing the joints of its body against each other, it thus supplies a stream of light which, if it allures the male, as we are told, serves for very useful purposes.

The Cantharis is of the beetle kind, from whence come cantharides, well known in the shops by the name of *Spanish flies*, and for their use in blisters. They have feelers like bristles, flexible cases to the wings, a breast pretty plain, and the sides of the belly wrinkled. Cantharides differ from each other in their size, shape, and colour, those used in the shops also do the same. The largest in these parts are about an inch long, and as much in circumference, but others are not above three quarters of an inch. Some are of a pure azure colour, others of pure gold, and others again have a mixture of pure gold and azure colours; but they are all very brilliant, and extremely beautiful. These insects, as is well known, are of the greatest benefit to mankind, making a part in many medicines conducive to human preservation. They are chiefly natives of Spain, Italy, and Portugal; but they are to be met with also about Paris in the summer time, upon the leaves of the ash, the poplar, and the rose-tree, and also among wheat, and in meadows. It is very certain that these insects are fond of ash leaves, insomuch that they will sometimes strip one of these trees quite bare. Some affirm, that these flies delight in sweet-smelling herbs, and it is very certain that they are fond of honey-suckles, lilac, and wild-cherry shrubs.

Another useful insect, is the Cochineal beetle. As they appear in our shops when brought from America, they are of an irregular shape, convex on one side, and a little concave on the other; but are both marked with transverse streaks or wrinkles. They are of a scarlet colour within, and without of a blackish red, and sometimes of a white, reddish, or ash-colour, which are accounted the best, and are brought to us from Mexico. The cochineal insect is of an oval form, of the size of a small pea, with six feet, and a

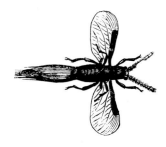

snout or trunk. It brings forth its young alive, and is nourished by sucking the juice of the plant. Its body consists of several rings, and when it is once fixed on the plant, it continues immoveable, being subject to no change. Some pretend there are two sorts, the one domestic, which is best, and the other wild, that is of

a vivid colour; however they appear to be the same, only with this difference, that the wild feeds upon uncultivated trees, without any assistance, whereas the domestic is carefully at a stated season, removed to cultivated trees, where it feeds upon a purer juice. Those who take care of these insects, place them on the prickly pear-plant in a certain order, and are very industrious in defending them from other insects; for if any other kind comes among them, they take care to brush them off with foxes' tails. Towards the end of the year, when the rains and cold weather are coming on, which are fatal to these insects, they take off the leaves or branches covered with cochineal, that have not attained their utmost degree of perfection, and keep them in their houses till winter is past.

THE GNAT AND THE TIPULA

There are two insects which entirely resemble each other in their form, and yet widely differ in their habits, manners and propagation. Those who have seen the Tipula, or Long-Legs, and the larger kind of Gnat, have most probably mistaken the one for the other, they have often accused the tipula, a harmless insect, of depredations made by the gnat, and the innocent have suffered for the guilty; indeed the differences in their form are so very minute, that it often requires the assistance of a microscope to distinguish the one from the other: they are both mounted on long legs, both furnished with two wings and a slender body; their heads are large, and they seem to be hump-backed; the chief and only difference, therefore is, that the tipula wants a trunk, while the gnat has a large one, which it often exerts to very mischievous purposes. The tipula is a harmless peaceful insect, that offers injury to nothing; the gnat is sanguinary and predacious, ever seeking out for a place in which to bury its trunk, and pumping up the blood from the animal in large quantities.

The gnat proceeds from a little worm, which is usually seen at the bottom of standing waters. The manner in which the insect lays its eggs is particularly curious; after having laid the proper number on the surface of the water, it surrounds them with a kind of unctuous matter, which prevents them from sinking; but at the same time fastens them with a thread to the bottom, to prevent their floating away. Thus the insects, in their egg state, resemble a buoy, which is fixed by an anchor. As they come to maturity they sink deeper, and at last, when they leave the egg as worms they creep at the bottom. They now make themselves lodgements of cement, which they fasten

GIANT TROPICAL LONG HORN BEETLE *Enoplocerus armillatus*

to some solid body at the very bottom of the water. The worm afterwards changes its form. It appears with a large head, and a tail invested with hair, and moistened with an oleaginous liquor, which she makes use of as a cork, to sustain her head in the air, and her tail in the water, and to transport her from one place to another. When the oil with which her tail

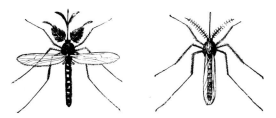

is moistened begins to grow dry, she discharges out of her mouth an unctuous humour, which she sheds all over her tail, by virtue whereof, she is enabled to transport herself where she pleases, without being either wet or any ways incommoded by the water. The gnat, in her second state, is properly speaking, in her form of a nymph, which is an introduction, or entrance into a new life. In the first place, she divests herself of her second skin; in the next she resigns her eyes, her antennae, and her tail; in short, she actually seems to expire. However, from the spoils of the amphibious animal, a little winged insect cuts the air, whose every part is active to the last degree, and whose whole structure is the just object of our admiration. Its little head is adorned with a plume of feathers, and its whole body invested with scales and hair, to secure it from any wet or dust. She makes trial of the activity of her wings, by rubbing them either against her body, or her broad side-bags, which keep her in an equilibrium.

ZOOPHYTES

In the class of zoophytes, we may place all those animals, which may be propagated by cuttings, or in other words, which, if divided into two or more parts, each part in time, becomes a separate and perfect animal; the head shoots forth a tail, and on the contrary, the tail produces a head; some of these will bear dividing, but into two parts; such is the earthworm; some may be divided into more than two, and of this kind are many of the star-fish; others still may be cut into a thousand parts, each becoming a perfect animal; they may be turned inside out, like the finger of a glove, they may be moulded into all manner of shapes, yet still their vivacious principle remains, still every single part becomes perfect in its kind, and after a few days existence, exhibits all the arts and industry of its contemptible parent! We shall, therefore, divide

zoophytes according to their several degrees of perfection, namely, into Worms, Star-fish, and Polypi; contenting ourselves with a short review of those nauseous and despicable creatures, that excite our curiosity chiefly by their imperfections; it must not be concealed, however, that much has of late been written on this part of natural history. A new mode of animal production, could not fail of exciting not only the curiosity, but the astonishment of every philosopher; many found their favourite systems totally overthrown by the discovery, and it was not without a wordy struggle, that they gave up what had formerly been their pleasure and their pride. At last, however, conviction became too strong for argument, and a question, which owed its general spread rather to its novelty, than to its importance, was given up in favour of the new discovery.

WORMS

Animals of the Worm kind, being entirely destitute of feet, trail themselves along upon the ground, and find themselves a retreat under the earth, or in the water. But though worms, as well as serpents, are without feet, and have been doomed to creep along the earth on their bellies, yet their motions are very different. The serpent, having a back bone, which it is incapable of contracting, bends its body into the form of a bow, and then shoots forward from the tail; but it is very different with the worm, which has a power of contracting or lengthening itself at will. There is a spiral muscle, that runs round its whole body, from the head to tail, somewhat resemblig a wire wound round a walking-cane, which, when slipped off, and one end extended and held fast, will bring the other nearer to it; in this manner the earth-worm, having shot out, or extended its body, takes hold by the slime of the forepart of its body, and so contracts and brings forward the hind part; in this manner it moves onward, not without great effort, but the occasions for its progressive motion are few.

As it is designed for living under the earth, and leading a life of obscurity, so it seems tolerably adapted to its situation. Its body is armed with small stiff sharp burrs or prickles, which it can erect or depress at pleasure; under the skin there lies a slimy juice, to be ejected as occasion requires, at certain perforations, between the rings of the muscles, to lubricate its body, and facilitate its passage into the earth. Like most other insects, it has breathing-holes along the back, adjoining each ring; but it is without bones, without eyes, and without ears. It has a mouth, and also an elementary canal, which runs along to the very point of the tail. In some worms, however, particularly such as are found in the bodies of animals, this canal opens towards the middle of the belly, at some distance from the tail. The intestines of the earth-worm, are always found filled with a very fine earth, which seems to be the only nourishment these animals are capable of receiving.

THE STAR-FISH

The next order of zoophytes is that of the Star-Fish, a numerous tribe, shapeless and deformed, assuming at different times different appearances. The same animal that now appears round like a ball, shortly after flattens as thin as a plate. All of this kind are formed of a semi-transparent gelatinous susbstance, covered with a thin membrane, and, to an inattentive spectator, often appear like a lump of inanimate jelly, floating at random upon the surface of the sea, or thrown by chance on shore at the departure of the tide. But upon a more minute inspection, they will be found to shoot forth their arms in every direction, in order to seize their prey, and to devour them with great rapacity. Worms, the spawn of fish, and even mussels themselves, with their hard resisting shell, have been found in the stomachs of these voracious animals; and what is very extraordinary, though the substance of their own bodies are almost as soft as water, yet they are no way injured by swallowing these shells, which are almost of a stony hardness. They increase in size as all other animals do. In summer, when the water of the sea is warmed by the heat of the sun, they float upon the surface, and in the dark they send forth a kind of shining light resembling that of phosphorus. Some have given these animals the name of sea-nettles, because they burn the hands of those that touch them, as nettles are found to do. They are often seen fastened to the rocks, and to the largest sea-shells, as if to derive their nourishment from them. If they are taken and put into spirit of wine, they will continue for many years entire, but if they are left to the influence of the air, they are, in less than twenty four hours melted down into a limpid and offensive water.

In all of these species, none are found to possess a vent for their excrements, but the same passage by which they devour their food, served for the ejection of their faeces. These animals as was said, take such a variety of figures, that it is impossible to describe them under one determinate shape; but in general,

1 CLUB-SPINNED SEA URCHIN *Cidartes imperialis*

2 LOBED SEA URCHIN *Echinus atratus* 3 SEA URCHIN *Echinus globiformis*

5 SAND DOLLAR *Scutella quinquefora*

Dujardin pinx.

Fournier sc.

their bodies resemble a truncated cone, whose base is applied to the rock to which they are found usually attached. Though generally transparent, they are found of different colours, some inclining to green, some to red, some to white, and some to brown. In some, their colours appear diffused over the whole surface, in some, they are often streaked, and in others often spotted. They are possessed of a very slow progressive motion, and in fine weather, they are continually seen, stretching out and fishing for their prey. Many of them are possessed of a number of long slender filaments, in which they entangle any small animals they happen to approach, and thus draw them into their enormous stomachs, which fill the whole cavity of their bodies. The harder shells continue for some weeks undigested, but at length, they undergo a kind of maceration in the stomach, and become a part of the substance of the animal itself. The indigestible parts, are returned by the same aperture by which they are swallowed, and then the star-fish begins to fish for more. These also may be cut in pieces, and every part will survive the operation; each becoming a perfect animal, endued with its natural rapacity.

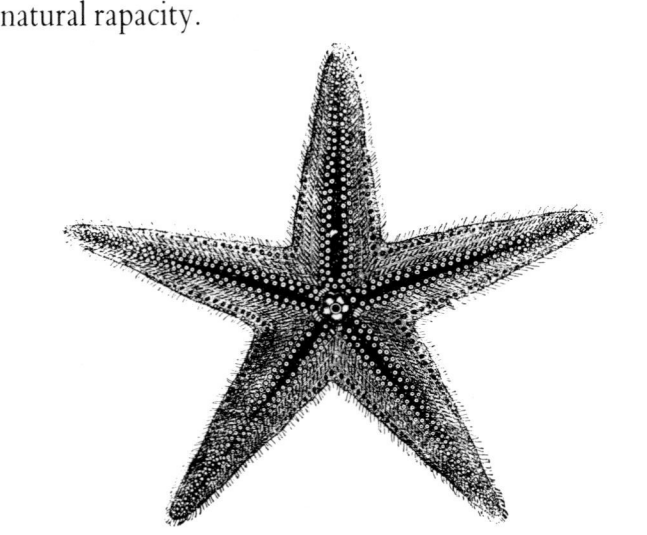

THE POLYPUS

Those animals already described, are variously denominated. They have been called the Star-fish, Sea-nettles, and Sea-polypi. This last name has been peculiarly ascribed to them by the ancients, because of the number of feelers or feet of which they are all possessed, and with which they have a slow progressive motion; but the moderns have given the name of Polypus, to a hydra that lives in fresh water, by no means so large or observable. These are found at the bottom of wet ditches, or attached to the under surface of the broad-leafed plants that grow and swim on the waters. The same difference holds between these and the seawater polypus, as between all the productions of the sea, and of the land and the ocean. The marine vegetables and animals grow to a mon-

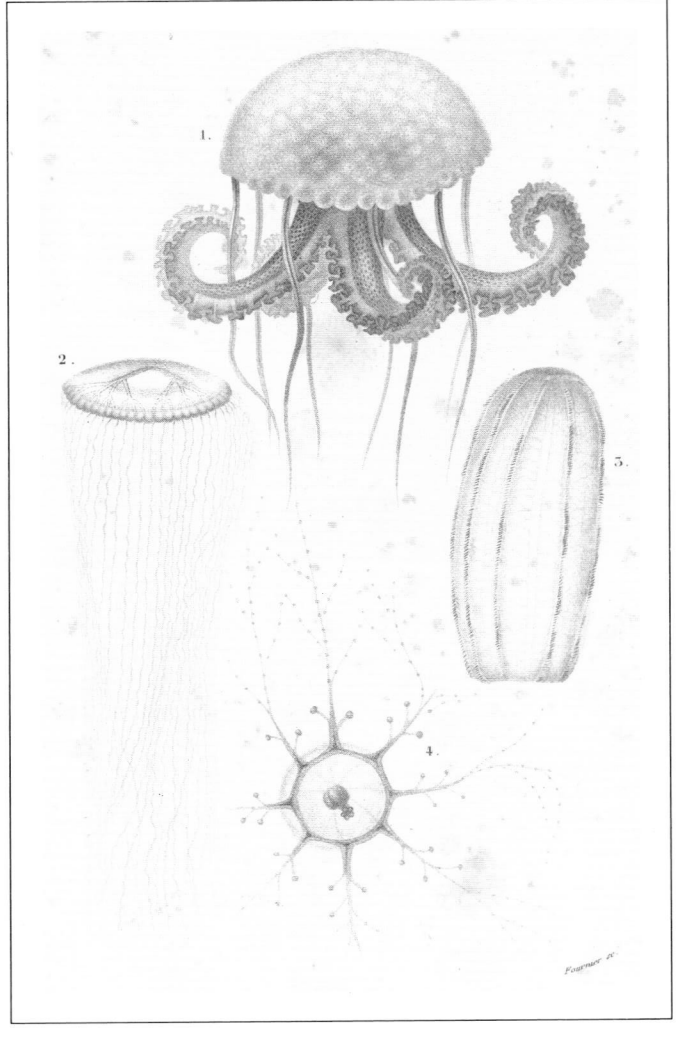

1 LUMINESCENT JELLYFISH *Pelagia noctiluca* 2 JELLYFISH *Berenice rosea*
3 COMB JELLYFISH *Beroe forskahlie* 4 *Cladonema radiatum*

strous size. The eel, the pike, or the bream of freshwaters, are small; but in the sea, they grow to an enormous magnitude. The herbs of the field are at most but a few feet high; those of the sea often shoot forth a stalk of a hundred. It is so between the polypi of both elements. Those of the sea are found from two feet in length to three or four, and Pliny has even described one, the arms of which were no less than thirty feet long. Those in fresh waters, however, are comparatively minute, at their utmost size, seldom above three parts of an inch long, and when gathered up into their usual form, not above a third even of those dimensions.

Mr. Trembley was the person to whom we owe the first discovery of the amazing properties and powers of this little vivacious creature: He divided this class of animals into four different kinds; into those inclining to green, those of a brownish cast, those of flesh-colour, those which he calls the polype de panache. The differences of structure in these, as also of colour, are observable enough; but the manner of their subsisting, of seizing their prey, and of their propagation, is pretty nearly the same in all.

Whoever has looked with care into the bottom of a

wet ditch, when the water is stagnant, and the sun has been powerful, may remember to have seen many little transparent lumps of jelly, about the size of a pea, and flattened on one side; such also as have examined the underside of the broad-leafed weeds that grow on the surface of the water, must have observed them studded with a number of these little jelly-like substances, which were probably then disregarded, because their nature and history was unknown. These little substances however, were no other than living polypi gathered up into a quiescent state and seemingly inanimate, because either disturbed, or not excited by the calls of appetite to action. When they are seen exerting themselves they put on a very different appearance from that when at rest; to conceive a just idea of their figure, we may suppose the finger of a glove cut off at the bottom; we may suppose also several threads or horns planted round the edge like a fringe. The hollow of this finger will give us an idea of the stomach of the animal, the threads issuing forth from the edges may be considered as the arms or feelers, with which it hunts for its prey. The animal, at its greatest extent, is seldom seen above an inch and a half long, but it is much shorter when it is contracted and at rest; it is furnished neither with muscles nor rings, and its manner of lengthening or contracting itself, more resembles that of the snail, than worms, or any other insect. The polypus contracts itself more or less, in proportion as it is touched, or as the water is agitated in which they are seen. Warmth animates them, and cold benumbs them; but it requires a degree of cold approaching congelation before they are reduced to perfect inactivity.

Though appearing blind, all animals of this kind have a remarkable attachment to turn towards the light, and it is most probable that, like several other creatures which hunt their prey by their feeling, they are unfurnished with advantages which would be totally useless for their support.

In the centre of the arms, the mouth is placed, which the animal can open and shut at pleasure, and this serves at once as a passage for food, and an opening for it after digestion. The inward part of the animal's body seems to be one great stomach, which is open at both ends; but the purposes which the opening at the bottom serves are hitherto unknown, but certainly not for excluding their excrements, for those are ejected at the aperture, by which they are taken in. If the surface of the body of this little creature be examined with a microscope, it will be found studded with a number of warts, as also the arms, especially when they are contracted; and these tubercles, as we shall presently see, answer a very important purpose.

If we examine their way of living, we shall find these insects chiefly subsisting upon others, much less than themselves, particularly a kind of millepede that live in the water, and a very small red worm, which they seize with great avidity. In short no insect whatsoever, less than themselves, seems to come amiss to them; their arms serve them as a net would a fisherman. Wherever their prey is perceived it is sufficient to touch the object it would seize upon and it is fastened, without a power of escaping. The instant one of this insect's long arms is laid upon a millepede, the little insect sticks without a possibility of retreating. The greater the distance at which it is touched, the greater is the ease with which the polypus brings the prey to its mouth. When the polypus is unsupplied with prey, it testifies its hunger by opening its mouth; the aperture, however, is so small that it cannot be easily perceived; but when, with any of its long arms, it has seized upon its prey, it then opens the mouth distinctly enough, and this opening is always in proportion to the size of the animal which it would swallow; the lips dilate insensibly by small degrees, and adjust themselves precisely to the figure of their prey. Mr. Trembley, who took a pleasure in feeding this useless brood, found that they could devour aliments of every kind, fish and flesh as well as insects; but he owns they did not thrive so well upon beef and veal, as upon the little worms of their own providing. When he gave one of these famished animals any substance which was improper to serve for aliment, at first it seized the prey with avidity, but after keeping it some time entangled near the mouth, it let drop again with distinguishing nicety.

SEA ANEMONES

Besides these kinds mentioned by Mr. Trembley, there are various others which have been lately discovered by the vigilance of succeeding observers, and some of these so strongly resemble a flowering vegetable in their forms, that they have been mistaken by many naturalists for such. Mr. Hughes, the author of the Natural History of Barbados, has described a species of this animal, but has mistaken its nature, and called it a sensitive flowering plant; he observed it to take refuge in the holes of rocks, and when undisturbed, to spread forth a number of ramifications, each terminated by a flowery petal which shrunk at the approach of the hand, and withdrew into the hole from whence before it had been seen to issue. This plant however was no other than an animal of the polypus kind, which is not only to be found in Barbados, but also on many parts of

the coast of Cornwall, and along the shores of the Continent.

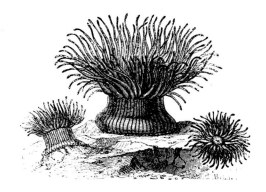

LITHOPHYTES AND SPONGES

It is very probable that the animals we see, and are acquainted with, bear no manner of proportion to those that are concealed from us. Although every leaf and vegetable swarms with animals upon land, yet at sea, they are still more abundant; for the greatest part of what would seem vegetables growing there is in fact the work of animals, palaces which they have built for their own habitation.

If we examine the bottom of the sea along some shores, and particularly at the mouths of several rivers, we shall find it has the appearance of a forest of trees under water, millions of plants growing in various directions, with their branches entangled in each other, and sometimes standing so thick as to obstruct navigation. The shores of the Persian Gulf, the whole extent of the Red Sea, and the western coasts of America, are so choked up in many places with these coraline substances, that though ships force a passage through them, boats and swimmers find it impossible to make their way. These aquatic groves are formed of different substances, and assume various appearances. The coral-plants, as they are called, sometimes shoot out like trees without leaves in winter; they often spread out a broad surface like a fan, and not uncommonly a large bundling head, like a faggot; sometimes they are found to resemble a plant with leaves and flowers; and often the antlers of a stag, with great exactness and regularity. In other parts of the sea are seen sponges of various magnitude, and extraordinary appearances, assuming a variety of fantastic forms like large mushrooms, mitres, fonts and flower-pots.

If a coraline structure is strictly observed, while still growing in the sea, and the animals upon its surface are not disturbed, either by the agitation of the waters, or the touch of the observer, the little polypi will then be seen in infinite numbers, each issuing from its cell, and in some kinds, the head covered with a little shell, resembling an umbrella, the arms spread abroad, in order to seize its prey, while the hind part still remains attached to its habitation, from whence it never wholly removes. By this time it is perceived that the number of inhabitants is infinitely greater than was at first suspected; that they are all assiduously employed in the same pursuits, and that they issue from their respective cells, and retire into them at pleasure. Like the shells which are formed by snails, mussels and oysters, these coraline substances effervesce with acids, and may therefore well be supposed to partake of the same animal nature. The ingenious Mr. Ellis examined their operations, just as they were beginning, putting it past doubt, that corals and sponges were entirely the work of an infinite number of polypi. Observing an oyster-bed which had been for some time neglected, he there perceived the first rudiments of a coraline plantation, and tufts of various kinds shooting from different parts of this favourable foil. It was upon these he tried his principal experiment. He took out the oysters which were thus furnished with coralines, and placed them in a large wooden vessel, covering them with sea water. In about an hour, he perceived the animals, which before had been contracted by handling, and had shown no signs of life, expanding themselves in every direction, and appearing employed in their own natural manner. Perceiving them therefore in this state, his next aim was to preserve them thus expanded, so as to be permanent objects of curiosity. For this purpose he poured, by slow degrees, an equal quantity of boiling-water into the vessel of sea water in which they were immersed. He then separated each polypus with pincers from its shell, and plunged each separately into small crystal vases, filled with spirit of wine mixed with water. By this means, the animal was preserved entire, without having time to contract itself, and he thus perceived a variety of kinds, almost equal to that variety of productions which these little animals are seen to form. He has been thus able to perceive and describe fifty different kinds, each of which is seen to possess its own peculiar mode of construction, and to form a coraline that none of the rest can imitate. It is true indeed, that on every coraline substance there are a number of polypi found, no way resembling those which are the erectors of the building; these vagabond organisms are only intruders upon the labours of others, taking possession of habitations, which they have neither art nor power to build for themselves.

1 HORNWRACK *Flustra foliacea*

2 PRECIOUS CORAL *Corallium rubrum*

3 CREEPING CORNULARIID *Cornularia elegans*

4 WHITE WEED *Sertularia pumila*

INDEX

All page numbers in italics denote illustrations

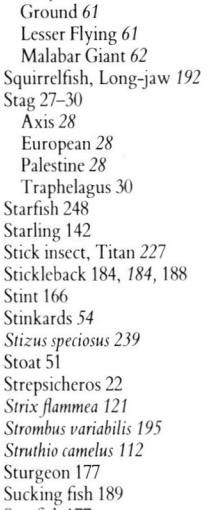
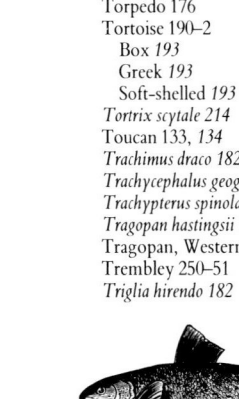